"Bisaha provides the most comprehensive and nuanced account now available of the attitudes of Western intellectuals to the Turks, the Byzantines, and crusading in Renaissance Italy, an important time and place for the formation of Western cultural identity."—James Hankins, Harvard University

As the Ottoman Empire advanced westward from the fourteenth to the sixteenth centuries, humanists responded on a grand scale, leaving behind a large body of fascinating yet understudied works. These compositions included Crusade orations and histories, ethnographic, historical, and religious studies of the Turks, epic poetry, and even tracts on converting the Turks to Christianity. Most scholars have seen this vast literature as atypical of Renaissance humanism. Nancy Bisaha now offers an in-depth look at the body of Renaissance humanist works that focus not on classical or contemporary Italian subjects but on the Ottoman Empire, Islam, and the Crusades. Throughout, Bisaha probes these texts to reveal the significant role Renaissance writers played in shaping Western views of self and other.

Medieval concepts of Islam were generally informed and constrained by religious attitudes and rhetoric in which Muslims were depicted as enemies of the faith. While humanist thinkers of the Renaissance did not move entirely beyond this stance, *Creating East and West* argues that their understanding was consider-

Creating East and West

Creating East and West

Renaissance Humanists and the Ottoman Turks

Nancy Bisaha

PENN

UNIVERSITY OF PENNSYLVANIA PRESS

Philadelphia

10   9   8   7   6   5   4   3   2   1

Published by
University of Pennsylvania Press
Philadelphia, Pennsylvania 19104-4011

Library of Congress Cataloging-in-Publication Data

Bisaha, Nancy.
    Creating East and West : Renaissance humanists and the Ottoman Turks / Nancy Bisaha.
        p.   cm.
    ISBN 0-8122-3806-0 (alk. paper)
    1. East and West.   2. Humanists.   3. Turkey—History—Ottoman Empire, 1288–1918.   I.
Title.
CB251.B57 2004
956.1′0151′004—dc22   2004043021

For my parents,
Joseph J. Bisaha (1929–1988)
and
Victoria J. Bisaha

Contents

Time Line of Key Events in the Ottoman Advance

1302	Death of Osman, founder of the Ottoman Dynasty
1345–52	Ottomans ally with Byzantine Empire and begin establishing a foothold in Europe
1389	Battle of Kosovo
1396	Crusade of Nicopolis defeated by Ottoman forces
1400–1402	Byzantine emperor Manuel II visits Western courts seeking aid against the Ottomans
1439	Union between Eastern Orthodox and Latin churches proclaimed at the Council of Florence
1444	Crusade of Varna defeated by Ottoman forces under Murad II
1451–81	Reign of Sultan Mehmed II
1453	Constantinople besieged and captured by Mehmed II
1458–64	Reign of Pope Pius II; Congress of Mantua (1459–60) and aborted crusade that ends in Ancona with Pius's death
1463	Bosnia annexed by Ottoman Empire
1463–79	Venice at war with Ottoman Empire
1470	Loss of Venetian colony of Negroponte to Ottoman forces
1480	Rhodes successfully defended by Knights of Saint John; Otranto in southern Italy falls to Ottoman invaders
1481	Otranto recovered by Christian forces
1499–1503	Venice at war with Ottoman Empire
1529	Vienna besieged by Suleiman I; successfully defended by Christian forces

Introduction

IN THE SPRING OF 1453 MEHMED II, the clever and ambitious young sultan of the Ottoman Empire, was laying siege to Constantinople, the still-formidable capital of the waning Byzantine Empire. Despite some help from Western European fighters primarily from Venice and Genoa, the Greeks were heavily outnumbered: approximately seven thousand fighting men within the city faced an army of eighty thousand camped without and armed with powerful cannons. Despite the city's redoubtable three sets of land walls and seaward walls, the courageous leadership of its emperor, and the military expertise of its soldiers and sailors, Constantinople could not resist Mehmed's overwhelming assault power. After an intense, yet brief siege the city fell to the Ottomans on 29 May and was brutally sacked.[1] In keeping with Islamic tradition, a three-day pillage was granted to the soldiers. Hundreds of citizens and soldiers managed to escape by ship, but most of the population were enslaved and their houses and churches looted.[2] Approximately four thousand inhabitants were killed in the siege; countless women and boys were raped. The last Byzantine emperor, Constantine XI Palaeologus Dragases, died while attempting to defend the walls of his city, dramatically hurling himself into the fray rather than fleeing, according to several accounts. (Mehmed reportedly had his head stuffed and sent around to Muslim courts to regale them with his victory.) A few hours after the city was taken, Mehmed entered in triumph. In only seven weeks the twenty-one-year-old sultan had accomplished a feat that had eluded numerous commanders before him. Given its strategic and symbolic import, the city became the new capital of the Ottoman Empire.

Western powers slowly mustering relief forces, secure in the belief that the city could withstand a siege of several months, were stunned by the news. The broader populace, particularly in Italy, was equally horrified; Roman citizens were so shocked that they refused to believe the news at first.[3] Accounts circulating in the West fed popular anxiety by depicting the sack as one of the bloodiest and most inhumane acts of history. The

Venetian Senate, for example, exaggerated tales of casualties by reporting that all inhabitants over the age of six had been slaughtered. Numerous laments were penned in Latin and the vernacular alike, and rumors abounded that Mehmed would not be content with the prize of the "new Rome" and would soon attempt to conquer the old Rome.[4]

Humanists as a group responded to news of the sack with great emotion. Calling the Turks "the most inhuman barbarians [*immanes barbari*] and the most savage enemies of the faith," Cardinal Bessarion exclaimed, "Men have been butchered like cattle, women abducted, virgins ravished, and children snatched from the arms of their parents. If any survived so great a slaughter, they have been enslaved in chains so that they might be ransomed for a price, or subjected to every kind of torture, or reduced to the most humiliating servitude."[5] In addition to the loss of life, humanists lamented the desecration of churches and the irreparable damage to famous buildings and libraries. Aeneas Silvius Piccolomini (later Pope Pius II) labeled the fall of Constantinople a "second death for Homer and a second destruction of Plato."[6] Hence, in the midst of a golden age of learning and the arts, Renaissance Europeans battled fears that a hostile, Islamic enemy to the East could at any moment destroy their world and hurl them back to the "dark ages."

The events and rhetoric surrounding 11 September 2001 serve as a grim reminder of just how powerful the perceived opposition between East and West continues to be—both for the Muslim extremists who planned the attacks and for the American and European politicians who responded with broad insinuations about the savagery of the Muslim East. Before this date, intellectuals had an open forum to argue leisurely about whether stark divisions of any kind mirror cultural realities, man-made and simplistic as they are.[7] Recent events, however, have revealed how easily such reductive rhetoric is resurrected, be it the West as the Great Satan or evil crusader, the East as the intolerant and cunning foe, or the "clash of civilizations."[8] The broad appeal of such biting sophistry is part and parcel of deeply rooted cultural constructs.

The myth of East and West as polar opposites was introduced over two thousand years ago by the Greeks and adapted by the Romans.[9] From about the eleventh century on, Europeans used the terms "Christian" and "Infidel" to articulate this renewed sense of cultural division.[10] By the modern colonial period Western European powers had come to view themselves as superior to Eastern peoples both militarily and culturally. Today, of course, the question of East and West is receiving renewed attention. All of the aforementioned periods have been carefully studied in terms of Western cultural perceptions of the East, but the period that in many ways links them all, the Renaissance, has suffered severe neglect. Later Renaissance attitudes toward other cultures have been explored in some detail, but few scholars think of the early Renaissance as a formative moment in cultural perceptions of any kind.

Perhaps the fifteenth century has been neglected because it was not an era of aggressive European conquests and contacts. On the contrary, Europeans—particularly Italians and Eastern Europeans—were on the defensive against a powerful enemy from the East. Between their rise in the late thirteenth century and their first attempt to capture Vienna (1529), the Ottoman Turks became masters of Anatolia, several islands in the Mediterranean, and a large portion of southeastern Europe, including the Byzantine Empire, the Balkan region, and the area around the Black Sea and the Danube.[11] Not until the seventeenth century did Europeans begin to believe that the ominous Turkish threat was slowing down.

Western Europe's response to the Ottoman Empire was complex and multifaceted, ranging from warfare and espionage, to diplomacy and trade, to religious, literary, and intellectual approaches. Some of these topics, particularly military and political efforts, have been studied in depth.[12] Recently a few scholars have examined commercial and artistic exchange between the Ottoman Empire and Western Europe.[13] Attention has also been devoted to the ways in which religious thinkers approached the Turks.[14] But one area of Western reactions to the Ottoman advance has received little scholarly attention until recent years: intellectual responses, particularly in the fourteenth and fifteenth centuries.[15] This long period of neglect is striking given the many works Italian humanists composed on this subject.

From the late fourteenth century to the early sixteenth century a large group of Italian humanists addressed the Turkish problem and the question of crusade. They composed letters and orations to princes and prelates calling for crusade, histories of the Turks and the Crusades, epic poetry, ethnographic and religious studies of the Turks, laments on areas lost to the Turks, and even tracts on converting the Turks to Christianity. The number of these works is impressive in and of itself.[16] Their content, however, makes them hard to categorize. Why so many humanists should write on a topic that was neither classical nor Western is a question that has puzzled scholars or, more often, led them to reject these texts as unrepresentative of "typical" humanist subjects.[17] The supposed anomaly of these

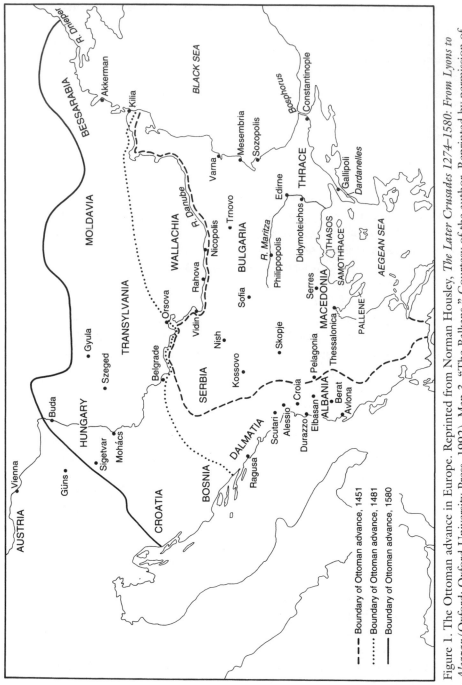

Figure 1. The Ottoman advance in Europe. Reprinted from Norman Housley, *The Later Crusades 1274–1580: From Lyons to Alcazar* (Oxford: Oxford University Press, 1992), Map 3, "The Balkans." Courtesy of the author. Reprinted by permission of

texts has also led to questions regarding the sincerity of the humanists who penned them; one scholar opined that humanists regarded crusade as nothing more than "a golden opportunity for rhetorical exercises."[18] More pointedly, another scholar dismissed these humanist works as silly, degrading, and venal.[19] Such views might persuade if humanists only touched on the Turkish advance, but they do not explain why prominent humanists devoted much time and energy to the crusade cause.[20] Nor do these assumptions jibe with the large number of manuscripts and crusade treatises that were disseminated throughout Europe—evidence that strongly suggests humanists were discussing and publicizing a timely and serious issue that drew a sizable readership.[21]

These texts were widely read because they spoke to central issues in Italian culture and humanism. Humanists wrote against the backdrop of a long history of Italian involvement in the eastern Mediterranean as well as a rich tradition of Italian and European support for crusading. On a very basic level, their texts are worth further study for the palpable fear of invasion that they convey—an attitude that brings human dimension to the battles and negotiations that were being conducted by rulers, diplomats, and merchants at this time. More important, these texts were hardly peripheral to humanism, nor were they, as one scholar has argued, mere footnotes to an established medieval tradition.[22] The rise of new intellectual currents in the early Renaissance, namely a return to classical texts, rhetoric, and ideas, enabled humanists to complicate and innovatively shape contemporary attitudes on countless issues, including the Turks. This study will show how humanists revolutionized Western views of Islam, transforming an old enemy of the faith into a political and cultural threat to their growing sense of "Europe."

Fortunately, the trend of indifference or disdain toward humanist writings on the Ottoman Turks is beginning to wane due to the work of a handful of scholars in the last few decades—much of which has been indispensable to the present study. In his monograph on Benedetto Accolti, Robert Black drew attention to the vast number of texts written by other humanists on the Turks and crusade, providing extensive bibliography on both primary and secondary texts.[23] More recently James Hankins published an article on humanists and crusade c. 1451–81, which includes an appendix of a dozen texts of this genre edited by him.[24] This article is a valuable introduction both to key humanist thinkers and to certain thematic strains in this area of humanist thought. Agostino Pertusi, Francesco Tateo, Ludwig Schmügge, Michael J. Heath, John Monfasani, Margaret

Meserve, and others have contributed substantially to the study of humanist literature on the Turks through editions of primary sources, monographs, and articles.[25] Finally, several studies on crusading, perceptions of
the East, or humanism contain helpful discussions of humanists writing in
this genre.[26]

The present study, in contrast to previous ones, includes close readings and extended analyses of a large sampling of humanist compositions
on the Ottoman Turks. The writings of about thirty humanists are examined closely and located within their various historical, intellectual, and
cross-cultural contexts. Though rarely applied to these texts, cross-cultural
theory is useful in that it places Renaissance thought on the East firmly
within the history of Western perceptions of other societies.[27] As such, a
clearer picture emerges of the ways in which humanists drew on medieval
and ancient traditions or broke free of their models and ultimately influenced later generations. Finally, on a more limited scale, cross-cultural
theory provides new ways of reading humanist texts within their own historical context.

Edward Said remains one of the most important thinkers on the inter-
section of cross-cultural and intellectual history. While aspects of his approach have been criticized, his vision of a Western discourse of the East as
a deliberately constructed exaggeration or fiction of otherness and cultural
inferiority has influenced scholarship in a variety of fields.[28] As Said explains, this sense of the East as a foil to the West constrains and limits
scholarly approaches to Muslim societies; all inquiries about the East
founded on the Self/Other dichotomy are bound to return to stereotypes,
or a "discourse" of superiority versus inferiority.[29] Renaissance humanists,
however, present some important challenges to Said's model. Where Said
focuses on colonialism as a key component in the formation of the West-
East discourse, the bulk of humanist rhetoric on the Turks and Islam
shows a highly developed sense of Europe as the cultural superior to the
East—precisely at a time when Europe was fighting for its survival.[30] Perhaps the clearest example of this can be seen in humanists' frequent designation of the Turks as "barbarians" who tore down the achievements of
civilization.[31] A second problem in applying Said's model is that, just as it
fails to address more open-minded views of a large number of orientalists,
it does not help explain expressions of relativism among a handful of humanists.[32] This study, then, presents not one monolithic humanist discourse but two or three discourses, each significant and influential in its
own way.[33]

Cross-cultural studies on other parts of the world by Stephen Green-blatt, among others, have also provided useful ways in which to frame humanist texts on the Turks and Islam. Greenblatt's literary critical ap-proach to the Age of Discovery resonates with humanist rhetoric in his discussion of "engaged representations" that rely more heavily on the imagination of the writer and his cultural and historical context than on any detached, scientific observations.[34] This imaginative approach to other cultures helps explain how many humanists could write with such confi-dence on the Turks when relatively few of them had firsthand experience of the Ottomans and their empire, apart from what they gleaned from ancient and medieval texts and contemporary reports.[35] In addressing the issue of cultural distance and perceptions, comparative historical studies, such as John Dower's *War without Mercy*, have also proved useful. Dower sheds light on the demonization of enemies and the malleability of cultural perceptions between America and Japan during World War II. Just as the Japanese were alternately demonized or portrayed as harmless monkeys, depending on the level of threat they posed, so too did humanists depict the Turks as inhuman savages or simple primitives.[36]

Of course, cross-cultural theory alone cannot fully illuminate human-ist rhetoric on the Turks and Islam. The discourse of "otherness" becomes a vague notion without more tangible reference points, specifically the intellectual world that humanists inhabited. Hence this study seeks to cre-ate a dialogue between cross-cultural theory and intellectual history by focusing on the language and context of the pieces under consideration. Such an approach reveals the subtleties of humanist concepts of cultural and religious alterity, but even more important, it reveals the Renaissance as a crucial moment of cultural self-definition: in responding to the Turk-ish outsider, humanists simultaneously crafted a compelling notion of Western society. As Denys Hay has argued, the Ottoman advance set the stage for the modern creation of European civilization—an idea based in part on ancient sources and in part on modern political and religious con-cerns.[37] Understanding the route by which humanists arrived at this point, however, requires a closer look at humanism itself.

The modern word "humanism," according to Paul Oskar Kristeller, derives from the *studia humanitatis*, which represented a group of schol-arly disciplines already well defined by the mid-fifteenth century. These included grammar, rhetoric, history, poetry, and moral philosophy; all of these studies revolved around the careful reading and interpretation of ancient Roman and Greek texts.[38] It was this emphasis on ancient authori-

ties that distinguished humanism from other studies. Classical concepts
became sounding boards for humanist thought on topics ranging from
political thought and history to social issues, ethics, and theology. When
it came to applying these skills, some humanists preferred the contemplative life, but most sought out career opportunities in secular or ecclesiastical chanceries or in teaching. They served as chancellors (high-profile
letter and speech writers), ambassadors and orators, as well as humble no-
taries and copyists. As teachers, some occupied prestigious chairs of rhetoric, poetry, or philosophy in state-sponsored universities and *studi*; others
were employed as tutors for individuals and families.[39] Hence, training in
classical rhetoric and literature as well as the ability to inspire and persuade
through rhetoric allowed most humanists to lead active lives and often
provided opportunities to address audiences of considerable size or influence. From delivered speeches to written works such as poems, letters, or
orations, the majority of humanists addressed in this study composed what
is known as primary rhetoric: works with a civic function, designed to be
broadly disseminated.[40]

While the activities of humanists are easily defined, there is some debate on the significance of humanism and its role in Renaissance culture.
Humanist texts on the Turks may be seen as representative of that debate.
Scholars have argued at length over whether humanism represents a break
with medieval culture or indeed sprang organically out of it;[41] whether it
was more secular or more religious in nature;[42] and whether it encouraged
individuality and a creative approach to the classics or a dry, formulaic
parroting of the same works, written to appease the elite who controlled
the message and paid humanists' salaries.[43] Some texts on the Turks demonstrate a strong attachment to the medieval past, almost all of them address religious concerns in some way, and many of them indeed reflect the
goals of the powerful men who commissioned these works. Still, the bulk
of humanist literature on the Turks more consistently reflects the opposite
tendencies.

A strong preference for classical models and concepts characterizes
most humanist treatments of the Turks, Islam, and crusade. This radical
departure from previous writings on Europe's confrontation with Islam
inspired a more secular outlook vis-à-vis the Turks. By engaging pre-Christian concepts of foreign cultures and adversaries, humanists were able to
see the Turks as more than just "enemies of the faith." Without discarding
expressions of religious superiority and concern for the faith, humanists
began to address new topics such as the Turks' record on learning, the

arts, civility, and government. The Turks could now be considered in lay cultural and political contexts alternately as members of a backward, barbaric society or as a virtuous, austere culture: as a foreign menace, or as worthy and capable adversaries, or even as potential allies.[44] This secular outlook, then, gave rise to two opposite approaches: Eurocentrism and, conversely, cultural tolerance. It may even be argued that one branch of humanist rhetoric on the Turks acted as a precursor for intellectual justifications of colonialism.[45] These two poles of perceiving the Turks (and increasingly all Muslims) through the secular lens show how humanist views of the Turks acted as a bridge between medieval and modern attitudes toward the East and Islam. They also helped shape new constructs of the "Western Self."

How exactly did an interest in the classical past bring about such a dramatic shift? As Kenneth Gouwens argues, Renaissance humanists cultivated an active relationship with the ancient world; for many this was a moving and transformative experience. Using the tools of cognitive psychology, Gouwens views humanist engagement in classical texts not simply as study or mindless imitation but as a reciprocal relationship, a cultural context, a state of mind, and a shared discursive field among fellow scholars.[46] This theory helps answer two important questions regarding humanism and the Turks. Their unique "cultural context" helped humanists create an original vision of the Turks and Islam—a vision that was very much their own and not that of the ruling elite whom they served.[47]

It also helps explain the emergence of a common discourse or "shared discursive field" on the Turks. Humanists' common educational and cultural context, nourished by their tendency to form intellectual circles comprised of friends, teachers, pupils, and professional associates, provided fertile ground for shared ideas and language.[48] The unique historical circumstances of the Ottoman advance were also important. Humanists were responding to a very real threat; they actively created a timely discourse instead of passively participating in a preexisting one.[49] Hence, instead of viewing common humanist rhetoric as repetitive or insincere, we should view the phenomenon as the joint creation of a powerful dialogue that involved a large group of scholars across Italy, and later Europe, in the act of speaking and writing about the Turks and Islam in similar, yet meaningful terms.[50]

Owing to the amount of humanist literature on the Turks, I have found it necessary to limit my inquiry both chronologically and geographically. The fifteenth century is the main focus as this period witnessed the first real surge of concern over the Turkish advance among Europeans in general and humanists in particular. To set the scene, I examine a few earlier humanists' texts as well as examples of medieval and early Renaissance crusade rhetoric and religious polemic. To assess the consequences and legacy of fifteenth-century attitudes, a brief look at some early modern thinkers is presented in the epilogue. In terms of geographical limits, Italy is the main focus because this is where most early humanist thought on the Turks was generated. In addition to Italian humanists, though, Byzantines such as Cardinal Bessarion and George of Trebizond appear, as do the northerners Nicholas of Cusa, Erasmus, and the Spaniard John of Segovia.

This study is divided into four areas or themes and thus into as many chapters, plus an epilogue. I should stress that humanists moved back and forth between these categories, often in the same work. The purpose in dividing them here is to facilitate an understanding of both a dauntingly large body of literature and the unique attributes of each genre, not to imply that humanists perceived them as hard and fast divisions. Chapter 1 acts as a fitting opening by exploring medieval influences on humanist thought regarding the Turks, particularly crusade and chivalric literature. It demonstrates the sense of continuity humanists felt with medieval traditions as well as the ways in which they experimented with these models. In Chapter 2 I come to the heart of my argument: the influence of ancient Greek and Roman literature and thought on humanist attitudes toward the Turks. Here I explore the ways in which humanists, with the aid of classical thought, departed from medieval rhetoric and began to formulate a more recognizably modern and secular discourse of the Turks and Muslim cultures in general. Chapter 3 is devoted to the influence of Byzantium as well as Greek scholars and refugees who settled in Italy. Issues explored here include Greek views of the Turks and the loss of Greece, Greek and Italian perceptions of the modern Greeks as heirs to ancient Greece, and the complexity and ambivalence of humanist attitudes toward the modern Greeks. Chapter 4 is devoted to religious approaches to the Turkish threat inspired by Christian thought and/or anti-Islamic polemic. These include both traditional and more-creative polemics against Islam, works inspired by prophecy, and calls to convert the Turks or simply to make peace with them. This chapter will show how certain humanists continued to view the Turks as a religious problem, and how some frequently blurred the distinctions between the Turks and Muslims from other cultures. The final

section is an epilogue that traces the humanists' impact on later generations of writers.

My goal, then, is to open the conversation and debate on an over-
looked set of works that challenge views of not only Renaissance humanism and culture but also the history of cross-cultural perceptions.
Humanist reactions to the Ottoman Turks are a legacy of the Renaissance
no less important than the dignity of man, republican thought, and three-
point perspective in painting. Scholars have been attentive to bleaker aspects of Renaissance attitudes, such as the position and treatment of
women, religious minorities, and the poor. This study aims to show how
the enlightened humanists, who in many ways broke free of the confines
of medieval perceptions of other cultures, created a darker heritage to re-
place it. It will also show how some humanists did in fact embrace the
more peaceful, relativistic aspects of the humanist tradition, echoing Herodotus. Humanists drew on earlier examples, both ancient and medieval,
both positive and negative, but they created something very new and influential that would affect Western thought for centuries to come. Humanists, in short, added dimension and depth to preexisting cross-cultural
and religious perceptions and rhetoric, shaping them for use in a modern
context with resonance from Petrarch's world to our own. Just as they
defined "Western civilization" in terms still used today, they shaped Western perceptions of other cultures.

I would like to clarify what this study is *not* attempting to imply.
My focus on negative views of the Turks should not suggest that cultural
chauvinism is the unique province of the West. Muslims too were guilty
of cultural and religious biases in their dealings with Christians. The practice of dhimmitude, often portrayed romantically as proof of Muslim tolerance, was a repressive system whereby Jews and Christians were protected
but treated unequally in many ways.[51] Cultural perceptions were no better
than legal and political practice. A similar discourse of otherness and cul-
tural/religious superiority had long existed in the Muslim East. During
and even after the crusading period Muslim writers dismissively labeled
Westerners from all over Europe as the "Franj," or the Franks, using harsh
stereotypes to describe them.[52] Also, while Westerners wrote often about
the world of Islam—regardless of accuracy—Muslims exhibited slight interest in the West, confident that it had little of value to offer.[53] While the
Ottoman Empire made greater efforts to deal with Western governments,
their cultural attitudes have been depicted as more cosmopolitan and enlightened than the sources can prove.[54] Today, of course, the demoniza-

tion of the West by radical Muslim clerics and their followers is a problem
that even the most liberal of postmodern thinkers can no longer portray
as innocuous. These are undeniably important issues, but they take us well
beyond the parameters of this study. (My focus on Western attitudes and
their tendency toward chauvinism and hostility, then, should not be read
as an implication that more open-minded attitudes prevailed in the Muslim world or that reductive, hostile attitudes are excusable on either side
of the debate. It is my hope that this study will be read in tandem with
others viewing the issue from the East looking West so that this complex,
two-sided problem will be examined in its entirety.

I

Crusade and Charlemagne: Medieval Influences

BECAUSE THE MIDDLE AGES WITNESSED the first European responses to Islam, Renaissance humanists naturally turned to this period for inspiration and authority on the subject of the Ottoman Turks, finding such sources as crusade histories, chivalric literature, sermons, and theological works.[1] While the humanists' most original contributions to Western perceptions of Muslims may be found in their use of classical exempla, it is undeniable that medieval themes and language also played a role. Indeed, as many scholars have argued, Renaissance thinkers were not so antimedieval and secular as Jacob Burckhardt suggested; nor was there a sharp break between medieval and Renaissance ideals.[2] Several Italian humanists researched and wrote on the Middle Ages; some, such as Benedetto Accolti and Donato Acciaiuoli, deliberately chose medieval topics to generate an interest among contemporaries in crusading against the Ottoman Turks.[3] Images and rhetoric of crusading and Islam, then, represent particularly powerful examples of continuity between medieval and Renaissance thought. Yet humanists did more than merely echo these ideas; they also transformed them.

Humanist explorations of the medieval past produced some interesting results. On the one hand, it enabled them to view the Ottoman threat within a longer historical framework, making the crusades more relevant to their own time. Simultaneously, however, forging links to the medieval past may have created an unrealistic view of the Ottoman Turks. Comparing them to Muslims encountered by crusaders or by Charlemagne (in legend or reality) could produce a simplification and distortion of the Ottomans to make them fit the crusading or chivalric model. In some ways this comparison may reflect what Anthony Grafton has called "schizophrenic reading," in which humanists simultaneously read texts historically and ahistorically.[4] The historical approach promoted a greater understanding of the Crusades, while an ahistorical reading allowed humanists to lift their messages out of a medieval context so as to inspire readers to battle the Ottomans. While this method offered a multilayered engagement in medieval texts, it might also lead to confusion. The Seljuk Turks were not the Ottomans; the crusade battlefront and the nature of European warfare had also changed considerably since the late eleventh century. Still, if drawing on the medieval past sometimes clouded humanists' perceptions of the present-day Ottomans, the medieval heritage, like the classical heritage, provided a rich array of materials for constructing perceptions of the Turks as a cultural and religious adversary.

Medieval Perceptions of Muslims and Crusading

Before humanist reworkings of medieval themes on Islam and crusading can be analyzed, it is necessary to gain a brief sense of these attitudes in their original context.[5] The early centuries of Europe's confrontation with Islam (c. 630–1095) have been characterized as an "age of ignorance," with Spain and Byzantium being important exceptions.[6] While this has been shown to be an overstatement,[7] it is fair to say that most Europeans thought little about the rival religion until the era of the Crusades, which dramatically raised European interest in Islam and decisively shaped perceptions. Pope Urban II preached the call in 1095 for the first "armed pilgrimage" to the Holy Land in order to protect Christians and their shrines from the alleged ravages of Muslim rulers. Soldiers, increasingly chastised by the clergy for fighting fellow Christians, were given a chance to achieve glory and to channel their violence in a manner more acceptable to the Church, and purportedly to God. In exchange for their labors they would receive "remission of sins" or die as martyrs if they were struck down. In addition to enormous spiritual rewards, Urban proffered visions of plunder and lands for the taking. This military campaign was the first of several such undertakings that would later be termed "crusades."[8] Something in Urban's appeal struck a chord with the warrior aristocracy; the response was overwhelming.[9]

An important question for this study is how crusaders perceived the enemy they set off to fight. From its inception the crusading movement was marked by propaganda calling for vengeance by Christians.[10] The imagery crusaders absorbed from sermons combined with their own warlike mentality left little desire to explore foreign cultures. Some of these notions were taking shape before 1095, but the call for the First Crusade seems to have had the greatest impact on their formation.[11] The First Crusade would be widely preached through France, Italy, and Flanders, acting as an important source for burgeoning perceptions of Islam. The most famous of these sermons was Urban's speech at Clermont in 1095, which became the cornerstone of crusade preaching and propaganda.[12] In one account of the sermon Urban is reported to have said:

From the confines of Jerusalem and the city of Constantinople a horrible tale has gone forth and very frequently has been brought to our ears, namely, that a race from the kingdom of the Persians, an accursed race, a race utterly alienated from God, a generation forsooth which has not directed its heart and has not entrusted its spirit to God, has invaded the lands of those Christians and has depopulated them by the sword, pillage and fire; it has led away a part of the captives into its own country, and a part it has destroyed by cruel tortures; it has either entirely destroyed the churches of God or appropriated them for the rites of its own religion.[13]

The sermon goes on to describe specific abuses that include evisceration, circumcision, and rape. These images appear to have been exaggerated.[14] Nonetheless, Urban's speech filled crusaders with expectations of finding bloodthirsty, godless savages who delighted in torturing and killing defenseless Christians and in desecrating their shrines. Islam was presented as a sham religion, founded upon violence and unrestrained lust. The only way to deal with such people was to annihilate them. The savagery of the first crusaders in taking Jerusalem (1099), for example, bears witness to their view of Muslims as inhuman enemies of Christ.[15]

And yet perceptions of Muslim antagonism toward Christians were only one factor in the crusading movement. European Christians had goals of their own: to possess the Holy Land—an area they already felt was rightly theirs—and to expand their faith, influence, territory, and wealth. Islam was perceived as an obstacle to these ambitions. Moreover, the Crusades were symptomatic of a growing sense of cultural and religious unity in the West in the High Middle Ages.[16] Crusade preaching spoke to these evolving notions of religious and ethnic pride—among Latins in general but particularly among the Franks.[17] Westerners defined themselves in a host of ways, presenting Muslims in opposite and largely inaccurate terms that recall Said's model of "positional superiority."[18] For example, if Christianity was founded on love and chaste behavior, then Islam could only be perceived as a religion of violence and lust; if Latins were brave warriors, then Muslims were cowardly men who fired arrows from a distance or harassed noncombatants.[19] It should come as no surprise, then, that the Crusades, at least initially, did not expand European knowledge of Muslims and their religion.[20]

To some degree the stunning victories of the First Crusade seemed to confirm the Europeans' view of their own superiority. Western Christians were convinced, now more than ever, that theirs was the true faith and that crusaders were doing God's work.[21] Even chronicles of the crusade written by eyewitnesses who traveled to the Holy Land did little to dispel fantasies about Islam. These works employed the model of early martyrologies, casting Muslims as pagans of the same stripe as the ancients who persecuted early Christians. The gross inaccuracy of these characterizations did not prevent readers at home or even crusaders themselves, who should have known better, from believing such powerful myths.[22]

But feelings of hostility engendered by the Crusades did not represent the sum total of European attitudes toward Islam in the Middle Ages. While theologians continued to develop and support the theory of crusade and tout the religious superiority of Christians over Muslims, others could not contain their curiosity and admiration for Islamic culture and learning.[23] Such contradictory tendencies have been difficult to explain. As David Nirenberg argues, coexistence was not always peaceful but was in fact partially predicated on violence; hence a pattern of tense interrelations, in which conflict functions as a meeting ground, seems more realistic.[24] This would seem to be the case in Christian relations with Muslims. Religious and cultural differences made for a great deal of discomfort and tension, but they did not prevent fruitful exchange.

If the attitude of most crusaders toward Muslims was decidedly hostile, Franks who were born in the East or settled there often attained a more nuanced perspective. Despite the violence of many battles in the First Crusade, the Latins soon learned the merits of diplomacy, alliance, and cooperation with Muslim leaders in the area.[25] This is not to say that generations of Eastern-born Franks faced lives of perfect amity alongside Muslim neighbors; hostilities would flare up on both sides until the final collapse of the crusader kingdoms in 1291.[26] Nonetheless, a generation or so after the First Crusade it was not unusual for Franks to "go native," adopting the dress, cuisine, hygiene habits, and medical practices of Muslim residents, not to mention befriending local Muslims, as the Syrian writer Usamah Ibn-Munquidh's fascinating anecdotes illustrate.[27] Nor was the Holy Land the only site for such interactions; a good deal of political and cultural exchange took place at the court of Frederick II (1194–1250) in Sicily and in both Muslim and Christian courts in Spain.[28]

One of the most significant exchanges between Muslims and Christians occurred in the field of philosophy. Beginning in the ninth century Arabs translated Greek works and soon produced original works and commentaries of their own. The Christian West's rediscovery of Aristotle and the growth of scholastic thought were, in many ways, predicated on these Arab commentaries and translated texts.[29] Did the role of Islamic scholars in the growth of scholastic philosophy create a sense of interest in or sympathy for their culture and religion? Yes and no. As Rodinson observes, many Western thinkers "began to create an image of the Muslim world as the birthplace of the greatest and most wide-ranging philosophers."[30] Alauddin Samarrai argues that both Muslims and Western Christians had much in common, such as their Hellenic cultural roots; however, he also suggests that neither side was well aware of these shared attributes.[31] Moreover, indebtedness to Muslim thinkers did not prevent Latins such as Aquinas and Dante from characterizing Islam in unflattering terms. As in the case of Europeans wearing turban-inspired hats, borrowing from Muslim culture did not presuppose approval of it.[32]

While contacts with Muslims in the Holy Land, Spain, and Sicily were important, few Western Europeans traveled to these areas as crusaders, pilgrims, missionaries, traders, or scholars. Any favorable impressions brought back to Western Europe had to compete with a powerful body of stereotypes circulating in Europe. For most Western Christians, at least in the High Middle Ages, their education about Muslims began and ended with crusade propaganda, sermons, and perhaps literary works such as chansons de geste. Propaganda and sermons were obviously negative, but chansons de geste and romances could be more ambivalent. These oral and written literary pieces are extremely important in gauging popular opinions of Islam and crusade—opinions not directly manufactured by the clergy.[33] Perhaps the most popular of the chansons de geste, the *Song of Roland*, acquired the form we know today around 1100, when crusade imagery was inserted into this epic celebration of martial valor.[34] The Saracens of Spain are repeatedly styled as pagans and idolaters with a vague connection to the devil.[35] All of these images may represent a trend that gained popularity around the time of the First Crusade—that of viewing the Muslims as impious idolaters.[36]

While some songs dealing with crusade clearly drew on the doctrine, information, and propaganda of preachers and clerks, others were designed to entertain a lay, courtly audience and portrayed Muslims much like their French counterparts: noble, courtly, brave, loyal, and attractive. They served the important function of catering to the ideals and self-image of the nobility.[37] Jo Ann Cruz calls for a more nuanced reading of the chansons de geste; Saracens in these works often appear nobler than Christians who are divided, antagonistic, and treacherous toward one another.[38] Even the *Song of Roland* has some bright depictions of Saracens, notably Baligant the Babylonian Emir.[39] In short, portrayals of Muslims found in epics and romances, despite their general inaccuracy, may have gone a long way toward forcing Western audiences to see Muslims in a more complex and human context. The same can be said for fables and stories such as those of Pedro Alfonsi and Giovanni Boccaccio, which sometimes portrayed Muslims in a positive or neutral light.[40]

By the early fourteenth century, especially in northern Italy, where literacy levels were relatively high, the distinction between learned and popular works had narrowed. A growing body of literature was written in the vernacular and enjoyed a wide distribution among the mercantile classes and the highly educated. Dante's *Divine Comedy* offered depictions of Muslims and their faith to a large audience.[41] His attitude toward Islam and a few of its adherents appears to have been complex but, in the end, largely orthodox.[42] In canto 4 of the *Inferno*, Dante praises the accomplishments of the Arab philosophers Avicenna and Averroes as well as the great Muslim military leader Saladin. He places them all in Limbo, on the same level of distinction as great ancient thinkers and heroes who "did not sin; but if they have merit, that does not suffice, for they did not have baptism."[43] Although Dante could not imagine placing a non-Christian in paradise, he envisioned an equal fate for both ancient pagans, who lived before Christ, and Muslims, for whom the choice of Christianity was theoretically available.[44] Nevertheless, Dante's respect and sympathy for a handful of Muslims did not extend to most of their coreligionists or to Islam itself.[45] Dante's complex attitude reflects a growing tendency among medieval Italians to treat Muslims as a group as enemies, while appreciating the talents of certain individuals who greatly distinguished themselves.

An even more accommodating attitude toward Muslims is found in Giovanni Boccaccio's *Decameron*, a collection of one hundred stories written in Tuscan (c. 1351.)[46] Perhaps because merchants, who regularly traded with Muslims, figure prominently both as characters in the work and as a large proportion of its audience, Boccaccio reflects a strikingly nonjudgmental attitude toward Muslims. They often appear as benevolent rulers, as in the case of Saladin—who was already a legendary figure of chivalry and fairness in the medieval West—as partners in trade, or simply as regular characters caught up in tragic and comic circumstances.[47] The attitude resembles that of the English work *Travels of John Mandeville* (c. 1357).[48] Both reflect the period of prosperous trade in the East for Italian merchants and increased travel for pilgrims in the fourteenth century. These circumstances, combined with Boccaccio's desire to entertain—similar to those of many authors of chansons de geste—reflect a brief moment of more cosmopolitan attitudes. This is not to say that crusade is absent from this work; in one story (10.9) a merchant, who unknowingly befriends Saladin, also goes on crusade for "the honor of my body and the salvation of my soul."[49] Again, conflict and coexistence were not mutually exclusive.

By the mid-fourteenth century, then, European views of Islam and its adherents had acquired a complexity and richness, marked simultaneously by intolerance and compassion, as well as knowledge and mythology. But at this moment the Ottoman Turks began pushing westward, threatening European borders as no Muslim empire had done for several centuries. As a result of this threat Renaissance thinkers adopted an attitude toward Muslims that was more hostile on the whole than was that of their medieval predecessors. Many scholars and statesmen tried to revive the spirit of Christian unity and crusade; likewise humanists turned to the rhetoric and history of crusade to support a war against the Turks. Still others turned to the chivalric legend of Charlemagne as holy warrior. What marks most humanist borrowings from the medieval past, however, is the tendency to draw on the more defensive tendencies in both crusade history and chivalric literature.

Humanists and the Crusades

The first stirrings of humanist interest in crusade appear in the writings of Petrarch (1304–74). A cleric in minor orders, Petrarch served patrons such as the Colonna and Carrara families but spent most of his time devoted to independent study of ancient texts as well as the composition of poetry and prose in both Latin and Italian.[50] Petrarch had relatively little to say about the Ottoman Turks, whose growing strength did not begin to concern most Europeans until the later fourteenth century, but he frequently remarked on the Holy Land, the Mamluks who controlled that area, and the stagnant state of crusading. Although Petrarch's lifetime seems a low

point in crusading activity, falling between the loss of the crusader kingdom (Outremer) and the rise of the Ottomans, many events drew his attention to the Muslim East.[51] The fall of Outremer in 1291 was followed
by decades of spirited discussion and plans for its recovery. King Philip VI
of France planned to lead a large-scale crusade in the early 1330s.[52] Pope
Clement VI's crusade to Anatolia captured part of Smyrna in 1344. Peter
of Cyprus briefly conquered Alexandria in 1365, and Amadeo of Savoy won
victories in Gallipoli (1366). These events, added to calls for a crusade
against Byzantium, kept Petrarch interested in the East.

Indeed, Petrarch wrote a great deal on crusading and Islam in poetry,
in various prose works, and in his correspondence. In several letters directed to lay rulers and the papacy, he addressed the need for a crusade in
conjunction with calls for peace between Venice and Genoa or a return
to Rome by the emperor or the pope.[53] In such works Petrarch laid the
foundation for future humanist discourse on crusade and Islam by showing how classical texts and rhetoric could be applied in innovative ways to
an old, "medieval" subject. Nonetheless, as a product of medieval culture,
crusade was bound to summon up images of pilgrimage, knighthood, holy
war, and the "Infidel." A good deal of Petrarch's writings on crusade
and Islam incorporate these themes, showing the resilience and cultural
significance of medieval themes even for scholars steeped in the ancient
past.

Petrarch draws on the medieval crusade tradition in poem 28, "O
aspettata in ciel beata e bella" (1334), using well-established images of Islamic idolatry and polytheism. Here Petrarch celebrates Philip VI's crusade plans, urging him on by invoking the figures of a vengeful Christ and
Charlemagne—Philip's glorious predecessor and reputed ancestor. We can
detect the influence of medieval polemic in line 55, in which the Turks,
Arabs, and Chaldeans are described as "those who hope in gods" (*tutti
quei speran nelli Dei*), attributing polytheism to Muslims,[54] much like the
Song of Roland. It is possible that Petrarch knew better than to believe this
of Muslims but found religious polemic better suited to his purpose than
accurate depictions of Islam. The literary medium that Petrarch was working in may also have influenced him to use poetic license.

De vita solitaria, which he began in 1346 and revised later in Milan
(1353–60), shows a more pronounced influence of crusade imagery. In
book 2, chapter 9, of this work exalting the contemplative life, Petrarch
abruptly switches gears and defends pursuit of the active life in such causes
as crusade; he specifically cites the example of a famous hermit named

Peter, who left his peaceful solitude in order to preach and help lead the First Crusade. Bringing the subject back to his own times, Petrarch lashes out against the sloth of Christian princes, who refuse to tear themselves from their soft beds in order to save their patrimony from the Mamluks. This digression, starkly different in tone from the optimism of poem 28, likely arose from his disappointment over Philip's aborted crusade and the general lack of effort by Western powers to reclaim the Holy Land.

Although modern scholars tend to see Peter the Hermit as a fiery but irresponsible leader of the disastrous People's Crusade, his image in the Middle Ages was considerably less blemished.[55] Petrarch introduces Peter as a challenge to the contemplative ideal, asserting that, for the benefit of Christendom, sometimes one must venture out into the world:

This is Peter the Hermit who once led the solitary life in the region of Amiens, where however he did not remain hidden. For when Christ was beginning to grow indignant and wrathful at his own inheritance having been so long trampled upon by his enemies and ours, he did not reveal his wishes to any of those Christian kings enamored of comfortable sleep on down and purple, nor to Urban, the Pope of Rome, who, though an earnest and accomplished man, was preoccupied, but to Peter, a poor, inactive solitary, sleeping on a humble cot.[56]

Peter the Hermit's role in the liberation of the Holy Land quickly becomes a springboard for a larger discussion of the neglect of crusade in Petrarch's day. His emphasis on Christ's supposed indignation and the need for placing the Holy Land once again in Christian hands are reminiscent of medieval calls for crusade.[57] He describes the Holy Land as the patrimony of Christians: "And now shall the Egyptian dog hold this land which was promised to our forefathers and snatched away from us, which was destined for us if we were men,—the center of our hope, the pledge of our eternal home?"[58] This echoes the rhetoric used by Urban II in 1095, describing Jerusalem as "your [the crusaders'] Jerusalem" and a "royal city . . . now held captive by His [Christ's] enemies . . . in subjection to those who do not know God. . . ."[59] It is also reminiscent of Peter the Venerable's use of the epithet "dogs" to refer to Muslims.[60] Petrarch draws on common medieval polemical devices in describing Islam and the Prophet, but what makes *De vita solitaria*'s treatment of crusade radically different from that in earlier works is Petrarch's innovative use of classical and pagan figures, namely Julius Caesar, as role models for his contemporaries. By invoking the example of Caesar, Petrarch attempts to infuse the crusading ideal with the unflinching sense of duty associated with classical warriors.[61]

In tracing medieval roots of humanist discourse, then, it is important to note the divergences that made humanist works on crusade more than reiterations of familiar themes.

Crusading rhetoric and propaganda continued to appeal to humanists, as may be seen in Coluccio Salutati's passionate response to the Battle of Kosovo in 1389. Today historians view the battle as an Ottoman victory or, at best, a draw.[62] In the immediate aftermath of the battle, however, the Serbs and Bosnians had good reason to believe they had broken Ottoman power. Sultan Murad was killed shortly before the battle by a Serbian assassin. Moreover, Murad's son Bayezid I (1389–1403) was soon forced to leave the Balkans in order to deal with rebellion in Anatolia brought on by news of his father's death. While the long-term effects of the battle would spell trouble for the Balkans, King Tvrtko of Bosnia rejoiced in his victory in communications with Western powers.

As chancellor of Florence, Salutati composed his government's official reaction to Kosovo, portraying 1389 as a moment of hope.[63] He congratulates Tvrtko on his divinely granted, glorious victory over the "arrogantly mad and madly arrogant Mohammed-worshipper, Amurad [Murad], who had taken the empire of the Phrygians or Turks by force and planned to destroy Christianity and the name of our dear Savior from the face of the earth, and—if he could—to erase it from the book of the living."[64] The violence of Salutati's language conjures up crusade propaganda, portraying Muslim rulers as idolatrous and antagonistic to Christianity. While it is likely that early raids and punitive expeditions had generated a terrifying image of Murad and the Turks at war,[65] Ottoman policy in the Balkans was very different from Salutati's depiction. Murad was far more interested in maintaining local rulers as vassals than in depriving them of their lands.

It was only after the battles of Kosovo and Nicopolis (1396) that Murad's heir Bayezid would reject this precedent and begin placing Turks of steadier allegiance in positions of local power. Even so, Christian families of proven loyalty continued to hold lands from the Ottomans until the late fifteenth century; in time, conversion rather than replacement of Christians would alter this arrangement.[66] Moreover, while some of their practices were oppressive, the early Ottomans demonstrated relative tolerance that reflected both their interest in peaceful and stable government and respect for long-standing Muslim traditions. In exchange for paying a special tax, Christians and Jews, or *dhimmis*, were permitted to continue practicing their faith but restricted in other ways. Ottoman rulers even allowed Orthodox Christians and Jews to form self governing religious communities called *millets*, in which religious issues and civil suits were handled internally.[67] Hence, Ottoman rule of the Balkans brought advantages and disadvantages to the peasant class, but it did not correspond to Salutati's scene of wholesale persecution.

One might wonder, then, about the broader effects of Salutati's rhetorical borrowing from crusade literature, particularly in works that served a public, political function. On the one hand, the use of crusading propaganda and rhetoric certainly provided a rich historical and cultural context to Renaissance humanists and their audience, allowing them to recall a more triumphant time in Christendom's past and to inspire contemporaries to strive for the same glory. On the other hand, the use of such rhetoric could produce a serious disjunction between actual circumstances in the Ottoman Empire and the way they were portrayed by humanists. While Salutati and others seem to be using the medieval past selectively or ahistorically, one cannot help but wonder if this practice skewed their notion of the present, encouraging a vision of the Ottoman Empire that was comforting, perhaps, but still a caricature. It demonstrates a lack of interest on their part in knowing the details of Ottoman rule; it also shows a preference for depicting the Turks in stark crusading terms as an absolute enemy of all Christians rather than rulers who were, in some ways, no worse than the Balkan Christian elite had been.[68]

A few decades later Poggio Bracciolini (1380–1459) drew on the crusading theme of Christian sacrifice against the evils of Islam. One of the most eminent humanists of the quattrocento, Poggio held posts as papal secretary and Florentine chancellor. In addition he was an avid manuscript hunter and author of widely read dialogues, letters, and orations.[69] Poggio, like other humanists, was devoted to classical studies, both Latin and Greek, and frequently used them in his works on all subjects, including Turks and crusade. Yet he shows a greater predilection for the medieval rhetoric of crusade sermons and histories in his earlier works, such as his funeral oration on Cardinal Cesarini (1444) and his letter to John Hunyadi (1448).[70]

Both of these figures were connected with the struggle against the Turkish advance in Eastern Europe. Hunyadi, governor (*voivode*) of the Hungarian province of Transylvania, buoyed Christian hopes in Eastern and Western Europe by winning several victories in the 1440s against the Turks. During this time Pope Eugenius IV was planning the crusade promised to the Byzantine Empire in exchange for their unification with

the Roman See in 1439. Cardinal Giuliano Cesarini was sent by Eugenius
as papal legate to organize and guide the movement in Eastern courts.[71]
By Cesarini's arrival, however, Ottoman Sultan Murad II had already concluded a ten-year truce with local leaders and gone off to Asia Minor to
retire, entrusting power to his twelve-year-old son, Mehmed II, and the
youth's advisers. But Cesarini persuaded Hunyadi and Ladislas III, king
of both Poland and Hungary, to break the truce and march their small
force toward Varna, and Murad returned to confront them. After considerable difficulty in getting around a joint papal and Byzantine blockade in
the Dardanelles, he managed to cross the straits with the help of Genoese
ships. At Varna on 10 November 1444, Murad won a resounding victory;
both Ladislas and Cesarini were killed.[72] News of the defeat at Varna excited concern among Christians for the future of Eastern Europe.

The Poggio's funeral oration laments Cesarini's death as the loss of a pillar
of the Church. While Setton summarily dismisses this piece as a "jejune
oration unworthy of its subject," it is worth some examination on two
counts.[73] It provides interesting portrayals of Islam and the Turks. Equally
important, as part of an established genre, this funeral oration presents a
picture of contemporary ideals, offering both praise for the dead and cen-
sure for the living who fail to measure up to his example.[74] As such, Poggio
reveals the power that holy war continued to exercise on Italian Renaissance society. Honoring a clergyman who lost his life "in defense of the
faithful" (*pro fidelium defensione*), Poggio equates Cesarini with the arche-
typal Christian martyr, rather than, say, a classical hero: "there were once
almost innumerable martyrs who gave testimony to the faith of our Savior
with their blood. But through the fault of our times, this type of sanctity
has ceased for many generations. . . . Yet this man had renewed this forgot-
ten custom."[75]

The despair over the loss of Cesarini in 1444 was tempered a few years
later when John Hunyadi rallied and raised the hopes of Poggio and other
Western Europeans. In Hunyadi, Poggio found a rare living model of the
crusading spirit that had been lost in Cesarini. Writing to him in 1448, he
asks: "What indeed can be more glorious than to wage war against the
enemies of the faith in defense of the faithful?"[76] The Turks, in stark contrast, are described as "infidels" (*infideles*) and "enemies of the faith"
(*fidei hostes*). Such language of infidels and martyrs shows the resonance of
the crusade ideal even in fifteenth-century humanist circles. It creates an
engaged representation of the Ottoman Turks as a nefarious religious and

cultural enemy.[77] This notion is underscored and intensified by a passage in the letter to Hunyadi in which Poggio connects Islam with Satanism.[78]

To a lesser degree in these texts, classical elements mix with traditional crusade rhetoric. Cesarini's goals, according to Poggio, were not only defense and augmentation of the faith but also freeing Europe from the oppression of the "barbarians" (*liberandam Europam ab oppressione barbarorum*).[79] Here Poggio employs two classical concepts, the notion of "Europe" as a cultural-political entity and the barbarian archetype—ideas more commonly found in an ancient Greek or late Roman treatise than in a crusade piece.[80] Moreover, in addressing Hunyadi, Poggio equates his military prowess with that of great leaders and emperors of antiquity.[81] With such a departure Poggio would seem to have found a new Julius Caesar defending the faith as envisioned by Petrarch almost a century earlier. The overall feel of both pieces is a blending of medieval and classical motifs, a common approach in humanist works on the Ottomans, particularly before 1453.

Moving beyond crusade rhetoric, the history of holy war inspired several humanists in their writings on the Ottoman advance. The first humanist to write a full-fledged historical treatment of the Crusades was Flavio Biondo (1392–1463), a native of Forlì who spent most of his career as a secretary in the papal curia. In his *Historiarum ab inclinatione Romanorum decades* (completed in 1453), a general history covering the fall of the Roman Empire to present times, Biondo devotes no less than four books to the Crusades. He presents a full account of events from the Council of Clermont in 1095, where the First Crusade was preached, to the fall of Acre in 1291.[82]

Biondo often made use of his knowledge of crusading history when composing orations, holding up the success and commitment of early crusaders as a model to modern-day rulers facing the Ottoman Turks. One example of this strategy is seen in Biondo's exhortation *De expeditione in Turchos* (1453), written to enlist Alfonso of Naples's support for a crusade. Like most crusade orations, it is an example of deliberative rhetoric, debating the advantages of a future course of action, and is meant to be broadly disseminated.[83] When news of the fall of Constantinople hit Rome, Biondo's concern about the imminent danger to Italy and his eagerness for the recovery of the Greek city were such that he interrupted work on the *Decades* and *Italia Illustrata* in order to devote the next three weeks to composing the work.[84] Not only does Biondo affirm that Alfonso can beat back the Turks but he also encourages him to liberate the Holy Land. In

so doing he will follow in the footsteps of Scipio and Pompey but especially the illustrious early crusaders. Biondo goes on at great length about
how each crusade was built on the notion of cooperation between Christians for a greater good. After this long discussion he invokes the example
of some of the greatest crusaders to inspire Alfonso: "Thus did our Christians . . . during the time of Urban II, the Roman pope, cross the Bosporus
and triumph over the infidels with their leaders Hugh the Great, brother
of the king of France, Godfrey of Bouillon, and Bohemond, son of Robert
Guiscard, who first established your Italian kingdom, and thereafter many
others, whom there is not time and space to name."[85] Biondo's implication is that Alfonso can be a new Godfrey of Bouillon or, even better, a
new Bohemond. In this way he will revive the reputation of his kingdom
as a crusading state, just as the Norman rulers of southern Italy once
fought back the Saracens and even pursued them in the Holy Land. In an
oration to the doge of Genoa on the same theme, Biondo praises the naval
power's own distinguished past as an important part of the Crusades.[86]
Thus, although Biondo often showed a preference for classical models and
examples, he obviously felt compelled to use the powerful and appropriate
examples from medieval crusading history when he discussed the subject
of holy war.

Following Biondo's example, Giannozzo Manetti (1396–1459) used
early crusaders and popes as examples to Pope Calixtus III in his oration of
1455.[87] Written on behalf of Alfonso of Naples with the hope of convincing
Calixtus to appoint Alfonso leader of the papal crusade, Manetti ends the
oration with a reminder of the great alliances between popes and crusaders
in centuries past:

If it is written that, for the recovery of the Holy Land, John granted to Heraclius,
and Gelasius granted to Godfrey, and again, if for aid of the besieged city of Constantinople, Eugenius granted to Louis,[88] liberally and beneficently the faithful
signs of the holy cross, for which they rejected ornaments of power, then indeed,
you, most excellent Calixtus, by all means seem capable of granting by sacred law,
more liberally and magnificently, that same sign of the holy cross to King Alfonso
as well, since he would take up [the cross] not for the recovery of the Holy Land
as did the aforesaid Heraclius and Godfrey, not for the aid of Constantinople
against the Turks as did the above mentioned Louis, but rightly for the defense of
the Christian faith. . . .[89]

By referring to previous popes who gave their blessings to great crusaders,
Manetti tries to persuade Calixtus that he can achieve the same glory as

past crusading popes by allowing Alfonso to lead his expedition. This argument is made even more intriguing by the fact that the larger part of Manetti's oration revolves around a classical theme, Cicero's oration on the Manilian Law—the proposal to appoint Pompey to crush the rebellion of Mithridates IV in Asia Minor. Despite his attention to classical themes, however, Manetti finds it impossible to sustain the discourse of crusade without making some medieval references. What better role models to offer Calixtus than other popes who preceded him? What better way to encourage him to organize a crusade than to use the examples from the Crusades themselves? As the orator's goal was to persuade and motivate his audience toward a specific end, finishing on a strong, emotional note was crucial.[90] Manetti's decision to close the work with medieval crusading examples illustrates his belief in the Crusades as a symbolic rallying cry for his generation.[91]

A decade later the Aretine humanist Benedetto Accolti (1415–64) found inspiration in crusading history when discussing his government's attitude toward the Ottoman threat. Accolti was chancellor of the Florentine Republic from 1458 to 1464, a period that coincided with the reign of Pope Pius II. During these years the republic actively supported Pius's crusade efforts, as did Accolti, whom Black describes as part of a "circle of ardent crusading enthusiasts" in Florence. Accolti's religious fervor and concern for the plight of Eastern Christians made official compositions on crusade a personal matter as well. Whether composing instructions for ambassadors or official letters to other states, Accolti promoted the cause of crusade by wielding his skillful rhetoric on behalf of the republic.[92]

Perhaps the most prominent example of this is Accolti's history of the First Crusade, *De bello a christianis contra barbaros gesto pro Christi sepulcro et Iudea recuperandis libri IV* (1464)[93]—a fitting topic for a crusade lobbyist as it was the most successful of all the campaigns to the East. Although by nature an intellectual and religious exercise, *De bello* had an ancillary political purpose. At a time when Florence suffered criticism for its trade with the Ottomans, its antagonism with Venice, and its hesitancy about contributing openly to crusade, Accolti wrote this "semi-official history" to demonstrate his state's commitment to holy war.[94] In the work's dedication to Piero de' Medici, Accolti draws a bold parallel between the First Crusade and Europe's confrontation with the Ottoman Turks. Accolti challenges his readers to emulate the early crusaders by erasing "the common blot, which has grown enormously in our time, namely, that the enemies of the Christian religion not only hold His sepulcher but have extended their power far and wide.''[95] The first crusaders provide a dual model for Accolti: their example urges not only recovery of the Holy Land but also the more immediate concern of protecting the borders of Europe. Of course, as with Salutati's case, such images simplify and reduce the Ottoman threat, despite their rhetorical power. By the mid-fifteenth century the Turks were so well entrenched in Europe that a campaign similar to the First Crusade could never hope to dislodge them; the Ottomans were not disunited as were Muslims of the Holy Land, nor was crusading warfare as stripped down and portable as it had been in 1095.

Accolti's description of Muslim treatment of Christian shrines and Christian residents in the Holy Land in the eleventh century serves as another potent comparison to the Ottoman advance. Following the lead of medieval writers, such as Robert of St. Remy and William of Tyre, Accolti relates lurid tales of Muslim desecration and cruelty in Palestine on the eve of the First Crusade:

Nothing was more bitter to good men than [to behold] the capture of the province of Judaea, the profanation of temples and all the places through which Christ had passed, where He had performed His greatest miracles, [and] taught the truth with his words. . . . The disgrace of the thing was increased by the cruelty of the barbarians, who almost exterminated the Christian population in that province; indeed, an example of every kind of cruelty, lust and inhuman arrogance was performed by such men as these.[96]

Despite its eleventh-century setting, readers who were familiar with Ottoman victories would also recall more recent disasters.[97] In fact, in an oration read by Florentine ambassadors at the Congress of Mantua (1459)—a meeting called by Pope Pius II with the purpose of organizing a European-wide crusade—Accolti had used similar rhetoric and imagery to describe the plight of Christians living under the Ottoman Turks. In attempting to rouse would-be crusaders to defense of the faith, Accolti charged the Ottoman Turks with religious intolerance, idol worship, and sin: "[The Turks are] the enemies of Christ, whom they continually denounce with blasphemies, whose worshippers they persecute with inhuman cruelty, whose sacred churches they plunder, where, what is worse, in the place of God, they worship abominable and accursed demons—they who like sheep lead lives without struggling virtuously to overcome vice."[98] The similarities to Accolti's description of the Holy Land circa 1095, not to mention Urban II's sermon at Clermont, are striking.[99] Not only does this show that Accolti was familiar with medieval sources long before he began his crusade history but, more important, it also illustrates his notion of the versatility of these images to describe events separated by several centuries.[100] While reading about alleged events in the Holy Land from centuries earlier, Accolti's audience would also be reminded of the shame of the loss of Constantinople; conversely, while reading about the loss of Constantinople (with the desecration of churches and the rape and murder of the populace), they may have been transported back to the eleventh century. Of course, repetition of these lurid images had a positive goal to Accolti's mind; readers could think ahead, historically, to what was accomplished as a result of Urban's sermon and thus hope for a similar outcome in their own time. If Urban was able to motivate more than ninety thousand men to take the cross in 1095, Accolti believed that such words might have a similar effect vis-à-vis the Ottomans three and a half centuries later.

Although Accolti received most of his inspiration from medieval authors such as William of Tyre and Robert of St. Remy and, to a lesser extent, the early Renaissance writer Marin Sanuto,[101] he departed from these models in significant ways. Showing his humanist training, he added classical elements to his history, such as the addition, or invention, of speeches from key players.[102] By bringing new rhetorical polish to an old theme Accolti hoped to persuade his audience of the moral lessons of the past in the tradition of writers such as Sallust and Livy—sometimes at the cost of accuracy.[103] Consider Accolti's account of Urban II's speech, which repeatedly features the anachronistic *barbari*—a term that connotes a sense of cultural superiority rarely found in Western accounts of Muslims before the fifteenth century.[104] The only time he uses *barbarus* in original accounts of Urban's speech is when he describes the "barbarous peoples" who lived outside of Christendom on frozen islands to the *north* of Europe.[105]

Accuracy, it seems, was not Accolti's primary goal. Rather than reproducing his sources' words, Accolti endeavored to make the crusaders' deeds come alive so as to inspire his contemporaries to emulate them.[106] As such, Accolti assumed the role of orator, educating his audience on ethics and practical issues by means of active persuasion rather than sterile, unadorned fact.[107] For a great many humanist historians, reporting an event or one's sources verbatim without an eye to its implications or utility for the present-day audience was pointless. Petrarch had addressed this issue by daring to question the value of reading Aristotle. The highest achievement that could derive from reading past authorities, he argued, was not to become more learned but somehow "better"—a quest in which the words of great orators such as Cicero and Seneca "sting and set afire and urge toward love of virtue and hatred of vice."[108] For Accolti, altering the language of his medieval subjects and even inventing whole speeches served to remind his audience of their own Muslim threat, in language that they could more easily comprehend. Thus, his history is a fascinating blend of a medieval subject, contemporary references, humanist oratory and historiography, and the discourse of the Ottoman "other"—a figure that, in the 1460s, represented as much a cultural threat as a religious and political problem.[109]

While the military effects of Accolti's crusade rhetoric are debatable, it is clear that his use of such imagery in his historical and diplomatic compositions helped bring some medieval concepts into Renaissance political discourse. Indeed, Accolti repeated themes in the history that he had discussed in chancery documents: the Turks/Saracens as enemies of the faith, persecutors of Christians, threats to civilization and high culture, and so on.[110] Finally, the broad appeal of Accolti's history should be noted; it enjoyed a wide readership and several printings in the sixteenth century.[111] Thus, Accolti's blend of crusading commonplaces with humanist rhetoric helped continue the conceptual divide between Christian and Muslim, with the added nuances of East versus West and civilization versus barbarism.

Charlemagne and the Chivalric Model

In looking back to the Middle Ages for inspiration, some humanists seized on the deeds and the legend of Charlemagne. His appeal to classically minded humanists may not be obvious, given his identity as a Frankish king and (Holy) Roman emperor. Yet Charlemagne and his paladins had long been fixtures in Italian literature and folklore and would continue to enjoy popularity for years to come.[112] In the Renaissance they stood as an enduring example of chivalry, service to the faith, and crusading zeal. Evidence has been found of the circulation of Carolingian legends and heroes in Italy as early as the twelfth century. From the popularity of heroic names to literary references by Brunetto Latini and Dante, it is clear that stories of Charlemagne and his paladins were circulating, at least in oral form, by 1300.[113]

Romances dealing with Charlemagne and his paladins spread through

Italy during the fourteenth and fifteenth centuries; most were adapted from French or Franco-Veneto romances, but some plots were original concepts of Italian writers.[114] Many of these romances dealt with Islam or Muslim protagonists. Among them was *Il Fioravante*, a mid-fourteenth-century romance by an unknown writer, which was later used by the Florentine Andrea da Barberino (c. 1371–1431/32) for the first three books of his *I Reali di Francia*. Andrea wrote two other romances dealing with a Carolingian and Muslim theme: *L'Aspramonte* and *Guerrino il Meschino*. Barberino's influence and appeal in Italy during the Renaissance and later periods was profound.[115] He drew his audience from both the wealthy, literate mercantile and banking class of Florence seeking to surround themselves in aristocratic trappings and the lower classes throughout Italy, who probably came to know his stories through public readings and puppet theater.[116]

Both *Il Fioravante* and *l'Aspramonte* deal with the concept of Christian knighthood versus the Saracens, or "pagans."[117] Like many medieval romances, they show both positive and negative portrayals of Muslims. *Guerrino il Meschino*'s depiction of Muslims is somewhat more complex.[118] The plot revolves around Guerrino, the story's hero and a descendant of Charlemagne, who is kidnapped as a child by pirates and spends his youth wandering around Africa and the Middle East. As Gloria Allaire argues, Andrea drew on Christian medieval polemic to criticize and, occasionally, insult Islam. For instance, Guerrino visits a mosque, where he mocks the Muslim praying position (kneeling, with one's face to the ground) by pointing his posterior toward "the altar" (presumably the quiblah), which all Muslims face in prayer. Yet, despite Andrea's antipathy for Islam, he depicts individual Muslim characters and culture in *Guerrino* with greater dignity.[119]

Aspramonte, unlike Barberino's other romances, seems to draw much of its inspiration from the Turkish advance, mirroring Italy's growing fear of Ottoman designs in the Adriatic. This is reflected in the plot line's considerable focus on struggles against the Saracens. The romance opens with one Saracen king attacking Sicily and southern Italy and ends with his son attacking Vienna. The forces of Charlemagne repel both advances.[120] Perhaps this was intended as a message of hope to Barberino's countrymen. Ciarambino sees a conscious parallel and suggests that, in fifteenth-century narratives, Charlemagne's conflicts with the Saracens came to represent the cause of the Christian West against their Turkish enemies.[121] Charlemagne, then, offered Italian writers a vivid role model when crusade propaganda needed an infusion of new blood. But Charlemagne's role as a crusading icon was not invented in Renaissance Italy. By the late eleventh century, if not earlier, Charlemagne and his paladins were portrayed as Christian warriors courageously defending their faith against the Muslim rulers of Spain. In the *Song of Roland* they conquer the better part of Spain for their faith and force its Muslim inhabitants to choose conversion or death, but the historical record tells a very different story.

In 778 the governor of Barcelona, Ibn-al-Arabi, requested Charlemagne's aid against his enemy, Abderrahman, promising several Spanish cities in return. Charlemagne campaigned in Spain for a few months, but on his return home his rear guard was attacked by Basque raiders at Roncesvalles.[122] Some accounts, such as that of Ibn al-Athir and the *Nota Emilianense*, suggest that Arabs were present at the battle in order to avenge the Frankish destruction of Pamplona.[123] Whatever the circumstances of the attack, Charlemagne's campaign was not a holy war, nor was the Battle of Roncesvalles a symbolic standoff between two faiths. Nevertheless, by the late eleventh century Charlemagne's involvement in Spain had been transformed into a holy war. In his sermon at Clermont, Urban II cited the example of Charlemagne, his son Louis, and other French kings who "destroyed the kingdoms of the pagans and have extended in these lands the territory of the holy church."[124] This concept certainly survived in popular romances, but it even appeared in chronicles such as that of the Florentine Giovanni Villani (c. 1276–1348).[125]

Humanists were drawn to the legend of Charlemagne conquering the Muslims of Spain; many appear to have accepted it as fact.[126] The Florentine humanist Donato Acciaiuoli (1429–78) did so when he composed his *Vita Caroli* in 1461. Donato came from an illustrious Florentine family whose members ruled areas of Sicily and Greece. He would make his mark as a statesman, serving as a high-level diplomat and in 1474 as *Gonfaloniere* of justice. He also produced philosophical and political works, such as translations of Aristotle, Plutarch, and Bruni; commentaries on Aristotle; lives of Scipio, Hannibal, and Charlemagne; orations; and a large body of letters to fellow humanists and other associates.[127] His letters and several of his works demonstrate his hopes and concerns about the Ottoman advance, as does his association with other crusading enthusiasts in Florence.[128]

Donato presented his life of Charlemagne on behalf of the Florentine government to King Louis XI of France at his coronation. As one might imagine, Donato's account flattered Charlemagne, whom Louis claimed as a direct ancestor. A desire to please Louis may, in part, account for Donato's willingness to portray certain legends as true.[129] Louis, it appears, was delighted by the gift.[130] Charlemagne's Spanish campaign, for example, is glorified as nothing short of a holy war, complete with the conversion of several cities to Christianity: "Since, assuredly, in that time the barbarian peoples, who were declaring perpetual war on our religion, held Spain in the oppression of onerous servitude, Charles, moved by the indignity of this thing, set himself to liberating them."[131] Charlemagne, according to Acciaiuoli, was entirely motivated by piety and concern for the welfare of the Christian faith; his political goals are not mentioned. This pious motivation is not stated so much as it is implied in legendary accounts such as the *Song of Roland*. But Einhard, Acciaiuoli's main and most valued source, states no particular reason for Charlemagne's journey into Spain.[132]

Acciaiuoli's account of Charlemagne's Spanish campaign continues on the theme of holy war when the topic of forced conversion arises. Having won great victories in Spain, Charlemagne turns his energies toward stamping out Islam in the peninsula before he returns home to France: "Thus, nearly all of Spain came under the power of the Franks. The abandoned false gods having been defeated, Charles ordered that they [the Saracens] accept the law of the Christian faith."[133] Again, Donato describes an event that Einhard does not corroborate. Nowhere in Einhard's *vita* do we read about Muslim cities converting to Christianity—these concepts come straight out of legend and literature.[134] Still, this mélange of fact and fiction was treated as history, even by the educated Donato.[135] The fabled Spanish campaign was probably invoked here as political propaganda for recruiting French aid against the Turks; a more direct example may be found in Venetian humanist Bernardo Giustiniani's oration to Louis XI (1461/62).[136]

So appealing was Charlemagne to later generations in Italy that he appeared in local legends; Florentines, for example, claimed a connection to him in order to bolster their city's historical significance.[137] Donato, for one, argued that Florence was deeply indebted to Charlemagne for its liberty, laws, and civil order.[138] His goal here was most likely to convince Louis XI that Florence was as much the beneficiary of Charlemagne's legacy as France was, thereby suggesting a kinship between the two states. Indeed, Florentine ambassadors to the French court were instructed to mention Charlemagne's legendary link to their city to demonstrate the ancient bonds that tied the republic to the French ruling dynasty.[139] If connecting Charlemagne to one's city increased its prestige, connecting him to a mission such as crusade held a similar promise.

Charlemagne's Spanish campaign, however, was not the only holy war with which he was credited. Several medieval and Renaissance writers asserted that he journeyed to the Holy Land and liberated Jerusalem— over three hundred years before the "First" Crusade. The origins of this legend are a bit obscure, but they seem to have sprung from an amalgamation of sources. While the earliest accounts of the life and deeds of Charlemagne do not mention a trip to Jerusalem, Charlemagne did nonetheless have some connections to the Holy Land. In 799 the patriarch of Jerusalem sent Charlemagne his blessings and some relics from the Holy Sepulcher. This visit, ostensibly paid to announce the election of a new patriarch, was most likely intended to seek a donation from the wealthy Frankish king.[140] In 800 another embassy from the patriarch to Charlemagne brought gifts: a banner and the keys to both the Holy Sepulcher and Mount Calvary. This act is often read as the patriarch's attempt to place himself and Jerusalem, or at least the Church of the Holy Sepulcher, under Charlemagne's suzerainty; Charlemagne's embassies to and from Harun al-Rashid, caliph of Baghdad and ruler of Palestine, have thus been construed as negotiations to effect this transfer of power.[141]

It is more likely that Charlemagne, who was already in contact with the caliph for political reasons, receiving the unusual gift of an elephant in the process,[142] sent another embassy (802–6) to arrange for a much smaller exchange: the transference of the Church of Saint Mary (later known as Sancta Maria Latina) to the use of Latin Christians. In 806 or 807 Charlemagne was granted some sort of protectorate over the site, and he later arranged for both a hostel for pilgrims and a library to be built near the church.[143] Einhard relates some of the above details, saying that Harun al-Rashid granted Charlemagne jurisdiction over the Holy Sepulcher, no doubt conflating Saint Mary's, which was part of the complex of buildings around the Holy Sepulcher, with the great shrine itself.[144] As a result of the above circumstances, both the average reader of Einhard and pilgrims to Jerusalem could easily have received the impression that Charlemagne once possessed great authority in that city. Many pilgrims seem to have left Jerusalem thinking that Charlemagne *personally* founded the buildings they saw there.[145] Monastic chroniclers, in an effort to legitimate their houses' relics, inflated these suggestions of Charlemagne's authority in the Holy Land into assertions that he had indeed personally visited the area.[146] One thirteenth-century account went so far as to claim that Charlemagne liberated Jerusalem from Muslim rule while visiting the East and gathering relics.[147] Even the Jewish scholar Moses Maimonides (d. 1209) refers to Charlemagne's conquest, which suggests that the tale was accepted in the East as well as the West.[148]

Charlemagne's fabled journey to the East soon found its way into more chronicles and histories, giving it an increasingly genuine appearance. During the twelfth and thirteenth centuries French chroniclers—Alberic des Trois Fontaines, Helinand, Gui de Bazoches, Pierre Mangeard, and Pseudo-Turpin—related the story of Charlemagne's travels to the East as historical fact. During the fourteenth century Giovanni Villani described the legendary visit as follows:

[Charlemagne] with a force of twelve barons and peers of France called paladins . . . crossed the sea at the request of Emperor Michael of Constantinople and the patriarch of Jerusalem, and conquered the Holy Land which the Saracens occupied, and restored to the emperor all of the Levant which the Saracens and Turks had occupied. Returning to Constantinople, the Emperor Michael wanted to give Charlemagne many rich treasures, but Charlemagne refused them all except for some wood from the holy cross, and nails from Christ's passion.[149]

Villani adds to this that the relics are currently in Paris.

Literature provided an alternate conduit for the dissemination of the Charlemagne legend. The earliest example of such literary attempts appears to be the *Journey of Charlemagne*. This twelfth-century French romance has been described by one editor as "a light and jocular poem narrating the comical adventures of Charlemagne."[150] In this farcical take on the Charlemagne legend, the emperor visits Jerusalem but does not conquer it; on the contrary, he finds the city empty and takes the opportunity to stroll around and see the sights. He then visits Constantinople, where he is received with honor by the Byzantine emperor and returns home with a bevy of relics. Comical conceits pepper the work.[151] The overall effect of this poem is a ridiculous rendition of Charlemagne's supposed trip to the East that could not possibly have inspired would-be crusaders to take up the cross. Nonetheless, the poem may have appeared to its audience to be based on an actual voyage made by Charlemagne to Palestine.

Humanists reacted to the legend of Charlemagne in the Holy Land in various ways. Petrarch appears to be drawing on this legend in poems 27 and 28 of his *Canzoniere* when he invokes the figure of Charlemagne as crusader and role model for Philip. In poem 28 he describes how all eyes now turn to the place where the Lord was crucified: "[Christ] breathes into the breast of the new Charles that vengeance whose delay has harmed us and made Europe sigh for many years."[152] The "new Charles" may be a reference to the legend of Charlemagne in the Holy Land. If Petrarch is referring to this, he may be using poetic license since he does not describe Charlemagne as crusader to the Holy Land in prose works such as *De vita solitaria* or personal letters. Still, it is an effective image. By calling Philip a "new Charles" (*novo Carlo*), Petrarch figures him as Charlemagne's successor in taking up the "vendetta" of Holy War—a war that Charlemagne, protocrusader and Philip's ancestor, began. Apart from any real or perceived ancestral connection, Charlemagne is a fitting model for Philip. Here was a king who reputedly took Jerusalem with only the help of his paladins; Philip was hoping to emulate that success as a king leading crusade, albeit with a much larger force. Nor were there other positive examples on which to draw. Three French kings—Louis VII, Philip II, and Louis IX—attempted to liberate the Holy Land, but all failed. Thus, Petrarch needed to dig deeper into history or even legend to find a successful royal French crusader.

Humanist historians were more careful in their approach to the legend of Charlemagne in the Holy Land. Bruni, Biondo, and Accolti do not mention the legend in their discussions of Charlemagne or the Crusades.[153] How surprising it is, then, that no less a scholar than Aeneas Silvius Piccolomini cited Charlemagne's conquest of the Holy Land when he wrote in a letter of 1453, "With great effort, Charlemagne first laid claim to the Holy Land; thereafter it was lost, but was reclaimed by Godfrey."[154] Donato Acciaiuoli pursued more of a middle course regarding Charlemagne's involvement in the Holy Land. Like most of his humanist predecessors, he was unable to confirm the legend of Charlemagne in the Holy Land. He feels compelled, however, to mention the legend when other humanist historians preferred to avoid it:

Some writers add a notable event to the great deeds and memory [of Charlemagne], which I dare neither to affirm as certain, since there is no mention of it among other writers, nor to ignore as uncertain. And yet, because it is uncertain, I do not dare to leave it unmentioned. Namely, they say that when Jerusalem was held in the oppressive domination of the barbarians, Charlemagne was summoned by the entreaties of the Emperor Constantine. Simultaneously he was moved by the indignity of the matter to liberate that holiest place, whence the salvation of all men was born. He attacked with a huge army, and, having expelled the wretched barbarians from the entire province, he restored the city to the Christians and left it protected by strong fortresses.[155]

As a humanist historian who valued a critical approach to sources, he is troubled by the lack of supporting evidence for this legend—particularly in Einhard. Yet, Donato was reluctant to abandon the idea of Charlemagne as an early crusader. Again, his desire to please Louis XI, whom Donato called Charlemagne's "successor," may have been a factor.[156] Moreover, Donato's personal interest in seeing the Ottomans defeated may well have made them part of the subtext of his discussions of crusading; hence rhetorical goals of supporting holy war in his own day took precedence over historical accuracy. Just as Donato was attracted to legends associating Charlemagne's campaign in Spain with crusade ideology, he was unwilling to reject the possibility that Charlemagne had waged a holy war in Palestine.

George of Trebizond used the legend to inspire a different sort of campaign—an attack on Mamluk Egypt and the Holy Land. A Cretan humanist who served the papacy for many years, he watched the Ottomans advance into Greek territory with increasing anxiety, calling on Western leaders to save the shrinking Byzantine Empire.[157] In a crusade exhortation addressed first to Alfonso of Naples (1443) and later to Holy Roman Emperor Frederick III (1452), he discusses Charlemagne's legendary eastern conquests as a means to rouse them to crusade:

I entreat you, recall to mind why Charles, even in these times, is said to be so great. That same Charles who transferred the Roman imperium from Greece to the Gauls, who, lord of nearly all of Europe, vigorously attacked Africa. From this thing, his greatness was established. Was not Jerusalem liberated and Egypt and Syria brought under his sway? For when the Arabs occupied that holiest place, that most prudent king understood not only that the kingdoms and empire of the Christians would come spontaneously to him, but that he would also gain eternal praise, in heaven and on earth.[158]

Perhaps the questionable nature of this tale was evident to scholars who researched it as a historical question, but it was not of crucial import to humanists such as Petrarch, George of Trebizond, and Aeneas Silvius Piccolomini, who invoked the myth for its rhetorical and inspirational applications; Acciaiuoli appears to have had both purposes in mind. Undoubtedly the legend was still viewed as a powerful crusade motif even as some scholars were beginning to question it.

In the late fifteenth century the legend of Charlemagne's journey east was taken up by the Florentine humanist and poet Ugolino Verino (1438–1516) with considerably more respect for Charlemagne and his paladins as

heroic figures and warriors of Christ than was displayed by the author of
the *Journey of Charlemagne*.[159] The *Carlias* (begun in 1465–66) is an epic
poem in fifteen books that describes Charlemagne and his paladins' journey to and conquest of the Holy Land, their travels and adventures in the
East and the afterlife, and their return home, where Charlemagne confronts and defeats the Lombard king Desiderius.[160] Epic was an unusual
genre for fifteenth-century Florentine humanists, but it provided Verino
with greater opportunities to make use of myth and fantasy, which abound
in the work.[161] Although the main characters are medieval, Verino pat-
terned the work after Virgil's *Aeneid*.[162] The result is a creative mix of
classical imagery and poetry with medieval legend, history, and ideals. Nor
was Verino's choice of topic and approach accidental; the work was dedicated to Charles VIII of France, who fancied himself both a crusader and
a successor to Charlemagne.

Verino's treatment of holy war and his conceptualization of the Muslim enemy in the *Carlias* present both similarities to and departures from
medieval views. The poem begins with Charlemagne and his barons getting shipwrecked on the shores of Epirus, where they are hosted by its
king, Iustinus. As in the *Aeneid*, the ruler asks the travelers to tell of their
adventures, which occupy the next few books. In book 2 Charlemagne
describes his motivation for coming to the Holy Land in language reminiscent of medieval anti-Islamic polemic. Describing Islam as Muhammad's
"impious fictions" (*impia inventa*), whose converts are won by "sweet
enticements" (*dulcibus illecebris*), Charlemagne laments the corruption
that these "dreadful laws" (*dirae leges*) have wrought on the world.[163]
Having vilified Islam, Verino, in the voice of Charlemagne, decries Muslim
possession of the Holy Land:

Moved to pity, for the misfortunes of the human race, we thought it vile to fight
under a northern sky and to extend our war to the Rhiphaean mountains,[164] ne-
glecting the land of God which, pressed into servitude, the barbaric enemy has
befouled with impunity for many years after the citadel of Christ had been completely overthrown. Mangers stood before the sacred temples there. Indeed the
intermediary Raphael, the agent of God, sent from God's heaven on high, meeting
me, ordered me to take up these wars when night cloaked the earth in shadow.
Then I often seemed to be swept along to fight by the warning voice of God: "Are
you delaying to wrench away our dwelling places that have been stolen by savage
tyrants?"[165]

Verino's depiction of Charlemagne's supposed holy war draws freely on
crusade rhetoric. His words convey a belief that the Holy Land is some-

how the property of Christians; as the scene of Christ's life and passion, it represents the terrestrial focal point for man's redemption. As in Urban II's sermon at Clermont, Verino has described the Muslims as "befouling" and desecrating the Holy Land—stabling their horses in holy shrines. So great is God's displeasure that he cries out for justice and sends visions to crusaders—a common device in crusade histories and legends, as well as in ancient epics, in which gods and goddesses frequently intervene. By liberating the Holy Land, Charlemagne will be doing "God's will." Moved by this heavenly plea, Charlemagne and his paladins set off with a large army for the Holy Land, signed with the cross as the first crusaders had been. While Petrarch clothed Julius Caesar in crusader costume, Verino has inversely adorned a figure of chivalry and holy war with classical speech and virtues.

The *Carlias* provided Verino with a means to show his poetic mastery, winning praise from fellow humanists such as Poliziano.[166] It also functioned as a means to call for crusade and express his resentment and fears concerning Islam, issues that he would take up again in his panegyric on Ferdinand and Isabella's conquest of Granada in 1492.[167] It was certainly composed with an eye to please the French kings Louis and Charles, who were avid Charlemagne enthusiasts.[168] But Charles VIII's ambitions may have been a factor in yet another way. He spent the better part of his reign looking for ways to recover the Angevin kingdom of Naples and make good on distant claims to the Kingdom of Jerusalem; in 1494 he would invade Italy and briefly achieve the first of these goals. Like his father, Charles argued that a successful crusade could be predicated only on recovery of Italian claims, which would serve as a base for the expedition to the Holy Land.[169] This raises yet another connection to the *Aeneid*. Just as Virgil sought to legitimize Rome's legendary founding, Verino created a parallel epic foundation story, supporting the French dynasty and, specifically, its claim to the Holy Land.

Apocalyptic thought may also have influenced Verino's fantastical representation of Charlemagne as a divinely inspired crusader. A branch of millenarianism enjoyed a rise in popularity in the late fifteenth century—"the Second Charlemagne" prophecy. The idea originated in the Pseudo-Methodian concept of a Last World Emperor, but it acquired its distinctive character from Joachism—a popular prophetic tradition that developed from the apocalyptic writings of the Cistercian monk Joachim of Fiore (d. 1202). Followers of Joachim layered prophecies of the Last World Emperor over those of Joachim; in time this Last World Emperor became equated with the French dynasty and the figure of Charlemagne.[170] According to this prophecy, either a second Charlemagne would be born or Charlemagne himself reborn, from his line of descendants—much like the Arthurian *rex quondam rexque futurus* myth—and save the world. One of the tasks this Second Charlemagne was expected to fulfill was the reconquest of the Holy Land. Given the prophecy's propagandistic possibilities, this concept became a political tool for the French dynasty and its supporters in the mid-fourteenth century. The prophecy and its link to France became popular in Italy during the mid- to late fourteenth century.[171] Petrarch's use of the phrase the "new Charles" in poem 28 may have derived from it. Christine de Pizan's *Ditié de Jehanne d'Arc* and Pierre Dubois's *recuperatio* treatise (a tract on the recovery of the Holy Land), too, mention the Second Charlemagne prophecy.[172]

Verino seems to allude to the Second Charlemagne legend in the dedication of his work to Charles VIII of France when he says: "I have dedicated it to you in particular King Charles, not only because you derive name and bloodline from him [Charlemagne]. You truly emulate his ways and deeds. Thus we foresee in you the founder, having driven out again and thoroughly removed the stench of Muhammad from Jerusalem as well as every region, to be clothed in the sacred truth and imperial dignity of Christ a second time. . . ."[173] We cannot be sure if Verino believed in the Second Charlemagne prophecy, but his hope that Charles VIII would perform such glorious deeds *a second time* is suggestive. We do know that the French king saw himself in such a role. Another telling bit of information regarding Verino and the Second Charlemagne prophecy was his own connection with the fiery prophet Savonarola.

The Dominican friar Girolamo Savonarola (d. 1498) became an influential preacher in Florence during the 1490s. He acquired spiritual authority among all ranks of Florentine society through his preaching and prophecy, convincing many wealthy Florentines to consign frivolous possessions to his famous "bonfire of the vanities" for the good of their souls.[174] Savonarola also achieved political power in the Florentine government as an adviser and, on the dramatic occasion of the French arrival in Tuscany in November 1494, as a member of the delegation sent to negotiate with Charles VIII.[175] Verino became an admirer of Savonarola as early as 1491, the year in which he dedicated his *Carmen de Christiana religione* to the friar. Verino turned against him, however, in 1498 when the preacher began to be suspected of false prophecy and even heresy.[176]

Savonarola embraced the Second Charlemagne prophecy and applied it to Charles VIII, but it was not until late 1494 that the friar began publicly preaching about it—sometime after Verino dedicated the *Carlias* to Charles VIII.[177] Still, this does not preclude the possibility that Verino either knew of the prophecy years before meeting Savonarola or had conversed with the friar about the prophecy.[178] In any case, it seems likely that Verino consciously played on the Second Charlemagne prophecy as a means to earn favor for himself and for the Florentine Republic; Florentine ambassadors presented the work to Charles in 1493 in hopes of furthering good relations with the king, whose aspirations in Italy were already well known.[179] Marsilio Ficino too cited the Second Charlemagne prophecy in the brief period when he supported Savonarola, mentioning the legend in an oration to Charles VIII.[180]

The use of Charlemagne as a crusade hero by Petrarch, Donato Acciaiuoli, and Ugolino Verino indicates the extent to which chivalry still informed Renaissance views of crusading. Although crusade warfare and policy had changed since the High Middle Ages, for humanists the notion of crusade still conjured up inspiring images of kings and knights taking up the cross when their faith was in jeopardy. Charlemagne and the first crusaders stood as consummate men of Christian conviction and fierce action in an age when princes and kings too often proved to be indecisive and full of excuses. On a different level, however, the figure of Charlemagne also allowed humanists, particularly in Florence, to flatter the French monarchy while asserting the dynasty's historical and even prophetic ties to their city. Finally, for some, the eschatological promise of an eventual Christian victory over the Turks was spiritually comforting.[181]

Medieval perceptions and rhetoric regarding crusade and the Turks were still influential in Renaissance thought, even for humanists who tended to focus on the classical period. Accolti, Pius II, Biondo, Acciaiuoli, Verino, and others recognized the power of the language and themes of crusade and sought to incorporate them into their writings on the Turks. Not all humanist inquiries into the medieval past resulted in procrusade or anti-Islamic fervor, as will be seen in Chapter 4. But, positive or negative, humanists maintained certain medieval perceptions of Islam and crusade and helped bring them into modern Western thought.[182] Sometimes the use of medieval ideas of crusade and chivalry might obscure the realities of the Ottoman threat and European disunity. But this is not to say that the humanists absorbed and reproduced the medieval heritage uncritically, without adding their own unique nuances. They frequently applied classical rhetoric, history, and literature to medieval models. As such, they stretched these models beyond their limited applications and began to examine the Ottoman advance in terms we would consider more secular and modern. Hence, the medieval heritage was important to humanists, but their use of the classical heritage allowed them to see holy war and the Muslim threat in entirely new ways.

2

The New Barbarian: Redefining the Turks in Classical Terms

HUMANISTS USED THE CLASSICAL PAST as a guide for every subject on which they wrote; the Turks and crusade were no exception to this rule. Nor was this engagement with ancient texts a dry, academic exercise in volving humanists laboring to extract eloquent turns of phrase or a fitting parallel from literature or history. As Kenneth Gouwens has argued, humanists felt an intimate association, or "active relationship," with the ancient past; they collected artifacts and tried to re-create ancient conviviality in sodalities and dinner parties among the ruins of Rome.[1] Petrarch commonly engaged in dialogues or arguments with ancient authorities such as Cicero; Machiavelli's description of his exchanges with classical authors to formulate solutions to modern political problems is also well known.[2] Hence ancient texts provided a cultural context and a discursive field in which humanists placed not only themselves[3] but also the Ottoman Turks. This might seem a strange approach since the ancient period preceded the rise of Islam, the Crusades, and most of Christian history. But, as with other nonclassical subjects, the humanists saw connections that elude the modern eye. They also, of course, stretched their ancient models in some very creative ways in order to *make* them fit the Turkish advance.

Carol Quillen calls this mode of reading transformative; in a slightly different vein, James Hankins describes such ahistorical readings as "scholastic," and Anthony Grafton uses the term "allegorical."[4] All of these models apply to humanist writings on the Turks, revealing a spirited dialogue with ancient times and texts that sometimes preserved the original context and other times altered it significantly. Perhaps the greatest shift that classical rhetoric brought to discussions of the Turks was its secular tone. Few historians have suffered the kind of ritual beating that Jacob Burckhardt has been subjected to in the last few decades, but there is something to be said for his vision of the application of classical ideals as a secularizing force; this is certainly the case in humanist texts on the Turkish advance.[5]

Did humanists begin applying classical motifs to the Turks simply because of their love of ancient texts, or were other factors at play? Because historical context weighs heavily in the adoption of any given discourse, the nature of the Ottoman advance must be taken into account. There was no denying that this conflict was different from the Crusades, despite some efforts to compare the two: whereas crusaders fought Muslim armies in the Near East, the Ottomans were moving across the borders of Europe, more like the "barbarian invaders" of late antiquity. Moreover, the fall of Constantinople in 1453 resonated with the classical past for its perceived parallels to the fifth-century attacks on Rome. One last variable that encouraged classical treatment of the Turks was the influence of contemporary Byzantine attitudes.[6] The result was not only an increase in classically inspired rhetoric on the Turks but also the development of a more unified discourse of European civility versus Asian barbarism.

The originality of humanist treatments of the Turks is generally underappreciated or dismissed as old wine in new bottles.[7] Norman Daniel has characterized all texts on Islam written after the mid-fourteenth century as derivative of medieval texts.[8] Even Robert Schwoebel, who devoted the better part of a chapter in *The Shadow of the Crescent* to humanist writings on the Turks, prefaced it by quoting Daniel's assessment. The antique models of the humanists, he adds, "failed them" in their lack of objectivity toward the "barbarians" of their day. Daniel and Schwoebel's point about the humanists' failure to build a more objective body of knowledge is well taken, if only partially correct; some humanists discussed the Turks in a spirit approaching relativism. That notwithstanding, a lack of objectivity on the part of humanists need not imply a lack of originality. Their use of the classics was not only creative but, more important, also enabled them to forge new and influential paradigms for their contemporaries and future generations of Western thinkers.

Ancient Concepts of the East, Barbarians, and Foreigners

In rediscovering classical texts and rhetoric, humanists resurrected cultural prejudices of "barbarians" and foreigners, many of which had receded over the centuries. They also rediscovered ancient constructs of East and West or Europe and Asia as hard and fast cultural and political boundaries.

Ancient texts were revered as great authorities; hence they were powerful tools for evaluating other cultures, even in the face of contradictory empirical evidence during the Age of Discovery.[9] Even today some classically rooted ideas, such as the antagonism of East and West, continue to hold sway. How much more influence, then, might classical definitions of other cultures have held over early Renaissance readers who had little contact with the Turks?

The earliest developed notion of cultural difference in the West appears to have been the concept of barbarism. Originally the term "barbarian" was linguistic, referring to peoples who spoke not Greek but unintelligible "bar-bar." Homer provides the earliest use of the term *barbarophonoi*, or "bar-bar-speakers," in the early eighth century B.C.E. In Homer's case the term was merely descriptive, not derogatory.[10] In the fifth century B.C.E. a mixture of xenophobia and stereotyping took hold in Greek society as a result of the Persian Wars; during this time *barbaros* came to be used as a noun denoting the entire non-Greek world.[11] The Persian invasion was repelled by an alliance of only forty Greek states—a small percentage of the seven hundred or more Greek states in the Aegean area—but the phenomenon was significant enough to engender among Greeks a sense of Self and Other, or pan-Hellenism and barbarism.[12] One of the first expressions of the more pejorative use of "barbarian" is found in Aeschylus's play *The Persians* (472 B.C.E.), written in the wake of the defeated invasion of Greece (480–79 B.C.E.).[13] Here the Persians appear cowardly, soft and luxurious, and servile as opposed to the implied or stated courage, austerity, and egalitarianism of the Greeks.[14] A generation later Euripides (485–406 B.C.E.) incorporated the barbarian, Asian stereotype into many of his plays. The character of Dionysos in his *Bakkhai* hails from the East; he is at once exotic and effeminate and yet a source of horrific societal instability.[15] On the whole, Euripides' depiction of other cultures tended to be more complex, yet he found Eastern stereotypes compelling enough to repeat.[16]

Nearly half of the extant tragedies from fifth-century Athens either are set in a non-Greek land or portray barbarian characters, and almost all of these plays make some reference to barbarian customs or the superiority of Greeks.[17] These cultural messages, moreover, could reach a broad audience, given the staging of Athenian tragedies as public events, which accommodated as many as seventeen thousand people per performance.[18] Dramas of the fourth and fifth centuries have been described as "elite/mass texts . . . written and produced by elites for presentation to a mass audience"; tragedies, therefore, helped to forge communal consensus by dramatizing political and social ideals.[19] By extension, a sense of cultural identity or "Greekness" might have been defined for this mass audience against an opposite barbarian archetype.

The historian Herodotus was unique among Greeks for his greater tolerance of other cultures, for example, the Scythians.[20] Offering few explicit criticisms of their way of life, he refused to dismiss them as barbaric simply because their ways conflicted with Greek practices. He took an interest in their oral history and customs, while injecting surprisingly little criticism.[21] This is not to say that Herodotus was a complete relativist; he had strong views on the governments of other cultures and frequently employed the discourse of Self and Other.[22] Nonetheless, because of his relative receptivity toward other cultures, Herodotus became known among ancient Greeks as "a friend of the barbarians," a bias that would survive with amazing tenacity until the sixteenth century.[23] At least one of Herodotus's principles, however, would appeal to Renaissance thinkers: his sharp division between Greece and Asia or the East. His analysis of the Persian Wars as a deeply rooted conflict between Europe and Asia established a sense of geographical and cultural poles that would shape future Western thought.

A century later Aristotle developed political and climatic notions of barbarism. Comparing it to servitude, he cited the Greek practice of referring to prisoners of war not as slaves but as "barbarians."[24] Greek freedom and nobility are absolute, inherent qualities, whereas barbarians can only be considered noble in their own country, not among the Greeks—the implication being that barbarian dignity is negligible compared to that of Greeks. Hippocrates attributed the supposed inferiority of Asiatic peoples to their steady climate, which serves to make a man feeble and tame; the Greeks, by contrast, are stimulated mentally and physically by changes in temperature. If the climate does not ruin an Asian of strong mind and body, Hippocrates adds, life under the monarchy is sure to break him.[25]

An even harsher definition of barbarians as "raw, uncultivated and cruel men" arose during the Hellenistic and Roman Republican period.[26] For the Greeks "polished and cultivated" most certainly applied only to those trained in Hellenic learning and culture. But such learning and culture were generally only available to the Greco-Macedonian elite who ruled the lands conquered by Alexander; this class, moreover, tended to place itself at a distance from the local peoples and their cultural heritage. While Hellenism became more of a homogeneous culture among the elite classes, native culture throughout the eastern Mediterranean and the Middle East—in the form of language, literature, and to a lesser extent history, religion, and art—was deliberately snubbed by the Greeks.[27] At the same time, however, Stoicism achieved a softening of the concept of barbarism by conceding that barbaric traits—primarily inhumane, animal-like stupidity—could be applied to *all* men, not just foreigners. As a result the Germanic peoples, despite their unintelligible language and foreign status, could be regarded as possessing a civilization of inherent value.[28] By the Hellenistic and Republican period then, three interpretations of "barbarian" existed: 1) non-Greek speakers; 2) foreigners, especially enemies; and 3) raw, uncultivated, and cruel men.[29]

While the Romans adopted many Greek ideals, their views of other cultures diverge in some ways. One does not, for example, find so hard and fast a concept of the barbarian among Roman writers. Perhaps this is due to the imperial and integrative nature of the Roman state. As its empire grew, Rome showed a willingness to incorporate non-Romans into its administration and army. In 90 B.C.E. Rome extended full citizenship to all Italians; in 212 B.C.E. citizenship was granted to all free inhabitants of the Roman Empire. If Romans had ever been as xenophobic as the Greeks—which seems unlikely—they would have needed to temper some of their biases in order to run their empire. Roman soldiers often campaigned with foreign auxiliaries such as Germanic tribesmen. Moreover, Romans did not need to travel to encounter foreigners since many of the capital's inhabitants were Greek or Eastern slaves or freedmen.[30]

Not all Romans were so cosmopolitan. Cato the Censor, among others, was a harsh critic of foreign—namely Greek—influence on Romans. Having been educated in Greek language and literature, he appreciated their merits but worried that they might diminish his countrymen's pride in Rome's substantial cultural achievements.[31] Roman attitudes toward Greeks were often marked by a sense of rivalry, owing to the accomplishments of Greek culture and the rapid advancement of the "hungry little Greek" (*Graeculus esuriens*) by Roman patrons.[32] Even Cicero, who greatly admired Greek culture and learning, did not shrink from employing the stereotype of Greeks as untrustworthy smooth talkers.[33] By way of contrast, Romans saw less to fear or compete with in northern barbarians, whom they admired in some ways but generally regarded as cultural inferiors.[34] Julius Caesar, for instance, described the Gauls as flighty, rash, and generally weak, but otherwise he did not go out of his way to criticize them.[35] In book 1 of the *Gallic Wars* he harshly depicts Ariovistus and the

Gauls as barbaric, but he does this to justify his controversial military attack on the Roman ally without formal sanction. Apart from the section on Ariovistus, his tone regarding the barbarians is markedly more open-minded; he praises the Atuatuci for their bravery and the Suebi for their heartiness.[36]

One can read a scathing account of the "barbaric" Gauls in Cicero's *Pro Fonteio* (70 B.C.E.). In an attempt to discredit the Gauls who testified regarding the corruption of Marcus Fonteius, praetor of Gaul, Cicero hurled an array of cultural insults their way. He accused them of capriciousness, inherent mendacity—as opposed to the sobriety and honesty of Romans testifying in Fonteius's defense—impiety, and human sacrifice.[37] Cicero even mocks their cloaks and breeches, their proud walks, and gestures, not to mention their coarse language.[38] But Cicero's speech is problematic. Momigliano calls it "cheap ethnography" and notes the "desperate vagueness," as well as paucity, of Cicero's thought on the Gauls.[39] Still, it shows a ready-made, hostile discourse, which could be turned against northern Europeans when needed.

In general, as long as the peace was kept, Roman attitudes tended to be benevolent. Polemical depictions of "barbarians" increased as barbarian invasions mounted.[40] Still, more-negative rhetoric comes from the eastern part of the empire, which largely escaped living in proximity to Germanic barbarians; in the West, where Roman and barbarian often dwelled together, there were fewer antibarbarian expressions.[41] In addition, barbaric origins were regarded as no serious handicap so long as the culture in question—such as the Turdetani in Strabo's account of Spain—took to Rome's civilizing influence.[42] We can probably attribute the increased hostility toward barbarians in the eastern part of the empire to the influence of Greek attitudes. These attitudes were echoed in Roman views of the East, though not necessarily of the North or South.[43] Greeks and Romans tended to produce similar images of Easterners as soft, effeminate, and unenterprising, unlike the warlike, if also crude, Westerners. Easterners showed their softness in their decadent dress and their cowardice in fighting at a distance with bows and arrows.[44] Living under kings and despots, they were viewed as slaves given to flattery and corruption.[45]

Some negative statements about the Germanic peoples can be found in Tacitus's *Germania*. Idleness and sloth among the Germans in times of peace are noted in chapter 15, for example.[46] Still, Tacitus portrays the Germans as possessing a certain austerity and moral backbone that he feared the Romans had lost. Tacitus's *Agricola* shows some admiration for the Britons and their attempts to preserve their freedom.[47] At one point in Chapter 21 it describes Agricola's efforts to bring Roman culture and religion to the Britons—not the action of an isolationist who refused to mix with the local barbarians. True, Tacitus, like Caesar, does refer to the Britons as "barbari" on occasion, but only in reaction to specific practices of the Britons, not their entire culture. Even Ammianus Marcellinus, writing about the Alans and the Huns in the fourth century C.E., presents a fairly balanced picture of these peoples. In some respects he finds them savage, but he admires their courage and skill in battle; on the whole his tone betrays more wonder than hostility for these most unusual peoples.[48] Of course, Ammianus can be brutal in his judgments on other peoples, such as the nomadic, half-nude, and wife-swapping Saraceni, whom, he states, "we never found desirable as friends or as enemies."[49] Finally, the poet Claudian openly praised Stilicho, a Vandal who rose to the rank of master of the soldiers and regent for Emperor Honorius in the late fourth century C.E.[50]

As Arnaldo Momigliano has noted, compared to the Greeks the Romans were simply more curious about other cultures. It was the Romans who learned Greek in large numbers, while most Greeks preferred not to learn Latin or other "barbaric tongues." It was the Romans who eagerly read Greek studies of peoples such as the Celts and Parthians and used this knowledge to further their conquests. It was in Italy where the most successful religious syncretism took place.[51] Perhaps the most widespread example of syncretism was the Roman form of Mithraism that imperial soldiers, merchants, and other travelers eagerly brought back from Persian territories.[52] Yet another important distinction between the Romans and the Greeks with respect to other cultures is that the Romans did not automatically designate all non-Romans "barbari" as the Greeks did with other cultures.

Adding to Rome's comparatively tolerant approach to foreigners and migratory groups was the spread of Christianity in the Roman Empire—a religion that attempted to reach out to all social groups, people in every religion and profession, and most important for our discussion, people from every land and culture. Barbarians were not pushed aside but rather welcomed into Christian communities and sought out by missionaries. In early Christian thought, barbarians were shown no bias: "Here there is not 'Gentile and Jew,' 'circumcised and uncircumcised,' 'Barbarian and Scythian,' . . . but Christ is all things and in all" (Col. 3:11).[53] Salvian found no reason to attack the barbarians as he attributed their shameful and vicious ways to their ignorance of the word of God; Christians were held more accountable for their bad behavior since they had no excuse.[54]

Christian thinkers began to shed this sanguine outlook as increased contact with barbarian peoples produced unhappy and unexpected results. Many pagan tribes snubbed the word of God, or worse, attacked and killed the venerable missionaries who attempted to convert them. Depending on which source one reads, the Scythians were believed to have killed either Saint Andrew or Saint Philip.[55] Furthermore, late antique Christians were horrified by tales of destruction of great cities and civilizations at the hands of barbarians. Saint Jerome, to cite one example, decried the abuses of the Goths in the sack of Rome (410 C.E.).[56] Christian rhetoric attacking the savagery of the barbarians was fully articulated in the later fifth century by writers in Constantinople such as Zosimus as more cities and kingdoms were lost to Vandals, and other invaders.[57] By Justinian's time such a view of the barbarians was well established in the works of writers such as Procopius.

Renaissance humanists found quite an assortment of approaches to foreigners and "barbarians" in classical texts, many of which were being rediscovered by manuscript hunters. In some humanist texts one can pinpoint the sources being used. Other texts seem to recall a more vague tradition of thought or historical memory. Whatever the case, classical examples opened up an entirely different approach to the Turks, allowing humanists to travel far beyond the medieval confines of religion and chivalry. For the first time in centuries they could view this foreign people in secular terms—terms that might prove as hostile as religious slurs or more open-minded political and cultural evaluations. In either case the use of classical sources gave humanists an opportunity to create a whole new discourse of the Ottoman Turks.

Early Humanist Appraisals of the Turks and Islam via Classical Sources (c. 1330–1453)

Even as humanists drew on traditions of crusade and chivalric literature in their early writings on the Ottoman Turks, they began experimenting with ancient rhetoric and history, combining classical and medieval motifs in surprising ways. This experiment was a bit hesitant at first, suggesting that the genre of classical approaches to the Turks was still being worked out. Petrarch was probably the first humanist to address crusading and Islam, especially via classical concepts, characters, and language.[58] In addition to Charlemagne references and medieval polemic, classical allusions abound in Petrarch's poem 28, "O aspettata in ciel beata e bella." Franco Cardini has noted the parallels Petrarch draws in the poem between Philip VI's planned crusade and the Persian War: "we enter a clash between 'civility' and 'barbarity,' that is not so much the collision of Christianity and Islam, but rather the Herodotean conflict between Europe and Asia."[59] Specific references to the Persian War include mentions of "the reckless daring of Xerxes" (*il temerario ardir di Xerse*) and the battle of Marathon.[60] The notion of antagonism between East and West may be seen in his description of "a western wind" (*un vento occidental*) blowing the soul to the Holy Land (*verace oriente*). It also appears in images of Europe's sighs over the delayed vengeance in the Holy Land and the defeat of "the unhappy folk of the East" in the Persian Wars.[61] The superiority of Europeans to Muslims is asserted in a verse contrasting the Germanic warrior spirit (literally, *tedesco furor*) of the people who live in a land "that always lies in ice and frozen in the snows, all distant from the path of the sun" to the softness of Muslim peoples: "Turks, Arabs, and Chaldeans . . . a naked, cowardly, and lazy people who never grasp the steel but entrust all their blows to the wind."[62] Here Petrarch echoes ancient Roman disdain for the "unmanly" Eastern tactic of archery and praise for the northern and western technique of hand-to-hand combat.[63] Note that Petrarch is silent regarding the Greco-Roman designation of northerners as dim-witted in comparison to quick-minded southerners. But his Western chauvinism does not rest solely and uncritically with the Germanic peoples; he concludes the canzone with praise and a challenge for Italy.[64]

Drawing on myth and history, Petrarch reminds fellow Italians of their distinguished military past with the examples of Romulus and Augustus. He cites Rome's generous practice of defending allies. How much more worthy of Italian aid, he asks, is Christ himself?[65] This is the first of several instances in which Petrarch uses classical heroes as models for late medieval crusaders—a strikingly innovative device. Before Petrarch, the most commonly cited examples of crusading valor were Christian warriors who could also exemplify piety and religious conviction. Charlemagne, kings of France, and crusaders such as Godfrey or Bohemond were logical symbols of Christian knighthood. Remember that Petrarch offered Peter the Hermit and Charlemagne as examples for would-be crusaders. Yet since such figures fall short of Petrarch's vision of an ideal crusader, he is compelled to consult the ancient past to find it. It is a testament to

Petrarch's humanism that even crusade, a concept so thoroughly medieval, is reshaped to correspond with classical precepts.

In no work is this more true than in *De vita solitaria*, in which Petrarch offers crusaders the unorthodox role model of Julius Caesar. Petrarch had already invoked the figure of Augustus in poem 28, but in *De vita solitaria* Petrarch tries to paint Julius as a would-be Christian. By doing so he symbolically unites the two Romes—ancient Rome and Christian Rome:

Say father, for it pleases me to put the question, if Julius Caesar should come back from the lower regions, bringing with him his former spirit and power and if, living in Rome, that is his own country, he should acknowledge the name of Christ as he doubtless would, do you think he would any longer suffer the Egyptian thief . . . to possess not only Jerusalem and Judea and Syria but even Egypt and Alexandria?[66]

This passage underscores two novel themes. First, Petrarch, in true humanist fashion, argues that the most virtuous and worthy of pre-Christian pagans would indubitably have accepted Christ. Second, as a Christian, Caesar would have brought all his military prowess to bear against the enemies of the faith—the implication being that holy war would take precedence over more secular pursuits of glory and gain.

These two concepts are presented together, lest the reader (or Petrarch) forget that Caesar was a pagan and that crusade was, in theory, a religious enterprise. Petrarch feels the need to introduce this caveat into the discussion because he is still somewhat hesitant about blending pagan and Christian virtues; a line exists between the two for him that he cannot completely ignore. Yet this does not stop him from extolling virtues and wisdom common to both pagans and Christians when he sees them.[67] The tension evident in Petrarch's use of classical figures or concepts to promote crusade shows us how tentative and fresh are his attempts to combine the cultural contexts of antiquity and crusade.

Eventually Petrarch arrives at his purpose in placing a pagan general in his discussion of holy war. Regardless of Caesar's personal life, his military prowess alone should inspire those who would crusade: "I do not inquire into the justice of the performance [conquering lands, supposedly, for Cleopatra], but I admire his force and energy of spirit and declare it necessary to our own time."[68] To Petrarch's mind, Caesar was one of the greatest heroes in history. He was both a brilliant and courageous general and the immediate predecessor of Augustus, who united the world into which Christ was born, thereby paving the way for the spread of Christianity and Latin culture. He is an excellent example for crusaders because of his heroism but also because of his ability to bring East and West together under the rule of Rome. Caesar's beliefs, then, are of less importance here than his masterful soldiery and ambition. Having redefined crusading role models, Petrarch set a powerful precedent for later humanists. They would enthusiastically follow his example of equating ancient heroes and victories with crusade endeavors, but with greater confidence.

Petrarch united a very different classical concept with crusade in *De vita solitaria* that may explain how he arrived at the notion of invoking Caesar. Hoping to shame Christians into fighting for the Holy Land and their faith, he reminds his readers how Christianity and Latin culture once dominated the known world. As an illustration of his point he draws from the life of Saint Augustine. Though born in Africa, Augustine's native language was Latin; Greek was a foreign language to him.[69] Describing the vast expanse of Africa and how much of the continent (according to medieval geographical knowledge) was once imbued with both Roman learning and Christianity, Petrarch then contemplates the expulsion of Latin culture from these regions: "I believe that you will not find any one there who understands or loves our literature, unless he chance to be some pilgrim, or merchant or captive."[70] This brief passage further illustrates Petrarch's association of the spread of Christianity with the dissemination of Latin language and culture. An empire once united by religion, language, and education has been fragmented through the advent of Islam.

Petrarch, then, sees a tangible divide between "good" Latin culture and "bad"—effete, perverted, and mean—Arab culture, which he disparages in one of his letters (*Epistolae Seniles*, 12.2).[71] Finally, Petrarch's view of Arab/Eastern culture takes on a deeper shade of meaning with a brief but intriguing passage in *De vita solitaria*. Here Petrarch appears to echo a classically based belief in Western cultural and religious superiority *predating* Islam; this occurs in a reference to Saint Jerome writing about the spread of Christianity through France, Britain, and other Western regions, as well as "Africa, Persia, and the East, and all the barbaric lands (*omnemque barbariem*)."[72] Petrarch's use of the term "barbarian" is not particularly well defined here, but it may point to the beginning of a trend that would mark most humanist discourse toward the Turks and Islam in general.[73]

While Petrarch's references to Julius Caesar as crusader and his sorrow at the decline of the Latin language, religion, and culture in African and Eastern regions may seem like random, awkward attempts to impose classicism on crusade, they form a compellingly coherent vision: passion for ancient Rome and a desire to see the resurgence of modern Rome. His letters to Charles IV, the Holy Roman Emperor, and Pope Urban V convey this longing.[74] Interestingly, in almost all of these letters he urges the leaders not only to return to Rome and help unite Christendom but also to lead crusades to the Holy Land. Petrarch's vision of the far-flung power of Rome and the once broad span of Christianity is inseparable from his support for crusade and his disdain for any culture that attempts to rival that of the Latins—Byzantium included.[75] Petrarch offers a particularly strong example of how vividly a humanist's love of ancient Rome could color and constrain his view of the world around him. The greatest period in world history was the era of the Roman Empire; if it were revived under Christian leadership, there could be no room for another empire or religion in the Mediterranean world. Blending elements of the pagan Roman past with the modern Christian world, he presents a transformative reading of both eras and an imaginative answer to the "Muslim problem."

The Turks rarely appear in Petrarch's works, but by the time Coluccio Salutati wrote in the late fourteenth century the Ottoman Empire was a threat to both European interests in the East and to Europe itself. Scholars and statesmen such as Salutati (1331–1406) began to comment more on this people and the threat they posed to Christendom. Chancellor of the Florentine republic from 1375 until his death, Salutati wrote numerous personal letters and works including *De laboribus Herculis, De fato et fortuna*, and *De tyranno*.[76] While much of his scholarly output was "medieval" in inspiration, Salutati's innovative use of classical rhetoric and ideals so much affected the course of humanism that Hans Baron regards him as a highly influential figure in the founding of a new movement called "civic humanism."[77] Salutati's treatment of the Turkish threat parallels his eclecticism as a humanist: in some ways he embraced the views of Petrarch; in others he struck out in radically new directions.

While Salutati's reaction to the battle of Kosovo (1389) reflected the fear and resentment most Europeans felt toward the Ottomans at this time and made use of medieval polemic on Islam, his discussion of the Turks in a letter of 1397 was considerably more complex.[78] Of course, much had changed in eight years on the Ottoman front. In 1396 a crusading force comprised primarily of Burgundian and French troops, released from hostilities of the Hundred Years' War by a recent truce, and Venetian ships headed east to battle the Turks. Joined by recruits from England, Germany, and Italy, the forces were still not as large as they could have been, which was the result of poor planning and timing. Still, the army was hopeful—spurred on by dreams of chivalry and hopes of erasing the stigma of the loss of the Holy Land a century earlier. The troops assembled at Buda, joined with King Sigismund of Hungary's army, and marched toward Nicopolis in August 1396. While besieging the city they were met by a large Ottoman army. The fighting was fierce and might have gone in favor of the crusaders, but the battle was decided by the arrival of Bayezid I's Serbian ally, Stephen Lazarevich. As eyewitness Johan Schiltberger recounts, the prisoners were initially slaughtered, but many were ransomed or sold into slavery.[79] This instance shows the complexity of political alliances in that a Christian, albeit an Orthodox Christian, decided to fight against crusaders on the side of the "Infidel."

The failed Crusade of Nicopolis would have two important ramifications. For the Balkans, the failure at Nicopolis helped to ensure that Serbia, Bosnia, and Albania would come directly under Ottoman control in the following century.[80] For Western Europeans, 1396 represented a tremendous psychological blow to the crusade ideal: the Turks proved superior to Hungarians trained on the Turkish frontier as well as French and Burgundian knights schooled in the Hundred Years' War.[81] Literary works such as Christine de Pizan's *Dit de Poissy* hint at the demoralizing effect of the loss on the French aristocracy years afterward.[82]

The stunning victory of the Ottomans against the flower of European chivalry may have forced Salutati to rise above his previous crusading polemic in order to consider the Ottomans' military and social organization. Nicopolis also stingingly symbolized the unity and vigor of the Ottomans at a time when Western Europeans were experiencing a long and frustrating papal schism.[83] For nearly twenty years the papacy had endured the embarrassing crisis of two popes representing the Roman and Avignonese factions, with each claiming to be the rightful pontiff. As a humanist and master rhetorician, he took up his pen on behalf of the Church torn by scandal and discord, addressing both the Schism and the Ottoman Turks in a letter (dated 20 August 1397) to Iodoco, Margrave of Moravia and a delegate at the Diet of Frankfurt. Letters of humanists, especially government officials such as Salutati, often functioned as essays on moral, philosophical, political, or intellectual issues; unlike most correspondence today, they were intended for broad dissemination and copied and collected by their authors as carefully executed rhetorical pieces.[84]

Initially, Salutati's purpose in discussing the Muslims seems to be to illustrate a simple analogy between Christian schism and the errors of Islam.[85] But his discussion soon expands to a lengthy consideration of the Turkish people. He introduces them as *Teucri*, not *Turchi*, defending his choice of spelling with the argument that the Turks presently rule the land of Troy, or *Teucria* and putting less importance on their place of origin, believed to be the Caucasus Mountains.[86] Here, Salutati appears to be invoking a medieval tradition placing the Turks among the descendants of the ancient Trojans, specifically an individual named Turchot.[87] While Salutati does not elaborate on his meaning or his intent, his reference to the legend has important implications. It links the Turks to a noble, ancient people regarded as the ancestors of the Romans.

Salutati describes the Turks as a fierce and determined people whose advance represents a grave threat to Europe: "The Turks are an extremely ferocious race of men with high expectations. Do not ignore what I mention here. They trust and believe that they will erase the name of Christ throughout the world and they say that it is in their fates to devastate Italy until they reach the city divided by a river, which they interpret as Rome, and they will consume everything by fire and sword."[88] Imagine how ominously this prediction would echo in the minds of fourteenth-century Europeans who had recently experienced the Black Death and were still living with the Schism. Salutati's depiction of the power and ambition of the Turks may have been designed to alarm his contemporaries, but the ethnographic discussion that follows provides more than a simple warning. The length and detail of Salutati's description of Turkish customs indicates a keen interest in their culture and more accurate knowledge than he demonstrated in 1389.

A conspicuous aspect of Salutati's discussion is his attention to the Turkish military machine. He examines battle tactics such as feigned retreat but focuses mostly on the individual soldier and his rigorous training:

It is astonishing how the leaders cultivate their men in the art of war; ten or twelve year-old boys are seized for military service. Through hunting and labors they inure and harden them, and through running, leaping and this daily training and experience they become vigorous. They eat coarse food and heavy black bread with many kinds of grains mixed into it; whatever delicate foods they eat are acquired by the sweat of hunting. They are so well trained that they live contentedly with only one set of clothing and on bread alone. Remarkably tolerant of cold and heat, they endure rain and snow without complaint.[89]

The statement regarding the seizure of ten- or twelve-year-old boys is most likely a reference to the practice of *devshirme* and the janissary corps.

Introduced by Murad I, the notorious yet highly effective *devshirme* has been described as "an institution of artificial kinship" in which boys between the ages of eight and eighteen were periodically levied from subject Christian areas (mainly the Balkans and, after the sixteenth century, Anatolia).[90] The boys were converted to Islam and hired out to Turkish farmers, who taught them the language and faith of their newly adopted culture. On completion of their training they joined an elite fighting force called the "janissaries." Probably beginning in Mehmed II's reign (1451–81), a select few of these youths were educated and placed into service at the palace.[91] While some individuals and families benefited from the opportunities inherent in the practice, most European Christians decried this system.[92] And yet Salutati does not. It is puzzling that apart from his use of *rapiunt*, denoting seizure, Salutati does not comment on the compulsory nature of the boy tribute, and he entirely neglects to mention that these were Christian boys who were forced to convert to Islam as part of their training. Instead he applauds the success of the Turks, judging them by the effects rather than the methods of their system, regardless of its exploitation of Christians.

In some ways this portrait of the Turks resembles the classical model of "the noble savage." Often Germanic or Scythian, the noble savage was idealized as uncorrupted by society's degenerative influences. As in Tacitus's description of the Germans, Salutati commends the Turks for their rigorous, simple lifestyle and military discipline. But as Salutati probably did not have access to this work, more likely models may have been Caesar or Seneca.[93] In other ways, however, his portrayal goes beyond classical models, certainly of the noble savage. This may be seen in his acknowledgment of the Turks' agricultural, military, and political organization—all regarded as signs of a highly developed civilization.

The strong and simple faith of the Turks and a willingness to die for that faith also attract Salutati's admiration: "Indeed they are not barbarians to the extent that they do not believe in the existence of God or a future life and glory; but they consider it a certainty that fighters for the Lord or his perpetual law are received into glory. To the extent that they believe more firmly, they live more simply and less learnedly."[94] What is so arresting about these brief, dispassionate statements is their hint of respect for the beliefs of Islam and the concept of *jihad*, so rarely seen among Salutati's contemporaries. Another intriguing aspect of the above statement is its contradiction of most humanist perceptions of barbarism, specifically a lack of education as an inherent evil.[95]

Toward the end of this discussion Salutati makes what is perhaps his most striking assertion. After praising their strengths in battle, including agility, speed, and the cunning technique of feigned retreat and counterattack, he boldly states: "believe me, when I observe the customs, life, and institutions of this race of men, I remember the religious practice and customs of the mighty Romans."[96] Just a few decades earlier Petrarch was modeling the ideal crusader and champion of the West on Julius Caesar, Pompey, and Scipio Africanus, but Salutati turns this model on its head. He does this by implying in not-so-veiled terms that the rough-and-ready Turkish infidels possess more of the ancient Roman spirit than do modern Italians. Perhaps this is a link to his description of the Turks as Trojans— the same people whom the ancient Romans claimed as their ancestors in works such as Virgil's *Aeneid*. Perhaps Salutati used this image to shame Christians into ending the Schism.[97] While Salutati's anguish over the Schism is apparent, this does not explain the effusiveness of his praise for the Turks. Even Tacitus, in exposing Roman degeneracy by contrasting his people with the Germans, passed many negative judgments on the latter group; in the end we still have a sense that Tacitus would not wish his culture to adopt more than a few Germanic customs. And yet Salutati's ardent praise for the Turks seems more than a mere literary device or a means of chiding Christian society. It certainly seems out of place with his political writings in which he claimed Roman ancestry, as well as republican virtues such as love of liberty, for contemporary Florentines.[98] To some degree Salutati seems to have admired the Turks who embodied Roman *virtus* and made Christendom look quibbling, weak, and divided.

Salutati's approach to the Turks in his letter of 1397 does not appear to have set major trends for early quattrocento humanists, but his innovation did not die with him. Some later fifteenth-century and early sixteenth-century humanists compared the Turks to Trojans or Romans: Giovanni Mario Filelfo did so in his poem *Amyris* (1471–76), and in the early sixteenth century some Venetian *baili*, or resident ambassadors in Istanbul, made such comparisons in their reports.[99] For the next few decades, however, humanist perceptions of the Turks tended to be harsh. Writing in the 1440s, Florentine humanist Leonardo Bruni (1370–1444) helped develop the concept of the Turks as barbarians by equating them with the ancient Goths who ravaged Rome. A central figure in quattrocento humanism, specifically civic humanism, Bruni served as papal secretary and, from 1427 until his death, chancellor of Florence. Accomplished in Greek as well as Latin, he authored such works as the *Panegyric on the City of Florence* and

The History of the Florentine People; he also translated Aristotle's *Ethics* and *Politics* and composed *The Constitution of Florence* in Greek.[100]

Bruni presents a brief but intriguing equation of the ancient past with the Turkish advance in a letter (dated 1440–44) to an anonymous recipient, probably Sicco Polenton.[101] The letter is an answer to the correspondent's queries regarding Livy's history of Rome, specifically the question of how many books in Livy's history were lost. Although some thirty books survive, Bruni replies, Livy had written over one hundred. The loss of these books is attributed to the occupation of Italy by the Goths and the Lombards: "To come to your question, assuredly, the cause of the loss, I imagine, is Italy's former affliction by the Goths and the Lombards who oppressed our people with a long invasion and such calamity that they wholly forgot books and studies."[102] During this long servitude—over 364 years, by Bruni's reckoning—the Goths and Lombards destroyed many cities. Education suffered terribly, and books nearly disappeared.[103] Here, Bruni echoes Petrarch's vision of the "dark ages," a perception of the Middle Ages that would survive well into recent years.[104]

But for Bruni the "dark ages" were even darker since the beginning of this period witnessed not only the loss of Rome's glory—which Petrarch especially laments—but also the loss of so much of its learning. In 1401 Bruni had complained that "it would certainly take me all day to name those [ancient authors] of whom our age has been deprived," citing the specific examples of Varro, Livy, Sallust, Pliny, and Cicero.[105] At that time he blamed no particular group for these losses, but in 1436 Bruni was placing the blame squarely on the shoulders of the Goths and Vandals, who brought Roman learning—already weakened under its tyrannical emperors—to a state of near obliteration.[106] Bruni may have been influenced in this view by reading Procopius's account of the Italian war against the Goths, which he paraphrased in 1441. His knowledge of this source undoubtedly helped him become more acquainted with the Goths than were most of his Western contemporaries.[107] Only in Greek accounts such as Procopius's could this period of history become accessible, Bruni explains, since "no record had survived [of the Gothic War] among the Latins— only a kind of myth, and this insubstantial and shadowy."[108]

These images of barbarians and lost texts, intriguing in and of themselves, take on yet another facet as Bruni compares ancient Rome and its barbaric adversaries to contemporary Greece and its new-style barbarians, the Turks: "As it was, to a certain degree, in Italy then, so it is now in Greece, occupied by the Turks. For the Greek nation is now so afflicted that, among those who were once teachers and leaders of learning, now there are hardly to be found any who have even rudimentary knowledge of letters."[109] Bruni accuses the Turks of destroying cities and, as a result, the learning that once flourished there.[110] Like Salutati before him, Bruni perceives a decline in Byzantine learning; unlike Salutati, he blames the Turks rather than Greek indolence.[111] Perhaps discussions with Greek delegates at the Council of Florence (1439) or his correspondence with Ciriaco of Ancona, an Italian scholar traveling in Greece at the time who blamed the Turks for the destruction of ancient sites, influenced this view.[112]

From a purely academic standpoint, the Turks alarmed humanists such as Bruni for the threat they posed to learning.[113] To appreciate his fears, consider the number of ancient texts being rediscovered in the early fifteenth century by manuscript hunters such as Poggio Bracciolini and Giovanni Aurispa.[114] Important ancient texts, thought to be lost forever, were recovered and brought back into circulation for the first time in many centuries. If the original loss of these texts was blamed on the "old barbarians," what might the "new barbarians" do to the treasures of learning if their depredations remained unchecked? This question, raised in an aside by Bruni in 1444, would be taken up with greater urgency by humanists after the fall of Constantinople.

While Bruni comes close to calling the Turks "barbarians" without directly using such terminology, other humanists began using this highly charged word around the same time. Poggio applied the term to the Ottomans in the aftermath of the crusade of Varna in 1444. Venetian humanist and statesman Bernardo Giustiniani exhorted Holy Roman Emperor Frederick III on his coronation in 1452 to lead Christians in crusade against "the barbarians."[115] Still, these early uses of the term "barbarian" had not yet reached the level of a "discourse" on the Turks. A stronger and more unified rhetoric and set of images would come as the result of one catastrophic event: the fall of Constantinople.

The Turks as Barbarian Enemies of Civilization: 1453 and Beyond

The fall of Constantinople in 1453 was a dramatic event with serious repercussions for both East and West.[116] A great strategic and symbolic victory for the Ottomans, the conquest made the Turks appear virtually unstoppable to Westerners and excited more horror and concern than any Ottoman

battle preceding or following it for some time to come. Greek and Turkish
accounts tended to present a slightly milder version of events, depicting
more looting and capture of the citizens than gratuitous slaughter,[117] but
Latin writers, whose reports circulated in Western Europe, painted a more
gruesome story.[118] Eyewitnesses such as the Genoese archbishop of Myti-
lene Leonard of Chios and Niccolò Barbaro of Venice[119] describe the sack
in violent terms with mass slaughter, rape, and enslavement. Regarding
damage done to the city in the siege and sack, there is little disagreement
among the sources from all sides: many churches and other buildings were
burned or looted. Precious relics were given no consideration by the invaders, who saw them only in terms of monetary worth or as idolatrous
objects to be destroyed.[120] While Greek and Latin accounts differed somewhat in tone regarding the Turks, they agreed that 1453 was a tragedy of
epic proportions. It represented thousands of lost lives and the end of a
once great and glorious empire, the seat of Greek learning and religion.

The shocking news of the loss of Constantinople was soon followed
by calls for a crusade to recover the city and head off a rumored Turkish
attack on western Europe.[121] Perhaps the most notable political response
was the Peace of Lodi (1454), a general truce between the major powers
of Italy, which afforded the peninsula a certain measure of calm for the
next forty years and established the Most Holy League to combat the
Turkish advance.[122] Despite numerous small campaigns, in the end no
large-scale crusade was mounted as political rivalries and tensions within
Europe proved to be insurmountable. Concern regarding the Turkish advance, however, should not be underestimated.[123] We can gain a sense of
the publicity that the Turkish advance was generating from the volume of
sermons and laments that survive from the period. Laments were often
sung as well as copied and printed; hence they could be transmitted to a
broad—literate and illiterate—audience, apprising them of specific details
and actors in the events of 1453. As "repositories of memory" and "erup-
tion[s] of political feeling," they kept 1453 and the Turkish threat alive in
the minds of several generations.[124] Nor were Christians the only contemporaries to mourn the fall of Constantinople; at least one Jewish writer
composed a lament in Hebrew.[125] The collection of crusading tithes, too,
is a testament to widespread concern and support of crusade.[126] The newly
developed printing press provided an effective means of informing many
people about planned crusades, victories and losses, and the character of
the Turks; one tract on the fall of Constantinople, probably composed in
1453 and printed for the first time around 1474, shows that the topic was

still significant two decades later.[127] Indulgences were soon printed and sold, and there were calendars that featured rousing calls for crusade at the start of each month.[128]

Few groups were more deeply affected by the fall of Constantinople than the humanists. The event had an enormous psychological and intellectual impact on them and intensified a growing interest in the Turkish advance; it also greatly increased the number of texts they wrote on the subject.[129] More important, 1453 affected the way humanists wrote, precipitating a crystallization of rhetoric into a recognizable discourse on the Turks.[130] One might well argue that this unity of rhetoric had less to do with 1453 per se than with the maturation of humanism as a school of thought—a process decades in the making that provided humanists a ready-made classical vocabulary. Given their training in the same sources and methods as well as their friendships and avid correspondence with one another, humanists may be viewed as working within a common cultural context or discursive field.[131] Such conditions help explain the similarities in language.

And yet the jarring experience of 1453 had much to do with the formation of this discourse and its rapid spread. The foundation may have been laid earlier, but the event and vivid reports that circulated in Europe made humanists choose their terms in specific, unique ways. This is not to say that either 1453 or their common educational background would lead all humanists to speak or write *one* discourse on the Turks. Still, a dominant characteristic of most humanist writings on the Turks after 1453 is their use, to the point of fetishism, of Greco-Roman concepts of civility versus barbarism. Most humanists would embrace, either passingly or passionately, the rhetoric of the Turks as "the new barbarian,"[132] strengthening and spreading their image as enemies of civilization as well as the faith. And yet—albeit to a much lesser extent—the reverse also applies after 1453. The military genius demonstrated by the Turks in their rapid seizure of Constantinople led some humanists to depict the Turks in more flattering classical terms, comparing them to ancient heroes—something few, if any, humanists had done since Salutati.

While it is clear that 1453 greatly increased and focused the discourse of Turks as barbarians, the precise cause or causes are not immediately apparent. This was certainly not the first disastrous loss to the Turks. Massive defeats had taken place at Nicopolis and Varna, among other places, but these events did not unleash a torrent of accusations of barbarism. Why was 1453 special? One reason is that the siege of Constantinople, unlike other military defeats, involved many noncombatants who were captured or killed. Equally or more important was the unique position Constantinople had occupied as a former Roman capital and a center of culture and learning. Both the loss of life and the political and cultural losses feature prominently in humanist responses to the siege.

Tales of unrestrained slaughter frequently appeared in reactions to the siege. Recall Cardinal Bessarion's horror over reports of Turkish barbarism and atrocities.[133] In his *Expugnatio Constantinopolitana* (1455) Niccolò Tignosi—a Florentine humanist, physician, and possibly the tutor of Marsilio Ficino—makes an acerbic pun: "they are not *teucri* [Turks] but rather *truces* [butchers]."[134] Aeneas Silvius Piccolomini repeated the popular image: "so much blood was shed that it flowed in streams through the streets."[135] Poggio Bracciolini described his countrymen's reactions to news of the fall of Constantinople, specifically their lamentations over "the harsh and savage cruelty of the barbarians that raged in the slaughter and blood of the faithful."[136]

Allegations of Turkish cruelty did not focus on slaughter alone but also on sexual violence.[137] Aeneas Silvius Piccolomini (1405–64), who received word of the siege in Germany while serving as secretary of the chancery to Emperor Frederick III, brought high drama to tales of the siege in some of the most eloquent and emotional laments to be composed. His letters, on 1453 and other topics, would receive wide distribution in several printed editions.[138] Given his long commitment to crusade, he was more passionate about the Turks than were many of his contemporaries; he would devote much of his clerical career, as bishop of Siena and Trieste and especially as Pope Pius II (1458–64), to promoting crusade.[139] Sparing no detail, Aeneas paints a lurid image of the Turks and their leader as wanton rapists:

What utter slaughter in the imperial city would I relate, virgins having been prostituted, boys made to submit as women, nuns raped, and all sort of monks and women treated wickedly? . . . Those who were present say that the foul leader of the Turks, or to speak more aptly, that most repulsive beast, raped on the high altar of Hagia Sophia, before everyone's eyes, the most noble, royal maiden, and her young brother, and then ordered them killed.[140]

While it is likely that the soldiers were guilty of rape, the story about Mehmed II publicly violating scions of the royal family on the high altar of Hagia Sophia is certainly apocryphal. For one thing, the emperor was unmarried and childless.[141] It is true that Mehmed took captives of both sexes into his seraglio, and those who were unwilling to accept his advances might face severe penalties. According to some sources, this was the fate of the son of the Grand Duke Lucas Notaras. The boy was executed, as were Notaras and his son-in-law for refusing to allow the boy to be dishonored.[142]

The myth of Mehmed's rape of the royal maiden probably attracted the attention of humanists such as Aeneas for its resemblance to the rape of King Priam's daughter in tales of the sack of Troy. Indeed, the use of ancient literary treatments of sieges was widespread in reactions to 1453. Leslie F. Smith rightly calls attention to the formulaic quality of these descriptions and demonstrates the extent to which the language echoes Virgil's description of the fall of Troy or Innocent III's reaction to the crusaders' brutal sack of Constantinople in 1204. This parallel to classical or medieval exempla does not necessarily mean that all the events described were invented, but it does raise some doubts as to whether they were exaggerated to correspond to these models. Smith perhaps takes his point too far when he argues that these formulas might lead us to question how genuinely shocked humanists were by news of Turkish atrocities.[143] Formulaic speech may render accounts of the siege less historically reliable, but the borrowing of language from other sources should not place the authors' emotions or horror in question. To humanists, 1453 was an epic event; it only makes sense that, as trained rhetoricians, they would seek to bring an epic quality to their writings on the subject. A conscious use of classical or medieval rhetoric was meant to empower their diatribes and to underscore the horror of the siege.[144]

With humanists repeating, and often embellishing, tales of unrestrained slaughter, enslavement, and rape of the population of Constantinople, the Turks began to occupy a most sinister niche of the European imagination—as cruel and lascivious barbarians. Although other scholars have argued that the lustful and cruel stereotypes of Turks only cohered and spread in the eighteenth and nineteenth centuries,[145] the popularity of these stories about the sultan and his soldiers implies that this stereotype may have been in place as early as the fifteenth century.

Compounding their sorrow over human suffering in 1453, humanists also lamented the great losses to Western security and culture. No ordinary Christian city, Constantinople was viewed as a barrier between Europe and the Infidel.[146] Despite complicated Latin attitudes toward the Greeks and the Turkish invasion of the Balkans, the image of Constantinople as protector still endured in both East and West.[147] Europeans felt vulnerable and frightened when "the bulwark of Christendom" fell. On a very different level, Constantinople possessed a rich heritage as an illustrious city, continuously occupied for many centuries. This fact, added to its famous monuments, churches, and libraries, made the city seem a living piece of ancient history to Western scholars—a vision shattered by reports of the sack.

Eyewitness and humanist Leonard of Chios described the looting of churches, adding further details in descriptions of how the soldiers vandalized altars and statues and even mocked the crucifix by parading it through their camp with a Turkish cap on its head while cursing it and spitting on it.[148] Perhaps the worst act of desecration was Sultan Mehmed II's conversion of the great cathedral of Hagia Sophia into a mosque. Humanists responded with great alarm to tales of the physical destruction of religious buildings and artifacts. Tignosi describes the spectacle of young Christians being disemboweled near altars and other holy places while the Turks trampled holy relics, violated tombs, and blasphemed and burned churches.[149] Aeneas Silvius Piccolomini also describes the damage done to churches as an unusual occurrence in the history of warfare.[150]

But Aeneas's reactions stand out more for their eloquent laments on losses to learning and high culture: "Until today, there remained a record of ancient wisdom in Constantinople, and as though it were the home of letters, no Latin seemed learned enough unless he had studied a while in Constantinople. The fame accorded to Athens as the seat of wisdom while Rome flourished, seemed to apply to Constantinople [in the fifteenth century]."[151] Aeneas underscores Constantinople's status as a venerable city that had preserved an unbroken connection with ancient Greek culture. Some Italian scholars had recently studied there; many more were taught by Byzantines or used books procured from the city. Clearly, by 1453 humanists felt a kinship with Byzantium; the historical and cultural connections it seemed to share with the West made it appear familiar and accessible to scholarly imaginations.[152] As a result, the destructive sack of Constantinople led humanists to view the Turks as a threat to culture as well as to European security.

One specific aspect of the sack puzzled and horrified humanists: reports that thousands of books were lost or deliberately destroyed. Many contemporary eyewitness and secondhand accounts, as well as modern studies, corroborate the story.[153] Just how many books were lost is difficult to say. Lauro Quirini, reporting a conversation with Isidore of Kiev, who escaped Constantinople during the sack, stated that more than 120,000 volumes were destroyed.[154] According to Kritoboulos, "holy and divine books, and others mainly of profane literature and philosophy, were either given to the flames or trampled underfoot. Many of them were sold for two or three pieces of money, and sometimes for pennies only, not for gain so much as in contempt."[155] And Doukas describes how innumerable books were loaded onto wagons, scattered east and west, and sold cheaply; richer books such as Evangelistaries were torn apart for their precious metals and jewels, while others were simply thrown away.[156] Julian Raby has expressed his doubts about the extent of the destruction, stating that such a scenario of wanton destruction ran counter to Mehmed's interests in scholarship and book collecting.[157] While Raby's point is valid, the sources also indicate Mehmed's lack of control over his soldiers during the sack. He only appears to have put his foot down when it came to protecting buildings such as Hagia Sophia, which some soldiers had begun hacking apart.[158]

Avid book collectors of any period can appreciate the humanists' profound regret on hearing such tales. Each of these books had been laboriously copied by hand; some of the lost texts may have been the last copies of their kind. For scholars attempting to uncover the ancient past and disseminate its wisdom to their contemporaries, this was an enormous blow indeed.[159] Constantinople was a storehouse of ancient Greek manuscripts, representing a culture that Western scholars were only beginning to understand and appreciate. Some humanists responded through direct action. Poggio, for example, extended his help to Greek scholars and attempted to recover many of these books through agents and dealers.[160] Cardinal Bessarion too devoted much energy and expense to recovering texts from Greek areas after 1453; he bequeathed his collection to Venice, where it became the core of the Biblioteca Marciana. He saw it as his duty to preserve the great cultural past of the Greeks even if their patrimony were lost to them.[161] Other humanists responded by expressing their outrage in writing.

The pained rhetoric composed by humanists shortly after hearing these reports reveals shock as well as an effort to comprehend this act of destruction. In their attempts to explain the loss of Constantinople's books and the consequences for learning, both Aeneas Silvius Piccolomini and Lauro Quirini proffer sharp diagrams of civility versus barbarism. Lauro Quirini (b. 1420; d. 1475–79) was a Venetian humanist who spent almost half his life in Candia, Crete, where he traded in such diverse commodities as land, alum, wine, and books—particularly Greek books.[162]

Quirini also actively gathered information on the Turks, which he diligently passed on to rulers and popes in letters featuring both stern warnings and advice on strategy.

Quirini was deeply affected by the alleged loss of thousands of books at Constantinople. In a letter to Pope Nicholas V he described the event with the words "the overthrow of an entire people has been accomplished—the name of the Greeks has been erased. . . . Consequently, the language and literature of the Greeks, invented, augmented, and perfected over so long a period with such labor and industry, will certainly perish!"[163] Two notions are at work here. First, Constantinople, more than any other Byzantine city, had preserved the ancient Greek language and literature as a *living* language and culture. Second, the loss of so many books in Constantinople would ensure that even the heritage of Greece would vanish. Quirini turns this concept against the Turks with a scathing indictment of their way of life. He calls them "a barbaric, uncultivated race, without established customs, or laws, living a careless, vagrant, arbitrary life. . . ."[164] With this statement Quirini echoes a common ancient topos about nomadic groups and lumps the Turks with other peoples whom they did not resemble in the least. He also revives ancient Roman and Greek value judgments that depict nomads—or those presumed to be such—as polar opposites to "civilized" peoples who inhabit cities, farm the land, operate courts of law, and so on.[165] Implicit in Quirini's words is the sense that the Turks are not only unworthy masters of so fine a city but also fundamentally inimical to high culture and learning. Unable to appreciate or support the beautiful architecture and learned arts of Byzantium, the Turks can only despoil or eradicate them.

This striking concept is further articulated by Aeneas, who mourns the death of Greek culture and the return of barbarism in his letter to Nicholas of Cusa. Constantinople, he argues, was unique among Greek cities in that it thrived continuously from ancient times while other cities crumbled. In all those years, even when the city came into enemy hands, basilicas were never destroyed, nor were libraries burnt or monasteries despoiled.[166] This attack on the fruits of high culture—churches and libraries—is unprecedented, according to Aeneas. Even among the dreaded Persians and the rugged Romans such destruction of the arts was unthinkable: "Xerxes and Darius, who once afflicted Greece with great disasters, waged war on men, not letters. However much the Romans reduced the Greeks to their power, they not only did not reject Greek letters, but they are reputed to have embraced and venerated them so much that a man was consequently considered to be very learned only when he seemed to be thoroughly practiced in Greek speech."[167] Aeneas then hammers home an attack on the Turks by adding, "Now under Turkish rule, the opposite will come to pass; [they are] savage men, hostile to good manners and to good literature."[168] He goes on to say: "they are steeped in luxury, study little, and are overcome by laziness. Into whose hands has Greek eloquence fallen, I do not know; who of sound mind does not lament it?"[169] This, incidentally, is one of the few references I have found in which Aeneas acknowledges the existence of *any* sort of learning among the Turks. Still, the statement offers neither praise for Turkish studies nor recognition of a structured system of scholarship. More often he places the Turks well outside the realm of cultivated men. For example, in an undated oration on the fall of Constantinople, Pius uses the Turks' supposed disdain of learning to help settle the debate about their ancient origins. Aeneas held that they were Scythian, vehemently denying the popular mid-fifteenth-century claim of Trojan origins, which would have made them distant cousins of the Romans: "The Turks are truly not, as many judge, of Asian origin, which they call Trojan; the Romans, who are of Trojan origin, did not hate literature."[170]

Given the short time between the composition of Quirini's and Aeneas's letters (15 July and 21 July, respectively), it is highly unlikely that Aeneas could have seen or heard of Quirini's letter before he wrote his own. It is striking, then, that they came to the same conclusion regarding the Turks based on reports of lost books. And yet it makes perfect sense. Old books and manuscripts were invaluable resources to humanists, particularly copies of rare texts such as ancient Greek works. Aeneas lamented the loss of so many texts "not yet known to the West," calling the fall of Constantinople a "second death for Homer and a second destruction of Plato."[171] The similarities in language between the two letters—the heights of civility brought low by the dregs of barbarism—indicate that both writers were drawing on a common cultural context of classical texts and ideals.

From only three days of plunder and careless destruction of books, which held little value for the foot soldiers who sacked the city, the Turks became known by Western scholars as one of the worst threats to high culture and learning Europe had ever faced.[172] It was not only humanists who heard and wrote about these deeds; even popular writers described the loss of learning and books in vernacular laments.[173] One of the better-known examples is Maffeo Pisano's ninety-nine stanza *Lamento di Costan-*

tinopoli.[174] Among the tragedies he mourns is the loss to learning: "And there was so great a number of books assembled, of so many kinds and of such value. There were a good sixty thousand in number; all were burned and thrown into the river. Weep now philosophers and learned men. Weep Greeks, weep Latins. Weep you who are zealous for study. Weep forever more since the Saracens have destroyed your honor."[175] Because Pisano tells the audience that his account is based on what he heard and read, it provides some perspective on the dissemination and content of reports regarding the siege among wider audiences. The loss of books and the blow to learning, then, were familiar topics in broader discussions of 1453, accompanying other tales of destruction and human suffering. The ruin of Greece, moreover, would continue as a powerful topic in the sixteenth century in vernacular as well as Latin works.[176]

Last but not least, the fall of Constantinople resonated with humanists for its perceived similarities to one of the greatest tragedies of the ancient past: the sack of Rome by the Goths (410) and later the Vandals (455). These comparisons provided humanists with a rich source of material for figuring the Turks and their own culture. Reacting to news of the fall of Constantinople, Poggio Bracciolini states in a letter of 25 July 1453: "I see the earth constantly tossed about in various surges of storms. I fear the times of the Vandals and the Goths may return."[177] Some humanists who drew a parallel to the Goths asserted that the fall of Constantinople was a greater calamity than the sack of Rome. Niccolò Tignosi begins his *Expugnatio Constantinopolitana* with the claim that the Goths' destruction of Rome cannot compare to the events he is about to describe. For one thing, many Romans who fled the Goths were able to return and reconstruct the city, unlike the Greeks who were either killed or drowned while trying to escape.[178] In a similar vein, Aeneas Silvius Piccolomini argues that the Goths did less damage to Rome because Alaric, their king, ordered that churches not be disturbed.[179] Possible authorities who may have influenced this perception of Gothic restraint were Augustine and the historian Orosius, who placed the (Arian) Christian invaders on a higher moral plane than the many pagans they conquered.[180] Aeneas, however, neglects to note that the Goths, unlike the Turks, were indeed Christian, which would explain their respect for churches. In general Aeneas refuses to place the Turks on an equal footing with ancient invaders; in every comparison the Turks are cast as worse than their ancient counterparts.

Comparisons to Goths or Vandals soon expanded beyond the immediate context of 1453. In his funeral oration on the Hungarian general John

Hunyadi (1456), Donato Acciaiuoli recalls the devastation wrought by these invaders on ancient Rome and depicts the Turks as a similar threat:

Did not our ancestors often experience this devastation in Italy? the destruction of the people? the overthrow of all Europe? I have learned of the savagery of the Goths, the Vandals and other barbarian peoples who devastated Italy through the chronicles of the ancients, and I reckon a similar calamity would have befallen Italy, had not Hunyadi thwarted it, who seems not so much to have been born to check the audacity of the Turks, as to have been given by divine favor to the Christian people.[181]

Exactly which ancient chroniclers Donato may have used is unclear.[182] It is likely, though, that Donato was following the lead of other humanists in representing the Turks as "new barbarians." There is no sense in Donato's rhetoric of the Turks as a settled people, who not only inhabited cities but built them—a people who ran their vast and diverse empire with efficiency and skill. Indeed, Donato argues that if the Turks took control of Italy they would destroy it just as the savage and uncouth Goths were thought to have done.[183] His comparison of the Ottoman Empire to classic barbarian stereotypes resembles Greenblatt's model of "engaged representations," which say more about the imaginations of the viewer and his culture than the subject.[184] Unable to view the Turks as competent rulers, Donato perceived them as a disruptive force threatening civilization—an inversion of his beloved principles of justice, freedom, and good government.[185]

Why did the destruction of Rome—rather than, say, the sack of Troy or Jerusalem—resonate so strongly with humanists?[186] Several explanations may be offered. First, both Rome and Constantinople were seats of the illustrious Roman Empire. Both had long and respected histories as imperial cities from which powerful empires were run. Both were important centers for art, architecture, literature, and scholarship. Both were the best places to find patronage, an appreciative audience, eminent scholars, and impressive libraries. Renaissance humanists clearly viewed the Goths as instrumental to, if not the direct cause of, the decline of Roman civilization. They saw that Rome had become a backwater with little cultural or political prominence until the papal curia brought new life to it in the fifteenth century. While the year 410 did not in itself inaugurate the end of late antique civilization and high culture, to Renaissance thinkers the sack of Rome was a decisive moment; it heralded the beginning of the dark, dreaded "Middle Ages" described by Petrarch, Biondo, and

Bruni.[187] Moreover, the humanists' sense that they had only recently emerged from this darkness is crucial to understanding their fear of the Turks: they saw themselves in danger of being plunged into another dark age by yet another barbarian horde. Therefore comparisons of the sack of Rome to the fall of Constantinople indicate humanists' belief that a profound cultural shift had taken place in 1453.

As Leonardo Bruni's writings before the conquest of Constantinople show, the equation could work in reverse as well: historical discussions of the destruction of Rome by the Goths and Vandals could bring to mind the current advance of the Turks. The same thought process appears decades later in Florentine chancellor Bartolomeo Scala's *History of the Florentine People*, in which the barbarian destruction of Italy functions as a reference point for contemporary despair over the Turks.[188] The Ottomans, then, were a foil for the various symbols of "Western civilization," past and present. The Turkish barbarians strengthened the humanists' perceived affinity with ancient Rome. Where there is high culture, barbarism lurks in the wings. As the modern Greek poet Constantine Cavafy (1863–1933) put it, barbarians provide "civilized society" with a sense of purpose and identity, to the point that their absence is almost lamented: "and now, what's going to happen to us without the barbarians? They were, those people, a kind of solution."[189] The Ottoman Turks provided just such a solution to humanists writing of the achievements of their golden age.[190]

Comparisons to the collapse of Rome could also stimulate philosophical questions. Evoking the tragedy in present-day terms was bound to set humanists to wondering whether their own recently founded cultural flowering was just as precarious. Equally apparent are fears of political dissolution at the hands of the Turks. One area ill suited to ancient comparisons, however, is the effect a Turkish attack on Western Europe might have on religion. The fall of Rome did not stop the spread of the Church; if anything, it freed it from many of the constraints of political patronage, lending it greater autonomy and temporal power. Why, then, did the humanists not compare 1453 to the Babylonian Captivity or the early Roman persecution of Christians? This is not to say that religious concerns or expressions of outrage were absent from humanist reactions to 1453 and other Turkish attacks. It is important to note, however, in instances such as this how boldly concerns over secular culture rang out in the years following 1453.

The rhetoric of barbarism, despite its inaccuracy, became a fixture in humanist discourses on the Turks for many years after 1453. In August 1454

Donato Acciaiuoli invoked this image in a letter to John Argyropoulos, a Greek refugee and eminent scholar who escaped Constantinople during the siege. In an effort to persuade the scholar to come live and teach in Florence, he called it a city "where no barbarians nor insolent men live, but rather civilized men . . . of good morals."[191] Others may have taken some time to absorb this new discourse and its implications. In the case of at least one humanist we can chart a delay in actual use of the term "barbarian." In 1444 Poggio Bracciolini used "barbarian" only once, preferring terms such as "infidel"; in a letter of 1453 he compares the Turks to Goths and Vandals but does not directly call them barbarians. By 1456, however, Poggio, like Donato, was using the term "barbarian" interchangeably with "Turk."[192]

So popular did the term "barbarian" become that Benedetto Accolti used it in his history of the First Crusade, *De bello a christianis contra barbaros* (1463–64), with even greater frequency than the medieval Christian designations "enemies of the faith" and "the Infidel." His letters and orations as chancellor (1458–64) also reflect a pronounced fondness for the term.[193] Later chancellors such as Bartolomeo Scala would continue to use this term with great rhetorical flourish or in passing references. In fact, during the mid- to late fifteenth century one can find examples of state records discussing the "barbarians" without clarifying *who* this group was supposed to represent.[194] Apparently the audience knew well enough what this signifier had come to mean. Such a consistent and straightforward use of "barbarian" to mean "Turk" suggests that within a few years of 1453 the term had acquired a broad currency and acceptance in political discourse. Nearly all the humanists surveyed in this study with few exceptions used the term for rhetorical effect. The Turks had become Europe's new barbarians, occupying a place beside the Persians and Germans of antiquity, not to mention the Vikings and Mongols. But for Accolti and Donato, among others, "barbarian" was more than a fashionable word. It reflected their abiding interest in cultural history as well as political history, particularly the decline in learning following the fall of Rome and its resurgence in the Renaissance.[195] Accolti, who viewed history and rhetoric as inseparable, believed that the past provided lessons and warnings to present-day readers. By constantly referring to the Turks as barbarians, he reminded audiences of potential losses to modern learning as well as those suffered in ancient times.[196]

The use of "barbarian" to signify "Turk" would be less surprising or noteworthy had it been a common designation for Muslims in the Middle

Ages. But, as W. R. Jones has demonstrated, it was not. In the medieval period the rise of powerful Germanic kings and the conversion of the Germanic peoples rendered "barbarian" a less biting cultural slur. By the late seventh century the term came to be applied most frequently to pagans. Only in the twelfth and thirteenth centuries did classical definitions of backwardness, ferocity, or cruelty reemerge. And yet, despite their status as non-Christians, Muslims escaped this epithet for centuries. Medieval thinkers probably sensed the incongruity in designating Arabs, who surpassed Westerners in learning and cultural achievements, as barbaric. Not until the fifteenth century was the term regularly applied to Muslims—most pointedly to the Ottoman Turks.[197] Humanists led the way in this trend. Perhaps because so little was known about the Ottomans they were more acceptable targets than the Arabs.

It hardly needs mentioning that Ottoman culture in no way resembled this picture of barbarism that Western humanists (and even Arab writers) delighted in painting.[198] Constantinople under the Ottomans was a thriving city, unlike abandoned Rome. No fifteenth-century Alaric, Mehmed took pains to rebuild and repopulate his new capital.[199] Mehmed also patronized education, building and supporting religious schools, or *medreses*. In this he followed an Ottoman tradition dating back to Orhan (r. 1326–62). Mehmed even displayed some innovation in reorganizing *medreses* to benefit the instruction of mathematics, astronomy, and medicine.[200] He also showed an interest in Western culture. Humanists discussed his familiarity with classical Greek and Latin texts, associating this curiosity with a desire to emulate the deeds of Alexander the Great and Julius Caesar.[201] Moreover, Mehmed's admiration of European portraiture resulted in the painter Gentile Bellini's mission to the Ottoman court as part of Venice's goodwill efforts after its long war with the Ottomans had ended (1479).[202]

While all these tendencies are important, they have been exaggerated. Some scholars present Mehmed as a kindred spirit to European Renaissance princes with his patronage and personal cultivation of art and learning—Western and humanistic learning as well as Eastern traditions.[203] But Mehmed was not a tireless supporter of learning and the arts; few works of originality, with the exception of those of the philosopher Hocazade, were produced during his reign.[204] Indeed, the bulk of his time and resources was spent on war, not on court poets, historians, or architects.[205] Moreover, his interest in Western literature, ancient and Renaissance alike, was at least partly grounded in a desire to learn strategic information or the tactics of its great generals. Culturally, Mehmed gravitated much more toward the Muslim East than the Christian (or ancient pagan) West.[206]

In many ways the Ottomans were no more culturally enlightened than Westerners were. The sixteenth-century Ottoman historian Sa'd ed-Din recalled the conquest of Constantinople as follows: "The temples of misbelievers were turned into mosques of the pious, and rays of light of Islam drove away the hosts of darkness from that place so long the abode of the despicable infidels, and the streaks of the dawn of the Faith dispelled the lurid blackness of oppression, for the word, irresistible as destiny, of the fortunate sultan became supreme in the governance of this new dominion."[207] While the theme here is clearly religious, the symbolism of the language is eerily similar to that of humanists describing the Turks' culture as one of darkness, versus the splendor of (Western) freedom and enlightenment. In fact, the entire record of Muslim interest in Europe before the modern period is paltry in comparison to the number of studies Europeans wrote on the Islamic world.[208]

Still, a lack of cultural diversity in the Ottoman court and Mehmed's modest patronage record do not add up to the image of Turkish barbarism touted by humanists—an image many fifteenth-century Westerners knew was inaccurate.[209] Why, then, were stereotypes of Turkish barbarism so enduring? This perception has more to do with narrow definitions of learning and culture prevalent in Renaissance Europe—definitions predicated on the classical canon.[210] The unfamiliar was relegated to lower cultural categories. Regarding the Turks, "barbarians" seemed an appropriate category for humanists who confused noninterest in "real" (that is, classical) culture with backwardness or simplicity.

By the later fifteenth century the term "barbarian" was used even more confidently. A major reason for its continued ideological relevance to Westerners was the unrelenting pace of the Turkish advance. Athens fell to the Turks in 1460, Bosnia in 1463, and Negroponte in 1470. The year 1480 was especially eventful, bringing both good and bad news to Western Europeans concerning two major sieges: Rhodes, which was successfully fended off; and Otranto, which was not. Otranto, located on the coast of Apulia in southern Italy, was captured and held for a year by the Turks.[211] On 1 October 1480 Marsilio Ficino, the Florentine humanist and Neoplatonic scholar, wrote a letter to Matthias Corvinus of Hungary entitled "An exhortation to war against the barbarians" (*Exhortatio ad bellum contra barbaros*). Ficino implores Matthias to help save Italy, and all of Christendom, from the ravages of the "inhuman Turks."

Ficino portrays the Turks as "savage beasts" and "barbarians": typical rhetoric used against the Turks, but all the more poignant given recent events. Oddly, Ficino does not dwell on the capture of Otranto or even mention it explicitly.[212] He chose instead to emphasize the damage the Turks had done to learning. Reflecting on the deterioration of Greek studies and the subjugation of the learned men of Greece, he states: "At length, after many generations of light, they [Greek scholars] have fallen down into darkness under the ferocious Turks. Alas what pain! Stars, I say, have fallen into darkness under savage beasts. Alas, the celestial lights of liberal teaching and arts have for a long time lain in limbo."[213] Ficino goes on to beseech Matthias, whom he now calls "Hercules," to protect Christendom from these "unruly monsters who wickedly ravage the countryside, destroy the towns, and devour the people."[214] Not content to "trample with filthy feet on the disciplines of all laws and liberal arts, and . . . on Holy Religion . . . as far as it is within their power, the [Turks] obliterate them from all memory of men."[215]

A sharp contrast appears between the barbarian Turks and Matthias, a protector of his people in the classical mode of Hercules. Matthias is also characterized as a protector of high culture, particularly learning—an image in keeping with his patronage of humanism and the arts.[216] Nearly three decades after the fall of Constantinople the Turks are still represented as uncouth ravagers of libraries and books—the greatest threat to European learning and culture since late antiquity.[217] Ficino's plea may very well have hit its mark. In 1481 Otranto was recovered with the help of Matthias's troops under the command of Blaise Magyar. Matthias also won important victories that same year against the Turks in Serbia.[218]

Humanism's fascination with barbarism provided one more avenue for conceptualizing the Turks via ancient sources: historiography. Some humanists, such as Aeneas Silvius Piccolomini and Francesco Filelfo, attempted to trace the origins of the Turkish people back to ancient times. Aeneas was particularly keen on dispelling the myth that the Turks were descendants of the Trojans, rather than the rough-and-tumble Scythians—a view expressed by Flavio Biondo before him.[219] Aeneas makes this argument in a few texts,[220] but it is best articulated in his *Cosmographia* (c. 1458). His most influential modern source was the *Liber de familia Autumanorum id est Turchorum* (1456) by the Greek scholar Nicholas Sagundinus—a work composed in honor of Aeneas, who was bishop of Siena at the time.[221] Among the ancient sources Aeneas cites are Ptolemy and Aethicus, but he also mentions medieval authors such as Otto of Freising and Jordanes.[222] Aeneas, however, mistakenly presumes Aethicus to be a classical source, when in fact he wrote in the seventh century.[223] This later date explains Aethicus's fabulous tales and legends, which more closely resemble the style of medieval chronicles than ancient Roman geography. It also explains Aethicus's "barbarous Latin," a defect that led many scholars of the Turks to reject him as a source.[224] As Margaret Meserve has shown, Aeneas chose a poor source in Aethicus, whose approach was more apocalyptic and fantastic than historical; he also rejected some of the better-informed, more recent medieval sources on the Turks, such as Haytho, Marco Polo, and Vincent of Beauvais. Aeneas, like other humanist historians of his period, relied instead on ancient (or presumed ancient) sources, which confirmed his bleak suspicions about Turkish origins.[225]

Apart from his error in assessing Turkish ancestry, Aeneas further complicates the narrative by offering a skewed picture of the Scythians. Herodotus does not appear in Aeneas's list of sources, which is odd considering the length at which he discussed the Scythians.[226] If Aeneas knew of Herodotus's treatment of the Scythians, he probably avoided it because of the Greek's more open-minded views.[227] Since he was described as friendly to the barbarians and labeled unreliable or mendacious by well-respected historians such as Thucydides and Plutarch, Aeneas—like other humanists—would have felt compelled to avoid using or acknowledging him.[228] In fact, one can imagine that Aeneas searched desperately for any classical source that inveighed against the Scythians since classical, pagan authors tended to praise them as "the noble savage."[229]

Aeneas introduces the Scythians in chapter 22 as the ancestors of the Huns. He calls them "a ferocious people, whom Jordanes and others believed were born of sorceresses and demon seed."[230] Aeneas then draws on Aethicus to describe the Scythian and Turkic peoples as "a fierce and ignominious people, fornicators engaging in all kinds of sexual perversions and frequenters of brothels, who ate detestable things: the flesh of mares, wolves, vultures, and, what is even more horrifying, aborted human fetuses."[231] Despite the sensationalism, the emphasis on the Scythians' unusual food is classical; it echoes a common trope of Greek historiography in which nomads or shepherds are almost automatically described as "eaters of flesh" and "drinkers of milk," unlike civilized people who consumed bread and wine. This division is not casual. Aristotle argued that the lazy pastoralist refuses to cultivate the land and is, hence, a slave to the land's caprices. Farmers, on the other hand, represent the highest form of civilization as they work the land and master it.[232] Aeneas's descriptions of the precise kinds of flesh eaten by the Scythians and of their wild sexual habits were probably thrown in to paint as lurid and disgusting a picture of the Turks' forebears as was possible.

Francesco Filelfo (1398–1481) concurred with Aeneas's assessment of the Turks as Scythian descendants.[233] Filelfo, who had commissioned a Greek, Theodore Gazes, to write a history of the Turks for him, may have arrived at this conclusion without the help of Aeneas.[234] At the Congress of Mantua in 1459 Filelfo delivered an oration on behalf of Francesco Sforza of Milan in which he expressed great ardor for crusade.[235] Attempting to rally support for the crusade, Filelfo spoke in the most derogatory manner about the Ottoman Turks and their history, beginning with the Scythians: "Who does not know that the Turks are fugitive slaves and shepherds of the Scythians, who descended from the prisons of the vast and inhospitable Caucasus Mountains into Persia and Media to practice banditry. They made their homes in no set place, except the bogs and the frightening hiding places of woods."[236] In this case the Turks are made to look like the dregs of Scythian society—a low insult indeed, given the image of the Scythians at this time. Here we see the Turks' supposed ancestors escaping the life of slaves in a vast wasteland to seek better opportunities in bogs and dank woods, coming out of them from time to time to rob defenseless travelers. Moving from slavery to banditry is not exactly progress toward civilization. What is particularly intriguing here is how the image of the Scythians worsens with each telling. This is a far cry from Herodotus's ethnographic study of a nomadic people, whom he described dispassionately, or with admiration. Moreover, while Filelfo's assertion that the Scythian-Turkish connection was common knowledge may be a rhetorical device, it seems to indicate a wide dissemination of this theory.[237]

Why did humanists push this agenda so vigorously? First, allowing for the possibility that the Turks were Trojan descendants was too humanizing a concept for comfort. It not only justified Turkish conquests in Anatolia and Greece as reconquest and revenge but also provided the Turks with a noble and legitimate past; this was no small matter given the importance of bloodline and ancestry in Renaissance Italy. Aeneas and Filelfo aimed to fire up their audience to righteous indignation against a foreign, lowly, barbarian people whose pretenses to ruling power were wholly invalid. Second, creating an image of the Turks as barbarians of the lowest sort played well into humanist notions of their own society as far more civilized. Apparently, humanists found the rhetoric of Christian versus infidel insufficient to the task of setting Europeans apart from the Turks and inciting a warlike mentality.

In conclusion, the image of the barbarian provided humanists with a powerful, multifaceted discourse of Self and Other. Deceptively simple and seemingly redundant of classical tropes, the Turks as barbarians invited a complex set of cultural, historical, and psychological tools with which humanists envisioned and sought to control them intellectually. It comforted humanists to feel that even as Europeans were losing ground to the Turks they were somehow "better" than their foes and would certainly rise again. And yet, despite the specific context in which "barbarian" became synonymous with "Turk," humanists soon began to stretch their use of the word. They started to apply the term indiscriminately to the larger Muslim world—even though for several centuries Westerners had regarded Arab culture as highly advanced.

Once the Ottoman Turks became new barbarians in Western eyes, however, the door was opened to other Muslim populations—regardless of their past or present achievements. Already in the mid-fifteenth century Benedetto Accolti, Donato Acciaiuoli, and Aeneas Silvius Piccolomini began applying the term to all Muslims.[238] In 1492 Ugolino Verino called the Moors of Spain "barbarians."[239] A few years later (1497) Marineo Siculo stated that Arabic was not widely studied because it was a barbaric language.[240] Verino's usage seems odd, given the cultural sophistication of Muslim Spain and the role it played in disseminating the Aristotelian corpus to Christian scholars; similarly, Siculo's dismissal of Arabic as a barbaric language misleadingly suggests that its literature and scholarship had no cultural value to Europeans. It is possible that Siculo's disdain is related to the antagonism many humanists such as Petrarch harbored toward scholasticism. It is also possible that humanists were aware that Arab learning was in a state of decline.[241] And yet the easy disregard of Arab learning and artistic traditions suggests that the humanist rhetoric of barbarism was gaining strength and, indeed, obscuring reality on a grand scale.[242]

Figuring the Turks in Political and Geographical Terms

While the concept of barbarism versus civility was indeed popular among humanists, other models from classical antiquity inspired them as well. Even as they continued to depict the Turks as enemies of Christian Europe and sought ways to promote enthusiasm for crusade, some humanists rose above cultural and religious polemic to engage in a more moderate discourse of the Turks as political adversaries and geographical outsiders. Such models might include comparing the Turks or crusaders to more heroic protagonists of famous ancient struggles. These parallels lack the vitriol commonly found in attempts to portray the Turks as barbarian enemies of the faith and arguably elevated humanist discourse on the Ottoman Turks to a more relativistic level.

A century after Petrarch's cautious invocation of Julius Caesar as crusader, Flavio Biondo looked back to the Romans for inspiration regarding Europe's conflict with the Turks. In one such work, *Roma Triumphans* (1459), he raises the subject of the crusade against the Turks.[243] Although holy war would seem to have little to do with a study on the customs, laws, and military genius of ancient Rome, Biondo works it into his dedication to Pius II, who was currently planning a crusade. He asserts that would-be crusaders can benefit by the ancient Roman example:

In the meantime, while you will be reading and rereading the triumphs of the ancient city of Rome, you will be awaiting a most resplendent triumph, which our great and holy God will give to you, Pius, over the ruined and emptied resources of the Turks, after Europe, first of all, has been liberated, thereafter, Jerusalem, then the Holy Land lying adjacent to it. In a short time, I hope and I am confident, yours will be a triumph, which is to be led with the highest approbation and glory of all.[244]

Optimistically, Biondo compares the splendid triumphs of ancient Rome to those that Pius hopes to achieve against the Turks. So direct are the parallels that he expects Pius to be reminded repeatedly of his crusade and inspired by reading about Roman victories; just as Rome ruled the world in ancient times, so too will Christian Rome extend her authority.[245] This motif of crusader as "new Roman" indeed harks back to Petrarch, but with one key difference: Biondo, unlike Petrarch, does not labor to portray the Roman Empire as Christian since, after all, it was most powerful when it was still largely pagan.[246]

Significantly, Biondo's dedication avoids the terms "barbarian" or "enemy of the faith," referring instead at one point to the Turks' cruel tyranny. Although this may not seem a great image improvement, it does present a subtle shift. Between his choice of terms for the Turks and the comparison of the pope's crusade to Roman expansion, Biondo's dedication creates a sense of the Turks as powerful, organized adversaries and the war against them as an undertaking both secular and religious. Even though he uses the term "barbarian" from time to time in earlier works and evokes it briefly at the end of this work, the parallel he draws in the dedication may suggest a growing appreciation of the Turks as serious opponents. Simply introducing the concept of tyranny at least suggested a system of government, as opposed to random, barbarous attacks.

Such an attitude toward crusade was perfectly in keeping with Biondo's general stance on ancient Rome. As Charles Stinger argues, Biondo led the way for other humanists by "abandoning the dichotomy of the pagan idolatry of ancient Rome and Christian Rome's martyr-sanctified soil."[247] Without making excuses or disclaimers Biondo asserts that the greatness of ancient Rome never completely left Italy. On the contrary, the grandeur of pagan Rome both prefigured the rise of the papacy and fused with the best aspects of Christian Rome to create one formidable society, whose greatest works were soon to shine forth—as in Pius's much-anticipated crusade. Through this example Biondo offers an additional means of viewing the Turks—as political enemies in a struggle for hegemony. Moreover, Biondo's equation of events from ancient history with the Turkish problem of his own time illustrates the growing trend of reading the Turks *into* classical texts.

Cardinal Bessarion (1403–72) presents a rather different classical comparison to the Turkish conflict in his Latin translation of Demosthenes' first Olynthiac oration.[248] Demosthenes wrote the orations in 348/49 B.C.E. in an effort to convince his fellow Athenians to align themselves with the besieged Olynthians and push back the imperialistic designs of Philip of Macedon.[249] The similarities between the Athenian position and that of Italy inspired Bessarion to use the oration as part of his anti-Turk propaganda. It was a task that became more urgent in late 1470 with the fall of Venetian Negroponte—just about the same time that Bessarion finished the translation.[250] In manuscripts and early printed editions of this oration, Bessarion's comments about the Turks are placed in the margins beside the Latin text of Demosthenes so as to make the connections crystal clear to the reader.[251] For example, the first of such marginal notes states: "Christian princes, hear Demosthenes, philosopher and orator, already dead for many centuries, arguing eloquently now on the state of your enemy, and demonstrating wisely what it behooves you to do, lest you fall to ruin in a graver situation."[252] For years Bessarion had been trying to gain support for a crusade. He tried a unique approach in using the words of another authority from another time. Many authors might be called on, but Bessarion took advantage of his audience's growing thirst for texts from Greek antiquity. The preface to the first Olynthiac oration states: "And so, since I judge his weighty authority and suitable oration to be more persuasive than my words, I have determined to let him speak these arguments himself."[253] After introducing the aim of Demosthenes' oration, Bessarion concludes the preface with the direct comparison to Turkish aggression: "Just as Philip threatened Greece in those times, so now do the Turks menace Italy. Therefore, let Philip play the part of the Turks, the Athenians the Italian people, and Demosthenes ourselves. Now you will easily understand how the entire oration is suitable to our cause."[254]

Like Philip to the Greeks, the Turks were a common threat to European governments. Demosthenes apprised the Athenians of the advantages of fighting a war away from home in defense of their liberty; Christian princes could do the same with the Turkish threat, heading it off before it damaged their realms. Bessarion also echoed the Athenian orator's themes of liberty versus tyranny, thereby opening the topic of war with the Turks to more secular considerations. For example, where Demosthenes holds forth regarding the struggles of the Olynthians—who were fighting Philip not for glory or land but to prevent their enslavement and the conquest of their patrimony—Bessarion's marginal note states, "We must also fight not for a piece of land, but for liberty, for life, and for the safety of our homeland."[255] Although he incorporates some Christian elements into his closing exhortation, he spends most of the work painting the Turks as a political threat, a theme he also underscores in his famous orations against the Turks, which were printed in 1470. In many respects the Olynthiac oration represents one of Bessarion's more practical attempts to enlist aid for a crusade in its blunt declaration of secular goals such as defense, effective strategizing, and relative cost.[256]

Just as Demosthenes' oratorical skill inspired Bessarion in his rhetoric against the Turks, Cicero was an inspiration to Giannozzo Manetti in an oration directed to Calixtus III in 1455. Descended from a respected Florentine family, Manetti (1396–1459) served on several important government councils and ambassadorial missions. He was a gifted orator, proficient in Latin, Greek, and even Hebrew, as well as a talented mathematician. Manetti also studied natural philosophy and metaphysics, rare interests for a humanist of his generation.[257] Fearing the intentions of his enemies, he went into voluntary exile in 1454, first to Rome and then to Naples. He spent the next several years working for King Alfonso and the papacy under Pius II.[258] His oration was written on behalf of Alfonso of Naples in an effort to convince Pope Calixtus to appoint the king military leader of the planned crusade.[259] In this long and layered work Manetti draws on examples from the medieval period and employs his share of Christian rhetoric depicting Alfonso as a model crusader against the enemies of the faith. But his comparison of the Turkish war to the rebellion of Mithridates in Asia Minor adds an innovative twist to his argument.

Cicero's speech "On the Manilian Law" (*Pro Lege Manilia*) is the source of Manetti's comparison.[260] Cicero delivered this speech in 66 B.C.E. in support of Manilius's proposal to grant supreme command and unlimited resources to Gnaeus Pompeius in the fight against Mithridates VI, king of Pontus. Rome's difficulties with Mithridates had begun many years before. Through a combination of aggression and intrigue, Mithridates had come to control most of Asia Minor by the year 92 BCE. In an attempt to assert his will concerning a dynastic dispute with Rome in the year 91, he defeated the Roman army in Asia Minor and ordered Manius Aquilius—the chief Roman official—to be tortured to death. But the greatest act of unwonted aggression took place one day in 88 when he ordered the massacre of every Italian in Asia Minor. Sulla defeated Mithridates' armies in 85, but he had to withdraw to Italy before Mithridates could be captured and punished. By 66 Mithridates, now joined by Tigranes, his son-in-law and the king of Armenia, was still at large and harassing the Romans. Lucius Lucullus had been campaigning against Mithridates on behalf of Rome for eight years without decisive results.[261]

Cicero's rhetoric lends itself to the Turkish conflict in several ways, such as a comparison of Mehmed to Mithridates. But rather than emphasize the similarities between Pompey and Alfonso, perhaps intentionally leaving it to the subtext, Manetti focuses on such rhetorical subjects as necessity, defense of allies, and honor. The urgency of the Turkish War is compared to the situation Rome faced with Asia Minor.[262] But the issue of honor in Cicero's oration concerns Manetti more. Cicero challenged the Romans to remove the stain (*macula*) placed on their honor by Mithridates, an insult that had gone unavenged for twenty-two years.[263] Pompey's successful campaign in the East redeemed Rome's honor and removed this blemish. Not only did Mithridates flee before Pompey's advance and commit suicide, but Pompey also rebuilt Roman authority in Asia Minor and went on to annex both Syria and Palestine for the empire.[264] Manetti describes Cicero's emphasis on vindication: "That stain which had been acquired in the previous Mithridatic War, and at the time had settled deeply and become fixed upon the name of the Roman people, had to be erased by the Romans."[265]

Manetti's emphasis on a belated restoration of honor is not difficult to comprehend. By 1455 Christendom had been beaten on several occasions by the Ottoman Turks, but Manetti avers that it is never too late to rally and avenge an insult. The Romans had proved this much. Christians who were watching the Turks seize more and more territory could benefit from the example of a commander who met a military threat in the East and ultimately took over Asia Minor, Syria, and Palestine, or "the Holy Land."[266] After years of humiliating Christians, Mehmed II—the modern Anatolian tyrant—might also be broken, paving the way for incorporating the East into Christendom. Hence, Manetti draws a parallel between two promising moments: one in the past, when Pompey stood ready to push Rome's borders far eastward; and one in the present, which he suggests could result in similar glory.

Cicero's discussion of obligations to one's tributaries and allies struck Manetti as resonant with his own times.[267] Manetti, however, puts a new spin on this point by arguing that a bond stronger than political alliance exists between Eastern and Western Christians: "In our case, as in that [of the Romans], it is not the welfare of allies and comrades, but assuredly the safety of all Christians that is in danger, or their destruction that is at stake; not for profits is this done, as was the case then, but for a great heritage; not for the goods of many Roman citizens, as it was then, is this [war] conducted, but for the precious and infinite treasures of the faithful. . . ."[268] With this statement Manetti draws attention to religious aspects of a proposed war against the Turks. In another passage he echoes reactions to 1453 with laments on the desecration of temples and relics and the willful slaughter of Christians. But he places equal importance on the Turks as a threat to the security and honor of Europe. The result is a secular point of view that supplements and expands traditional Christian rhetoric. More important, it presents an alternate image of the Turks not solely as barbarians but also as serious adversaries who required a serious response—a much less reductive rhetorical comparison than many others, for all its creative flair. This more respectful approach to the Turks comes through in other ways too, such as Manetti's description of Mehmed as "the young leader of the Turks, young in age, great in spirit, even greater in power."[269] He also compares ambitious Mehmed not to a barbarian but rather to Alexander the Great.

A very different political, or geopolitical, theme inspired by classical sources was the concept of Europe versus Asia or West versus East. From the time of the Persian Wars the Greeks began conceptualizing the East as more than a simple geographic distinction; they saw it as a political and cultural antagonist whose exact opposite was not always clear, perhaps because it varied. Greece was the most likely Self to Asia's Other, but many may have viewed it more broadly than that, as Herodotus's tale of Europa and Strabo's praise for the continent of Europe suggest. Still, "Europe" and "West" were seldom used in the ancient period as developed cultural concepts.[270] What did develop without question was a discourse of East and Asia. For the Greeks, their neighbors to the west might appear as barbaric as those to the east, if not more so, but the seeds were sown with the identification of an Eastern outsider.[271]

The rise of Christianity complicated East/West distinctions; "Christendom" (*Christianitas*) became the only entity of import, transcending geographical and ethnic boundaries. By the High Middle Ages, however, Christendom became associated with what we would call "Western Europe."[272] And yet in this period the East, particularly Jerusalem, was often perceived in a more positive light, as every Christian's focal point or destination—a concept that can be seen in maps as well as in the Eastern orientation of churches. This brings us to the question of the "West": when did it emerge as an idea, and when did Europe really take shape? Suzanne Conklin Akbari has argued that "East" always existed and was constantly being reshaped but that "West" really only became recognized in Europe in the fourteenth century when northern and Western Europeans began to take a more "us"-centered view, focusing not on their spiritual destination but on their location, enabling freer choice of one's direction, according to her, what this signifies is the "transition from the primacy of the sacred object to the primacy of the seeing subject."[273] Hence the conceptual opposition of East and West was, in some ways, a fledgling discourse when taken up by humanists. They would shape these concepts into more clearly defined cultural and political poles accompanied by an aggressive discourse of cultural difference and superiority.[274]

Petrarch used concepts of East and West—specifically the Persian Wars—in his poem 28 to hail Philip VI's commitment to crusade (1334). Over a century later, when Constantinople was directly threatened by the Turks, Greek humanist George of Trebizond invoked the idea of Europe versus Asia. In an exhortation to Pope Nicholas V, *Ad defendenda pro Europa Hellesponti claustra* (1452), George describes Constantinople and all of Greece as the bulwark of Europe against the barbarians of Asia. To bring authority and force to his argument he cites ancient examples of Greek generals who defended their shores against the Persians and of Alexander the Great, who launched his conquest of Asia from Greece; he also portrays Constantine's decision to establish a second Roman capital on the Bosporus as defensive in nature. He hoped to recruit aid for Byzantium by convincing the pope and other Europeans of the military supremacy of the West in its many struggles with the East.[275]

Poggio Bracciolini employed the rhetoric of East and West from an Italian perspective in 1455. As chancellor of Florence, Poggio wrote to Alfonso of Naples shortly after the king had joined the Most Holy League.[276] In this letter Poggio praises Alfonso's efforts toward peace in "Italy," indicating the sense of peninsular unity that he and other "Italians" felt in the optimistic period following the conclusion of the Peace of Lodi.[277] But he soon moves on to the larger concerns of Europe and Christendom, exhorting the king of Naples to lead a naval attack against the Turks. He argues that the only way to push the Turks out of Europe is by a joint naval and land offensive, which, significantly, Poggio never calls "crusade." Poggio urges Alfonso to lead this enterprise, given his abundance of troops and sailors and his proximity to the front.[278] In doing this, Alfonso will perform a great service for Christendom and win fame and glory for himself: "Truly, these things that are taken up and must be carried out for the defense of the Christian name, for the veneration of God, for the common utility, for the growth of religion and the faith, must be celebrated by all with one voice, with one speech, with one applause."[279] Here, Poggio deals with the concept of the *respublica christiana*, or the commonwealth of Christendom. Thus, having begun with a discussion of the safety and political stability of Italy, he expands his definition of the political entity to which they belong as ultimately being the community of Christendom and the continent of Europe.[280]

The Turks are cast in opposite terms as Asians, despite their firm control of the Balkans: "I have heard some men, eminent in peace and war, assert that never will the Turks be pushed from Europe while the sea affords passage to them, since their aid is furnished by Asia. . . . Europe, they say, is the body which summons its heart and spirit from Asia."[281] The Ottoman foothold in the Balkans must have seemed weaker than it truly was to Poggio if he believed that cutting off the Balkan Turks from Asia would leave them helpless. This becomes clear when he cites the examples of Xerxes and Themistocles, intimating that the Turks are as superficially established in Europe as were the Persians and that a few good battles might send them packing to their remote Eastern homes. Poggio's dichotomy of Europe and Asia, while a fascinating adaptation of classical rhetoric, downplays the political realities of his time; it may also reflect a lack of awareness in Europe regarding the strength of Turkish rule in the Balkans.

Still, we can see the hold that the concepts Europe, Christendom, and Asia continued to exercise on Poggio's mind. He uses these themes to define the ideological as well as geographical boundaries that kept Europeans distinct from the Infidels in Asia. As such, he renders the distinctions between civilized West and uncivilized East a topic for political discussion, as Accolti would do with greater force; it is now a criterion by which one may judge and classify allies or enemies of Europe and Christendom. Other examples of the rhetoric of Europe versus Asia may be found in Flavio Biondo's crusade exhortation to Alfonso of Aragon in 1453, Bernardo Giustiniani's oration to Sixtus IV (1471–72), and Donato Acciaiuoli's funeral oration on John Hunyadi.[282]

More than any other humanist, Aeneas Silvius Piccolomini (Pius II) defined and gave force to the concepts of West and East, Europe and Asia. As Denys Hay has shown, not only did he repeatedly use the term in works such as his *Cosmographia* and numerous letters, but he also took the important philological step of coining the term "European" as an adjective.[283] This shift substantially expanded the discourse of East and West, allowing humanists and others to think and speak of themselves, their ways of life, their learning and arts as belonging to a larger, coherent collective. It is crucial to note that Aeneas's sense of this cultural unity arose from a perception of opposition to the Turks and "Asia"—not from any genuine sense that European countries shared many strong similarities beyond religion and the common language of Latin among the elite. Indeed, his political experience taught him all too well about the antagonism between Christian states.

Perhaps Aeneas's boldest assertion regarding the perceived superiority of Europe and the West may be found in his letter to Mehmed II (1461). Although the letter's ostensible aim is to convert Mehmed to Christianity, there are many points of tension and even belligerence in the letter. Warning Mehmed not to imagine that he might conquer Western Europe just because the East fell so easily, Aeneas affirms: "you will not fight against women if you invade Italy, Hungary, or other occidental areas; matters here are decided with the sword. Not with Asian spears does a Chalibean cuirass cover chests."[284] He also underscores Western superiority by denigrating the state of learning in the East while boasting of the vitality of liberal arts in Europe.[285] While the letter's true purpose has not yet been conclusively determined, one of its likely goals is to offer Europeans a bold vision of their cultural and religious superiority over Asia.[286]

In sum, humanists played a crucial role in defining modern notions of Europe and the West—concepts created in dialectical opposition to Asia and East. Humanists did not simply invent the West or rediscover it from ancient texts in a scholarly vacuum. While the idea had been developing since the fourteenth century, it was mainly through their own confrontation with "the East"—similar to the Greeks' threat from Persia—that the idea of East as well as West suddenly took on force and significance. Greek refugees may have influenced this trend as well, as suggested by George of Trebizond's rhetoric. In their attempts to distinguish themselves from their enemy, humanists, like the ancient Greeks, fell into the seductive and dangerous trap of oversimplifying their adversary as a cultural other. "Easternness" or "Asianness" became synonymous with a host of unbecoming and threatening qualities, which served to offset the mythical greatness of the West.

Positive Comparisons: Noble Savages or Heirs to the Trojans and Romans?

A different approach to viewing the Turks in classical terms was to equate them and their leader with noble individuals and peoples of antiquity. Such parallels implicitly or explicitly suggested favorable judgments of the Turks. Before the fifteenth century Coluccio Salutati was one of the few humanists who could consider the Turks without allowing their aggression against Christian kingdoms to obscure their virtues entirely. But after the mid-fifteenth century, as the Turks' power increased, more humanists found themselves comparing the Turks to the ancient Romans and their leaders to some of the great generals of antiquity. The fall of Constantinople proved to be a considerable influence in this regard. Some of the same humanists who called them barbarians made more flattering classical comparisons at other moments.

Niccolò Tignosi provides a good example, pausing to express amazement at the Turks' success in the midst of his invective against their barbaric treatment of the Greeks. He styled the common soldiers in the Turkish army as new Goths or Vandals but surprisingly compared Mehmed II to some of the greatest generals of the classical period. Tignosi states that Mehmed admired and tried to emulate Alexander the Great, Julius Caesar, and Augustus. He even identifies Mehmed's well-disciplined janissary corps with both Alexander's argiraspides—a crack force trained from an early age—and Caesar's tenth legion.[287] Some classical parallels were less flattering, however. Tignosi also compares Mehmed to Caligula when describing the sultan's quick temper, acts of cruelty, and unrestrained sexual habits.[288] Admiration of the Turks' military talents, then, did not preclude condemnation.

More frequent pairings of Mehmed with classical figures are found in descriptions of his siege tactics. Leonard of Chios, a Genoese Dominican trained as a humanist, was present in Constantinople during the siege and watched the movements of the Turkish army. Despite his hostility toward the Turks and Mehmed, he expressed wonder and admiration for their strategy: "A Scipio, a Hannibal, or any of our modern generals would have been amazed at the discipline that they showed in arranging their weapons, and the promptness and evidence of forward planning which their manoeuvres showed."[289] Yet Leonard's opinion of Turkish efficiency and success in battle could be quite ambivalent. He went on to say, "But tell me pray, who was truly responsible for this encirclement of the city? Who but traitors from the Christian side taught the Turks their work? . . . Greeks, Latins, Germans, Hungarians, Bohemians [who converted to Islam]."[290] Leonard continues to enumerate and name, when he is able, all the Christians who helped the Turks during the siege. Perhaps he is trying to suggest that Mehmed and his army could not possibly have imagined such brilliant tactics on their own. This is surely the case when he claims that the Turks were merely imitating a Venetian strategy in carrying their ships overland into the harbor to get past the Byzantine sea chain. Leonard's ambivalence is again evident when he describes Mehmed's construction of a bridge of casks across the harbor as a "brilliant stroke (*hoc ingenium*)" but then says of the sultan, "in this way he imitated the might of Xerxes when he led his army from Asia to Thrace over the Bosporus [by means of such a bridge]."[291] This may have been meant as a flattering comparison, but it also seems to deny Mehmed credit for his clever strategies.

Many humanists were careful never to credit the Turks for their amazing victories, but some of the most vehement supporters of crusade could not help but wonder at the success of the sultan. Even Cardinal Bessarion, in his letter to the Doge of Venice, expresses awe at the Turks' speed in taking the city: "This city, which was most heavily protected by its situation, its walls and supplies, and by all manner of defence [*sic*], this city, which, it was hoped, would be able to withstand a total siege for an entire year, the barbarians stormed and overthrew."[292] Such statements lend complexity to humanist views of the Turks. It is as if an occasional expression of surprise, even admiration, slipped past them when they were not careful. These expressions of amazement betray moments when, if only briefly, some of the most xenophobic humanists accepted the Turks' strengths at face value without the blinders of their own hostility or classical stereotypes of barbarism. Indeed, one notes a profound tension between two seemingly incongruous ideas in Bessarion's statement: the near impossibility of anyone capturing the city in so short a time and the fact that this was done by so-called "barbarians." It proved impossible for all humanists to maintain the discourse of barbarism at all times.

Even Pius II on one occasion imparted words of praise for these so-called "barbarians." Pius's case is especially striking given his customary contempt for the Turks. His letter to Mehmed II (1461) contains a passage in which he compares Mehmed to Constantine the Great. It also includes praise for the Turks as noble descendants of the Scythians—in direct opposition to his earlier statements in the *Cosmographia*.[293] These statements are complicated by the letter's problematic nature and cannot be read at face value. But regardless of Pius's sincerity or insincerity, his use of both positive and negative classical models proves an important point. If nothing else, the letter demonstrates the tremendous malleability that classical texts and examples offered humanists; Aeneas perfectly illustrates that the ancients could provide both fodder for negative propaganda and shining examples of praise.[294]

By far the most intriguing example of positive classical comparisons to the Turks is Giovanni Mario Filelfo's *Amyris*, a work that deals with the *Turci-Teucri*, or Turk-Trojan, debate. Building on the medieval and Renaissance myth claiming the Turks as heirs of the Trojans, Filelfo invokes the fall of Troy as just cause for Mehmed's conquest of Constantinople and other Greek areas. Other humanists, such as Salutati, Leonard of Chios, and Orazio Romano, preferred to use the form *Teucri* in their works; even Aeneas Silvius Piccolomini used *Teucri* in his earlier writings. This form seems to have attracted some humanists because it sounded more classical and pleasing to the ear; it is likely that most humanists used it without reference to the Trojan ancestry theory. Other humanists, such as Salutati, consciously used *Teucri* or even *Troiani* to denote an association with the Trojans. Still others, for example Tignosi, used both spellings without commenting on the Trojan myth. Adding to the confusion was the use of two different endings for the root *Turc*. While the preferred spelling was *Turci* or *Turchi*, some scholars used the form *Turcae*.

Poggio Bracciolini expressed his own uncertainty about the *Teucri-Turci* issue in a letter of 1454 to Alberto Parisi. Acknowledging that *Teucri* was an ancient name stemming from Teucer and the Trojans, Poggio also knew that it had not been used to designate any race (*gens*) in Asia after the fall of Troy. In fact, only recently had it come into use again.[295] Perhaps, he considers, he would do better to call them by the new name of *Turci*, which applies to many other peoples of whom no (ancient) account exists.[296] He goes on to list groups who are now called by new names. For instance, the name *Tartari* is used for the people who were once called Scythians. It is worth noting that Poggio considered the history of the Scythians but assumed that their descendants were Tartars, not Turks. Poggio then relates a brief history of the Turks in Asia Minor and Greece but concludes this discussion without resolution: "Which name, however, is more appropriate to them, will be discerned by those who are more diligent in this matter."[297] For his own part, Poggio continued to use the form *Teucri* after writing this letter, despite his admission that this form made little sense.[298] Perhaps he judged that maintaining consistency was best if neither name could be established with certainty.

It was precisely this careless, or sometimes calculated, use of *Teucri* to signify the Turks that angered and frustrated crusade advocates who wished to discredit them. A popular fifteenth-century source that helped spread this rumor was the spurious letter from Mehmed II to Pope Nicholas V. According to this letter, "Mehmed" asserts that the Turks have every right to recover their patrimony from the Greeks and to subjugate them in the process. Furthermore he expresses wonder that the Italians would want to crusade against his people since they are of the same Trojan blood and should therefore share a bond of love.[299] Aeneas Silvius Piccolomini spearheaded the campaign to eradicate the myth of the Turks' Trojan ancestry and appears to have achieved considerable success.[300] By the sixteenth century historians and humanists such as Andrea Cambini, Jean Lemaire de Belge, and Erasmus denied the Trojan connection, favoring a "barbaric" or nomadic origin.[301] During the fifteenth century, however, some humanists and other writers still chose to describe the Turks as Trojans.[302]

Francesco Filelfo agreed with Aeneas regarding the supposed Scythian origin of the Turks. Hence it is odd that his son, Giovanni Mario, wrote what may be the boldest and most fully articulated humanist work in support of the Turks as Trojan descendants and legitimate rulers of the former Troy. The work in question is the epic poem *Amyris* (1471–76), which derives from the Arabic word *emir*.[303] It was composed at the behest of an Italian merchant from Ancona, Othman Lillo Ferducci, whose family had connections to the Ottoman ruling family. In fact, Othman's unusual name, a variant of Osman, derived from his father's wish to honor his friend Murad II (Mehmed II's father).[304] Hoping to capitalize on his family's connections and to win favor with Mehmed, Othman asked his friend Giovanni Mario to compose a work that would exalt the young sultan.[305] In at least this one case, then, the interests and attitudes of Italian traders affected literary portrayals of the Turks in a way perhaps not seen since Boccaccio's *Decameron*. Like most humanists charged with writing a panegyric, Filelfo sought to incorporate classical themes into the work so as to lend both the work and the subject greater dignity. But he also chose the genre of epic poetry, which allowed him to draw freely on mythology and heroic language to celebrate his subject all the more. He does this most prominently in recurring references to the Trojan-Turk legend and in the machinations of gods and goddesses.

In book 1 a youthful Mehmed receives a visitation from both Venus and the Roman goddess of war, Bellona.[306] As in the contest of Paris, they each try to win him over with tempting promises. Venus offers Mehmed a long life of pleasure and ease, while Bellona offers a life of trials and war but also glory. In order to spur him on, Bellona describes the injustices done to the Trojans, Mehmed's ancestors (*tui parentes*), by the Greeks in the Trojan War, including the enslavement of the people and usurpation of their homeland—all for a lascivious woman (*pro muliere tamen lasciva*), the infamous and beautiful Helen of Troy.[307]

Bellona goes on to assert the Turks' birthright: "Who does not know by now that your ancestors are of Phrygian stock? . . . Othman was begotten from this race, derived from Priam's stock; you are the descendant of Priam, and the distinctions of this once unconquerable blood-line, which were lost then by fraud, accompany you."[308] The prospect of vengeance and recovering the Trojan inheritance, among other considerations, convinces Mehmed to accept Bellona rather than Venus as his guide, as did other great leaders such as Camillus, Fabius, and Metellus.[309] Mehmed's choice of Bellona, goddess of Romans as well as war, provides another link not only with Romans but also with modern Italians;[310] it also stands in stark contrast to Paris's fateful choice of Venus. Whereas Paris's judgment resulted in the destruction of Troy, Mehmed's opposite decision will bring about a series of reversals for the modern Trojans and Greeks alike.

Mehmed vows from that moment to do all in his power against the Greeks: "I have determined by means of war either to lose my soul or to defeat the wicked Greeks [*Mermidonas*], who once caused so much damage to our race."[311] The rhetoric of Trojan versus Greek culminates in Mehmed's satisfaction on entering Constantinople in triumph after his troops have taken the city: "You [Thracians] were once Greek subjects, you will now bear the rule of the ancient Phrygians, under a new king with a new law."[312] Filelfo has created a surreal scenario pitting the descendants of the Trojans against their ancestral enemies, the Greeks. Even though Filelfo paints this as a past injury with words such as *quondam* and *olim*, this ancient, legendary war is used as a present-day justification for obliterating the Byzantine Empire. Filelfo, then, does not limit his indictments of the Greeks to the ancient period but rather extends his invective to modern Greeks.[313]

The path that Filelfo chose seems logical at first. It allowed him to incorporate the classical past, or at least the mythical past, into the work. More important, it provided a noble and illustrious lineage for his subject, thereby "exalting" Mehmed as Ferducci asked him to do. Filelfo's approach, however, becomes more enigmatic when we recall that most humanists were traditionally anti-Turk and that Filelfo was part Greek. Moreover, those humanists who showed some respect or sympathy for the Turks tended not to represent them as a noble and ancient people who possessed the same legendary ancestry and greatness as the Romans. The tensions in his approach therefore are anything but subtle. We have no record of Filelfo's personal motives in writing this piece, but it seems unlikely that he strongly supported the Turkish cause. He later dedicated the poem, of which only one manuscript survives, with some awkward procrusade additions, to Galeazzo Maria Sforza.[314] This indicates a loss of interest in the project on his part, difficulty selling it to a broader Christian audience, or both. Even more telling is his later exhortation to Christian princes to crusade against the Turks.[315] Unless Filelfo was exercising pure poetic license in the *Amyris*—which is certainly possible, if not likely—we can only conclude that his views of the Turks were highly ambivalent. Regardless of his feelings about crusade or the Turkish advance, the *Amyris* suggests that Filelfo felt a degree of admiration for the Turks. He may have feared their advance and wished to see it halted, but this need not have prevented him from appreciating their tremendous, even epic, achievements from a distance.

The classical past provided humanists with a variety of new perspectives on the Ottoman Turks. Whether they were seen as "new barbarians" or worthy adversaries, there was a pronounced shift from medieval rhetoric in regard to the Turks. No longer were they simply classified as "enemies of the faith" and the struggle against them as purely religious, it was now also cultural and political. Perhaps the classical past was more malleable than the medieval tradition, in that the latter emerged specifically in reference to Islam while the former reacted to a host of cultural, political, and social differences. Medieval themes arguably invited less creativity than did ancient concepts, which were invented centuries before Islam and never applied systematically by anyone before the fifteenth century. Putting aside the question of which tradition can be seen as richer, it is clear that a revival of ancient models at the very least expanded and complicated the dominant religious discourse.

Some classically inspired images of the Turks were less hostile than medieval examples were. For instance, Manetti's Ciceronian discussion of the Turks as a political problem may be seen as a step toward realpolitik. Even Aeneas's insincere compliments in his letter to Mehmed paved the way for thinkers to perceive and discuss the Turks more impartially by means of classical discourse. More often humanists gravitated toward ancient models that denigrated the Turks. The popular view of the Ottomans as barbaric enemies of high culture replaced one negative (medieval) stereotype with another. The result was a more secular discourse of the Turks as an inferior, backward society. Classically inspired, secular images would prove vital and enduring over the course of time, surviving the vicissitudes of religious and antireligious sentiment in the early modern and modern eras as the crusade ideal began to deteriorate. Even when the concept of the "noble savage" emerged to occupy early modern European imaginations, "the barbarian in his Ottoman form still continued to thrill Europe."[316]

Straddling East and West:
Byzantium and Greek Refugees

BYZANTIUM PLAYED A CRUCIAL ROLE in the development of European attitudes toward the Turks and crusade. The empire's history of extensive contact and conflict with Muslim neighbors in the East enabled Byzantines to develop firsthand knowledge about Arabs, Persians, and especially Turks. As such, the Greek Empire functioned as mediator between the Muslim East and the rest of Europe. Despite tensions over the unresolved Schism of 1054, contacts between Byzantium and Western Europe increased dramatically as the Ottoman advance began to threaten the empire's stability and future viability. Greek scholars, churchmen, and diplomats struggled to convince Westerners of the fearsome Turks' inexorable approach; in the process they became an important source of information and propaganda regarding the Ottomans in fifteenth-century Europe.[1]

This role as cultural intermediary takes on yet another dimension in the close intellectual relationship between many Greek scholars and Italian humanists. Byzantine émigrés served as teachers and translators of ancient Greek as well as purveyors and editors of the Greek texts Italians craved. But, as Deno Geanakoplos has argued, "the émigrés were not merely transmitters but also interpreters in matters of textual meaning and nuances of style"; themselves products of the Palaeologan Renaissance—which, like Italian humanism, emphasized the arts of rhetoric and philology—Byzantine émigrés helped shape the course of ancient Greek studies in Renaissance Italy.[2] While Italians were primarily concerned with émigré scholars as links to the slowly unfolding mysteries of ancient Greece, Greek humanists often used their connections in Italy to recruit support against the Ottomans. They consciously played on ancient Greek history and culture in order to encourage a sense of cultural difference and antagonism between Europe and Asia/West and East. Western humanists, who had only begun to rediscover and appreciate the ancient Greek past and were simultaneously making such connections, as seen in the previous chapter, were a ripe audience for Byzantine rhetoric on the Ottoman Turks.

As important as the Byzantines were to Italy as mediators between Christian West and Muslim East, we should not imagine that relations between the Greeks and Latins were always warm. On the contrary, the Byzantines themselves sometimes required go-betweens when it came to dealing with Western Europe. Although they were technically European and Christian, the Schism between the Orthodox and Latin churches as well as considerable cultural differences could make them appear as antagonistic as the Muslims. For centuries Latins regarded Byzantines with scorn and suspicion, while the Greeks gazed warily back. Byzantines, then, occupied a changeable position in Western eyes, continually shifting between the realms of cultural and religious siblings to outsiders.

Background: Byzantium and Eastern Europe between Islam and the Latin West

During the High Middle Ages, Byzantium was the powerful empire that shielded Europe from the threat of the Infidel. Although the Greeks lost possessions in Asia and North Africa to Arab armies in the seventh century and would continue to lose more territory to Muslims and Christians alike, the Byzantine Empire showed enormous resilience and even recovered some lost territory.[3] This strength and longevity made Byzantium appear to be the protector of Christendom, constantly maintaining the frontier between Christendom and the forces of Islam. However, Byzantium was not always regarded by Latins as an ally. In many ways it seemed an outsider. Some of these perceptions were grounded in reality since compelling forces pulled medieval Byzantium away from its western orbit, such as the loss of Byzantium's imperial influence in the West. The Greeks' continued insistence on designating themselves "Roman" and portraying the West, at least theoretically, as part of their empire only served to irritate or incense many Latins, especially those who followed Germanic Roman emperors.

The greatest source of friction between Latins and Greeks, however, was religion. Owing to the split in 1054 between the Latin and Greek Churches, Byzantines were viewed as "schismatics" and even "heretics," who persisted in doctrinal errors and stubbornly resisted papal jurisdiction.[4] Moreover, the Byzantine tendency to form alliances with Eastern neighbors rather than increasingly hostile Western powers led Latins, however unfairly, to question their loyalty to Christendom. For many Western Europeans, Byzantium appeared as foreign, exotic, and decadent as the Persians had once appeared to the Greeks. Tensions could, indeed, run high between Greeks and Latins.

The Crusades, intended to heal the breach between Byzantines and Latins, only served to widen it. Wary Byzantine observers regarded the first crusaders as dangerous interlopers in lands they viewed as Greek territory, not as the patrimony of all Christians. Over time the mutual suspicion and frequent clashes between Latins and Greeks during the Crusades were potent enough to divert some of the Western hatred away from the Muslims and focus it on the Byzantines.[5] By 1204 many Latins viewed Byzantium as a grave threat to Christian unity—almost as threatening as the Muslims. It was in this year that the Fourth Crusade, which had been summoned to liberate Jerusalem, ended with the seizure and sack of Constantinople. From 1204 until 1261 Constantinople was governed by Latin rulers and Roman Catholic bishops; Venetian and French adventurers continued to seize Greek islands and mainland possessions in the years after the capture of Constantinople.[6] This act of extreme aggression and the ensuing years of foreign rule and religious intolerance did more than any other event to sow feelings of mistrust among the Byzantines toward the Latins and the Roman Catholic Church. Pope Innocent III was pained and disappointed by the attack on Constantinople.[7] The Byzantines, for their part, never forgot the outrage. Even when the Turks encircled their city in 1453, the majority of Byzantine Christians could not accept union with the Latin Church in order to secure aid. Most Latins regretted the loss of Constantinople in 1261 more than the shameful attack on the city in 1204. It was not until 1320 that plans for an anti-Byzantine crusade were abandoned.[8]

As rocky as Byzantium's relationship with the West became at times, its contacts with Muslim neighbors were even more troubled. Byzantium's involvement with the Turks, though not always violent, was generally tense. Beginning in the eleventh century Seljuk Turks began conquering the Anatolian peninsula. The remaining local Greek and Armenian population assimilated with the Turks by conversion, intermarriage, and/or an eventual acceptance of Turkish hegemony and culture.[9] In the late thirteenth century under the leadership of Osman, the Ottomans began to consolidate power in the northwest corner of Anatolia, conquering several Byzantine cities; the most important of these was the trading center Bursa, which would become their first capital.[10] Within a few decades the Byzantines would attempt to bring the Ottomans over to their side.

Seeking aid in his civil war against the legitimate heir to the throne, Emperor John VI Cantacuzenus (r. 1347–54) turned to Orhan, Osman's son, in 1345, giving his daughter Theodora to him in marriage the following year.[11] Cantacuzenus's first choice, Umur Bey of Izmir, was busy defending his city from Latin crusading forces.[12] Orhan later formed an accord with the Genoese (1354 or earlier) during one of their wars with Venice. This web of alliances shows how Turks and Eastern Christians openly and readily cooperated to suit their political interests at this time.

The Byzantine alliance offered the Ottomans an opportunity to cross the Dardanelles into Europe in 1352 while aiding Cantacuzenus against rivals for the throne at Adrianople. Historians disagree on how and when the Ottomans, led by Orhan's son Suleiman, began taking over and raiding Thracian cities, or whether they violated their pact with Cantacuzenus. It is clear, however, that by 1353 or 1354 they had established themselves in Europe and were raiding throughout Thrace.[13] Nor did Suleiman's death in 1357 slow the process of conquest; his brother Murad stepped into the Thracian arena, expanding on Suleiman's victories.[14] Pope Urban V responded to these developments in 1365–66 by trying to fit an anti-Turkish campaign into his plans for a crusade to the Holy Land; at least one ruler, Amadeo of Savoy, answered the call, winning some victories at Gallipoli and along the Black Sea.[15]

Byzantium continued to lose ground to the Ottomans during the reign of Murad I (r. 1362–89), who simultaneously centralized his power and expanded his dominions.[16] Perhaps the greatest loss of this period was that of Adrianople (Edirne) in 1369. This victory gave the Ottomans both a new capital and easy access to Bulgaria, which came under Ottoman vassalage in the 1370s.[17] Some Balkan rulers accepted Ottoman overlordship; while others fought strenuously against it.[18] Pope Gregory XI, alarmed by these events, struggled to organize a crusade but met with little concrete response, despite Catherine of Siena's supportive letter-writing campaign. Venice and Genoa's engagement in their Fourth War (1376–81) ensured that they would be too busy to consider helping a crusade effort. When not at war, Venetian and Genoese trade interests in Ottoman areas generally complicated their commitment to crusade. Macedonia soon came under Ottoman control, leaving Serbia and Bosnia open to Turkish raids. Even Byzantium became a tributary in 1372–73.[19]

As these developments indicate, the complexity of Balkan politics prevented a simple unification of Christians versus Muslims. Bitter rivalries between Orthodox and Catholic interests only intensified the divisions and diminished hopes for a crusade.[20] One by one the Ottomans made vassals of the Bulgarians, the Byzantines, the Serbs, and the Bosnians, thus establishing suzerainty over large portions of the Balkans. Ottoman rule over the Christian peasant population was even more indirect and hands-off than their control over the elite.[21] Despite the appeal of these arrangements to many Balkan rulers and peasants, there was enough discontent with Ottoman suzerainty to bring about revolts. Prince Lazar of Serbia and King Tvrtko of Bosnia fought the Turks separately in the late 1380s and jointly at Kosovo in 1389.[22] In an attempt to reestablish control, Murad's heir Bayezid initiated a process of more direct Ottoman rule and tighter control over his Christian vassals.[23] He assembled them at Serrai in late 1393 to reaffirm their vassalage, but Byzantine emperor Manuel II (r. 1391–1425) fled this meeting, claiming that his life was in danger from Bayezid; Bayezid responded by besieging Constantinople, where the emperor was trapped.[24] Preferring resistance to cooperation with the Ottomans, Manuel actively sought help from Western powers; he received a response in the crusade of Nicopolis, which ended in utter defeat in 1396.[25] The crusade provided a brief respite from Bayezid's siege of Constantinople, but the blockade was not fully lifted until 1402.

Still, Manuel did not give up on the prospect of aid from the West. From 1400 to 1402 he traveled through Europe, personally petitioning rulers and governments to join him in another crusade. Constantinople, meanwhile, escaped an imminent assault by Bayezid when the Ottoman Empire was attacked on its eastern flank by Timur Lenk, or "Tamerlane," a Tatar warlord, who had built up a loose empire in central Asia. After suffering defeat to Timur, Bayezid died in 1403 in captivity; civil war soon broke out between Bayezid's sons. During these years of upheaval, many local rulers in the Balkans and Anatolia regained some of their former territory and began to rule independently. Byzantium profited by regaining some of her lands while playing Bayezid's sons against each other. It was not until the reign of Murad II (r. 1421–51) that Ottoman power was resurgent.[26] Manuel once again became an Ottoman vassal, but he kept looking for ways to undermine Murad's power.[27]

Murad won victories against Hungary and Venice but decided in 1444 to make a truce with his enemies and retire, for reasons that are still debated.[28] Precisely at this time, however, another crusade was forming under joint papal and Balkan leadership: the crusade of Varna. In many ways 1444 was an opportune time for a crusade. The Ottoman hold in Europe was looking rather shaky, its presence having been greatly reduced in Thrace, Macedonia, and Greece; Constantinople, of course, would never be secure without a crusade.[29] Varna, however, was another military disaster for the crusade movement.[30] For Greece the consequences would be heavy; following Varna, the withdrawal of Hungarian forces and Western aid allowed the Turks to move easily into the Peloponnesus. Varna also enabled the Ottoman process of annexation inaugurated by Bayezid I to proceed with little resistance.[31]

The reign of Mehmed II (1451–81) spelled the end of the Byzantine Empire, beginning with his spectacular conquest of Constantinople (1453).[32] Mehmed went on to capture the city of Athens (1456), which had been ruled for several generations by the Acciaiuoli family of Florence. Serbia was fully conquered by the Turks in 1459, the Morea fell in 1460, the tiny empire of Trebizond followed in 1461, and Bosnia was annexed in 1463. Mehmed also won crucial victories on the eastern front in central Anatolia in this period. Despite the violence of his conquests, a contemporary chronicler argued that Mehmed took pains to help the Greeks recover and wish to remain in Ottoman dominions. After the fall of Constantinople he tried to reverse the damage by freeing captives, forcing slave owners to pay their slaves wages in order to earn their freedom, and rebuilding and repopulating the city. Within a short time Constantinople was thriving commercially and culturally.[33] In some ways the lives of most Greeks, that is, the peasant class, were no worse than they had been under Christian overlords; economically they were better, given the comparatively lighter taxes. Later sultans would not be so generous, but Mehmed granted many privileges to the Orthodox Church—no small relief to Greeks who had been pressured for centuries to return to Roman Catholicism. Under the millet system religious life went on as before, and many legal issues were left to Christian control.[34] For many Greeks, however, exile in such places as Italy, Venetian Crete, or Spain was preferable to life under the Ottomans.

Byzantium's last few centuries were beset by political and religious pressures from both the Muslim East and the Latin West. While the Greeks were able to mediate between the two poles for many years, they suffered too many losses in the process to survive. It is against this background of constant tension between East and West that we should examine Byzantine contacts with Renaissance humanists. Humanists mirrored the political and religious ambivalence seen in Byzantium's larger relationship with the West. At times they treated Byzantine losses to the Turks as their own. At other moments they affected a righteous stance toward Greek defeats, claiming that they had gotten what they deserved. Hence, affinity or enmity for Byzantium could directly impact one's view of the Turks; in this sense the Greeks were more than mediators but almost a medium through which humanists viewed the Turks. Conversely, the Ottoman advance helped foster some intriguing (and disturbing) views of the Greeks.

Italians in the Greek East

In addition to the political and religious tensions sketched above, a great deal of travel and peaceful exchange took place between Italy and the Greek East. The eastern Mediterranean of the late fourteenth and early fifteenth centuries acted as a meeting ground as well as a battlefield for Italians, Greeks, and Turks.[35] Although the Turks would come to dominate the eastern Mediterranean, the Italian presence in that area was strong until the late fifteenth century. In addition to their settlements and trading privileges in key Byzantine and Muslim cities such as Constantinople and Alexandria, Italian maritime powers also had political control of some eastern colonies. Most prominent of the Italian powers in this arena was Venice, which possessed Crete, portions of the Morea in Greece, and the better part of Euboea. The Genoese controlled Chios; Famagusta in Cyprus; Pera, which lay across the harbor from Constantinople; and Caffa on the Black Sea. Florence too had ties to the eastern Mediterranean in the Acciaiuoli family. A branch of this family ruled over parts of the Morea in Greece, including at one time or another Corinth, Athens, Attica, and Boeotia until 1458, when the last Acciaiuoli duke of Athens was deposed by Mehmed II.[36] Pisans too were responsible for a significant amount of trade in and around Greece, and non-Italian groups such as the Catalan and Navarrese companies made several attempts to win power in Greece.

The Italian commercial presence in the eastern Mediterranean helped ease the way for fellow countrymen who wished to travel in the East for reasons other than trade. Scholars especially profited from these connections. In the first half of the fifteenth century many Italians journeyed east either to study with Greek masters or to observe the material culture of the Greek East. Two scholars who ventured out on their own to learn about Greece and its culture were Cristoforo Buondelmonti and Ciriaco d'Ancona. The Florentine priest Cristoforo Buondelmonti was an early quattrocento enthusiast of Greek geography and topography. While most Italian scholars were content to satisfy their curiosity about the Greek East with Ptolemy's *Geography*—an inaccurate text held in high esteem for its "ancient authority"—Buondelmonti preferred to explore the area first-hand.[37] After learning Greek on the island of Rhodes in 1415, Buondelmonti traveled to various islands in the Aegean and Mediterranean, gathering information about their size, topography, monuments, and inhabitants. His *Book of Islands* (*Liber Insularum*), "a best seller throughout the fifteenth century," and *The Description of Crete* were the results of his inquiries.[38] But Buondelmonti was not interested in contemporary Greek civilization alone. To gain a better sense of what ancient Greek art, architecture, and communal spaces once looked like, he often searched for ruins of various ancient edifices and statues from history and mythology.[39]

A slightly younger contemporary, Ciriaco d'Ancona, also traversed and wrote about the Greek East. Born into a mercantile family, he was almost wholly self-taught in both Latin and Greek. Ciriaco focused much more on the physical remains of ancient Greece than did Buondelmonti, copying down many of the Greek inscriptions he found on his travels; this rare and painstaking activity has led historians to consider him the only archaeologist of Greece during the humanistic age.[40] Far from secretive about his unique work, Ciriaco eagerly spread his knowledge to the uninitiated. He shared his discoveries with such humanists as Leonardo Bruni, Niccolò Niccoli, and Francesco Filelfo in his correspondence, keeping them apprised of his antiquarian pursuits as well as current political matters.[41]

Ciriaco's views of the Turks and crusade have been a subject of debate among scholars. While he supported crusade and served Christian rulers on diplomatic missions in the Mediterranean, he also seems to have had cordial relations with Murad II, who granted him safe-conduct to travel through Ottoman areas. It was once widely thought that Ciriaco served Mehmed II, teaching him ancient Greek and Roman history, and that he was even present in the conqueror's camp during the siege of Constantinople.[42] This rumor has led some to call him an opportunist and turncoat, and others, a cosmopolitan man of the world. Such conclusions proved baseless, however, when the story of Ciriaco's presence at Mehmed's camp was discredited; his loyalties, then, were not so divided.[43] Despite his reservations regarding the Greek Schism, he worked tirelessly to help Eastern Christians achieve security against the Turks, assisting Emperor John VIII and others.[44] Ciriaco's letters further demonstrate his commitment. On many occasions he apprised Western European recipients of the current dangers and urged them to help the crusade cause. A letter to John Hunyadi written in the summer of 1444 before the battle of Varna is particularly telling. Ciriaco explains his own moderation concerning the "barbarians" in previous letters from Adrianople—then the Ottoman capital—as a necessary means to protect his life. Writing now from the safety of Constantinople, he urges Hunyadi to take advantage of "the tyrant" Murad's absence by breaking his peace with him and attacking his armies in Thrace.[45] If Ciriaco were a partisan of the Turks, would he have held so cheap solemn oaths, a ten-year peace, and the attractive concessions Murad had made to the Hungarians and Serbs? Clearly he distrusted the Turks. He also knew that if the truce held, two important parties would suffer: the Greeks, who had received no concessions or hope of safety from Murad; and, of course, the papacy and Cesarini, whose crusade was still in the offing.[46] Ciriaco's good relations with the Ottomans, then, appear to have been a necessity of negotiating his way through what was once Greek and Roman territory.

Ciriaco's antipathy for the Turks was not only political and religious but also intellectual, as may be seen in accounts of his visits to ancient Greek sites. On a journey to the Propontis (1444), Ciriaco laments the sorry state of the ancient site of Artace (Erdek), which he had seen in much better condition seven years earlier: "But alas! What a degradation it was which we now revisited compared with what we had seen twice seven years previously; for then we had seen thirty-one columns standing upright, but now indeed, I saw only twenty-nine remained and those had partly lost their architraves. But the glorious walls, which had almost all then stood intact, now seemed for the most part to have been reduced by the barbarians and fallen to the ground"; And at Cyzicus he grieves not only for the sorry state of that ancient site but also for the news that "within days it would be utterly destroyed by the barbarians."[47] Ciriaco's reaction to the state of Greek monuments is not surprising for an antiquarian, but what stands out is his assumption that the Turks had vandalized these areas. Whether or not they were actually responsible, it is notable that Ciriaco sees them as agents of cultural destruction, as the new barbarians who threaten the precious ancient heritage of the Greeks as well as their freedom. This is a perception that resonates with accusations from

Italian humanists that the Turks had deliberately set out to destroy ancient Greek learning in their treatment of books in 1453.

But Ciriaco's use of "barbarian" may be significant in yet another way. By 1444 a few other humanists, for example, Poggio, Bruni, and Aeneas Silvius Piccolomini, had used the term in a loose fashion, only vaguely or infrequently related to the Turks. Ciriaco uses the term not only in the context of the Turks but also as a cognomen for them. What may account for this difference is his time spent among the Greeks, who had been using the term as a cultural designation for Easterners for centuries.[48] Ciriaco's use of the ancient concept of barbarism points strongly toward the influence of Byzantine perceptions of the Turks in the formation of his views. A similar case might be made in regard to other Western Europeans. For example, in a letter of 1406 Florentine Pier Paolo Vergerio laments the return to Greece of the great scholar Manuel Chrysoloras, where he is "exposed to constant danger of becoming a captive of barbarians."[49] Chrysoloras had spent several years in Florence teaching Greek. Since the application of "barbarian" to the Turks is rarely found among Italian humanists before the 1440s, it seems likely that Chrysoloras introduced his circle to such a use of the term. Greek delegates at the Council of Florence may have revived its popularity in 1438/39. The year 1453 too had a significant impact on humanists in increasing the concept and language of barbarism vis-à-vis the Turks. Perhaps, then, Greek rhetoric helped promote familiarity with this term, providing a discourse that humanists readily chose to adopt following the fall of Constantinople.

Other Italian scholars traveled to the Greek East, not for independent study but to seek instruction from Byzantine scholars. The most famous of these students were Guarino da Verona, Jacopo Angeli da Scarperia, Giovanni Tortelli, and Francesco Filelfo. A native of Tolentino, Filelfo (1389–1481) came to Constantinople as secretary to the Venetian consul general; shortly after arriving he began learning Greek under the instruction of John Chrysoloras. The two developed a close relationship; Filelfo boarded with his professor and even married his daughter Theodora in 1424.[50] In Constantinople Filelfo and other Italians learned not only Greek but also methods of philology and textual interpretation, showing that the city maintained its image as a bastion of high culture and learning until its capture.[51] In addition to studies in classical texts, training in philosophy, theology, astronomy, medicine, and mathematics flourished. Ironically, it was only when the Byzantine Empire was on the verge of extinction that Westerners exhibited the greatest enthusiasm for the fruits of Byzantine learning.[52] This may be due to expanding Western interests, but it is at least as much a consequence of the Palaeologan renaissance in learning and the arts during the final two centuries of Byzantium's existence.

For the first time in centuries Western scholars, who had previously relied on Arab sources, could examine ancient Greek texts without the filter of a translation or paraphrase. Excited humanists finally returned *ad fontes*, to the sources, in their original language and form.[53] Their enthusiasm for Greek learning and their reverence for Greek scholars gave humanists an appreciation of the scale of the Turkish threat; the opportunity to see Greece firsthand also reinforced their appreciation of what was at stake. Accompanying this cultural resurgence was a preoccupation among Byzantines with their own "Greekness," that is, history and culture, both pagan and Christian.[54] All of these elements would greatly affect attitudes toward Byzantium and the Turks in fifteenth-century Italy.

Greeks in Italy

As time went on, fewer Italian scholars traveled to Byzantium, largely because Byzantine Greeks were going to Italy in increasing numbers. A combination of pressure from the Turks and growing opportunities in the West led many Greeks to leave their homelands in search of employment in Italy, while others relocated to different areas of Greece and Venetian Crete.[55] Scholars were in great demand, but so were soldiers and sailors, who found work in southern Italy. While the history of the Byzantine Greeks in Renaissance Italy cannot be easily summarized, a few key individuals stand out for their impact in shaping Italian views of the Ottoman Turks. One of the earliest of these figures was the emperor of Byzantium, Manuel II Palaeologus.

Seeking Western aid against the Ottoman Turks, Manuel arrived in Venice in May 1400, whence he traveled through Italy, proceeded to Paris, and spent Christmas at the English court. He continued to travel through Europe until he was summoned home due to an impending Turkish attack on Constantinople in 1402.[56] While he commanded great respect and sympathy, he returned to Constantinople without any firm promises of aid from the Western potentates he had visited.[57] This is not to say that his audiences were unmoved. He aroused pity in those who saw his reduced state of begging for his once glorious but now shrunken and endangered empire. An English lawyer at King Henry IV's court remarked on the sadness of these affairs: "I thought within myself, what a grievous thing it was that this great Christian prince from the farthest east should perforce be driven by unbelievers to visit the distant islands of the west, to seek aid against them. My God! What dost thou, ancient glory of Rome? Shorn is the greatness of thine empire this day. . . ."[58] Clearly, it was not lost on Western observers that the Turks were responsible for Byzantium's fall from power and glory. Reactions to Manuel's plight stand as an early instance of Western antipathy for the Turks as the reckless banes of the Christian empire of Byzantium.

Over thirty years later an even larger delegation of Greeks visited Italy to attend the Council of Florence (1438–39).[59] Over seven hundred Greek clergy and laymen were at the council, whose purpose was to unify the Greek and Latin Churches. Even the emperor and the patriarch attended the council. Although some thirty union negotiations had previously been attempted, this was arguably the most crucial: the very survival of the empire was at stake since papal assistance and crusade were generally only offered to the Greeks on the condition of their acceptance of Latin authority. Emperor John VIII Palaeologus, like several previous emperors, eagerly solicited a union for this reason. But submission to Rome was a price that few Orthodox clergymen and even fewer Greek laymen were willing to pay. Lingering enmity and distrust for the Latins, stemming from the Fourth Crusade and subsequent Latin rule, as well as doctrinal differences (over precise wording of the Nicene Creed, papal authority, purgatory, and the nature of transubstantiation) were rifts too great to be bridged.[60] Nonetheless, the Turkish threat had so intensified that even the more stubborn Orthodox clergy could recognize the merits of attempting a union.

The council also offered potential benefits to Westerners. Latin churchmen welcomed the chance either to repair the old breach between the two rites or simply to assert the supremacy of Rome. Florentines, for their part, were happy to host the council for several reasons. The council helped boost the city's international prestige and economy. It also stimulated Florentine humanism, which was developing a strong interest in Greek studies and language.[61] Underscoring Florence's growing support of Greek studies, Leonardo Bruni delivered two orations in Greek on the arrival of the patriarch and the emperor.[62] Emperor John VIII, who happened to arrive in the city on the Sunday of Carnival, was greeted with fanfare and celebration, as was the pope. Therefore, a mood of celebration and curiosity marked the Greeks' arrival.[63]

In their appearance and bearing, the Greek delegates at the Council of Florence made a vivid impression. Humanists were especially moved. Studies in the language and literature of ancient Greece had blossomed in Italy to such a degree that Italian humanists saw the council as a unique opportunity to commune with the heirs of ancient Greece. Vespasiano da Bisticci wrote in his *Vite* about the striking appearance and dress of the Byzantine Greeks, saying, "For the last fifteen hundred years and more they have not altered the style of their dress; their clothes are of the same fashion now as they were in the time indicated."[64] Evidently, Vespasiano was unaware of the impact of Asian fabrics and styles as well as the change of fashions on Byzantine dress and hairstyles. As one modern author has remarked, "when looked at, these turbaned, bearded and long-robed Platonists appeared more like the denizens of Susa [the ancient Persian city] than Athens."[65] Some Florentines, however, did notice the Eastern aspect in the delegates' appearance; the painter Benozzo Gozzoli depicted Emperor John VIII and Patriarch Joseph II as magi in his Palazzo Medici fresco (*The Procession of the Magi*).[66] Carlo Ginzburg has shown how the emperor and Cardinal Bessarion, another prominent figure from the council, were portrayed in Piero della Francesca's *Flagellation of Christ*.[67]

On closer acquaintance, however, some Byzantines shattered this image of ancient nobility or magian benevolence. Squabbles over ceremonial procedure and doctrinal issues encouraged bad behavior on both sides. In their concern for protecting the Greek Church's dignity and Constantinople's episcopal parity with Rome, the Greek delegates refused to greet the pope by ceremonially kissing his foot. Because of this the Byzantine clergy were obliged to meet the pope unceremoniously and in private, lest the Italian public view this affront to their pontiff.[68] Some Orthodox clerics, such as Mark of Ephesus, were so zealous to preserve their church's rights and doctrines that their pronouncements took the form of thinly veiled insults. Mark went so far as to compose an essay in the pope's honor, ostensibly praising his efforts toward union while debunking Roman doctrines and denouncing Roman pride. His vehemence embarrassed the Latins and infuriated the emperor, who was narrowly prevented from having the metropolitan punished.[69] Moments such as this did little to endear the Greeks to the Latins, who already harbored suspicions of Greek pride. Thus in some respects the council only served to ingrain negative Byzantine stereotypes in Western imaginations—stereotypes that were reinforced by the later repudiation of the union by the citizens of Constantinople. After this development, in addition to other epithets, the Greeks were commonly labeled perfidious and unfaithful—unfair charges since the people were not consulted when the union was being discussed. Mark of Ephesus refused to sign the declaration of union and became a prominent voice of antiunion sentiment in Constantinople.[70]

But Mark of Ephesus's attitudes were not representative of the delegation as a whole. Most of his cohorts were more accommodating; their fears of Turkish conquest outweighed their desire to stand firm on all matters of doctrine. Through compromise and careful wording the union of the Greek and Latin Churches was formally declared on 6 July 1439. Throughout the council, then, disagreement and discomfort were balanced by understanding and communication. Aside from official gatherings, Latins and Greeks met in small, informal groups to discuss matters of theology and philosophy as well as books and manuscripts, forging long-lasting friendships and useful connections.[71] George Gemistos Plethon, an eccentric Greek Platonist who openly embraced paganism, gave informal philosophical lectures. His enthusiasm for ancient Greek culture and his characterization of the Turks as barbarians may have influenced Western thinkers such as Bruni to view the Turkish advance as a threat to civilization.[72] Cardinal Bessarion and John Argyropoulos, among others, made important contacts with Italian scholars and clergymen that would later help them find a new home and worthy positions in Italy. Also, as John Monfasani has shown, academic interests were fed on both sides. Byzantine scholars were genuinely interested in Latin scholarship, particularly scholasticism, and eagerly conversed with Latin scholars or studied at Western schools.[73]

The eventual settlement of Greek scholars in Italy, most of whom arrived for good after 1453, made an even stronger impression on Italians than did the widely attended Council of Florence. Byzantine scholars who taught in Italy represented the richness of the Greek heritage to their Western admirers. As Westerners began to appreciate Byzantium's position as a steward and interpreter of antique culture, the Turkish menace to Byzantium took on new meaning. The Turks were not only threats to Christianity and European security; they were also perceived as threats to the culture and learning of the increasingly vulnerable Byzantine Empire.

The first major Greek scholar to teach in Italy was Manuel Chrysoloras. He traveled to Venice as a Byzantine ambassador in 1394/95, but his mission excited less reaction than did his reputation as an eminent scholar. Shortly after Chrysoloras and his fellow ambassador Demetrius Cydones arrived in Venice seeking military assistance for their emperor, two Florentines, Jacopo Angeli da Scarperia and Roberto Rossi, solicited their services for instruction in Greek. While Angeli journeyed back to Constantinople with the ambassadors to continue his education, Rossi returned home to Florence, where he sang the praises of the two Greeks to the chancellor Coluccio Salutati. In 1396 Salutati wrote Chrysoloras offering him a position teaching Greek in Florence on a public salary.[74] Chrysoloras lived in Florence for three years (1397–1400) and taught well-known locals such as Leonardo Bruni, Palla Strozzi, and Niccolò Niccoli, as well as scholars from outside of Florence, for example, Pier Paolo Vergerio.[75] He spent the next three years in Milan and Pavia, where he taught Uberto Decembrio among others.

While Chrysoloras's time teaching in Italy was relatively short, his impact on the course of humanism was pronounced. In addition to training some of the best humanists of the early quattrocento in Greek and composing a Greek grammar,[76] he was by all accounts an inspiration to his Italian students and colleagues. Chrysoloras opened a world of learning to Italians, acquainting them with great Greek poets, thinkers, and orators such as Homer, Plato, and Demosthenes. He inspired his students with his enthusiasm not only for the Greek language but also for classical civilization.[77] Between his efforts in Italy and those of Italian students in Byzantium, knowledge of the Greek language soon became widespread among humanists. Numerous Italian students schooled at home and abroad became important translators and teachers of Greek to succeeding generations of Italian students.[78]

It is likely that Chrysoloras, who also actively supported the empire by serving as an envoy, inspired his Italian students to share in his fears and biases regarding the Turks.[79] As James Hankins has argued, Chrysoloras probably viewed his teaching and his diplomatic work as serving the same purpose. His cultural activities offered an important medium to convince Latins of Byzantium's valuable and vibrant heritage—a rich resource that merited protection against the Turks. Thus, Greek studies, particularly ancient works, acted as common ground between modern Greeks and Latins that transcended the tensions of the lingering Schism.[80]

While Chrysoloras laid the foundation in Italy for a renewed love of Greek learning and an enthusiasm for Byzantine pedagogy, the Greek scholars who followed in his wake probably did more to impress on Italian scholars the extent to which Byzantium and Greek learning were imperiled by the Turkish advance. Indeed, as many of these scholars arrived in Italy fleeing the Turkish advance, the connection was readily apparent. The Byzantine scholar most closely associated with the Turkish problem was also a prominent member of the Church: Cardinal Bessarion. Bessarion was born in Trebizond (1403) and educated in Constantinople and Mistra. After entering the priesthood he became an important member of the emperor's court and was nominated metropolitan of Nicaea in 1437.[81] At the Council of Florence the following year Bessarion began to expand his interests beyond the Greek East to the Latin West. He was one of the few high ranking Greek clergymen who both accepted the union of the Latin and Orthodox Churches and maintained his unionist stance throughout his life. After a brief visit home to Greece in 1439, Bessarion returned to Italy to help solidify the work of the council; he spent the rest of his life in the service of the papacy, receiving the cardinal's hat in late 1439.

Bessarion's scholarly interests ranged from Platonism to theology to translating. He was well trained in Latin, producing many fine orations and translations in a language foreign to most Greeks.[82] But a great deal of his time and energy was consumed by the Turkish threat to Byzantium and the West. Both alone and in concert with other Greeks and the papacy, he worked tirelessly to publicize the problem and to garner military and financial aid in the war against the Turks. To analyze all of Bessarion's works in which he discusses the Ottoman advance would require a study of its own. Still, by examining some key works on the subject one may form a fair impression of his attitudes toward the Turks and crusade, specifically in relation to Byzantium.

One of the earliest instances when Bessarion publicly discussed the Turks was in an oration delivered at the Council of Florence. The body of the long *Oratio Dogmatica* was devoted to theological issues, demonstrating the fundamental agreement of both churches on doctrinal matters. The epilogue, however, included a rousing discussion of the Turkish advance, using deliberative rhetoric to persuade both sides of their common need to unite against the Turks. Bessarion claims that there is a correlation between the division of the Orthodox and Latin Churches and Ottoman successes in the Greek East: "Who, indeed, does not know what temporal evils are about to pursue us as a result of this division? What misfortunes? Who does not know that we make our common enemy and the hostile leader of the Turks stronger against ourselves? Any and all Christians who follow our rite are in danger, with the result that nearly all are perishing, and the name of Christ there is being utterly obliterated."[83] While acknowledging the dangers of disunity, Bessarion manages to demonstrate the shared circumstances that bind Greek and Latin Christians: the bond of a common faith and a common enemy. The danger that threatens them both far outweighs the petty disagreements between the two churches. Bessarion's point is clear: the Turks are a threat to both East and West; should the two churches not reach an accord, the Christian religion will be destroyed. He closes this argument by asking the Eastern Orthodox Christians: "Who does not know that our only remaining refuge was the friendship of and a future union with the Latins, and that, hoping in this thing, we are able to protect ourselves and to conquer our enemies? And that this thing alone deterred our enemies and checked their fury against us?"[84] Clearly for Bessarion, as for many Greeks, religious accord and military alliance with the West were part of the same elusive goal. Bessarion's rhetoric, however, continually stressed the commonalities between East and West rather than the need for submission or capitulation, showing his sensitivity to the easily wounded pride of Greek delegates as well as his ability to assuage Latin doubts. His diplomacy and optimism were no doubt factors in his advancement within the Church, as was his knowledge of Turkish policy and attitudes.[85]

On hearing that Constantinople had fallen, Bessarion, now a cardinal, wrote to the doge of Venice (13 July 1453) exhorting him to recapture it.[86] The letter stands as one of the most eloquent and fully descriptive reactions to the loss among humanists. In addition to lamenting the loss of life, he vividly illustrates the losses to Western culture:

A city which was recently flourishing, with such a great emperor, so many illustrious men, such very famous and ancient families, so prosperous, the head of all Greece, the splendor and glory of the East, the school of the best arts, the refuge of all good things has been captured, despoiled, ravaged and completely sacked by the most inhuman barbarians and the most savage enemies of the Christian faith, by the fiercest of wild beasts. The public treasure has been consumed, private wealth has been destroyed, the temples have been stripped of gold, silver, jewels, the relics of the saints and other most precious ornaments.[87]

This description of the fall of Constantinople is representative of the kind of language and imagery seen in a variety of Western accounts.[88] Bessarion lamented the loss of an ancient and prestigious empire; the destruction, pillage, and desecration of sacred buildings and relics; as well as the murder, rape, and enslavement of the city's inhabitants. If Ciriaco of Ancona was impressed by Greek rhetoric concerning the Turks during his travels, Bessarion may have had a similar effect on Italian humanists, especially after 1453. Of course, the revival of Latin classics had much to do with the revival of the discourse of barbarism. Indeed, it seems unlikely that any

one humanist was responsible for inventing and disseminating it wholesale. That said, Bessarion stood out as an authority on Greece and the
Turks; the ground may already have been fertile for a revived discourse of
barbarism, but his letters and other works may well have helped the idea
spread more rapidly and widely after 1453. If nothing else, Bessarion's account created a vivid impression of all that was lost in 1453 for Westerners
who had never seen Constantinople.

Throughout his career in the Roman Church, Bessarion remained
loyal to his homeland and helped many fellow Greeks, acting as a patron
and a host to refugees seeking a new home and livelihood in Italy. Combining patriotism with scholarship, Bessarion, like many other Byzantine
humanists, sought to improve Greece's public image in the West.[89] Given
the bad press it had received, their task was by no means easy. One approach favored by Bessarion was to remind Westerners of the rich religious
and cultural heritage of Greece—a heritage that Christians and scholars of
the West could appreciate as formative of their own culture. While working with Pope Pius II to garner support for the papal crusade, Bessarion
delivered a speech filled with references to Greece on the occasion of the
transferal of the head of Saint Andrew the Apostle from Patras in Greece to
Saint Peter's Church in Rome (1462). In his flight from the Turks, Thomas
Palaeologus, despot of the Morea, brought the precious relic with him to
assure its safety. Rich ceremony surrounded the reception of the relic; both
Pius and Bessarion delivered speeches to mark the occasion. Pius described
the importance of the event for all of Christendom and called on the apostle to bring success to the papal crusade, but it was Bessarion who stressed
the role of Greece in Andrew's life and in the early Church.[90] In the voice
of Andrew, Bessarion exclaimed: "after traveling through many and diverse nations whom I dedicated to the true Faith and the name of Christ,
I came at last to Achaia, a province of the Peloponnese filled full of men
not only noble but learned; there I sowed the truth of the Gospel so widely
that I converted the entire province from the worship of idols to the religion of the true God."[91] Implying that Andrew owed his success in Greece
partly to the nobility and erudition of its inhabitants, Bessarion presents
his homeland as a cradle of ancient Christianity, a land fortunate in its
people and blessed by the work of the great apostle. In this way Bessarion
counters accusations that Greek Christians practiced an inferior religion;
on the contrary, like the Romans, they were converted by one of Jesus'
disciples. After decrying Achaia's subjugation by the "Mohammedans,"
Bessarion uses Andrew's voice to express incipient nationalistic sentiments:

"I have come to thee, most holy brother [Saint Peter] . . . so I too taking refuge with thee, may by thy power and help restore to their former liberty the sons whom I had begotten to myself, or rather to thee, nay to Christ our Lord, who are now subject to an impious and most savage enemy and not only deprived of physical freedom but in danger of losing the integrity of their faith. . . ."[92] Not only, then, is Bessarion calling for crusade and the defense of Christendom in his oration on Saint Andrew, but he is also calling for the reestablishment of a Greek homeland in the East. Bessarion, still speaking as Andrew, goes on to exhort Saint Peter to take up arms against the Turks. The heavy-handed parallelism of Andrew's plea to Peter becomes a plea from Bessarion himself (Andrew's successor as a high-ranking Greek churchman) to Pius (pope and direct successor of Saint Peter).[93] Bessarion is endeavoring to demonstrate both the apostolic tradition that links him to Pius, and his obvious dependence on the pope for help with a crusade in Greece. As in the *Oratio dogmatica*, he tried to convince Latin Christians that the shared history and interests that bound them to Greek Christians outweighed their differences.

In 1470 a dreadful loss occurred that prompted Bessarion to renew his rhetorical energies in the service of crusade: the fall of the Venetian colony of Negroponte on the island of Euboea (12 July 1470). Venice had been at war with the Turks for seven years when this event took place. The local citizenry and the Venetian garrison fought bravely for three weeks against a siege as powerful and obstinate as that of Constantinople. Mehmed II led the operations. The city refused to surrender; even when it was finally stormed, inhabitants put up a great struggle against the invaders. Having previously blockaded the streets with tree trunks and barrels, they proceeded to throw roof tiles, quicklime, and boiling water from upper windows on the soldiers; the Turks' retaliation was reported to have been exceedingly violent.[94] News of the fall of the Venetian colony was received in Italy with great shock and alarm. Negroponte had been a crucial possession for Venice and a friendly port to Christians sailing to the eastern Mediterranean and the Levant. Many European powers and private citizens mourned the loss of one of the few remaining Christian footholds in the Aegean.[95]

In the wake of Negroponte, Bessarion composed his famous *Orationes* in 1471, calling on Christian princes to halt the advancing Turks.[96] The main theme of these orations directed to the princes of Europe is a call for unity among Christian powers so that they might battle the Turks together.[97] He calls attention to the lost glories of Byzantium in his second oration, and in his fourth oration he discusses at length how division among the Greeks had been their downfall in both ancient and modern times: "Nothing else destroyed miserable Greece, except discord; nothing else destroyed that part of the world, except civil war, and not only in our memory,[98] but in ancient times."[99] The example of Greece is mentioned as a lesson to the West, but it also affords Bessarion an opportunity to dispute claims that Greece fell to the Turks as a punishment from God for its schismatic beliefs and failure to uphold the sacred union.

During this period Bessarion drew once again on the example of ancient Greece in his translation of Demosthenes' *Olynthiac Orations*.[100] In the prologue, epilogue, and marginal notes he cites parallels between the situation in ancient Athens, with Philip of Macedon menacing all of Greece, and that of modern Europe facing the Turkish threat. Bessarion's choice of Demosthenes to plead his case for extending aid to one's allies was carefully considered, not only for the parallels inherent in the two cases. By translating and disseminating the eloquence of Demosthenes to a Latin public, he was advertising the heritage of ancient Greece as the home of democracy, liberty, and especially learning—learning that Western scholars were increasingly coming to appreciate and claim as their own. Demosthenes, then, represents one shining example of the riches that might still be saved from the Turks in Greece and perhaps also proof of the worth of the modern Greeks as descendants of such great men.

Still, Bessarion was not complacent about would-be Latin saviors and took steps on his own to preserve what he could of Greece's cultural heritage. To this end he gathered and copied many manuscripts in danger of being destroyed in the Turkish advance—both before and after 1453. Near the end of his life in 1468 he donated his library to Venice, where it became the core of the Biblioteca Marciana.[101] While it has been suggested that Bessarion chose Venice for its cosmopolitan and commercial character, the republic's current war with the Ottoman Empire and the presence of a large Greek community in the city no doubt played a larger part in his decision.[102] His gift would simultaneously reward the one Western state that took up Bessarion's cause and act as a great resource for his countrymen and Latins alike. Bessarion described the sentiments that motivated him to preserve Greek learning in his dedicatory letter to Doge Cristoforo Moro:

However much I have devoted myself to this thing [collecting Greek manuscripts as a young man] with all my mind, nevertheless, I have with even more ardent zeal consumed all my powers, all my care, all my energy, and all my means and industry, since the ruin of Greece and the mournful captivity of Byzantium, in diligently searching for Greek books. I feared and was indeed terribly frightened that with other things so great a number of the most excellent books, the labors and vigilance of the greatest men, so many lights of the world would be endangered and perish in so short a time.[103]

We see in Bessarion's words the same fears expressed by humanists such as Aeneas Silvius Piccolomini and Lauro Quirini following the fall of Constantinople and by Marsilio Ficino in 1480: the Turks were a serious threat to the survival of Greek culture.[104] Like the Goths and Vandals, they would neglect the arts and learning or even speed their demise. To Bessarion, the only solution was to spirit away high culture in the form of books for its own protection and survival. For Latin scholars a great deal of rich learning and literature was at stake, but for Bessarion and other Greeks an entire heritage was slipping away. As Geanakoplos has argued, Bessarion's actions showed his desire to continually remind his countrymen of their glorious ancestry and prevent their descent into "barbarism or slavery" as they faced the indignities of Turkish rule. But *which* ancestral tradition was he preserving? For centuries Greek identity had been bound up in Orthodoxy and separation from the Latin Church. However, as more and more Greeks, Bessarion included, were coming to the West and embracing the Roman rite—many less sincerely than the cardinal—focusing on the Orthodox tradition was no longer a viable option. Unionists such as Bessarion could still maintain a sense of self and Greek pride by turning to their more secular and ancient heritage.[105]

Drawing on a different period of ancient, yet Christian, Greek history, the Athenian-born scholar Demetrius Chalcondyles (1423–1511) delivered an exhortation for crusade and the recovery of his homeland.[106] At the end of the first of his "Discourses on the inauguration of Greek studies at Padua University" in 1463, Chalcondyles calls on Venice and "all of the Latins" to aid the Greeks against "the abominable, monstrous, and impious barbarian Turks."[107] He does this by reminding the Latins how the Byzantine Greeks once came to Italy's aid against their supposed oppressors in the Gothic Wars (535–53 C.E.):

just as she [Greece] had expended in their behalf [the Latins] all of her most precious and outstanding possessions liberally and without any parsimony, and had restored with her hand and force of arms the state of Italy, long ago oppressed by the Goths, they [the Latins] should in the same way now be willing to raise up prostrate and afflicted Greece and liberate it by arms from the hands of the barbarians.[108]

Calling attention to Greece's glorious and magnanimous past while asking the Latins to come to its aid, Chalcondyles seems not to be begging for help so much as calling in an overdue debt. Moreover, like Bessarion, he reminds the Latins of the unity that once existed between Greek East and Latin West—in this case back when the Italians still acknowledged the Byzantines as "Romans."[109]

Reaching further back into the ancient Greek past, George of Trebizond (1395–1472/73) invoked the Persian Wars to support crusade. Born in Crete, George converted to Roman Catholicism and began a new life in Italy, all the while remaining devoted to the Greek cause. For most of his career he was attached to the papal court as a secretary and translator of Greek, but he also lectured and taught in Florence, Rome, and Venice on rhetoric, poetry, and the Greek language. In addition to his pedagogical and translating skills, he was an eloquent Latin rhetorician. As an avowed Aristotelian, he devoted much time and energy to debates with and attacks on Platonists, often coming to blows with Cardinal Bessarion over this issue.[110]

In his exhortation to Pope Nicholas V, *Ad defendenda pro Europa Hellesponti claustra* (1452), George paints an adversarial picture of Europe and Asia. He does away with the notion of Greece as a foreign, Eastern land and places it firmly within Europe, stressing its identity as a Western, Christian culture—the "bulwark" (*claustra*) of Europe against the barbarians. George discusses the strategic value of a Christian empire on the Bosporus in preventing the Turks from unleashing their full power on the West.[111] But then again, he argues, Greece has protected Europe from Asia since antiquity: "Militiades, having defeated the armies of Darius, and Themistocles, having repulsed the powerful Xerxes and destroyed his army, both took triumph away from the invaders. Alexander the Great devastated all of Asia. The Asiatics often tried, nevertheless, to cross into Europe, but they were repulsed at the gates of the Hellespont."[112] George goes on to demonstrate how the use of the Hellespont as a defense against invaders continued under Roman rule. On seeing the devastation wrought by the Parthians in Europe, Constantine moved his capital to the Bosporus in order to protect the empire from such invasions.[113] Just as Constantine once fortified the city "at the gates of the Hellespont" and thereby protected Europe from Eastern invaders, so too could the pope refortify the beleaguered city and allow it to maintain its position as protectress of Europe.[114] While George uses apocalyptic thought to help stress his point, he avoids engaging contemporary religious arguments here, as Bessarion often did. On the contrary, George acknowledges the Greek schismatics' failure to uphold the union. But punishing the Greeks by refusing them aid, he asserts, will only end in the invasion of Catholic lands as well.[115] By focusing on Greece's position in antiquity as defender of all Europe, and therefore as a crucial *part* of Europe, he firmly brings Byzantium within the Western cultural identity.[116]

This is not to suggest that George showed little interest in religious issues in his writings on Greece and the Turks. His oration to both Alfonso of Aragon and Emperor Frederick III (1442) exhorted them to recover not Greece but the Holy Land. Still, George used this method in the hope that a successful crusade to the Holy Land would return the Mediterranean to its former status as a Christian lake; as such, Constantinople would eventually be rescued.[117] George's most controversial religious-inspired works on the Turks are the eschatological treatises written after 1453.[118]

At least one Greek humanist helped promote the crusade cause by means of espionage. Working on behalf of Lorenzo de' Medici, Janus Lascaris (1445–1535) went on two missions between 1489 and 1492 to the former Byzantine Empire.[119] Ostensibly his goal was to collect Greek manuscripts for the Medici library, but Lascaris was also secretly collecting information that might shed light on the prospects of a crusade against the Ottomans: the size and strength of their army and navy, the commitment of their soldiers, particularly the Christian-born janissaries, and the disposition of the Greeks toward revolting against their Ottoman overlords and joining the crusade.[120] There is no way of knowing what Lorenzo might have done with these reports since he fell ill and died in 1492. But Lorenzo's sponsorship of such a mission certainly complicates the widely accepted notion that he cared little for crusade or was a friend of the Turk.[121] As for Lascaris, he continued with his efforts to generate interest in battling the Turks. In 1508 he composed a treatise entitled *Informatione ad impresa contro a' Turchi*, exhorting Christian powers to crusade and providing a sanguine account of what he learned on his travels.[122] In 1525, at the age of eighty, he was sent by Pope Clement VII to plead with Emperor Charles V for the release of Francis I following the battle of Pavia; he was also instructed to urge Charles to lead a crusade against the Turks.[123]

Bessarion, Chalcondyles, George of Trebizond, and Lascaris are just a few examples of Greek scholars who settled in Italy in the fifteenth century as their homeland was losing its battle against the Turks. There were others, such as John Argyropoulos, who taught in the Florentine Studio, Theodore Gazes, who translated texts and taught in Ferrara, Rome, and Naples; and Marcus Musurus, who worked with Aldo Manuzio as an editor and taught in Padua.[124] We cannot even begin to account for all the scholars who were unable to find a more dignified position than copyist.[125] By examining some of the crusade exhortations composed by Greek refugees in Italy, however, a few common themes have emerged. Greek scholars living in the West used their newfound connections to promote concern and interest in the Ottoman advance. Their approach to the subject, though, says much about their role in the humanist movement, specifically their skillful manipulation of the deepest concerns of their Latin audience. The whole of Greek learning, the integrity of Europe, the Christian faith, and even civilization itself were at stake, they argued. They spoke of matters that were at once very Greek and yet universally humanist and "Western." Above all, Greek scholars symbolized for their patrons, colleagues, and students all the glory that was ancient Greece. They were undeniable proof of the heritage of learning that Byzantium had maintained till its end. They also fancied themselves, and were often perceived to be, the heirs of ancient Greece. In this way they fostered a certain empathy with Latin humanists who touted their own ancient Roman pedigree.

And yet, despite their efforts to fit in and their tendency to adopt Roman Catholicism, most Byzantine émigré scholars tenaciously held on to their Greek cultural identity. They closely associated themselves with other Byzantine refugees and tried to maintain ties to their homeland. Even the physical appearance of the Byzantine refugees served as a potent reminder of their origins. Many persisted in cultivating beards, which were not fashionable in fifteenth-century Italy.[126] An integral part of maintaining their Greek cultural identity was an embattled view of the Ottoman Turks. Drawing on their knowledge of Eastern affairs, they tried to warn Western powers of impending disasters—Bessarion and George of Trebizond easily saw the fall of Constantinople coming long before it did—but rarely were the efforts of the Greeks rewarded. Ironically, sometimes the harshest indictments of Greeks living in the East came from the same humanists who embraced the refugees settled among them.

Italian Humanist Perceptions of the Greeks and Their Plight

While perceptions of the Greeks may seem to lie beyond the realm of this study, they are more closely related to perceptions of the Turks than one might initially suppose. The Greeks were indisputably bearing the brunt of the Turkish advance, but what was disputable, at least to Western Europeans, was whether the Greeks *deserved* such a sad fate. The literary and popular image of the "ruin of Greece," which found a largely sympathetic audience by the sixteenth century, was by no means a broadly accepted view in previous years.[127]

In humanist eyes, the Greeks were constantly shifting between West and East or Christian and heretic—in many ways occupying a triangular relationship between Muslims and Latins. Some humanists embraced the Greeks and Byzantine culture, sympathizing with their hardships. Others were hostile, attacking their religion, their pride, and their strange ways; such individuals were not sorry to see Byzantium crushed by the Turks. Most humanists, however, were ambivalent. The same humanist who bemoaned the fall of Constantinople in one text might attack their religious error or greed in another. The tensions can be found as far back as Petrarch.[128]

On the one hand, Petrarch was a great admirer of Greek culture—namely ancient Greek culture. His appreciation for certain ancient Greek writers made him eager to read their works in the original language. To that end, he took lessons from the Calabrian monk Barlaam (d. 1348), a southern Italian Greek who adopted Catholicism and supported church union.[129] He was employed by the papal curia at Avignon as a lecturer in Greek and as a diplomat in attempted negotiations in Constantinople to heal the Schism (1342–46). Moreover, Barlaam was a keen observer of the tensions between the Greek and Latin Churches and offered personal insights on resolving the stalemate. A major obstacle to church union was not dogma, he argued, but rather "the hatred which has entered into [the Greeks'] spirit against the Latins" as a result of years of conflict centering on the Latin rule of Constantinople.[130] He recommended that the curia first send aid to the weakened Byzantine Empire as a show of good faith; only then might the Byzantine church come willingly to the bargaining table regarding a union.[131]

Petrarch became Barlaam's student and friend during their residence in Avignon. One might expect Petrarch to have developed a degree of sympathy for the Greek position, given his relationship with Barlaam, but

Petrarch's works, even those written after this acquaintance began, betray a palpable sense of animosity toward the Byzantines. One aspect of Petrarch's hostility was his desire to assert the superiority of Latins over Greeks in matters of culture and history. In a letter to Boccaccio (*Sen.*, III, 6), Petrarch rails against the Calabrian Greek Leontius Pilatus for fancying himself Greek rather than Italian: "Our Leontius is really a Calabrian, but would have us consider him a Thessalian, as though it were nobler to be Greek than Italian."[132] After proceeding in his description of Pilatus by mocking his long, shaggy beard and hair, and naming various character flaws such as a lack of virtue and wisdom, Petrarch informs Boccaccio that Pilatus had the gall to ask him to write to the Byzantine emperor on his behalf. Petrarch ridicules the very notion.

Moving from personal invective against Pilatus to an attack on his countrymen, he seizes the opportunity to attack the Byzantines for their persistence in referring to their empire as Roman: "the Greeks call Constantinople another Rome. They have dared to call it not only equal to the ancient city, but greater in monuments and graced with riches. But if this were true on both counts as it is false (I would say it without offense to Sozomen who wrote this) surely no little Greek, however impudent, would dare to call them equal in men, arms, virtues and glory."[133] In an earlier letter to Cardinal Giovanni Colonna (*Fam.*, I, 4), Petrarch argued that a Greek cannot rightly consider himself nobler than an Italian because "whoever says this would also say that a slave is more noble than a master."[134] Petrarch supports this audacious claim by pointing to ancient Greece's subjection under the Roman imperium. An ironic coincidence was that Latin traders at this time were selling Orthodox Christians as slaves, including thousands of Greeks taken by Turks in razzias, or raids. Barlaam had complained about this to the pope in 1339.[135] One wonders if Petrarch was making some reference to this practice.

Clearly, Petrarch was a Latin chauvinist who gleefully subverted Greek pretensions. The "real" Romans, Petrarch implies, were Italians who spoke Latin; they became masters of the world, sweeping up all of Greece in the process. The only true descendants of the ancient Romans are those who now occupy Italy, while the modern-day Greeks are no more than the descendants of an enslaved and subjugated people who unjustly usurped the dignity of the Roman Empire. As he argues in his *Itinerarium ad sepulcrum Domini*, the Byzantine Empire became famous for its *emulation* of the Roman Empire.[136] In 1354 the idea appears again a letter to Nicholas Sygeros—a letter written in thanks for a manuscript of

Homer that the Byzantine official had sent to him. Petrarch's gratitude to Sygeros did not restrain him from belittling the Byzantine emperor, who still styled himself "Roman Emperor"; Petrarch demotes him to "emperor of Constantinople" (*constantinopolitanus imperator*), as opposed to the *real* Roman emperor, whom he names as Charles IV.[137]

So strenuously does Petrarch deny the merits of the Greeks that one wonders whether he was not overcompensating for some insecurity or anxiety. Given his great love of learning and antiquity, his inability to fully appreciate Greek culture is curious. Perhaps his religious and ethnic prejudices against modern Greeks clouded his judgment. Perhaps, too, Petrarch's paltry knowledge of Greek and Greek texts, which he read in poor Latin translations when he could find them, narrowed his sense of the richness of Greek learning and literature.[138] We might well ask, however, if this postmodernist view does justice to Petrarch's larger worldview and the context of his times and scholarship. His consuming passion for ancient Rome appears to have shaped his condescension toward Greece—ancient and modern—just as it did toward Islamic countries. All these lands were once under Rome's benevolent aegis; breaking away from Roman rule only sent them into cultural decline, heresy, and political anarchy—or so Petrarch would argue.

Petrarch's antipathy for the Greeks went beyond cultural criticisms; on a few occasions his message became bellicose, as in his letters to the rulers of Venice and Genoa.[139] In these letters he begs the two governments to stop fighting one another and to embrace their connection as fellow Italians. Much worthier battles, he argues, can be fought against the Muslims and even the Greeks. Religious antagonism also played a large part in Petrarch's views of Byzantium, as can be seen in his letter to Doge Giovanni di Valente of Genoa, who took office in 1352, and the Genoese Council (*Fam.*, XIV, 5). Petrarch repeats his plea for a cessation of war among Italians in exchange for a joint attack on Greece and the Holy Land: "Yea indeed, not only do I not grieve, but I greatly rejoice over the deceitful and indolent Greeks [or "Greeklings"] who dare nothing on their own.[140] I desire to see that infamous empire, that seat of error, destroyed at your hands, if by chance Christ has chosen you avengers of their wrongs, if He assigned to you that vengeance which all Catholic peoples have unfortunately deferred."[141] With this statement the Greeks are compared to Muslims or to heretics such as the Albigensians—groups whose existence was believed to pose a great danger to the faith, which could only be met with crusade.

Rather than mellowing over time, Petrarch's resentment of the Greeks intensified. In a letter to Pope Urban V (*Sen.* VII) written in 1366, Petrarch urged a return to Rome and aid to the beleaguered Christian East. While he initially seems to sympathize with the "wretched Greeks," encouraging the pope to lead a crusade to Constantinople to help the Byzantines push back the Turkish advance, Petrarch's objectives soon take a sinister turn. More than military aid or an alliance, Petrarch advocates a return to Latin rule of Constantinople—a hope still cherished by Westerners, now over a century after the Greeks had reestablished their control of the imperial city.[142] The aims of defense and stability in the East soon give way to desires for vengeance and punishment of the arrogant, schismatic Greeks who hate the Latins so much that they reconsecrate their churches when a Latin so much as enters them. In an astonishing statement, he goes so far as to advocate a crusade against Byzantium—a move that had not been seriously contemplated since the 1320s. Jerusalem is possessed by enemies, while the Byzantines, as heretics, are "worse than enemies" (*peioris hostibus*):

The fact remains that a great sea lies between us and our enemies who now hold Jerusalem. So, as matters now stand between us and them it is no small effort. . . . On the other hand, nothing stands between us and these petty Greeks except our lethargy and our laziness, since, while they have the utmost hatred, they have no power, and it is a simple matter for any two Italian states that want to [attack]; if you would begin to favor it, I can guarantee you that whether together or just singly they can either overthrow that unwarlike empire or lead it back to the yoke of the Mother Church.[143]

In short, Petrarch calls for crusade against a weakened, Christian (albeit schismatic) empire because it is *easier* than a full-scale assault on the Holy Land.

Petrarch's friendship with Barlaam, we may assume, would have been greatly complicated, even impossible, had the Calabrian monk not accepted Roman Catholicism. The mass of faceless modern Greeks in the East who lived among the ruins of ancient Hellas, and who held the key to the Greek classics he endeavored to learn, were as great an enemy of Italian maritime powers as the Muslim peoples were. More precisely, Petrarch viewed them as an obstacle to crusade and Christian unity; if they could not help the common Christian cause, then they were fair game for destruction by Italian fleets. While most fourteenth-century Western Europeans envisioned the Greeks as neither allies nor full-fledged enemies but somewhere in between, to Petrarch's mind the Greeks more often emerged as adversaries. On occasion, however, he relented somewhat in his enmity by recognizing that "our [Latin] pride" may have turned them away from desiring union.[144] In this aside he was closer to the truth than he could have imagined.

A generation later Coluccio Salutati expressed greater ambivalence toward the Byzantines. He saw them as a rich resource for learning the Greek language and ancient texts. For certain Greeks, such as the scholars Demetrius Cydones and Manuel Chrysoloras, Salutati expressed only esteem. Addressing Cydones in 1396, Salutati gushes with admiration for his teaching in Venice, "where as soon as you took on and began to teach Roberto [Rossi] in your friendly fashion, you fired many hearts with the desire to learn the language of the people of old Hellas, so that already I perceive there will be many earnest students of Greek literature within a few years."[145] In Cydones and Chrysoloras, Salutati found a doorway to the language and literature of ancient Greece. Yet this admiration by no means extended to the Greeks as a people. Byzantium was not a breeding ground for great scholarship in Salutati's eyes. On the contrary, Cydones and Chrysoloras were rare exceptions among the Greeks: "I perceive you have appeared, like a light in darkness, for the study of literature, almost lost among the Greeks, because the minds of all are taken up with ambition, pleasures and avarice."[146] Here, Salutati echoes common Western cultural biases against the Greeks—recall that Petrarch described them as "deceitful and indolent." Interestingly, these are the same kinds of classical stereotypes ancient Greeks and Romans had used to describe Asians and that Petrarch used to describe the Arabs in particular.[147] Hence here are clear examples of Byzantium shifting closer to the Eastern axis in the cultural imagination of Westerners.

The liberties that Salutati takes with Cydones are astonishing; he is so confident in his opinion of the Greek people that he feels comfortable insulting them before one of their own countrymen. One reason for Salutati's familiarity may be that he is addressing a fellow scholar and enthusiast of Latin learning.[148] The other reason becomes clear as the letter unfolds: Cydones, unlike the majority of Greeks, was a Roman Catholic who supported Church union. Salutati states: "But there is one thing about you, by which I am greatly pleased: clearly, I can tell that you are not held by the errors of your race regarding the faith without which we cannot be saved. Thus, my discussion with you is not only with a learned man, but even with an orthodox [Catholic] one."[149] In fact, Salutati's main goal in writing Cydones was to enlist his aid in convincing other Greeks to accept the union. It is questionable whether Salutati would have held Cydones in such high esteem had Cydones not been a Catholic. Chrysoloras, who later taught in Florence, converted to Catholicism in the first decade of the fifteenth century. In light of Salutati's religious prejudices against the Greek Orthodox community, it seems doubtful that he would have used his influence to help a non-Catholic obtain this teaching position.

Humanists continued to lash out against Greek "error," but these pronouncements were tempered to a certain degree by sympathy for the misfortunes of the Byzantine Empire. Greek refugees played no small role in disseminating tales of misfortune at the hands of the Turks, but some Greek writers, it must be noted, depicted their Turkish rulers in a more complicated fashion. George of Trebizond began to interpret Mehmed II's successes as a sign of divine favor, envisioning him as the prophesied universal Christian emperor who would usher in an era of world peace.[150] Some Greeks who remained in the East, such as the chronicler Kritoboulos, saw Mehmed II as a competent ruler and a great general. Favorable attitudes toward Turkish rule, however, were not well accepted in the West, as may be evidenced by the troubles George encountered over his later beliefs.[151] Moreover, the balanced accounts of Mehmed written by Greeks who remained in the East were not well known or used in the West, certainly not among Latins.[152] Hence, when Latin humanists thought of Greek losses in the East, they tended to view the Turks as a hostile force with few redeeming qualities; their opinions on the Greeks, however, were quite mixed.

Some humanists were strongly sympathetic to the Byzantines who had lost so much in the terrible siege. Lauro Quirini's reaction to the fall of Constantinople suggests an affinity for Greek culture and perhaps the Greeks themselves. This may be attributed to his residence in the Venetian-controlled island of Crete. There Quirini not only availed himself of the increased opportunities to study Greek but also came into greater contact with Greeks than did his fellow humanists in Italy.[153] Quirini's respect for his patron Cardinal Bessarion may also have been a factor. Venetians in general came into more contact with Greeks who formed the bulk of the population in Mediterranean colonies such as Crete, Modon, or Coron, or who settled in Venice. Ironically, many Greeks prospered as merchants, soldiers, and scholars in the city that took part in conquering their capital in 1204.[154]

Lampugnino (or Lampo) Birago (d. 1472), an enthusiast of ancient Greek culture appears to have seen their modern descendants in an equally positive light. A Lombard scholar who spent most of his career as a translator in the papal curia, Birago offered a solution to halting the Turkish advance in his *Strategicon adversus turcos*, a treatise outlining the state of the Ottoman military and suggestions for its defeat. The *Strategicon* (presented to Nicholas V in 1454) apparently made use of oral and possibly written Greek reports,[155] showing a familiarity with and appreciation of Greek perceptions of the Turkish advance. Birago, like other humanists reacting to the fall of Constantinople, drew a connection between liberating Greek areas from the Ottomans and protecting Greek learning. No one, he argued, would provide a better example to Western princes of military leadership in the face of formidable enemies than Themistocles and other ancient Greeks. Offering these models to a wide readership may have been part of his intention in translating Greek works by Plutarch and Xenophon.[156]

In Florence at least one scholar, Donato Acciaiuoli, appears to have fully empathized with the misfortunes of the Greeks, particularly those of John Argyropoulos, the eminent Greek scholar who taught at both Florence and Rome.[157] Argyropoulos had received degrees in both Constantinople and Padua. In Constantinople he eagerly pursued philosophical studies, while at Padua he studied letters and medicine, acquiring fluency in Latin along the way. In addition Argyropoulos served the Byzantine Empire both as a delegate at the Council of Florence and as an ambassador seeking aid against the Turks. He was present at the fall of Constantinople in 1453, where he lost his family for several years to slave traders. While Argyropoulos does not appear to have written anything on the Turks that survives, Donato wrote of his plight on several occasions.

Donato's letters say more about his own views than those of Argyropoulos, but they are of great interest for their insights into humanist opinions of Greek scholars turned refugees by Turkish conquest. In a letter dated 5 August 1454 a young Donato expressed his excitement over meeting Argyropoulos in Florence, describing him as a symbol of Greek culture: "The man seems to me to be not only erudite, as I had heard, but also wise, venerable, and worthy of the ancient Greeks."[158] Despite his enthusiasm for Argyropoulos's learning, Donato was sensitive to the scholar's "miserable fortune": "Therefore, his most noble country having been overthrown, his children left behind in the hands of barbarians, and despoiled of all of his goods, he chose to seek refuge with the pope, whom he trusted would be the only protection of his well-being among so many losses."[159] Donato's opinion of Argyropoulos combined empathy for his adversity with respect for his achievements. To heighten the pathos and drama of Argyropoulos's fate, he poignantly contrasts the characters of the victim and the victors. Argyropoulos's losses were heavy indeed, but they become more tragic with Donato's skillful rhetoric of a man who matched the ancient Greeks in learning and character being brought so low by mere "barbarians."

Still, one might ask whether Donato would have been so generous to Argyropoulos had he not converted to Catholicism and supported the union; most successful and respected Greek émigré scholars accepted Roman Catholicism before or during the Council of Florence.[160] Donato, however, did not draw sharp distinctions between Orthodox and Catholic Greeks in decrying Turkish abuses. Nor does he appear to have viewed the destruction of Byzantium as a display of God's wrath toward the Greek "schismatics." Indeed, Donato's high opinion of Argyropoulos seems to have applied to Greek refugees as a group; in another letter he refers to them as "vestiges of ancient Greece."[161] Perhaps Donato's family connections to Greece engendered greater sympathy for Greece's plight than the average Italian would have felt.

Lest one think, however, that all learned Greek refugees received so warm a reception in the West, it is important to remember the bitterness of scholars such as Constantine Lascaris, who worked as a copyist and teacher of Greek in various Italian cities and courts. Writing around 1475, Lascaris compared his posts to servitude, lamenting the low appreciation of Greek learning he found among the "barbarism" of the West—not a casual choice of terminology by any means.[162] So much for the united cultural front! If Westerners could come off as barbarians, Greeks could appear irritatingly conceited about their cultural achievements. Even as their empire crumbled, their sense of cultural superiority over the Latins remained so strong that some refugees, for example, Demetrius Chalcondyles, felt comfortable reminding the Latins of their cultural indebtedness to ancient Greeks who taught the Romans everything they knew.[163]

Most Latin humanists who discussed the Greeks, even following 1453, cannot be classified as wholly positive or negative in their views. Poggio Bracciolini, for example, reacted with both sorrow and grim righteousness to the fall of Constantinople. In his letter to Piero da Noceto, dated 25 July 1453, he described the sadness that the event and the present war in Italy had aroused in him: "Truly, I am unable, amidst this universal sor-

row, not to be dejected myself."[164] Yet, Poggio's dejection gave way to
resentment in his *De miseria conditionis humanae* (1455).[165] In dialogue
format, Cosimo de' Medici voices popular sympathies regarding the
Greeks who were captured and killed in the siege of Constantinople, while
Matteo Palmieri asserts that the Greeks "deserved every punishment."[166]
After accusing the Byzantines of sabotaging the Crusades, he claims that
they brought the fall of their empire on themselves: "Twice already they
have denied the profession of the Catholic faith they made in the councils.
Idleness and greed then flourished so strongly in them that, although they
overflowed with gold and silver, they were not willing to pay even a penny
toward the protection of their city. In this way, I believe, they left a more
opulent plunder to the Turks."[167] Poggio, speaking as Palmieri, supports
this argument by mentioning reports that great hidden treasure had been
found in the city when it fell. He then castigates the Greeks for their greed
and cowardice in continually seeking aid from the pope when they possessed the resources to defend themselves, adding, "that calamity seems
to have come upon them, not by chance, but by divine judgment."[168]
Any question as to whether these statements represented Poggio's own
opinions or were merely rhetorical may be resolved by examining Poggio's
De rebus gestis memorabilibus.[169] When he comes to the year 1453 in this
historical work, Poggio angrily blames the Greeks for the loss of their city,
describing their greed in almost the same words as those used in his dialogue.[170]

Poggio's charge of Greek parsimony deserves further comment since
Westerners often accused the Greeks of avarice and hoarding following the
fall of Constantinople. But such charges seem overstated. While Greek
historians of the event, such as Kritoboulos, mention the wealth found in
the city by the Turks, they do not blame the Greeks for withholding precious resources while their city was under siege.[171] It is also known that
the emperor went to great lengths to recruit aid, offering in exchange
important Byzantine possessions to at least two rulers. Poggio's efforts to
blame the Greeks for the loss of their city appear to be little more than an
attempt to stanch common feelings of guilt among Westerners who had
abandoned fellow Christians to so harsh a fate.[172]

Other humanists were more sympathetic to the Greeks, although they
still faulted them for their schismatic beliefs. In his *Expugnatio Constantinopolitana* (1455) Niccolò Tignosi was not afraid to praise the Greeks, and
especially their emperor, for their brave efforts to fight off the Turks. Nor
did Tignosi shy away from criticizing Western powers for ignoring Byzan-

tium's call for assistance: "And, oh! they were given no aid in their re-
quests by Nicholas V, the exalted pope of the Christians, and by Alfonso,
king of Aragon, lord of the Sicilian kingdom, and even by the Venetian
people and the king of Hungary."[173] Yet, Tignosi, like most Latin Christians, could not ignore the Greeks' supposed perjury in reneging on their
promise of union with Rome. Echoing Poggio, he labeled the fall of Constantinople divine punishment: "Thus, true worshippers of Christ assert
that the triune and one God, whom we truly cherish, permitted such devastation and wanted revenge taken against his enemies by other enemies.
As you see, God chastened those who merited it with an iron scourge."[174]
This judgment is somewhat tempered by Tignosi's statement that the
Greek clergymen who agreed to the union and later denied it were more
culpable than the Greek laity. In this statement he shows a more complex
understanding of the Greek rejection of the union than most Westerners
had. Furthermore, Tignosi's lamentations on the sufferings of the Byzantines who were slaughtered, raped, and enslaved on that day indicate a
good deal of compassion on his part.[175]

When taken as a whole, Tignosi's attitudes toward the Greeks were
mixed. On the one hand, he admired their courage and mourned the
tragic loss of so many lives and so great a city. On the other hand, he
coolly labeled the demise of Byzantium as the expression of God's wrath
against those who had strayed from the "true faith." This pronounce-
ment, harsh though it seems and out of keeping with Tignosi's more com-
passionate views of the Greeks, is not unusual when read in historical
context. Medieval and Renaissance Christians almost always sought religious explanations, such as divine intervention or judgment, for catastro-
phes. The Byzantine Greeks believed that they were being punished for
their sins when their empire fell. But, unlike Western explanations, the
Greeks identified their sin as their original *acceptance* of Latin doctrine—
which they regarded as unorthodox—rather than their later denial of it.[176]

Aeneas Silvius Piccolomini's differing attitudes toward Greece may
have been more a product of change over time than ambivalence. He lamented the human tragedies in Constantinople as well as the destruction
of the glorious city, its architecture, religious art, and countless books,
describing the loss of the city as a "brand of infamy" on the reigns of
Pope Nicholas V and Emperor Frederick III.[177] Aeneas's sorrow in early
reactions to the fall of Constantinople appears to have been unmitigated
by any charges against the Greeks. Like Tignosi, he accuses Western powers of leaving Byzantium to its cruel fate; but unlike Tignosi and Poggio,

he does not criticize the Greeks for their religious beliefs or for a lack of effort or generosity toward their defense. His sympathy for the Greek plight was rendered all the more sincere by his efforts toward crusade—an enterprise to which he devoted the better part of his papal reign.

Yet, in his famous Letter to Mehmed II (1461),[178] Aeneas, by this time Pope Pius II, makes some antagonistic statements regarding Eastern Christians. While trying to warn Mehmed against pursuing conquests in Western Europe, he ends up insulting Eastern Europeans. Juxtaposing the ease with which Pompey and Caesar had conquered Greek lands with the difficulty of conquering Western areas, he asserts: "You will not fight against women if you invade Italy, Hungary or other occidental areas; matters are decided with the sword here."[179] Moreover, Aeneas points to the religious differences between Eastern and Western Christians. True Christians, Aeneas asserts, will not allow themselves to be ruled by Muslims. Because of his conquests of Eastern Christian lands Mehmed may believe that he is capable of dominating Christendom, but Aeneas objects that these are not proper Christians (that is, Latin Christians): "Very few are the Christians under your rule who walk in the truth of the New Testament. . . . The Greeks had abandoned the unity of the Roman Church when you invaded Constantinople, and they had not yet accepted the Florentine Decree and were in error."[180] These statements complicate Aeneas's attitude toward the Greeks, but it has been argued that he wrote them more for rhetorical effect than out of personal conviction. In a recent article Jean-Claude Margolin interprets Pius's passage regarding the Greeks as a bluff by which he insinuates: "you may have conquered the Greeks, but do you dare to fight us Westerners?"[181] Another possibility is that Aeneas's views simply evolved during the eight years since the fall of Constantinople, especially given his promotion in the Church and election as pope in 1458. Perhaps he became persuaded by the idea that Greek Christians were less firm in their convictions than were the Latins—as pope, he could certainly not voice any opinion to the contrary. Even if Aeneas was sincere in his rhetoric against the Greeks, his statements regarding the Greeks and Eastern Christians in general are comparatively mild when placed beside those of Petrarch or Poggio. It is reasonable to say that Aeneas, while not remaining free from Western prejudice against the Greeks, was moderate in his criticisms and, for the most part, sympathetic to the Greek plight.

Francesco Filelfo's complex attitudes toward the Greeks are particularly interesting given his close connections with Byzantium. Recall that

Filelfo was an Italian by birth who developed a strong affinity for Greece and its inhabitants during his years in Constantinople (1421–27). Filelfo's interest in and knowledge of Byzantium quickened his concerns about the Turks. While in Constantinople he took part in an embassy to Murad II, and after his return to Italy he eagerly sought news of the Turkish advance and the welfare of the Greeks. He also attempted to influence princes such as Charles VII of France to save Constantinople from the Turks. After the city fell, Filelfo aided Greeks escaping Turkish domination in various ways. His public efforts to generate support for crusade include his oration at the Congress of Mantua.[182]

Filelfo's enthusiasm for Greek learning and culture is evident in his letters. Writing to Marco Lipomano shortly after his return to Italy from Constantinople in 1427, Filelfo asks: "Who would doubt that I deeply loved not only the literature, but even the nature of the Greeks, on account of which I have myself become entirely Greek."[183] More than simple admiration for Greece, this quote suggests a sense of cultural absorption on Filelfo's part. On several occasions Filelfo asserted the inestimable value and even necessity of Greek studies among Latin scholars. In a letter to Lampugnino Birago (1449) he stated that one could not become an able Latin scholar without first acquiring a good knowledge of Greek.[184] Furthermore, Filelfo welcomed the immigration of Greek scholars into Italy, often going out of his way to support their efforts to gain teaching positions. He is known to have written letters on behalf of both Argyropoulos and Andronicus Callistus, and he actively corresponded with resident Greeks in their own language.[185] In one sympathetic reference to Greek refugees he states: "they are, in fact, a lamentable part of the ruin of Constantinople, who desire to redeem both themselves and their people from the impious Turks."[186]

Despite Filelfo's zeal for Greek culture and his support of crusade, at certain moments in his career he betrayed ambivalence toward their conquerors, the Turks. The most notable of these incidents occurred in 1454, when he wrote an adulatory letter to Mehmed II praising him in a Greek ode. Filelfo, of course, had ulterior motives. In an appended letter he requested the release of his mother-in-law and her daughters, who had been captured and enslaved in the fall of Constantinople. In addition he reminded Mehmed of his connections with Francesco Sforza of Milan by offering to help promote a possible alliance with the Turks. Filelfo's in-laws were promptly released without ransom—indicating, it would seem, his influence in the Ottoman Porte.[187] The tone and content of Filelfo's

ode to Mehmed II stand in sharp contrast to his crusade rhetoric and
Greek sympathies; he extols Mehmed for his valor, his generosity, and his
glory—claiming that he surpasses the greatest of the Argives and Romans.
Congratulating him on his great triumph, he closes by saying that, were
Mehmed a Christian, he would rule the world and Filelfo would serve
him.[188] Even worse, in the letter that accompanied the ode, he claims that
God sent Mehmed to carry out his divine will on the Greeks, who merited
the catastrophe through their own sinfulness.[189] Even the Jews come
under attack in Filelfo's strenuous efforts to avoid assigning any blame to
the Turks. Cowardly, avaricious, and "barbaric" Jews had enslaved his
family members, he claims, rather than implicate Turkish soldiers.[190]

Although Filelfo's goal to secure the release of his in-laws was an
effort most Greeks would applaud, they would no doubt have resented his
attack on them as well as his obsequious praise of a man whom they regarded as a vicious usurper. After all, they had chosen to defend their
empire to the death. This incident, of course, might be seen as a onetime
occurrence motivated solely by Filelfo's desire to free his relatives; he referred to it with distaste in a later letter, in which he calls Mehmed a
tyrant.[191] Still, his language describing the sultan is effusive enough to raise
questions about his true opinions.

Another notorious statement made by Filelfo suggests that his perceptions of the Turks were conflicted, to say the least. Filelfo's tensions
with Pius II over an unpaid pension led him to attack the pope's sincerity
in regard to crusade. In a letter to Cardinal Ammanati he went so far as to
say that if Pius did not pay his pension, he would "move to a place that
would greatly displease the pope. For all the world was the fatherland of
the scholar." He then added that he considered "as barbarians only those
who showed it in their actions"—truly a progressive statement from a
Latin humanist at this time, if it can be believed.[192] Schwoebel describes
Filelfo's gesture as "an idle threat" but rightly points out that it did nothing to enhance Filelfo's reputation. As proof of Filelfo's mercurial personality, consider his next letter to the cardinal—a reply to Ammanati's stern
warning to Filelfo against such outbursts—in which he offered to join the
pope's crusade army.[193]

It is impossible to simplify Filelfo's attitude toward the Turks. Both
his initial interest in Greek culture, which first led him to the East, and his
relationships with numerous Byzantine Greeks and refugees engendered
feelings of sympathy for the Greek people and a desire to help them. There
is evidence of hostility toward the Turks in his scathing rhetoric at the

Congress of Mantua. Yet this same involvement in the Greek East brought him in contact with the Turks, and he developed some respect for their power, or at the very least learned the necessity of negotiating with them. Filelfo's attitudes toward and contacts with the Turks complicated, but did not necessarily diminish, his philhellenism. Like Ciriaco of Ancona before him and like countless Greeks, he appears to have adapted to Turkish rule while still hoping for crusade. Perhaps his inconsistent behavior should be seen as a sign of realistic diplomacy rather than vacillation or self-interest.

For all his ambivalence regarding the Turks, Francesco Filelfo never criticized the Greeks as harshly as his son Giovanni Mario did in his poem *Amyris* (1471–76).[194] As if he found it impossible to praise the Turks without defaming the Greeks, Giovanni Mario levels an assortment of invectives against both the ancient Greeks and the modern-day Byzantines. Above all, he attacks the ancient Greeks for their role in the legendary Trojan War, which led to the downfall of Troy, and paints the fall of Constantinople as a long-awaited exaction of justice: "Thence the Greeks, who, after having fought so many wars with fraud and evil intentions, carried off the banners of victory and led away your ancestors, Mehmed, as slaves, received [in 1453] rewards worthy of their guilt."[195] The charge of fraud is a recurring motif that refers to the very foundation of the Trojan War. The traditional reason for the war was punishment for Paris's crime of kidnapping Helen, the wife of his host Menelaus. But Giovanni Mario argues that Helen was not abducted; rather she chose to follow Paris of her own volition. This explanation clears Paris and the Trojans of any guilt and lays full blame on the Greeks for deception as well as aggression.[196]

In addition to causing the Trojan War, the Greeks, argues Giovanni Mario Filelfo (as did Petrarch before him), usurped the imperial glory of Rome—founded by another of Mehmed's Trojan ancestors, Aeneas—by transferring the capital to Constantinople. From Constantinople they set about dominating the lands of Mehmed's ancestors.[197] And if these supposed ancestral crimes were not enough reason for Mehmed to chasten the Greeks, Giovanni Mario provides an additional excuse by denigrating the character of the modern Greeks. The ancient Greeks, he argues, had some virtues, but these were not passed on to the modern generation of Greeks, who are greedy, lascivious, unlearned, and heretical—as if Mehmed cared a whit about Christian orthodoxy![198] Such slurs are surprising as they follow Giovanni Mario's open acknowledgment of his own Greek background through the Chrysoloras family. The only moment in the poem where he relents is in the speech of Halil Pasha to Mehmed II when the grand vizier tries to convince the young sultan to leave Constantinople in peace. In defending the Greek people, Halil ("Chalyles") calls attention to the supposed blood tie existing between Byzantines and Turks through Aeneas, not to mention the historic preference of Byzantium for cooperation rather than war with the Ottomans.[199]

Still, Giovanni Mario Filelfo's attitude toward the Turks may have been more complicated than the *Amyris* suggests.[200] Such vacillation between praise of the sultan and support for crusade rightly raises questions about Giovanni Mario's sincerity, but it should not lead to a summary dismissal of a complex and rich work. For the purposes of this chapter, we might ask why Filelfo would go to such lengths to malign the Greek people in a work designed primarily to flatter the sultan. Perhaps he found it difficult to praise Mehmed without attacking the Greeks; even his philhellene father, Francesco, found himself insulting the Greeks in his 1454 letter to Mehmed.[201] Indeed, it was hard to fulfill the rhetorical goal of honoring a powerful dedicatee without praising his justice and condemning his enemies (or victims). Given this circumstance, it seems safer to regard Giovanni Mario as ambivalent in his attitudes toward the Byzantines rather than hostile. In this respect he resembles many other humanists who wrote on the Turkish advance.[202]

A clearer model of open hostility toward the Greeks is found in Ubertino Puscolo's *Constantinopolis*. A Brescian humanist who was living in Constantinople when the city was taken in 1453, he presented a wholly unsympathetic account of the last days of the imperial capital. After studying with Guarino da Verona, Puscolo had traveled east to further his education, but unlike Francesco Filelfo, he developed no marked affinity for the Byzantines.[203] Rather than sympathize with the inhabitants of Constantinople or applaud their last efforts to defend their city, Puscolo, like Leonard of Chios, condemned the Byzantines at every turn for the loss.[204] He especially blamed the Greeks for failing to uphold the union—a move that he claims arose from sheer stubbornness. Through it they lost everything: "O perfidious race of Greeks! What cruel fury drove you straight on toward the abyss, possessed you to fall, O men of Greece, that you should dig the gulf in which you sank your land, your cherished homes, your wives, your children?"[205] Puscolo did not share Giovanni Mario Filelfo's enthusiasm for the Turks, but he surpassed his fellow humanist in his enmity for the Greeks.

This chapter has shown the complex web formed by Greek attitudes toward the Turks and Western Europeans and Western attitudes toward the Greeks and the Turks. The development of these perceptions is not easily summarized or explained, given their marked ambivalence, but some common patterns do emerge. Greek attitudes toward the Turks in the decades surrounding the fall of Constantinople ranged from hostility and fear to accommodation and even admiration.[206] By "Greek attitudes" here I mean Greeks living throughout the Mediterranean and Europe. Narrowing the focus to Italy, we see that refugees' attitudes toward the Turks were marked by resentment and a driving desire to defeat the Turks in any way possible.[207] So strong were their convictions regarding their lost homeland and the illegitimacy of Turkish rule that Italy soon became a seedbed of Greek protonationalist thought.[208] Indeed it was in Italy that the remarkable transformation from "Byzantines" to "Hellenes" began to ripen.

Despite the hostility Europeans once felt toward the Byzantines, and which some individuals continued to express, the year 1453 marked the beginning of a change in Western perceptions of the Greeks. Greeks had been settling in Italy before this date, and thousands more came to settle afterward. Given their new status as residents, if not full-fledged citizens, their air of exoticism began to fade. Since many Greek scholars adopted Latin Christianity and others accepted certain Roman practices, it became difficult to see them as stubborn heretics who showed no respect for the Latin Church.[209] Certainly after 1453 no one could possibly see the Greeks as powerful adversaries who stood in the way of Western trade or crusade designs. Their aura of power and pride had diminished, leaving Italians little cause to envy or fear them. On the whole a spirit of coexistence, if not assimilation, began to pervade Western and Greek interactions. Most significant of all, the Greeks became an integral part of Western, especially Italian, society. As teachers, copyists, merchants, and soldiers they served important purposes in the community. Although they may have kept to themselves somewhat, they were not forcibly marginalized, as were the Jews, and in general found it much easier to cross over boundaries of religion and culture.[210]

Finally, we must not forget the significance of the fall of Constantinople to developing Western perceptions of the Turks. This event intensified the Greeks' growing awareness of their distinguished heritage and made the Turks appear as barbaric destroyers of that glory and usurpers of their ancient homeland. In a direct sense philhellenism became inextricably linked to anti-Turkish sentiment.[211] By extension Westerners, above all humanists, viewed the fall of Constantinople not merely as a Greek loss but as a blow to Christendom, Europe, and Western culture.[212] Only sixty-four years earlier the Balkan defeat at Kosovo did not create such a stir as the fall of Constantinople.[213] While ambivalent views continued for a time, Western hostility toward the Greeks began to ebb noticeably, and Italians embraced and expanded on Greek perceptions of the Turks. Humanists were especially important in the process, given their notions about the Turks as threats to culture. As Greek manuscripts continued to reach Italy and Greek learning became indispensable to Western scholars, humanists became all the more convinced that the Turks were barbarians capable of devastating the highest forms of learning and culture.[214]

4

Religious Influences and Interpretations

WHILE HUMANISTS FOCUSED MUCH ATTENTION on the Turkish advance as a secular problem, they were also concerned with its impact on the Christian faith. After all, the Turks practiced a faith that was, in many ways, antithetical to Christianity, and crusade was, in theory, a "holy war." From simple descriptions of the Turks as "enemies of the faith" to more detailed theological discussions of Islam, humanists underscored religious concerns that accompanied the Ottoman conquests of Christian lands. Hence the classical and secular discourse on the Turks created by humanists was employed alongside religious rhetoric; the two approaches were often interwoven in the same works. To be sure, humanists were inspired by medieval religious thought on Islam and incorporated some aspects of it into their works, but they blended these traditions with distinctly different rhetorical approaches and classical concepts. As a result humanists added some surprising new twists to Western views of Islam.

These religious interpretations of the Turks and crusade could vary substantially. Just as religious thinkers in the Renaissance disagreed on ecclesiastical, doctrinal, and spiritual issues, humanists reflected that diversity in their religious interpretations of the Turks and crusade. Some humanists were heavily influenced by more-traditional forms of medieval polemic against Islam. In harangues against the Turks they echoed tall tales about the Prophet and the rise of Islam, reducing the rival faith to idolatry, Satanism, or a cult of carnal pleasure. Combining religious polemic with cultural critiques, such as the charge of barbarism, humanists endeavored to strip the Turks of any sense of decency or goodness. Religious polemic was even employed as a means to minimize the intellectual foundations of Islam and, hence, the great scholarly achievements of Muslim scholars.

Other humanists were drawn to apocalyptic thought and attempted to pinpoint where the Turkish advance fit into the trajectory of sacred history. Given the variety of apocalyptic schemes already in circulation, the answers to this question could take radically different forms. Some creative thinkers envisioned the Turks as potential converts and saviors of Christendom, while some thinkers depicted the Turks as God's scourge on Christians. The latter suggestion offered humanists and other writers an opportunity to criticize Christian society for its failure to live up to its own religious standards. The Turks might be an evil force, they argued, but the Christians were to blame for inciting God to justly punish them.

Still other humanists applied peaceful religious principles to the Turks, embracing the Gospel virtue of proselytization. By combining aspects of medieval conversion treatises with humanist rhetoric, they hoped to persuade the Turks to accept the enlightened path of Christianity. Hence religious approaches to the Turks could and did take on many different forms. They all, however, underscore how important the divine continued to be in discourses of the Muslim East. Whether they were applying Christian principles or a flawed understanding of Islam, their belief that theology offered a key to solving the Turkish problem is apparent.

Background: Medieval and Renaissance Thought on Islam

Medieval approaches to Islam ranged from hostile propaganda to more-learned theological treatises.[1] The latter was more influential for humanists who wished to understand Islam on a deeper level—if only to deconstruct it. Christian theological treatises on Islam usually took one of three forms: learned polemic regarding the Prophet Muhammad and Islam; efforts to convert the Muslims; or eschatological works. To make matters more interesting (and confusing), many thinkers wrote on more than one theme, sometimes in the same work. All three of these tendencies led scholars to seek more information on Islam. As Southern argues, the period from 1140 to 1290 saw improvement in Western understanding of the religion. Knowledge of Islam came from two sources: increased contact with Muslim areas and study of the Qur'an. The earliest serious attempt at Qur'anic studies in Western Europe began with Peter the Venerable, the abbot of Cluny. On a visit to Spain in 1141 Peter witnessed "the progress and power of the Saracens" and determined to learn more about their religion in the hope of converting them.[2] Like many of his contemporaries, Peter appears to have perceived Islam as a Christian heresy that could easily be righted.[3] To achieve this goal he commissioned Robert of Ketton to translate the Qur'an into Latin, which was completed in 1143. Though expensive for

Peter and full of errors, this translation was the only one known in the West until the seventeenth century. Modern opinion of its poor quality, however, was not shared by medieval readers; numerous copies were made and disseminated in Europe.[4]

Peter's interest in the Qur'an stands as one of the first peaceful efforts to deal with the Muslim "problem" since the Crusades had begun. In fact, he commissioned this work at the same time Bernard of Clairvaux was helping to organize the Knights Templar. Though far from a religious or cultural relativist, Peter appeals to modern thinkers as a man who accepted Muslims as fellow human beings, as deserving of salvation as were Christians born to the faith. In the *Liber contra sectam Saracenorum* (1143) he explained to prospective Muslim readers: "I approach you, not as some of us often do with arms, but with words; not with force, but with reason; not with hatred but with love. I love you; loving you, I write to you; writing to you, I invite you to salvation."[5] While these peaceful solutions to religious division may reflect the influence of Gospel love and charity, they do not represent the sum of Peter's attitudes toward Muslims. Peter strongly supported the Second Crusade (1147–49) and wrote procrusading tracts describing Muslims as "dogs" or "blasphemous and wicked men."[6] Whether Peter experienced a change of heart or saw crusade and conversion as compatible remains a topic of debate.[7]

If Peter's proselytizing hopes are hard to gauge, Saint Francis, who journeyed to Egypt in an attempt to convert the sultan, is a clearer demonstration of conversion in action.[8] Jacques de Vitry, bishop of the crusader city of Acre (r. 1216–28), also made a sustained effort to convert local Muslims and to convince his fellow clergymen of the ease of such a project—an opinion he would later change.[9] William of Tripoli, a Dominican friar residing in Acre, also expressed hopes for peaceful conversion.[10] During the mid-thirteenth century the Franciscan Roger Bacon (d. 1292) more openly expressed opposition to conquest or forcible conversion in the name of the faith; he recommended instead learning the languages and beliefs of the Muslims and peaceful preaching as the only way to enlarge Christendom.[11] It must be stressed, however, that none of the above-mentioned conversion advocates has been shown to have opposed crusade. In fact, several medieval thinkers such as Ramón Lull and Humbert of Romans openly supported both crusade and conversion, and ultimately support for crusade far outweighed calls for pacifism.[12] Nonetheless, arguments for peaceful conversion of Muslims found an appreciative audience in the Middle Ages and would be echoed in the Renaissance when the question was posed regarding the more proximate and menacing Ottoman Turks.

The majority of medieval theologians who addressed Islam were less ambiguous, focusing defensively on the evils of the rival faith. In general, learned writers were better informed and more attentive to detail in their discussions of Islam than were writers or performers of works such as chansons de geste. Theologians, chroniclers, and other types of scholars were far less likely to portray Muslims as idolaters or polytheists. On the contrary, they recognized that Muslims were strict monotheists who regarded Muhammad as prophet, not deity. Many of them also knew of Islam's points of agreement with Christianity. This may be attributed to the improved sources available to Latin scholars.[13] And yet, despite their general accuracy on most tenets of Islam, scholars were just as likely as the unlearned to gravitate toward sensationalized accounts of the Prophet's life and the rise of Islam. This preference, Daniel argues, led to the creation of an enduring, "deformed image" of Islam in medieval Europe between the twelfth and fourteenth centuries.[14]

Pedro Alfonsi's influential work *Dialogi contra Iudaeos* (c. 1106) features a dialogue on Islam containing slanderous charges against the Prophet and the foundations of the faith. He portrays Muhammad as a greedy and lustful impostor, who did not restrain himself from enjoying other men's wives. Muhammad is also accused of recruiting converts to his religion by promises of carnal pleasure in this life and the next. Moreover, Alfonsi explains certain Muslim practices and beliefs as holdovers from Arabia's pagan past.[15] This portrayal of Islam proved to have vast appeal. Vincent of Beauvais's popular *Speculum historiale* copied this dialogue and others by Alfonsi, helping to spread these notions to an even wider audience. The same ideas can be found in Jacopo da Voragine's widely read compilation of saints' lives, *The Golden Legend*.[16]

No less a scholar than Saint Thomas Aquinas added his own twist to anti-Islamic pronouncements. If Aquinas read Ketton's translation of the Qur'an, he chose not to use it, relying instead on contemporary polemic in his *Summa contra Gentiles*.[17] In addition to portraying the Prophet as an impostor who preached a religion of carnal pleasure, he ridiculed Muhammad's followers as ignorant, brutal men and desert wanderers, who used force of arms to gain converts.[18] To his credit, however, Aquinas argued against forcibly converting Muslims and stated in the opening of his work that Muslims, like all men, are capable of being persuaded by natural reason.[19] Still, this vote of confidence is complicated by Aquinas's later assertion that those who place any faith in Muhammad's words believe foolishly.[20]

Eschatology offered medieval scholars an entirely different approach to Islam. By studying the Bible and prophetic works, they tried to rationalize the rise of Islam and predict its future—all in terms of Christian thought. The first apocalyptic work of this genre, *Revelations of the Pseudo-Methodius*, was composed in Syria in the seventh century, shortly after the rise and rapid spread of Islam. The work, which was translated into Latin by the early eighth century, was highly influential in Western Europe. These revelations brought hope to Christians by prophesying the appearance of a Last World Emperor, who would defeat the Muslim enemies of Christ or "Ishmaelites" and restore the glory of Rome.[21] Such a vision explained the appearance and strength of Islam to Christians unaccustomed to religious competition in the region.[22] It also implicitly encouraged armed resistance against the "enemies of Christ" by offering Christian rulers who fought against Islam the chance to be heralded as this Last World Emperor. In 1190 Joachim of Fiore identified Muhammad and Saladin with the fourth and sixth heads of the Dragon of Apocalypse 13. But Joachim believed that the turmoil of the sixth age under Saladin would soon be followed by the Age of the Holy Spirit. In order to bring this about, Joachim supported the Third Crusade led by Richard the Lionheart. Later, however, he predicted that the Saracens might be overcome by preaching instead of warfare. Joachim's writings greatly influenced future apocalyptic thought, and his views on conversion seem to have found a sympathetic audience in later generations.[23]

By the fourteenth century learned interpretations of Islam found their way into vernacular works of a more popular nature, such as the *Nuova Cronica* of Giovanni Villani (d. 1348).[24] By way of introducing the "Saracen" invasions of Italy and Sicily, Villani devotes book 3, chapter 8, to a discussion of their "sect." While this discussion draws on well-established polemical themes, it deserves mention given its air of historical authority, its literary embellishment, and its broad readership. Muhammad appears in Villani's account as a cunning impostor who fabricated a heretical offshoot of Christianity, set himself up as a prophet of God, and converted the masses through violence and coercion.[25] Both Muhammad and his religion are depicted as concupiscent and luxurious. One of the prophet's supposed laws, Villani claims, decreed that a woman caught in adultery was sentenced to death, unless, of course, she was caught with Muhammad himself, "because it was the commandment of the angel Gabriel that he [Muhammad] use married women to generate prophets."²⁶ Many quattrocento humanists echo images used by Villani—showing that they were persuaded by the same medieval sources he used, or that they perhaps drew directly on his work.

Medieval polemic was only one source of information on Islam available to Renaissance audiences; the papacy and the clergy provided another channel through crusading bulls and sermons. They frequently reminded humanists of the threat the Turks posed to the Christian faith, lest they become too wrapped up in political and intellectual concerns. The role of the papacy in leading crusade and shaping Western policy toward Muslim powers in the Renaissance is a topic of enormous size and significance, as shown in the seminal study by Kenneth Setton.²⁷ The majority of popes from the mid-fifteenth to the later sixteenth century made at least some effort on the crusade front.²⁸ Nicholas V (r. 1447–55) responded to the fall of Constantinople by trying to bring about peace in Italy and a joint crusade to rescue Byzantium. His successor Calixtus III (1455–58) spent the better part of his papacy organizing crusade efforts, which resulted in the relief of Belgrade (1456) and the Aegean victories of the papal fleet captained by Cardinal Ludovico Trevisan (1457); he also sent aid to the Albanian rebel Scanderbeg. Calixtus's zeal even led him to raid the treasures of the incipient Vatican library in order to raise money for the war effort.

Pius II (1458–64), the greatest crusading pope of the century, worked tirelessly at his dream of organizing a European-wide crusade against the Ottomans. In 1459 he called the ambitious Congress of Mantua in hopes of achieving this elusive goal. He wrote countless letters and speeches in support of the project, going so far as to attempt to lead the crusade himself until his death at the port of Ancona. Pius's successor, Paul II (1464–71), a Venetian with little love for his native city, still provided some assistance to the republic in its war against the Turks; he probably sent more funds to Hungary, however, which was also fighting the Ottoman advance. More committed to the crusade cause was Sixtus IV (1471–84), who issued frequent bulls, spent large sums on building a fleet, and worked with Naples and Venice on a joint enterprise. He even attempted to enlist the aid of Russia by arranging a marriage between Zoe Palaeologina and Ivan III, grand prince of Moscow.²⁹ Of course, his attempts to destroy the Medici undermined the idea of Christian unity against the Turks, but the Ottoman conquest of Otranto helped Sixtus to revive the tattered Most Holy League. Efforts continued to be made by popes in the following decades, including Innocent VIII (r. 1484–92), who convoked a congress in Rome in 1490 to plan a crusade.[30] While Rome's efforts often ended in frustration, at least one initiative led to a rousing victory: the crusade of Lepanto (1571), in which papal, Venetian, and Spanish forces defeated the Ottoman fleet.

Leadership of crusade was only part of the efforts made by popes and the cardinals and bishops who assisted them; they also acted as publicists and rhetoricians on the Turkish advance. One of the more important theoretical concepts the papacy helped to develop and spread was that of Europe and other Christian areas as an ideologically and culturally united *respublica Christiana*. Such rhetoric underscored cherished concepts of papal monarchy as well as a harmonious and militant Christendom capable of answering the formidable unanimity of the Ottoman Empire. Despite its potency, this imagery could not overcome the political divisions within Europe as successive attempts to launch large-scale papal crusades faced insurmountable problems.[31] Nevertheless, the dream of a united Christendom continued to appeal to a broad audience until the Protestant Reformation nullified the concept. Humanists were especially fond of the image of "Christendom," frequently employing it alongside secular concepts such as civilization, Europe, and the West.[32]

Broadcasting the dangers of the Turkish advance to a much wider population were numerous Renaissance preachers. In the quattrocento preachers such as Giovanni Capistrano, who helped organize the joint campaign of 1456, were vital to the crusade cause, playing an important role in the recruitment of soldiers and the collection of donations.[33] Over time, crusade funds were regulated and formalized into indulgences and church taxes, or tenths (tithes), twentieths, and thirtieths. These taxes were not voluntary by nature but rather were levied by the pope as Church taxes and were collected with varying levels of success.[34] Indulgences, offered for sale by preachers to all Christians, theoretically, enabled the purchaser to pay for a soldier to crusade in his or her stead while receiving all the benefits of *remissio peccatorum*.

The sermons delivered by crusade preachers varied in inspiration and content, but common features may be noted. Some sermons revolved around the text of a recently issued crusade bull, explaining to the populace the dangers that threatened Christendom and the heavenly rewards that awaited crusade participants.[35] In this respect sermons could serve as a medium for apprising the populace of the Turkish advance, as seen in Roberto Caracciolo's *Specchio della fede* (c. 1495), which lists Ottoman conquests, city by city, and provides gory details of atrocities.[36] Many preachers dramatically emphasized tales of atrocities so as to move the audience to a spirit of vengeance. Cardinal Bessarion used the example of Constantinople in his instruction to preachers of crusade (1463), directing them to dwell at length on the killings, enslavements, rapes, and desecrations of holy buildings and artifacts. As he bluntly states, the goal here was to engender a desire to avenge fellow Christians and even God.[37] While themes of vengeance and assistance to fellow Christians echo standard crusade sermon material dating back to the eleventh century, Bessarion's last category, defense of Italy, is a newer topos—indicating that crusade preaching, though conservative in most ways, was adapted to changes in the political scene.[38] After all, a preacher's audience was best addressed with relevant, immediate arguments. Perhaps the most common homiletic theme, however, was that of sin and repentance: the Turks were God's instrument, punishing the Christians for their sins, and it was the responsibility of Christians to repent and expiate their sins by the act of crusading.[39]

It is worth noting that many crusade preachers, such as the Franciscans Giacomo della Marca, Giovanni Capistrano, and Roberto Caracciolo, found ample time to preach against the Jews living among Christians in Italy. During the later Middle Ages and early Renaissance, Jews were increasingly marked out in northern Italy, literally in some cases, as members of an outmoded and inferior faith. San Bernardino and others preached that the Jews ought to be separated from Christians by wearing patches, certain colors, or jewelry.[40] The Jews had become indistinguishable in their clothing and styles; even more shocking, they were forming social bonds with Christians who had begun attending their weddings, circumcisions, and funerals with greater frequency.[41] Such mixing with Jews was believed to endanger a Christian's soul and pollute "good" society; they had to be marked out and avoided like prostitutes.[42] In the end the friars succeeded in marginalizing the Jews and casting suspicion on them as a group, while simultaneously trying to incite crusade fervor against the Turks.[43] Hence a growing attitude of religious intolerance in Italy applied both to internal and external non-Christian groups.

As important as these preachers were to the crusading movement, they also impeded its progress at times. In the fifteenth century the tactics and motives of certain preachers were heavily criticized. Some preachers absconded with collected funds, while others were reported to have employed reprehensible tactics in raising money.[44] Even the personalities of some preachers raised eyebrows. Erasmus caricatured the dramatic style of Roberto Caracciolo (also known as Roberto da Lecce): one day while scolding his listeners for their failure to take up the cross, he offered to join battle, threw off his habit to reveal a suit of armor, and then continued to preach in this attire for a full half hour.[45] Ludovico Domenichi, a sixteenth-century collector and editor of *facetiae* (amusing short anecdotes) recounted a similar tale about Caracciolo, adding that his motive was not to stir his audience but to impress his lady love.[46] According to Vespasiano da Bisticci, Caracciolo put off certain members of his audience, such as Cosimo de' Medici, by adopting fine dress and expensive habits— unbecoming conduct for a Franciscan.[47] Preachers could also be a source of instability when the subject matter turned to apocalyptic themes. The papacy had to caution them in the early sixteenth century to stop frightening impressionable listeners with predictions such as *when* the world would end.[48]

In sum, a range of religious traditions and rhetoric was transmitted to Renaissance humanists via medieval texts, papal pronouncements, and popular preachers. Hostile reactions were the most common results of scholarly inquiry into the nature of Islam during the Middle Ages and Renaissance. However, not all religious considerations of the Muslims degenerated into polemic and calls for crusade. A few religious thinkers approached the problem of Islam with a desire to know and guide the Muslims toward salvation rather than advocate their extinction. While it is true that the path by which they wished to help the Muslims involved not tolerance but eventual conversion, this approach was at the very least peaceful and less accusatory.

Conversion, Internal Reform, and Apocalyptic Thought

Some conciliatory and irenic views of Islam appeared in humanist circles even as calls for crusade were at their most intense. These include attempts to learn more about Islam, arguments for theological acceptance of Islam as part of God's plan, calls for peaceful conversion, and criticism of Christian society. Like their medieval predecessors, Renaissance proponents of such views could also exhibit profound ambivalence, expressing hostility toward Islam and calling for crusade at less peaceful moments. Yet Renaissance calls for a nonviolent approach to Islam were more surprising, perhaps even more earnest than earlier efforts, since the Turks were now a serious threat to Europe—a difference that truly tested the commitment of its advocates.

Renaissance thought on Islam differed from medieval approaches in another striking way: the same quattrocento spirit of conciliarism and reform that healed the papal schism led some humanists and churchmen to question not only aggressive papal initiatives such as crusade but also the very ideological foundations on which such initiatives depended. Implicitly challenging the papacy's arrogance concerning its enemies, they proposed a dialogue involving a large body of clergy and laity in place of univocal papal directives. It is no coincidence that two active proponents of the progressive conciliarist ideal—John of Segovia (d. c. 1458) and Nicholas of Cusa (1401–64)—were also among the greatest innovators in religious approaches to the Turks.[49] Since the two men saw eye to eye on the Turkish problem and proposed similar solutions, their ideas can be discussed together as expressions of an ongoing dialogue.[50]

It is debatable whether Cusanus and especially John of Segovia may be classified as humanists.[51] It is clear, however, that both of their approaches to the Islamic problem were heavily informed by humanist philology and hermeneutics. Both believed that the key to solving the problems posed by Islam lay in the study of textual sources—namely the Qur'an, which was still one of the most misunderstood texts in Europe. There is perhaps no technique that characterizes Renaissance humanism more than a return to the sources for careful and critical readings, and in this approach they found their inspiration.[52] Moreover, it has been argued that the art of rhetoric, given its emphasis on peaceful persuasion, led humanists naturally toward an attitude of toleration.[53] This study has shown that the opposite was true in regard to the Turks—that rhetoric was more often employed as a weapon of cultural chauvinism. Still, it makes sense that for some, humanism inspired a more peaceful, tactful approach. Cusanus spent a good deal of time in Italy and was well acquainted with humanists such as Aeneas Silvius Piccolomini and Lorenzo Valla.[54] Moreover, Cusanus's abiding interest in Plato and Neoplatonism as well as his innovative development of ideas of the harmony between different schools of thought and toleration of other faiths put him in the company of humanists such as Marsilio Ficino and Pico della Mirandola.[55]

The plans of Cusanus and John of Segovia to convert the Turks relied on a respectful approach to the Qur'an, acknowledging the Muslim belief that it contained the revealed word of God.[56] Both Cusanus and John of Segovia believed in the necessity of a clear understanding of the Qur'an—

and hence the need for a revised and accurate translation—but it was Segovia who spent many years trying to realize this dream. After finally securing an Arabic text of the Qur'an and a translator, a Muslim jurist from Salamanca, John watched the long-awaited project unfold. Although the work was never fully completed or distributed to a European audience,[57] it represents an important attempt to understand the faith of Islam on its own terms and not those of uninformed, culturally biased Christians.

Careful study of the Qur'an was only part of John of Segovia's plan; his ultimate goal was an interfaith conference, or a *contraferentia*, where the similarities and differences between Islamic and Christian doctrine might be discussed.[58] John of Segovia, along with Cusanus, had participated in the Council of Basel (1431–49) and witnessed the possibilities of such an undertaking. If councils could bring the Hussite problem under control and end the papal schism, what might a council between religions achieve in Europe's intractable conflict with the Turks?[59] While John of Segovia's primary hope for such a meeting was conversion of the Muslims, he was able to list thirty advantages of the *contraferentia* even if it did not lead to conversion; at any rate, he firmly believed that his approach was far superior to war.[60] John of Segovia's answer was innovative because it required both a greater understanding of Islam than earlier attempts at conversion and a willingness on the part of Christian participants to listen and discuss, not just to recite Muslim errors versus Christian virtues and truth. John of Segovia could envision such an approach because he, unlike the vast majority of his contemporaries, recognized some divine truth in Islam and stressed its commonalities with Christianity.[61]

Even after the fall of Constantinople (1453), John of Segovia and Cusanus continued to formulate peaceful solutions to the Turkish problem.[62] Given the climate of these years, it is not surprising that they won few adherents.[63] This is not to say that they opposed any type of war against Muslims. They agreed that Europe needed to halt the Turkish advance militarily; Cusanus even responded to the Christian military victory at Belgrade (1456) with rejoicing.[64] For the most part, however, they were progressive and pacifistic thinkers, who distinguished wars of defense from aggressive "holy wars." Cusanus responded enthusiastically to John of Segovia's letter of 1454 and made suggestions as to how the *contraferentia* might best be realized.[65]

Cusanus had already completed a tract of his own on the Muslim problem when he received John of Segovia's letter. *De pace fidei* is a dialogue between seventeen wise men from different world religions, among them an Arab and a Turk. In it Cusanus promotes the irenic concept that God sent many prophets to many nations but that over time certain customs were incorporated into the message and accepted as truths. These customs make religions diverge, but their essential belief in God is the same: "there is only one religion in a variety of rites."[66] As Southern put it, "he tried to embrace what was good in the religions of all peoples and to see through the details to the inner core of truth and unity."[67] Nonetheless, Nicholas measured "what was good" by Christian standards, mainly the acceptance of Christ, the Trinity, and the authority of the Church and firmly believed that true religious unity could only be achieved by common adherence to basic elements of Christian doctrine.[68] And yet the *De pace fidei* grants surprising concessions to other religions. Cusanus sees them all as genuine attempts to comprehend the Divine and even sympathizes with other sects for their errors or difficulties in accepting Christian doctrine. But he is confident that differences between religions are easily overcome through intelligent dialogue with their members. Regarding the Muslims' denial of the Trinity, he optimistically states: "Also the Arabians and all wise men will understand that to deny the Trinity is to deny the divine productivity and creative power; and that to admit the Trinity is to deny plurality and equality of gods . . . the Arabians will much better be able to grasp the truth in this way rather than in the way in which they assert that God has an essence and a soul and that he has a Verbum and a Spirit."[69] Incompatible beliefs, then, stem from surmountable differences in perception rather than willful heresy, stubbornness, or impiety.

A later work by Cusanus, the *Cribratio Alkorani*, or "sifting" of the Qur'an (1460), dealt exclusively with Islam and its tenets. Although it is less irenic than *De pace fidei*, the *Cribratio* still reflects Cusanus's desire to explicate common beliefs in Islam and Christianity. Essentially he sifts the Qur'an to find connections with Gospel truths.[70] It seems unlikely, however, that Cusanus had a Muslim audience in mind for the *Cribratio*, which would explain his callousness when addressing certain perceived tenets of Islam.[71] Drawing on such medieval works as that of Riccoldo da Montecroce and the Toledan collection of Peter the Venerable, Cusa indicts the Prophet for sensuality, worldliness, dishonesty, and use of force.[72] As Biechler asserts, however, we must not be quick to dismiss the entire work as hostile: "eight years of anti-Muslim polemic after the fall of Constantinople had decidedly dampened the pious irenicism of the *De pace fidei*, but the remarkable fact is that it had not destroyed it."[73] Though

Cusanus was writing for Christian readers, namely the pope, he still managed to give Muslims more credit for their beliefs than did most contemporary Christians. For example, he was one of the few Christian thinkers who explained the Qur'anic image of paradise as anything but a place of sensual indulgence and a sinful enticement for potential converts; instead, Cusanus posited that Muhammad described paradise in such terms as a metaphor for absolute bliss.[74] In chapter 18 of the *Cribratio* he suggests that the Prophet simply "wanted to persuade the uneducated Arabs . . . that in the everlasting, future age the Creator was also going to give them a life without deficiency."[75] Cusanus also tried to explain Muslims' denial of Jesus' crucifixion as an indication of their reverence for Christ; that is to say that such a lowly death was unworthy of him.[76] Drawing on common beliefs and interpreting certain Muslim tenets in a generously pro-Christian manner (*interpretatio pia*), Cusanus presents methods for leading Muslims by the hand (*manuductio*) toward Christian truth.[77]

Given both Cusanus's and John of Segovia's emphases on a textual evaluation of the Qur'an as a means to understanding the faith of Islam, one would expect to learn that humanists eagerly followed their lead. But, as we have seen throughout this study, few humanists were willing to consider the Turks, much less Islam, in a positive light. Perhaps cultural biases were too strong to pull them away from their cherished Latin and Greek texts toward the study of a dramatically foreign culture and religion, not to mention a difficult language.[78] Perhaps John of Segovia and Nicholas of Cusa also had a unique advantage over the bulk of their humanist contemporaries: they had both come in extended contact with Muslims, providing them ample opportunity to discuss matters of faith and to form positive impressions of the so-called Infidel on a firsthand basis.[79] Still, one wonders if events would have unfolded differently had John of Segovia completed and published his translation of the Qur'an. But, as he did not, we must grimly remember that it was not until the seventeenth century that Western audiences had a decent translation.

One of the most controversial conversion pieces composed by a Renaissance humanist is the famous letter of Pope Pius II (Aeneas Silvius Piccolomini) to Mehmed II (1461).[80] It has often been argued that Pius was influenced by the views of John of Segovia and especially of Nicholas of Cusa in the conception and composition of the letter. But Pius's ostensible aim in writing the letter—to head off war by converting the sultan to Christianity—is a question that must be examined in comparison to other conversion pieces as well as Pius's other writings and efforts. One of the greatest puzzles surrounding the letter is whether or not Pius was genuine in his designs and truly intended to send the letter to Mehmed.[81] Are we to believe that Pius, who more commonly referred to Mehmed as a "cruel and bloody butcher" (*crudelis et sanguinarius carnifex*), "that foul leader of the Turks" (*spurcissimus ille Turchorum dux*), and "the most repulsive beast" (*teterrima bestia*)[82] would—in the midst of planning a crusade—sincerely praise his good nature? Moreover, does it seem plausible that Pius would offer his archenemy political legitimation and papal support in his worldly endeavors, even in exchange for his conversion? Many scholars have argued that he had experienced a change of heart and was indeed earnest in his offer of conversion, even if the letter was never sent.[83] In the words of one biographer, "Several years had elapsed since Constantinople fell; the emotional Aeneas Sylvius who had deplored the Sultan's actions and moral character at the time was older now, and wiser, and sat upon the papal throne. . . . To later readers it is interesting . . . as an instance of Pius's indomitable faith in the powers of persuasion."[84] R. W. Southern went so far as to describe the letter, along with John of Segovia's and Cusanus's efforts, as "a moment of vision" in the history of Western attitudes toward Islam.[85]

The first few books of the letter do suggest that Pius was genuinely inviting Mehmed to convert. The opening of Pius's letter to Mehmed II, whom he addresses as "illustrious prince of the Turks" (*illustri principi turcarum*), is promising enough.[86] His tone is optimistic and respectful: "We do not seek you out with hatred nor do we threaten your person, although you are an enemy of our religion and press hard on Christian people with your weapons. We are hostile to your actions, not to you."[87] Pius warmly asks Mehmed to open his ears and his heart to the truths of Christianity. With surprising accuracy he points out some similarities between his faith and Mehmed's, such as their common belief in Old Testament doctrines.[88] He also invokes Christ, "whom the Mohammedan law in which you [Mehmed] were born calls a holy man, a great prophet, son of a virgin, and famous for his miracles."[89] Such statements not only reflect a degree of accuracy but also would seem to demonstrate an irenic tendency.[90] Pius's persuasions reach their peak in book 5 when he states: "You are a creature of God, and are his lamb, but you go astray and feed beyond your home in other pastures far from the Lord's fold. . . . We feel for you and deplore the unhappiness of your subjects who perish with you. We do not believe you willingly go astray since we have faith that your nature is good. The ignorance of the truth holds you back."[91] This tone of accommodation and understanding in the first part of Pius's letter is bolstered by his use of positive historical examples. He champions the benefits and honors of conversion to Christianity, citing the examples of Constantine, among others: "But why do we delay and not mention the greatest example of all? The Emperor and Monarch, Constantine himself, opened the way which you and all like you could have entered without delay."[92]

Constantine is one of the last people we would expect procrusade Pius to compare to Mehmed. Constantine's role as a capable Roman emperor, combined with his legitimation and support of Christianity, earned him Pius's respect as a man of action and faith. For Pius, Constantine combined the best of both worlds: Roman culture and devout Christianity. This can be seen, ironically, in an unfinished dialogue in which Pius depicts Constantine pleading with Christ on behalf of fifteenth-century Christians for help in destroying the wicked race of Turks.[93] And yet in his letter to Mehmed, Constantine is portrayed as a leader who rose to great heights with God's support and protection.[94] By offering the example of Constantine to Mehmed—either in earnest, or as a rhetorical device—Pius intimates that such glory is within Mehmed's reach should he simply convert.

Pius even goes so far as to praise the Turks' supposed Scythian ancestors in an effort to flatter Mehmed. Recall Pius's description of the Scythians in the *Cosmographia* as barbaric, backward, and even cannibalistic. In the letter to Mehmed, however, he reverses this judgment completely:

We understand that your origin is Scythian and tradition holds that among the Scythians there were many renowned warriors who held Asia in tribute for many centuries and who pushed the Egyptians beyond the swamps. The Egyptians and the Arabs cannot be compared with Scythians because there can be no comparison between a society of brave men and cowards. It is a cause for wonder how the Arabs fascinated and lured the bold, great Scythians into an alliance.[95]

A likely source for this passage is book 1 of Herodotus's *Histories*, although Pius would have been reluctant to cite it.[96] In direct contrast to Pius's earlier comments about the Scythians, they appear in this passage to be the best and the bravest of the peoples who would later convert to Islam; hence a race of noble warriors inexplicably allied themselves with cowards. Christians, Pius argues, would make far more suitable allies; since "courage attracts courage," theirs would be "a friendship between equals."[97]

What would compel Pius to reverse his opinions—and his own previous scholarship—regarding Mehmed and the Turks so completely? Most likely he did not reverse his views at all. Indeed, this abrupt shift casts some doubt on the sincerity of the letter. Moreover, the jarring disjunctions between the letter and Pius's other works are mirrored by unresolved tensions within the letter. In the later books of the letter Pius's tone shifts to condescension toward Mehmed and candid hostility for Islam, complicating and throwing into question the more positive aspects.[98]

An abundance of religious polemic appears in the letter. In one passage Pius states: "Your religion promises rivers of milk, honey, and wine in the next world, as well as delicate foods, plentiful women and concubines, relations with virgins, angels to assist in these foul pursuits; in short, all that the flesh desires. This is the paradise of an ox or an ass, not of a man!"[99] In another passage he argues that the Prophet's discovery was "of the devil," who used Muhammad to seduce mankind away from the power of Christianity only to devolve into idolatry.[100] Finally, he describes the law of Islam as "innumerable [in its] errors, its old woman's tales, and its puerile prattlings."[101] Could Pius have hoped to succeed with such scathing attacks on the religion of his correspondent?

To most modern readers this language would be enough to prove that the letter was no heartfelt conversion effort. But numerous medieval and Renaissance thinkers, including Nicholas of Cusa, employed polemic in conversion treatises. The use of polemic, therefore, and even simultaneous support of crusade, did not necessarily preclude a genuine desire to convert willing listeners. That being said, the methods of Cusanus and Pius share few resemblances under close scrutiny. While Pius charged that the Muslim paradise was fit only for beasts, Cusanus had the sensitivity and insight to challenge dismissive Christian assumptions regarding the Qur'anic vision of paradise. Moreover, while Pius called Islam an invention of Satan, Cusanus viewed Islam as a monotheistic faith and an instrument of providence—that is, a crucial step toward converting the Ishmaelites from idolatry to Christianity.[102] In short, Cusanus focuses on points of agreement between Christianity and Islam, whereas Pius only dabbles in comparisons before spending a good three quarters of the letter on acrimonious attacks. Pius's letter to Mehmed, as other scholars have noted, has little or none of Cusanus's irenic balance, nor does it demonstrate Cusanus's originality in religious argument; Cusanus strives to rise above the confines of religious polemic regarding Islam, while Pius is content to let it guide his sentiments.[103]

The main reason for such a difference in approach is that Pius's main source and possibly his inspiration was not Cusanus but Juan de Torquemada.[104] This highly polemical work aimed neither to understand Islam nor to convert its followers but rather to promote crusade. Pius's choice of Torquemada's work over that of Nicholas is telling. Also revealing was his unwillingness to give audience to the eager George of Trebizond, whose fascinating scheme to convert Mehmed II will be discussed shortly.[105] Combining Pius's unwillingness to meet with, much less employ, George of Trebizond with his failure to adopt Nicholas of Cusa's or John of Segovia's ideas adds to the general impression that Pius had other goals in mind.

An equally compelling reason to disregard the letter from a religious standpoint concerns a flippant remark Pius makes on baptism. This passage, which has shocked even scholars who accept the letter's ostensible intent, occurs in book 2 where Pius states: "A little thing can make you the greatest and most powerful and illustrious man of all who live today. . . . It is not difficult to guess, not far to seek, and is everywhere to be found: it is a little bit of water by which you may be baptized and brought to Christian rites and belief in the Gospel."[106] Baptism, the sacrament regarded by Catholics as most crucial for eternal salvation, has been reduced to a mindless initiation and a commonplace event. We see nothing like this in the works of Nicholas of Cusa, George of Trebizond, Aquinas, or other conversion theorists. Scholars have tried to justify this passage as either an attempt to mirror the "simple" confession of faith required of Muslim converts or as a humanistic argument for a cultural conversion,[107] but such arguments ring hollow. Pius took his faith and his position as pope far too seriously to treat so important an act as acceptance of Christ as *aquae pauxillum*. To understand this, one need only read a passage in the *Commentaries* book 12, in which Pius specifically cites defense of the sacraments as a cause for crusade.[108] Perhaps Pius cleverly designed this appeal to persuade Christian readers that the letter was directed toward an unbeliever, but it seems safe to say that it could not have been serious in any case.[109] Ironically, to accept Pius II's overture to Mehmed as genuine is to view Pius as far more cynical than if one rejects the entire letter as a conversion piece. Rejecting the letter also allows us to see Pius as a figure of greater consistency, whose views on crusade did not alter, no matter how frustrated his efforts became.

The history of the letter provides additional factors that bolster this interpretation. There is no evidence that the letter was sent or translated into Greek or Turkish. Moreover, nowhere else does Pius make such statements, and nowhere else does he even mention the letter or the idea of conversion.[110] Indeed, at the same time that he was revising the letter—in spring 1462—Pius announced to his cardinals his intention to lead a crusade personally.[111] Why would he continue to work on a conversion piece amid plans for a crusade? Furthermore, what should we make of his statements to his cardinals during this same meeting that his "old blood boiled with rage against the Turks" and that with the armies he planned to mobilize they could "wipe out the Turkish race"?[112] Where is there any mention of compassion, much less conversion? Pius's brash approach in the letter to Mehmed is even more jarring when we consider that he was a former diplomat and high-ranking prelate who appreciated the subtleties of tactful persuasion. We can understand his lack of theological training in comparison to Cusanus and Segovia, but surely he was accustomed to dealing with difficult and powerful men in more convincing ways.

Renaissance conversion treatises could be quite abrasive in tone, but they tended to be more balanced and learned than Pius's letter was. While the lack of information that exists on the letter has not yet allowed us to determine its exact purpose, it was clearly not intended for a Muslim audience. The letter may have been a bluff, designed to convince Western readers of either the pope's despair over their apathy or the imminent danger to Christian rulers if Mehmed ceased to be an enemy of the faith.[113] Yet another motivation for Pius may have been rhetorical. Whether or not Pius *believed* all the lies he told about Islam—which is another question entirely—he made a conscious choice to use the polemical approach, presenting the Muslim faith in the worst possible light. The letter belongs more to the realm of humanist history and pro-Western rhetoric than it does to any other genre.[114] Perhaps one of Pius's goals was to edify fellow Christians on the dangers of succumbing to Islam, cloaking his anti-Islamic polemic as a conversion piece, as did Peter the Venerable before him. Although Pius's letter cannot be classified as an original and enlightening religious work, it is still highly significant as an example of the longevity of medieval polemic regarding Islam in the Renaissance. It reveals a strong tendency to accept, or at least to employ, old superstitions and tales instead of pursuing more accurate information. Whatever the purpose of Pius's letter, whether it was a rhetorical exercise for himself or a propaganda piece designed for distribution among Christians, it does not belong in the same category as the efforts of John of Segovia or Nicholas of Cusa.

If Pius did not fulfill the goals of John of Segovia and Cusanus in his work, one quattrocento humanist tried to do so in his own way: George of Trebizond.[115] George molded apocalyptic thought to include the Otto mans in the Christian plan of salvation, presenting the Turks not as the greatest threat to face Christendom but as a key component in the future of Christian Europe. George wrote works dealing with crusade against the Turks. But his most controversial pieces were written in Greek and addressed to Sultan Mehmed II: *On the Truth of the Faith of Christians to the Emir* (1453), *On the Eternal Glory of the Autocrat* (1466), and *On the Divinity of Manuel* (1467). The unifying aspect of these texts is their praise of Mehmed II as not only a great ruler but also as the one man who might bring together all religious groups. Mehmed, George argues, could change the course of history, bringing peace and prosperity to all nations by accepting Christianity. Given their unusual content, these works attracted some suspicion. Cardinal Bessarion interpreted the singular works as treasonous and heretical; George was jailed by the papal curia for four months (1466–67) before Pope Paul II intervened to free him.[116] Although the charges were probably unfounded, it is easy to see how contemporaries viewed George as a political opportunist with his fulsome overtures to Mehmed, lauding the young sultan's greatness and repeatedly offering his own help.[117] Modern scholars too have speculated on the meaning of George's works, calling him an irenic spirit or an eccentric political thinker.[118]

But John Monfasani has offered an explanation, based on extensive study of George's life and works, that makes sense of the humanist's shift in attitude toward the Turks: "It was not as a precocious ecumenist nor as an insane political dreamer, but as a central actor in the final act of salvation history that George of Trebizond wrote to Mehmed II and risked life and limb to get to him."[119] But how exactly did this shift in attitude take place? How do we reconcile George's identification of Mehmed as an apocalyptic hero with his earlier calls for military efforts against the Turks? As late as 1452 he had claimed that the Turks would inaugurate the last dreadful days of the world. The Turks, he feared, were either the fabled hordes of Gog and Magog or the force that would open the gates that had kept them confined.[120]

The answer to this difficulty lies in the shocking events of 1453. George appears to have undergone a crisis in his perception of the Turks and the future of Christendom when Mehmed dealt the final crushing blow to Byzantium, becoming the undisputed leader of the Greek East.[121] George describes this turning point in *On the Eternal Glory of the Autocrat*: "in my opinion there has never been a man nor will there ever be one to whom God has granted a greater opportunity for sole dominion of the world than He has granted to your mightiness. . . . I arrived at this opinion immediately after I heard how God bestowed Constantinople on you. For, as the wondrous Aristotle teaches us, God does nothing in vain."[122] Clearly, the conquest of Constantinople led George to change his theory regarding the Turks as scourges of God. Since "God does nothing in vain," God allowed Mehmed to accomplish such a feat for reasons of cosmic importance. George began to wonder, however, if God had not chosen Mehmed for a positive purpose rather than as an instrument of destruction.

According to the Byzantine sources that informed George's eschatological vision—namely, Methodius and pseudo-Methodius—the Ishmaelites (here taken to mean the Turks) would be key players in the end of the world. After establishing dominion over Asia they would conquer first the Greek and then the Latin Empires. Theirs would be a reign of terror, ending only with the appearance of the last true Christian emperor, who would conquer the Ishmaelites and inaugurate a reign of peace. Following this reign Gog and Magog and the Antichrist would arrive on the scene. After the fall of Constantinople, however, George began to think that many of the tragedies associated with the last days of the world could be deflected if Mehmed II turned out to be not just the fabled leader of the Ishmaelites but the universal Christian emperor. In George's eyes, Mehmed's conversion could save the world from the fury of the Ishmaelites, "transforming two centuries of hell on earth into an age of universal bliss and peace."[123] Many of George's contemporaries viewed the Turkish conquest as the fulfillment of apocalyptic prophecies, but, as Monfasani argues, it was George's attempt to "change the script" that made his vision so fascinating and original.[124]

Of course, it would take some doing to transform Mehmed into a Christian of any kind, let alone a Christian ruler with a mission to bring the world to the one "true" faith. This is where George's learning as a humanist and skilled rhetorician comes into play. Fired by the religious convictions of his apocalyptic vision, he set himself the daunting task of persuading this mighty ruler through the power of eloquence. He began by explaining his unique ideas to Mehmed in *On the Truth of the Faith of Christians*, describing the sultan's newly augmented power and authority as being granted by God for the purpose of uniting Christianity and Islam into one faith.[125] He envisioned the "unification" as a recognition of common beliefs but primarily as Muslim acceptance of the superiority of Christianity and conversion. George may have been more open-minded than most of his contemporaries, but he was unwavering in his belief that Roman Catholicism was the truest expression of faith.[126]

He had once spoken of Muslims as infidels and barbarians,[127] but in 1457 he presented the Prophet Muhammad and Islam as more sensible and moral than the "corrupt" Byzantines. This takes place in his *Comparatio philosophorum Aristotelis et Platonis*, one of his many attempts to defend Aristotelianism and decry Platonism as immoral and heretical.[128] Platonic "hedonism," he argues, ruined the Byzantine Empire but was less successful with Muhammad and his followers:

> a second Plato arose: Muhammed. Muhammed learned his hedonism from a monk who was expelled from Alexandria because of his Platonic ideas and morals and who eventually came across Muhammed in Ethiopia. However, being much more sensible than the first Plato, Muhammed purged this instruction of its perversions and added practical rules of conduct. Consequently, after the perverse philosophy of the first Plato enervated Byzantium from within, the devotees of the second astuter Plato conquered it from without.[129]

Although George, like the majority of his contemporaries, depicts Islam as a heretical offshoot of Christianity, he grants it more dignity and austerity than most Christian contemporaries do. Muhammad, according to this picture, is no immoral seducer of the people, drawing them in by permitting vice and luxury; on the contrary, he improved on the religion he learned from the fallen monk. This concept is all the more striking when we consider that, in George's eyes, Muhammad and his followers were able to practice their faith—albeit a heresy—more purely and uprightly than were the Byzantines.

George, no doubt, presented such an example to strengthen his argument regarding the corruption of Platonism and its place in eschatological thought. But simultaneously, by elevating Islam to a higher moral plane than Greek Christianity, George supports his apocalyptic vision: Muslims, particularly the Turks, are a people worthy of both conversion and playing a great role in the last days of world history. Similarly, in *On the Eternal Glory of the Autocrat*, George describes how "God . . . raised up Mohameth" against the "schismatics of the Church, indeed against also the four Eastern patriarchs and the kingdom of Constantine, who were abettors of the schism."[130] Mehmed II, he proceeds, represents the culmination of God's plan to eradicate the Eastern Church and to unify all faiths into one: "In your [Mehmed's] victory, God transferred the kingdom to you in order to gather through you all the races into one faith and one church, and to exalt you as the autocrat of the whole world and king not merely of things perishable, but also of the very heavens."[131]

The rise of Islam and Mehmed II's ascent to power, then, are positive factors in God's plan for world salvation. Ironically, global conversion to the one true faith will be accomplished not by the Latin Christians or by the Church but by a group of future converts far more worthy of the task: the "Ishmaelites," or Turks. In this, George's scenario differs substantially from Western apocalyptic traditions of the Last World Emperor and Second Charlemagne, which viewed conversion of the Muslims as the result of the battles and other efforts of a prophesied *Christian* ruler. As George explains in *On the Divinity of Manuel* (1467), the Ishmaelites are truly God's chosen people. Although Isaac's line would produce Christ, Ishmael was more beloved of God and Abraham than Isaac was. He cites proof from the Bible when he states: "The verse, 'into a great multitude because he [Ishmael] is your [Abraham's] seed,'[132] signifies nothing if not those who will enter into Christ through the descendant of Ishmael."[133] In short, the descendants of Ishmael would complete the work begun by Christ and the early Church. More specifically, one descendant of Ishmael, none other than Mehmed II, will lead his people in this divine task. Given his "prudence and courage, his justice and liberality towards all," he is the obvious choice; for this reason "God has adorned [him] with every virtue [and] . . . every wisdom."[134]

Another area of nonviolent religious discourse on the Turks concerns neither conversion nor crusade but Christian reform. Some Renaissance thinkers viewed the Ottomans' military success and reports of their brutality as divine punishment for the sins of the people—an idea that goes back to the Old Testament. In the Christian Holy War tradition it dates back to at least the First Crusade. Preachers did a great deal to inspire and spread such notions, calling on Christians both to support crusading and to avert God's wrath with individual repentance. John O'Malley discusses the popularity of the Turkish advance as a topic of sermons at the papal court; preachers recalled the days when Christians possessed not only all of Europe but even the Holy Land, as opposed to the fifteenth century when the Ottomans won victory after victory. As Rodrigo Sánchez de Arévalo opined in a sermon of 1469, God permitted the Turkish advance because of the sins of the Christian flock.[135] After 1470 many wandering prophets lamented the state of Christian spirituality and talked of momentous signs from God.[136] In addition to the Turks, Jerusalem was a common subject for popular sermons in the fifteenth century. The image of Jerusalem became prominent as the geographical location of some of Christianity's most sacred events, or in an apocalyptic sense as a theater for the final events of world history.[137] The most popular (and notorious) preacher who used many of these topoi in his sermons was Girolamo Savonarola.[138] Ottavia Niccoli has also shown how this trend of associating the Turks both with tribulation in their attacks and renewal by their conversion was a popular theme of preachers in the early sixteenth century, alongside other prominent themes of flood, monstrous births, apparitions, Lutheranism, and other, non-Turkish invasions.[139]

What all these prophecies have in common is the link between calls for repentance and the Turkish advance. They encouraged ordinary Christians to take responsibility for Ottoman victories and to reverse them with their own seemingly mundane actions. In a way, the message was empowering and even optimistic: God was neither arbitrary nor unyielding in his judgment. In the end, moreover, the righteous would prevail and the Turks would eventually fall and/or be converted.[140] In more secular terms, prophecies of Turkish defeat were sometimes employed in a rhetorical fashion as a means of proving the supposed ease of a military strike against the Turks: divine providence or fate would assist in victory.[141]

The capture of Otranto in southern Italy (1480) inspired a good deal of apocalyptic thought among preachers and even some humanists.[142] The siege of Otranto was one of two campaigns launched by Ottomans against Christian powers in 1480. From late May to August 1480 an army of sixty thousand led by Mesih Pasha besieged the island of Rhodes, which was successfully defended by the Knights of Saint John (also known as the Hospitallers).[143] Europeans would take heart from the impressive victory, but their jubilation was cut short by news of another event even closer to home.[144] Just as the siege of Rhodes was lifted, another Turkish force landed on the shores of southern Italy.[145]

Mehmed had ordered a second great assault, this time aimed at the Kingdom of Naples. On 28 July 1480 Gedik Ahmed Pasha and a force of some eighteen thousand landed on the shores of Apulia and headed toward Otranto, looting and burning along the way. After the citizens of Otranto rejected the pasha's offer to surrender the city and be spared their lives, a furious assault began. King Ferrante was in Aversa, near Naples— the opposite corner of his kingdom. His son, Alfonso, duke of Calabria, was besieging Siena in Tuscany. Both made hurried preparations to relieve the city, but they could not arrive soon enough. Ill equipped to withstand a siege of any strength, Otranto fell to the Turks on 11 August. Alfonso arrived after the city had been taken, but his army was routed.[146]

Accounts of the siege vary, due in part to embellishment over time. According to several modern historians, a bloodbath ensued. One estimate claims that half the population, some ten thousand out of twenty-two thousand inhabitants, perished; this would include the entire male population.[147] More horrifying accounts describe a mass slaughter that followed the capture of the city three days later. Gedik Ahmed Pasha supposedly committed an unusual act in Muslim sieges of Christian cities: he ordered eight hundred inhabitants of Otranto to be taken to a nearby hill and offered the choice between conversion to Islam or death. When they refused to profess Islam, they were brutally cut down. The victims were canonized by Clement XIV in 1771, and the hill where they were killed is known today as the "Hill of the Martyrs."[148] Recently, though, historians have begun to question the veracity of these tales of mass slaughter and martyrdom. Francesco Tateo argues that the earliest contemporary sources do not support the story of the eight hundred martyrs; such tales of religious persecution and conscious self-sacrifice for the Christian faith appeared only two or more decades following the siege.[149] The earliest and most reliable sources describe the execution of eight hundred to one thousand soldiers or citizens and the local bishop, but none mentions a conversion as a condition of clemency.[150] Even more telling, neither a contemporary Turkish chronicle nor Italian diplomatic reports mention martyrdom.[151] One would imagine that if such a report were circulating, humanists and preachers would have seized on it. It seems likely that more inhabitants of Otranto were taken out of Italy and sold into slavery than were slaughtered.[152]

Across Italy news of Otranto elicited strong reactions from both the ruling hierarchy and the general populace.[153] The Turks had landed a large, organized force in Italy and captured key areas in Apulia. Pope Sixtus IV quickly began negotiating for peace in Italy. He addressed members of the poorly functioning Holy League and asked for pledges of aid in the reconquest of Otranto. The majority of Italian powers agreed to contribute to the cause, with the exception of Venice, which had just concluded a peace with the Turks in 1479 after a long and arduous war.[154] For Florence and other states it meant a halt in Naples's aggression in their territory. Reactions around Italy, then, were mixed.[155] But the alarming proximity of the Turks was a matter of serious concern; their acquisition of a base in Italy from which to attack the rest of the peninsula was a situation few Italian states could ignore. On a psychological level alone the presence of the Turks was demoralizing. Florentine humanist Angelo Poliziano tried to take hope in news of the Neapolitans' attempts to rout the Turks but still stated, "it will always seem as if the funeral cross is borne before me while these barbarians remain in the boundaries of Italy."[156] Italy's fears would be put to rest when the Turks were expelled from the peninsula the following year—partly because of a naval defeat at the hands of papal, Neapolitan, and Hungarian forces and partly owing to the disorder arising from Mehmed II's death on 3 May 1481.

The shock of Otranto combined with the rise of popular preaching and apocalypticism, mentioned above, set the stage for a unique response from a woman humanist from Brescia, Laura Cereta (1469–99). Cereta stands as one of the more confident and outspoken women humanists, daring to attack both male and female detractors in a spirited style of invective.[157] Her response to the Turkish advance, in a letter of 1485 to Elena de Cesare, shows the same talent for social criticism as is seen in her writings on women and education. She did not respond to the Turkish scourge with a call to arms, as did most humanists, but with a call for reform. Cereta begins the letter in standard humanist fashion, depicting the Turks as barbarians without mercy and citing their recent victories, including Otranto. When she moves to discuss the topic of Italy's defense, however, instead of calling for crusade she rails against the vices of the Italians: "We alone, turned away from God, continue to strive; we alone have become lawless and have shaken off every yoke of humanity from our savage minds. Our pardon, however, comes from heaven. Let us be aware, and let us correct the errors of our ways"; Cereta ends the letter with a stirring call for rejection of "the fruitless desires" and "the pomp of the age."[158] This brief comment on the Turkish advance is intriguing in its bold divergence from common humanist opinions and approaches. Rather than dwelling on classical texts for support—as she often does in other works—Cereta mimics the rhetoric of preaching, using Scripture as proof of her assertions.[159] She cites Jon. 3:1–10 comparing God's decision to save the people of Nineveh from destruction because of their fasting and repentance.

Vespasiano da Bisticci echoed these concerns with more emotion and detail. Vespasiano (1421–98), though not a humanist, had close connections with humanists as well as an interest in their studies. He was a prosperous producer and dealer of manuscripts whose clients included Cosimo de' Medici, Niccolò Niccoli, Popes Eugenius and Nicholas, King Alfonso of Naples, and Federico da Montefeltro, duke of Urbino.[160] His bookshop was a meeting place for intellectuals, and he enjoyed the companionship of such eminent humanists as Donato Acciaiuoli, John Argyropoulos, Giannozzo Manetti, and Alamanno Rinuccini.[161] In addition, he was a perceptive observer of his contemporaries, composing a book on the lives of famous men.

In 1480 Vespasiano wrote an emotional lament on the fall of Otranto, *Lamento d'Italia per la presa d'Otranto*.[162] Perhaps his greatest inspiration, and a leitmotif throughout the work, was Jeremiah's prophecies regarding the fall of Jerusalem and the Babylonian captivity. He begins the text with a quotation from Jeremiah: "Who will give water to my head? And a fountain of tears to my eyes, so that day and night I may weep for the wounds of my people."[163] This biblical reference prefaces an indictment of Florence and all of Italy for their indolence in the wake of Otranto:

One must lament and regret the blindness, not only of our city, blinded, hardened, and made obstinate in its sins. One would wish to God that she were alone, but all of Italy is mired in this stubbornness and calamity. Seeing so great a scourge come upon them, as is this of the Turk, no one is moved, blinded and shadowed and obstinate in sin as they are. And seeing the beginning of such ruin, there is not one person who is moved, or thinks or believes that this calamity will touch him.[164]

Echoing themes commonly exploited by preachers after 1453, Vespasiano portrays the Turkish advance as both a punishment and an unmistakable message from God that the Italians must repent. Italy's deficiency, he suggests, is not so much its weak military response to the Turkish invasion as the spiritual poverty of its people, who are "obstinate in sin."

The failure of his compatriots to recognize the Turkish invasion as divine intervention frustrates Vespasiano all the more since the Bible repeatedly illustrates such events: "Read the Holy Scriptures, and you will see how the omnipotent Lord has always used these methods for his punishments; he has always castigated his enemies with their own enemies."[165] To demonstrate his point Vespasiano cites the examples of the Flood, Sodom and Gomorrah, and Jerusalem during the time of Jeremiah and the puppet King Zedekiah. In the end Zedekiah's failed revolt against Babylonian overlords led to the eradication of the sovereign state of Judah, the enslavement of many Jews, and the utter destruction of Judean fortified cities.[166] A similar fate, Vespasiano asserts, awaits Italy if its people do not repent and take action.

Moreover, Vespasiano criticizes Italians for ignoring and mistreating their own modern-day prophets: "The prophets are the most holy preachers who have come to announce and preach in Italy the coming of the Turk, and the emendation of sins, showing the reason why God permitted the coming of the Turk. And never are they believed. Everyone makes fun of them, and no one wishes to change his perverse life or perverse customs."[167] Vespasiano points to no specific modern-day Jeremiah, yet it seems likely that he was inspired by one preacher in particular: Roberto Carracciolo, who preached in Florence in 1449, 1458, and 1480—a few months after the siege of Otranto, probably the same time when the lament was written.[168] Drawing on prophecy enabled Vespasiano to describe divine punishment of biblical proportions while demonstrating that God does not punish his people without warning. Also notable is Vespasiano's claim that such preachers are lightly dismissed or derided; this might indicate that prophecies of doom had not yet begun to sway as many Italians as they would after later disasters, such as the French invasion of 1494. Still, it would be wrong to assume that the fall of Otranto was not widely lamented by Italians.

Like Laura Cereta, Vespasiano perceived the Turks not as a military threat to be met with force but as a punishment from God that might be averted if Christians should make changes within their own hearts and community. Vespasiano's *Lamento* is a fascinating and unusual piece that appears to have sprung out of current trends in late quattrocento prophecy. Written in the vernacular and evocative of popular preaching, it is a different type of genre than most works examined in this study. Its intended audience, like that of most sermons, was the entire Christian community, whereas humanists, who tended to write in Latin, directed their pleas to a smaller group.[169] Still, Vespasiano addressed the same concerns that affected his humanist associates. His work provides a link between the vibrant apocalyptic culture of the period and both the spiritual interests of humanists and their concerns regarding the Turks—concerns that other humanists merely allude to in their writings.[170]

Polemical Approaches to Islam

Given their appeal to modern-day sensibilities, pacifistic approaches to Islam have been emphasized as representative of Renaissance thought. But polemic far outweighed more-charitable rhetoric for humanists and non-humanists alike. The reasons for this imbalance are manifold. Above all, the Ottomans inspired a strongly defensive reaction, given their encroachment on Europe. Most Europeans saw armed resistance, not religious persuasion, as the answer. In addition, the xenophobic aspect of humanism promoted an image of the Turks as foreign and undesirable in every way; the religion of the Turks received no more enlightened treatment than their cultural practices. Finally, humanists' applications of medieval sources in addressing Islam led to a perpetuation of the biases inherent in these sources.[171]

The most prevalent use of medieval polemic can be seen in humanists' repetition of formulaic asides on Islam. Humanists often described the Turks as infidels (*infideles*) or "enemies of the faith" (*fidei hostes*) when they were not referring to them as *barbari* or simply *Turci* or *Teucri*. Europe was frequently described in religious terms as well, such as *respublica christiana*; its inhabitants were simply "the faithful" (*fideles*). Such references to the Turks and Christians reflect the influence and use of medieval crusade rhetoric and do not demonstrate any innovation on the part of humanists. Other areas of medieval influence were charges of polytheism, but these tended to be employed with greater creativity as they invited classical comparisons.

Recall that Petrarch and Salutati employed medieval polemic depicting Muslims as polytheists.[172] Even worse, some humanists readily employed allegations of Satanism. For medieval writers this was mostly a poetic device, but some humanists appeared to have used it as a historical or ethnographic description. In his letter to John Hunyadi in 1448 Poggio Bracciolini implies that Muslims worship and sacrifice to Satan: "What is more hateful to God than the shedding of innocent blood [by the Turks], in which practice not only the bodies, but the souls of the faithful are destroyed in detestable sacrifice to Satan."[173] Similar accusations were made by Benedetto Accolti, who described the Turks as worshipping demons, in addition to other vices.[174] Pius II, as mentioned above, described Islam in his letter to Mehmed II as being "of the devil."

The most fully developed humanist expression of Islam, or at least of the Turks, as Satanic was voiced by Leonardo Dati. After the fall of Constantinople, Dati composed the epic poem *Carmen ad Nicolaum Papam V in Thurcum Mahomet*. More precisely, the poem is an epyllion, or epic fragment, modeled on Ovid or Catullus.[175] This genre allowed Dati to incorporate mythical classical elements, such as the river Acheron, Cerberus, and the Furies, and to mimic the poetic language of epic without having to match the length of an *Iliad* or *Aeneid*. The work, however, is not wholly classical in inspiration: Sultan Mehmed II is portrayed as a minion of the devil—a poetic conceit seen in the *Song of Roland* as well as other medieval and Renaissance texts on Islam.[176] Given its mixing of diverse traditions and imagery, it stands as one of the most creative humanist contributions to religious polemic against the Turks.[177]

Born in 1408 to a moderately prominent Florentine family, Dati was trained as a humanist and a cleric. He was employed as papal secretary from the reign of Calixtus III to that of Sixtus IV and was nominated bishop of Massa in 1467.[178] Even before the fall of Constantinople, Dati had shown concern for the crusade cause. He composed an epitaph on Cardinal Cesarini, who died in the crusade of Varna (1444). In 1447 he directed a poem to the Florentine people in which he attempted to put a favorable spin on Alfonso of Naples's intentions in Tuscany, depicting him as eager to take up the cross against the infidels.[179] The *Carmen ad Nicolaum*, most likely written in late 1453, was his greatest work concerning crusade and the Turks.[180]

Instead of attacking Islam directly, Dati weaves an imaginary narrative involving Satan and Mehmed II on one side, and the Virgin and Christ on the other. The poem opens in the aftermath of the fall of Constantinople; the devil has emerged from the underworld[181] and spies "the harsh Mehmed, that victor stained with the blood of Constantinople coming from the despoiled city."[182] On seeing the cruel and bloodied conqueror, Satan exclaims: "He is mine; he is the one whom I desired with all my heart. This is that sharer of evil deeds to whom I will give ghastly scepters of the world. To him, nothing can appear deadly."[183] In essence Dati has portrayed Mehmed as so wicked that Satan would handpick him as his partner in crime, an accomplice in eradicating Christianity. Satan then presents himself to Mehmed and offers him dominion of the world and more glory and fame than Alexander or Caesar.[184] In some respects there is a resemblance to the late classical poem *In Rufinum* by Claudian, in which one of the Furies, Megaera, choses Rufinus as her partner in bringing sorrow and disorder to the world.[185]

Drawing on classical images of the forces of darkness and the underworld, Dati describes an occult ritual sealing the pact between Satan and Mehmed:

He [Satan] said this, and shortly thereafter places [on Mehmed] a diadem, horrible to see, woven of one hundred serpents. In his right hand, he places an implacable scepter on which dreadful Cerberus rears it head with its triple-throated mouth.

He presents the implacable scepter, and having grimly examined the glowing eye on the shield of the Fury, he dedicates it with a nimble finger. And then he ties above his thigh a sword, a sword dipped in the black waves of the Acheron from which he anoints his face and whistles into his spreading ear.[186]

Here we see a macabre play on the ceremonial coronation and anointing of kings by popes and bishops. Instead of a crown of precious metals, Satan offers Mehmed a crown of snakes. In place of a sword blessed with holy water, Mehmed's solemn gift is immersed in the waters of the Acheron, the river of the underworld. Finally, Satan anoints Mehmed with the same dark water. This sinister inversion of a Christian rite shows Mehmed receiving his power and legitimacy from the devil; he will rule as Satan's servant, just as Christian kings pledge to reign as God's servants. As if this scene were not enough, Dati even represents Mehmed in a later passage calling Satan "my father in faith" (*Sathan fide pater*).

The association of Islam with the devil is further hinted by certain turns of phrase. Satan, for instance, refers to the prophet Muhammad as "sacred prophet" (*sanctus propheta*),[187] whereas he calls Christ "the fisherman godhead" (*piscator numen*). The suggestion that the devil honors Muhammad and insults Christ serves only to draw a sharper contrast between Islam, as a false and satanic faith, and Christianity, as the true cultivation of God. As further proof of the danger the Turks posed, he portrays Mehmed and Satan as setting their sights on Rome and all of Italy.

Not since medieval epics such as the *Song of Roland* had so a bold poetic comparison of Islam and Satanism been asserted. But the Muslim association with Satan is never made to look especially threatening in *Roland*; on the contrary, it serves to minimize the Saracens' existence and prove that they were "wrong" all along. The Frankish Christians, who are "right," seem destined to win the day. For Dati, however, the equation is neither as clear nor as comforting. Mehmed may be wicked and wrong in following the devil, but for Dati, this alliance renders him a powerful and grave adversary whose eventual defeat is by no means assured. The problem lies in the Christian fold, who are not so "right" as their Frankish literary counterparts.

This is demonstrated when the poem shifts to a dialogue between Christ and the Virgin about the sad state of affairs in the temporal world. She begs her son for help and mercy, but he is angry at the sins of Christians: "You know the pope, whom no one surpasses, who possesses the highest virtue—this same excellent father obtained a church that was shaken and fully hastening to its end, besieged by the vices and greed of a thousand tyrants."[188] This is a reference to the state of Rome and Europe when Nicholas V began his reign in 1447. Nicholas, Dati continues, brought stability to the Church and lifted the shadow of the Schism. But his flock has gone astray: "The ungrateful people tear themselves apart on all sides with discordant wars, and they sully themselves with plunder and blood."[189] A few lines down Christ exasperatedly asks, "Are these people Christians? Are these the men whom I myself redeemed?"[190] At first this seems a condemnation of Christian aggression, despite the Gospel's repeated calls to turn the other cheek. But Christ's indignation arises from Christians attacking one another instead of the Infidel.

Dati's purpose in writing the *Carmen*, then, was to call attention to the Turkish threat, and to chastise Christians for their apathy. At the end of the poem, in an exhortation to Pope Nicholas, Dati avers that God, having been angered by quarreling and internal strife among Christians, will not help them unless they reform and meet the Turkish threat head on.[191] Such a warning echoes the rhetoric of preachers and religious thinkers. Hence, Dati supported both holy war and internal reform without seeing any conflict between the two approaches.

By the fifteenth century fewer wild accusations were circulating against Muslims, such as Satan worship, than had been in previous centuries. And yet, as the examples of Poggio and Dati show, extreme assertions were still used for polemical and dramatic effect. Those uneducated about Islam might gather the impression that Islam was Satanic; those who knew better at the very least came away with a sinister view of Islam. Generally, however, when humanists composed polemic about Islam it was more measured and scholarly, showing at least some understanding of Islam. Sometimes the same author used both forms. Petrarch may have preferred the poetic and epic charge of polytheism when he wrote poem 28, but in his *De vita solitaria* he seems to have been working under the influence of more scholarly writers such as Jacques de Vitry and perhaps Vincent of Beauvais. Here the charge of polytheism is absent. Instead, Muhammad is described as a prophet who never maligned Jesus, at least not publicly. However, Petrarch uses some of the same accusations as did scholarly polemicists of the Middle Ages, as seen in his comparison of Muhammad to the rulers of his time. Petrarch states that they sympathize with him as a kindred spirit who pursued only luxury and hated virtue. He goes on to call Muhammad a "robber," a "butcher," and an "adulterous and licentious fellow" (*mechus et impurus homo*).[192] With this statement he makes a pun on Mecca, the holiest of Muslim cities, asserting that Muhammad blessed it because its name reflected his own debased (*mechus*) character. Furthermore, just as Aquinas described the teachings of Islam as consisting of some truths mixed with fables or doctrines of the greatest falsity, so Petrarch too refers to Islam as "a wicked superstition" (*nefanda superstitio*).[193]

What seems to be the unifying concept and motivation behind humanist polemic on Islam is the belief that crusade or some type of armed response was the only way to confront Muslims, specifically Ottomans. By presenting Muslims as idolaters, Satanists, or morally bankrupt, they become enemies of the faith. If their affinities with Christianity and the pious practices of Islam are exposed, it is much more difficult to justify a crusade against them. As scholars of cross-cultural aggression have suggested, an enemy must be effectively demonized in order to justify harsh tactics used against it.[194] Salutati makes this embattled stance clear in his letter of 1389 to the King of Bosnia, in which he portrays Murad I as planning to "destroy Christianity and the name of our dear Savior from the face of the earth, and—if he could—to erase it from the book of the living."[195] Like Petrarch before him, Salutati defines the Turks not simply as military threats but as adherents of an illegitimate and irreconcilably hostile religion. Their only goal, it would seem, is to attack the "true faith" and eradicate Christianity.

Historical Approaches to the Origins of Islam and Arab Learning

An effective medium for humanists to grapple with Islam on their own terms was to approach the religion via historiography. By applying the tools of historical inquiry they were able to examine and deconstruct Islam on a more rational and scientific level. Here, as in other writings on the Turks, their biases certainly obstructed objectivity, but humanists took comfort in exploring Islam via research into authoritative sources. Benedetto Accolti's history of the First Crusade (*De bello a christianis contra barbaros*) and Pius II's letter to Mehmed II combined historiography with anti-Islamic polemic.

Employing a common device in medieval crusade histories, Accolti opens his work with a propagandistic discussion of Muhammad and the rise of Islam. Since Muslim possession of the Holy Land in and of itself might not seem an acceptable excuse for waging large-scale holy war, the Muslim rulers of Palestine had to be vilified in every way possible in order to render their claims to the Holy Land illegitimate and their presence there a danger to the faith. One of the most effective means of doing this was to portray their religion as a pack of lies—the fabrication of "the great impostor" Muhammad.

Drawing on the elder Marin Sanuto's *Liber secretorum fidelium crucis* and William of Tyre's *Historia rerum in partibus transmarinis gestarum*,[196] Accolti introduces Muhammad as a false prophet who cunningly manipulated the Arab people into following his "sect":

a certain Arab, called Mohammed, who, although born in a humble and sordid place, . . . dared to say that he was a prophet sent by God to reveal perennial laws and new rites to mortals, nor did he lack a sharp wit or knowledge of sacred matters which he took from Jews and Christians. And although his morals were depraved, nevertheless he hid his sins artfully . . . adding also feigned prodigies, ridiculous to behold and hear, in order to increase his ability among men and enhance the authority of his deeds and laws.[197]

Accolti depicts Muhammad as a shrewd con artist seeking only to elevate his position in the community. In this respect he echoes not only Sanuto and William of Tyre but also the larger tradition of medieval Christian legend. True signs of prophethood for Christians were probity of life, proof of genuine miracles, and the constant truth of all his utterances— none of which medieval Christians would believe of Muhammad.[198]

Pius II inquired into the life of the Prophet and the rise of Islam in his letter to Mehmed II. Despite the declared goals of the letter, it was Pius's true intention to discredit Islam and encourage crusade. Even more bluntly than Accolti, Pius challenges Muhammad's legitimacy as a prophet by asking: "What are the signs, what are the miracles which prove the Law of Mohammed? . . . Your law, therefore, lacks testimony. . . ."[199] Pius also echoes the medieval fallacy that Muhammad's religion was a pastiche of Christian heresies[200] when he argues that "it was not Mohammed who originated this error, but the madmen Arius, Nestorius, and Macedonius. . . . Mohammed discovered [their virus] with the help of his teacher, Sergius, and diffused it widely."[201] Accolti too mentions the alleged contribution of Sergius in his history.[202]

Much as humanist historians enjoyed depicting Muhammad as an impostor, they faced a more daunting task in explaining his success in attracting converts to his religion. Here again medieval scholarship came to the rescue with the claim that the Prophet appealed to people's baser instincts. According to Aquinas, "he seduced the people by promises of carnal plea-sure to which the concupiscence of the flesh goads us. . . . In all this, as is not unexpected, he was obeyed by carnal men."[203] In the same vein, Pius derides the followers of Islam, affirming that Muhammad's most success-ful method of propagating his religion was "to promote things pleasurable to his listeners [polygamy, concubinage, feasting, and drinking] and espe-cially to the masses who are like cattle. His discovery did not fail in this regard, for it was pleasing, and in a little while it struck root and was received by many peoples of many languages because its foundation was pleasure."[204] Similarly, Accolti states: "Not unaware that the people are more prone to vice than virtue . . . he [Muhammad] instituted laws which scarcely seemed strict nor did he order anything which might prevent the gratification of lust, for he believed that many, weary of Christian severity, would forsake their faith and follow his sect."[205] Behind this rhetoric lies a palpable discomfort with a prophet who proclaimed a religion that shared so many common beliefs with Christianity—a religion that found a multitude of followers stretching from India to Spain. We can imagine that these justifications somehow comforted medieval Christians who saw their religion as the one true faith and their culture and values alone as pious.

The imputation of conversion by force also helped explain Islam's success to troubled Christians. When combined with charges of Islam's supposed sensuality, it created a sense that only the spiritually corrupt or the physically defenseless would take up Islam.[206] In his letter to Mehmed, Pius tried to explain away both conversion to Islam as an issue of force and Mehmed II's victories as merely the result of superior numbers in the field. Such a view need not contradict Pius's explanation for Christian losses in battle—that is, as God's punishment for their sins—since neither this view nor that of Islam's use of force suggested that God wished to reward Islam.[207] But Christian thinkers such as Pius encountered difficul-ties when they tried to explain Christian victories—for example, those of the crusaders—as shows of divine favor.[208] Seeing the difficulty of this proposition, Pius argued that victory was not necessarily a sign of correct faith, as seen in the victories of Alexander or the pre-Christian Romans. Still, he reveals a flaw in his logic regarding military victory and divine favor. How could victors be in the wrong if one believed in the principles of trial by combat? Pius, like other Christian writers, had trouble explain-ing Turkish military success while simultaneously calling for crusade, claiming that God would help bring victory to Christians.

Humanists continued their inquiry into the history of Islam by ques tioning its intellectual principles. Pius asserts that Islam, by its very nature, was irrational and opposed to intellectual inquiry. In book 16 of his letter to Mehmed, Pius bluntly states: "If there were no other argument against your religion, this one alone would suffice, that its founder prohibited disputing it."[209] This view represents a common medieval perception of Islam: it could not withstand the power of reason. Among the proponents of this view were San Pedro Pascual, Peter the Venerable, and Riccoldo da Montecroce; Riccoldo even added that wise Muslims did not actually be lieve in Islam and that was why they refused to dispute with members of other religions.[210] It is ironic that Catholics accused Muslims of abusing a tool—the act of condemnation without dispute—that the Church itself employed on occasion. While the Church did permit theological disputa tions by university faculty, condemnations, heresy trials, and inquisitions were also common.

The concept that Islam thrived on ignorance may have been medieval in origin, but humanists took it much further.[211] The question for human ists had much to do with classical definitions of what it meant to be civi lized and educated. Building on the assumption that Islam was supported by carnality and violence, they asserted that no such religion could support learning. As Accolti argues:

In this new way of life, virtue and learning were neither honored nor at all re warded, since nothing could be more inimical to a sham religion than virtue and knowledge of the arts and sciences, and so men turned to debauchery and idleness, abandoning the pursuits worthy of a free man; . . . with their minds captured and their spirits enervated, they changed their way of life and morals, and as though buried in the most profound darkness, they were able neither to lift themselves up nor to behold the light.[212]

Pius's view is fascinatingly similar in his letter to Mehmed. While discuss ing the role of religion as an agent of wisdom, he claims that Islam, by its very nature, inhibits intellectual growth: "There was once a great and flourishing school of philosophers in Alexandria. . . . But ever since the Law of Mohammed won the day, few have attained renown for revealing the secrets of nature. This is because neither your prophet nor your law, which is founded on pleasure and maintained by the sword, imparts wis dom to those lacking it."[213] Pius had already touched on this theme in his *Cosmographia*. Commenting on the advanced state of pagan and Christian learning in ancient Asia, he claimed that the arrival of Islam ended this intellectual vitality.[214] Moreover, both humanists depicted Islamic beliefs in identical terms as "old woman's tales."[215]

The increased emphasis on intellectual questions in the fifteenth century appears to be more a product of humanist thought than medieval precedent. The sense of education as a sign of worth, whether individual or societal, was a keystone of Renaissance intellectual life, much more so than in the medieval period, when some of the greatest heroes and saints were uneducated. Implicit in Accolti's and Pius's statements is the idea that Islam thrives on willful ignorance, while Christendom's strength lies in its support of learning. As Pius asserts: "The study of the liberal arts flourishes among us. Philosophy is read in public. Theology is taught in universities. No branch of learning is ignored."[216] Humanists, in their struggle to discredit the Turks and build up Western culture, made the giant leap of portraying all Muslims as backward dullards. Pius and Accolti, in short, superimposed on the entire religion of Islam their cultural stereotypes of the Turks as barbaric adversaries of learning. Misguided as this assumption was, Western thinkers in centuries to come would find themselves wielding it uncritically about any number of Islamic cultures.[217]

It seems peculiar that Muslim culture could become the object of humanist intellectual attacks when it produced some of the greatest philosophers of the Middle Ages. And yet some humanists, for example, Petrarch, completely dismissed Arab learning as valueless and even harmful to Western readers. In a 1370 letter criticizing modern medicine Petrarch seized the opportunity to assail the entire "race" and culture of Arabs, who were respected as great medical authorities: "Keep your Arab authorities in banishment from any advice to me; I hate the entire race. . . . [Y]ou know what kind of physicians the Arabs are, I know what kind of poets they are. There is nothing more charming, softer, more lax, in a word, more base. . . . I shall scarcely be persuaded that anything good can come from Arabia."[218] Petrarch's knowledge of Arab poetry may be a matter of debate,[219] but his use of ancient stereotypes of the Easterner seems clear. Francesco Gabrieli calls attention to the classical elements of this diatribe: the Easterner as weak, effeminate, and corrupt, yet also seductive in his cultural attainments.[220] Another source for Petrarch's aversion to all things Arabic may have been his hatred of scholasticism,[221] a method heavily associated with Arab commentaries, but Petrarch's sensibilities are shaped more by his own Western chauvinism and love of the Roman (and sometimes Greek) heritage. Quattrocento humanists continued to debate the merits and problems of scholasticism relative to humanism; Arab texts also

came under negative scrutiny when the full range of Greek texts and com
mentaries became available. But a humanist's praise or condemnation of
scholasticism and Arab scholarship did not necessarily correspond to his
position on Muslim religion and culture.[222]

As Greek learning became a prominent part of Florentine humanism,
ancient philosophers and their Arab commentators enjoyed increasing
popularity and respect. This is particularly the case among the Neoplato
nists. Marsilio Ficino drew heavily on Arab philosophers, physicians, and
astrologers in his studies. Ficino's *De Vita*, for example, is full of favorable
references to Arab scholars such as Abu Mashar, Al Kindi, and Avicenna.
Al Kindi was a Christian, but Abu Mashar and Avicenna were Muslims. On
one occasion Ficino refers to "the wise Avicenna"; in another reference he
mentions his "favorite authority Avicenna."[223] Ficino's enthusiasm for
Arab learning was surpassed by that of his friend and colleague Giovanni
Pico della Mirandola (1463–94), who also freely cited Arab sources in his
works. He opens his "Oration on the Dignity of Man" with a quotation
from "Abdallah the Saracen" and draws on other Arabic sources throughout the work, such as Alfarabi, Avicenna, Averroes, and Al Kindi.[224] Pico's
abiding interest in Arab scholarship may be connected to his studies in
scholasticism—a pursuit that brought him to the universities of Padua and
Paris.[225] Arab learning so interested Pico that he tried to learn Arabic so as
to read philosophical texts and even the Qur'an in the original language.
Pico also read the Qur'an in Latin—a copy that he borrowed from
Ficino.[226]

The enthusiasm Ficino and Pico shared for Arab learning does not
provide easy answers regarding their position on Islam. Ficino, it has been
argued, had a more open-minded outlook on other religions than most of
his contemporaries did; the tradition of irenicism and tolerance in Neoplatonism influenced him in this respect.[227] According to Kristeller, there are
several themes in Ficino's thought that point toward the concept of universal truth: Ficino believed that "all other religions [in addition to Christianity and ancient Judaism] are based on man's fundamental desire for
God [and] that they aim, though unconsciously, at the one true God."[228]
Although Ficino saw all religions as "species of the same genus religion,"
he clearly believed that Christianity "constituted the most perfect species"
of all religions. When it came to defending Christianity from the charges
of Islam, he was not above using arguments from medieval polemic against
Muhammad and his followers.[229] Owing to this conviction, he tried to
combat the errors of Muslims and Jews.[230]

Pico had little to say about Islam, but we may infer his stance on the religion from his views on universal truth. Benefiting from Ficino's somewhat tentative thoughts on universal truth, Pico developed the concept further and with greater confidence, albeit a confidence that earned him suspicion of heresy. Pico firmly believed that "a share of truth may be found in the works of thinkers of all times, places, and religions"; but such seemingly open-minded views did not prevent Pico from trying to bring his Jewish friends to the Catholic faith.[231] Although Pico did not specifically dwell on the place of Islam in his vision of universal truth, it has been suggested that the Turkish advance triggered both Pico's and Ficino's interests in accommodating Islam—a connection inspired by Nicholas of Cusa's and John of Segovia's plans to convert, rather than battle, Muslim enemies and thereby establish peace and unity.[232] Clearly, the two Neoplatonists valued Arab learning, and it is unlikely that they perceived Muslims as ignorant. Ficino wrote a few orations against the Turks, but his quarrel with the Turks does not appear to have been primarily religious.[233] On the contrary, he saw them as enemies of European security and Western culture; they were enemies of civilization as well as the faith. While Ficino freely labeled the Turks *barbari*, he did not treat all Muslims as such, despite his concerns about the foundations of their religion.

Yet it is important to remember that many humanists transferred their disdain for the Turks to other Islamic peoples—the conflict of West versus East was not limited to the Turks alone. Recall that several humanists applied the term "barbarian" indiscriminately to non-Turkish Muslims.[234] The intended effect was probably rhetorical, but other cultural biases in their writing would seem to indicate an acceptance of the idea behind it. Accolti's and Aeneas's views on Islam affected their perceptions of all Muslims. Marineo Siculo's assertion that the study of Arabic was neglected because it was a "barbarous language" seems to reflect the broadening of views described above.[235] The syllogism is embarrassingly naive—Turks are barbarians; Turks are Muslim; therefore Muslims are barbarians—and yet we find several humanists subscribing to such a notion. Despite such biases, some European schools began founding more and more chairs in Arabic in the sixteenth century; Guillaume Postel's chair at Paris (1535) is an early example. This trend has been seen as a sign of appreciation for Arab and Muslim culture.[236] But it appears that for a long time Europeans most often used Arabic as an aid to their religious inquiries, that is, to understand Hebrew Scriptures and kabala. In the end it was a very Christian-centric viewpoint.[237] Arabic had certainly ceased to be an important means of transmission for ancient Greek texts—as it was in the High Middle Ages—once Greek was reintroduced in Renaissance Italy.

Renaissance religious thought led humanists to approach the Turkish problem in some surprisingly diverse ways. It inspired Dati to describe Mehmed II as a disciple of Satan and to call for crusade. It led Pius II and Accolti to treat Islam as a sham religion. And yet it motivated some to examine Christendom's sins. Christian apocalyptic thought inspired Cereta and Vespasiano to describe the Turks as God's punishment personified or as a final warning to all Christians to repent. Contrastively, George of Trebizond used apocalyptic thought to present Mehmed and the Turks as saviors. In short, humanist interpretations of Christian thought regarding the Turks were a microcosm of later Christian attitudes toward Islam. Many thinkers, as Daniel argues, would continue in the vein of medieval polemic, perpetuated and expanded by humanists. Others would begin to view Islam as a faith with its own divine purpose—a purpose that Christians ought not to question.

Epilogue: The Renaissance Legacy

HUMANIST RESPONSES TO THE OTTOMAN advance continued to influence Western views of the Turks and Islam for centuries; even today their impact is felt. In some ways the humanist legacy promoted a greater openness and understanding of Muslim cultures and religion. In other ways its hostile take on the Ottoman Turks only served to nurture incipient ideas of Western superiority to Eastern rivals. In all its richness and diversity humanism helped cultivate both trends. While a thorough examination of early modern and modern attitudes toward the Muslim East transcends the scope of this work, it is useful to consider some ways in which humanism may have influenced Western attitudes toward other cultures. By simultaneously fashioning both a chauvinistic sense of "Western civilization" and a more relativistic approach to other societies, humanists would shape early modern and modern perceptions of not only the Muslim East but also other non-Western cultures. The negative impulse was the more dominant of the two legacies, but we will begin with the positive.

A handful of writers in the sixteenth and seventeenth centuries applied and expanded the more relativistic methods of earlier humanists. Erasmus of Rotterdam (1466–1536) discussed the Turks from a Christian humanist standpoint, applying skills of critical reading and argument to Scripture and early Church texts. By using this approach he challenged contemporary European notions of holy war and the Infidel.[1] Writing in a time when crusade appeared increasingly unachievable, Erasmus was a strong proponent of Christian nonviolence. Not only had papal initiatives and lay promises amounted to little over the preceding century, but also the Church's practice of selling crusade indulgences was coming under fire as a corrupt moneymaking scheme. The air of optimism regarding crusade that had swept Europe in the decades following 1453 was beginning to ebb in the early sixteenth century. Still, Erasmus was unique in challenging the very ideals of crusade, which most Christians continued to support despite their concerns about how the actual effort was going.[2]

In his letter to Paul Volz (1518) Erasmus criticizes the crusade ideal by exposing the harshness of prevailing attitudes toward the Turks.[3] Drawing on early Christian thought—not medieval accretions or crusade apologias—he asks what will become of the Turks if Leo X's proposed crusade succeeds.[4] Christians should endeavor to convert the Turks, just as Christ bade his followers do with all unbelievers. But Christians, in their present state, are by no means up to the task: "If the Turks should observe our ambition because of our loud, tyrannical clamoring, our avarice because of our plundering, our lust because of our debauchery, our cruelty because of our oppressive rule, how shall we press upon them the doctrine of Christ, so contrary to all these things?"[5] After centuries of crusade thought in which Islam was treated as the problem, Erasmus offers a fresh and introspective approach: the Christians are a greater threat to their own tarnished faith than any outside force—an idea briefly discussed by Laura Cereta.[6] If Christians truly desire to convert the Turks, he continued, they would have to present a better example of piety and charity. Violent confrontations such as crusade defy Gospel principles and disgust the Turks who are, after all, "men, nor are their hearts of iron or steel."[7] With this statement Erasmus questions earlier humanist dismissals of the Turks as inhuman barbarians.[8]

This is not to suggest that Erasmus was immune to the rhetoric of Turkish barbarism or that he completely opposed war against the Turks. The crusade ideal was still strong in Europe, and in the face of frightening events such as the siege of Vienna (1529) Erasmus relented somewhat in his anticrusade views. In his *Consultatio de bello Turcis inferendo* (1530) Erasmus echoes popular designations of the Turks as a "barbarous race" (*gens barbara*);[9] he also admits that war, under certain circumstances like defense, does not run counter to Christian principles.[10] Still, Erasmus did not cease in his attacks on crusade and his calls for more charitable views of the Turks. He echoed Nicholas of Cusa's optimistic view that the Turks were already "half-Christian."[11] Most early modern Christians, however, saw the Turks and Islam in very different terms. A host of writers, Protestant and Catholic alike, depicted the Turks as Antichrist; they brandished the word "Turk" as a slur against Christian adversaries. Luther frequently placed the papacy and the Turks in the same camp, and John Milton depicted Satan in *Paradise Lost* as a Muslim potentate surrounded by Eastern trappings and minions.[12]

Many sixteenth- and seventeenth-century writers mirrored Erasmus's tendency toward relativism, but they complicated such views with energetic calls for crusade. In his *History of Italy* (1537–40) Francesco Guicciardini praises the political and military strengths of the Turks and commends Sultan Bayezid II (1481–1512) for his treatment of Christians and his peace with Venice. The sultan is described as "a prince of mild ways, very unlike his ferocious father [Mehmed II], and dedicated to literature and to the study of sacred books of his religion, . . . by nature indisposed to warfare."[13] Guicciardini also notes Bayezid's successful attempts to intervene on behalf of his friend, the Marquis of Mantua, who had been imprisoned in Rome; he might just as easily have been describing a Christian Renaissance prince who used diplomatic pressure and alliances to secure this favor.[14] With an unwarlike ruler such as Bayezid, the Turks do not appear to be such troublesome neighbors; they may even become allies. Suleiman the Magnificent, while not commended, is at least noted for his agreement to let the Knights of Saint John and all other inhabitants of Rhodes take their possessions and leave the island unharmed in 1522 after the sultan had successfully besieged the Christian stronghold.[15]

For the most part, however, Guicciardini casts the Turks in an unfavorable light. He was troubled by their aggression in Christian lands, by reports of their cruelty, and by the inactivity of Christian princes. For example, Guicciardini notes a Turkish raid into Friuli in northern Italy, where "finding that country unguarded and unsuspecting of such an occurrence, the Turks overran it, pillaging and burning up to Liquenza; and having taken an innumerable quantity of prisoners, when on their return they reached the banks of the Tagliamento River, in order to march more easily, they kept those prisoners whom they thought they could lead with them, and cruelly massacred all the rest."[16] This type of cruelty was personified in leaders such as Selim, who succeeded the mild-mannered Bayezid. Selim's "greed for domination, his skill and ferocity" (*la cupidità del dominare, la virtù e la ferocia*) were well known, as was his tendency to kill off family members, including his own father.[17] Suleiman, despite some clemency at Rhodes, is depicted as an enemy of the faith who, "for the greater contempt of the Christian religion, made his entrance into that city on the birthday of the Son of God . . . had all the churches of Rhodes converted into mosques of the Mohammedan religion, and according to their custom all Christian rites exterminated."[18] Perhaps the worst part of this victory to Guicciardini is that Christian princes should have prevented it, or at the very least learned from it.[19] He had expressed high hopes for Pope Leo's proposed crusade of 1516 and was disappointed by its failure to move forward.[20] Judging from his *History of Italy*, then, Guicciardini appears to have had mixed feelings regarding the Turks. He holds onto the crusade ideal even as efforts to mobilize are disintegrating. Yet he also sees the Turks as potential political neighbors in times of peace.

On occasion Niccolò Machiavelli lamented the advances of the Turks, as in the *Florentine Histories,* in which he calls the loss of the Negroponte an event of "great disgrace and harm to the Christian name"; and in his play *Mandragola* (act 3, scene 3) he notes popular fears that the Turks might again attack Italy.[21] But on the whole his attitude toward the Turks is marked by political curiosity. In *The Prince* (1513) Machiavelli analyzes the Ottoman style of government. He mentions their rule of the Balkans in book 3 not to lament or criticize it, as so many of his contemporaries had done, but to praise their foresight in colonizing the area and thereby strengthening their position: "This move [the conquerors' decision to live in a newly acquired region] would make that possession more secure and more permanent: just as the Turk did with Greece; for in spite of all the other precautions he took to hold on to that dominion, if he had not gone there to live, it would have been impossible for him to hold it."[22] This attitude of cool appraisal is continued in book 4 when Machiavelli compares the governments of the French and the Turks. He makes no attacks on Turkish rule when his contemporaries might point to the tyranny or despotism of the sultan's rule. In fact, the only "barbarians" who appear in the work are the French, whose removal from Italy Machiavelli passionately urges in book 26; in some ways it reads as a bizarre reversal of Marsilio Ficino's letter of 1480 to Matthias Corvinus, begging him to expel the (Turkish) barbarians from Italy.[23]

Machiavelli's praise of the Turks reaches a high point in *The Discourses* (1513–17). In the preface to book 2, in which he discusses his theory of history and the balance of good and evil in the world, Machiavelli argues that the world's virtù, for centuries centered in Rome, has since been redistributed to other nations. The Franks, the Germans, and even the Saracens and Turks have shown the same virtù that once distinguished Rome. The tendency to praise the (Roman) past and to criticize the present, however, may cloud men's perspective as to the merits of one's present rulers: "anyone born in Italy who has not become at heart an ultramontane, or anyone born in Greece who has not become at heart a Turk, has good reason to criticize his own times and to praise others, since in the latter there are plenty of things to evoke his admiration, whereas in the former he comes across nothing but extreme misery, infamy and contempt. . . ."[24] In essence, Machiavelli views the Turks as founders of a great and impres-

sive empire. In this respect Machiavelli echoes Salutati: the worth of a
nation depends more on the character of its people and the level of their
success than on their bloodline or even religion.

Several scholars and travelers writing on the Turks in the sixteenth
century reflected this growing tendency to view the Turks from a less biased perspective—if only, in most cases, to help Westerners combat them
more effectively. Sixteenth-century Italian historians and treatise writers
such as Giovanni Menavino, Andrea Cambini, and Paolo Giovio spoke
highly of the Turks' organization and honorable behavior, exhorting Europeans to see beyond the barbarian stereotype and come to know their
enemy. Ironically, they still fell back on the rhetorical designation of "barbarian" from time to time, showing what an indelible mark the term had
made on European imaginations; they could not discard the term even
though they argued against the notion at other times.[25]

While connections between humanist thought and relativistic early
modern views are compelling, one should not ignore other important factors at play. Erasmus's views on Catholic reform played as great a role as
his humanist training when it came to his attitude toward the Turks. For
diplomats such as Guicciardini and Machiavelli, long careers as envoys in
war-torn Italy likely enabled them to see neighboring powers in a more
realistic, dispassionate light than did their humanist predecessors. Also
their positions may have made them privy to less biased information on
the Turks.[26] As for sixteenth-century scholars such as Cambini, Giovio,
and Menavino, not only did they have access to more accurate reports
than did earlier scholars—Menavino actually spent years in the Ottoman
Empire as a captive—but they also had a longer historical perspective.[27] By
1500 it was much harder to dismiss Turkish military successes or Ottoman
political stability as the work of aimless barbarians. Hence, when it comes
to evaluating more open-minded early modern perceptions of the Turks,
one should not claim exclusive credit for humanist predecessors. Humanists did, however, set the stage for more relativistic views by broadening
the discourse to secular issues. By comparing the armies and government
of the Turks to those of ancient peoples, scholars such as Salutati, Manetti,
and Bessarion emphasized the political over the religious, thereby reducing the sting of previous perceptions dominated by religious antagonism.

More direct and obvious links between humanist thought on the
Turks and later Western views emerge in negative rhetoric. Appealing
though they are to a twenty-first-century audience, the more liberal pronouncements of Erasmus and Machiavelli were atypical for their time.[28]

Far more often sixteenth-century writers echoed humanist concepts of the Turks as a threat to both Christianity and high culture. This may be partially attributed to the wide readership of Italian works on the Turks and crusading. Despite the errors and biases of humanist texts, they constituted the main source of information on the Turks in northern Europe as well as Italy. Better sources on the Turks may have existed, but humanist eloquence continued to attract and impress audiences.[29]

From vernacular poetry to Latin orations, sixteenth-century works kept readers in touch with the connection between Turks and barbarism. Torquato Tasso's popular *Gerusalemme Liberata,* an epic of the First Crusade, repeatedly applied the term *barbari* to Muslims encountered in the Holy Land. Inspired by Benedetto Accolti's history of the crusade, he uses the same humanistic terminology in a backward-looking fashion—bringing classical, learned disparagements into the realm of vernacular and chivalric poetry.[30] Two French writers of the 1580s, François de La Noue and René de Lucinge, composed separate treatises on the Turks that drew heavily on the concepts, style, and structure of humanist crusade orations, particularly those of Pius II and Bessarion. At times La Noue and Lucinge were more restrained regarding the Turks, praising their military and political order and allowing for possible alliances with Christian powers under certain circumstances. They cautioned contemporaries against viewing the Turks as a disorganized rabble and even deconstructed some aspects of the barbarian stereotype, arguing that a lack of interest in high culture made the Turks strong and vital, unlike effeminate overcivilized nations.[31] Still, far from entirely rejecting the notion of the Turk as barbarian, they affirmed its accuracy in regard to learning and culture, echoing fifteenth-century refrains of Western intellectual superiority and expressing concern for the heritage of Greece under Turkish domination.[32] Since the goal of their works was to encourage a joint European effort to drive the Turks out of Europe, humanist commonplaces proved useful to both writers.

The "ruin of Greece" at the hands of the Turks was a popular topic among Latin and vernacular writers alike in the sixteenth century. French poets such as Jean Molinet and Pierre de Ronsard lamented the sorry state of Greece: once the home of ancient heroes, poets, and philosophers, it lay desolated by barbarians.[33] They described as a fait accompli what humanists feared would happen in the years after 1453; the vantage points were different, but the messages were the same. Given sixteenth-century poets' use of the vernacular and the spread of printing, these ideas reached an even broader audience. Sixteenth- and seventeenth-century English writers such as Francis Bacon and George Sandys echoed the notion of the barbarous, unlettered Turks destroying the achievements of Greece.[34] The perception of the Ottomans as inimical to learning continued to impress writers and thinkers for many years to come. Even Giambattista Vico (1668–1744), who developed the first truly relativistic approach to other cultures in his *New Science*, still described the Ottoman Turks in good humanist fashion as a people opposed to the study of letters.[35]

If armchair ethnographers, poets, and historians still struggled with the biases set forth by humanists, perhaps travel writers fared better. It has been argued that Europeans who were able to spend time in the Ottoman Empire came away with a far more positive perception of so-called barbarian enemies of the faith. Modern scholars have made much of the commendations of Turkish justice, moral virtues, and military excellence in the works of Ogier de Busbecq and Guillaume Postel, among others.[36] But they often fail to note how many writers returned home with blinders intact and prejudices confirmed; they also minimize how ardently even writers of more liberal treatises on the Turks supported crusade.[37]

Postel and Busbecq came to the Ottoman Empire as part of diplomatic missions.[38] Their dispassionate or positive descriptions of the Turks may be partially attributed to their humanist educations, but a larger factor was probably their role as reporters and the unique political circumstances of their visit; they wrote at a time when alliances or truces were being discussed—a very different situation from the embattled stance of fifteenth-century humanists. And yet, despite all of these circumstances and their praise for the Turks, both writers remained convinced that the best approach to the Ottoman Empire was quick and decisive warfare. As Postel stated in *De la république des Turcs* (1560), his goal in writing was "to provide, through a well-founded knowledge of the enemy, the means of resisting him." Similarly, Busbecq used his knowledge of the Turks to compose a treatise in 1581 outlining his plan for defeating them.[39]

Busbecq is better known, though, for his famous *Turkish Letters*—addressed from Turkey to a friend in France and not intended for publication but printed in the 1580s. Modern scholars often depict the letters as a paragon of relativism, citing Busbecq's praise of Ottoman soldiery, the Turks' sense of social equality, and their hospitality to travelers and care for the poor. But these scholars have tended to downplay the letters' harsher judgments.[40] For example, Busbecq repeats the common refrain of the ruin of Greece, decrying the losses to its ancient heritage and the selfish reluctance of Christian princes to save it: "The land which discovered all the arts and all liberal learning seems to demand back the civilization which she has transmitted to us and to implore our aid, in the name of our common faith, against savage barbarism."[41] His belief in Western intellectual superiority emerges again when he chides the Turks over their inability to grasp the principles of historiography.[42] Contemporaries were probably less confused by Busbecq's overall stance; his first letter was printed in 1581 together with his treatise on crusade.[43]

Other travelers' accounts displayed more consistent attitudes toward the Turks, leaning heavily to hostile and critical statements. Royal geographer Nicolas de Nicolay accompanied a French embassy to the Ottoman Empire in 1551 and later produced a richly illustrated account of his journey.[44] Humanist influences appear throughout the work: Nicolay discusses numerous classical authors and figures, cites an unnamed work by Pope Pius II (probably his *Cosmographia*), and frequently uses the term "barbarian" throughout his account.[45] Where Turkish customs differ from his own, he tends to disparage them. Also convinced of Turkish barbarism was Pietro della Valle, a Roman aristocrat and humanist who spent many years in the Holy Land, Persia, India, and North Africa. Despite his stay in Constantinople for over a year learning Turkish (1614–15), he remained unimpressed by Ottoman culture, finding it brutish and barbarous. He was much more enthusiastic about Persia and aspired to fight with the forces of Shah Abbas I against the Turks.[46] Clearly for these travelers, spending time among the Turks did not soften preconceived, humanist-inspired notions of Ottoman brutality and backwardness. Not only did travelers often return to Europe repeating the same biases they had left with, but they began to create new, equally damaging stereotypes about the Turks, such as the lascivious and cruel Turk.[47]

If humanist concepts of European civility versus Turkish barbarism were tenacious enough to hinder objectivity in travelers to the Ottoman Empire, perhaps they extended to other non-Western cultures. While not specifically commenting on humanist responses to the Turkish advance, scholars have noted the link between humanism and perceptions of Native Americans. This connection is evident in the widespread use of classical texts as guides in the encounter. As Anthony Grafton has shown, the classical canon continued to influence Western thought on the Americas despite its conflict with empirical evidence. Instead of forcing Europeans to see the lacunae in their intellectual heritage, the New World encounter actually bolstered confidence in their cultural superiority.[48]

This idea emerges even more clearly in justifications for imperialism.

A large part of these arguments centered on religion: Christians had a duty to save heathen souls. But another important and enduring factor for colonizers from several countries was the quest to bring civilization, in the classical sense, to those lacking it.[49] Anthony Pagden notes the frequent discussion of civility in sixteenth-century Spanish treatises on the New World. While some notions of civility reflect the scholastic bent of theologians in Spain and are Aristotelian in origin—such as the concept of the natural slave—others are decidedly more humanistic in tone. For example, in addition to characterizing Indians as barbarous for practicing human sacrifice and cannibalism, theologian Francisco de Vitoria engages the humanist definition of culture by claiming that Indians lacked "all the arts and letters, both liberal and mechanical, a diligent system of agriculture or artisans and many other things necessary for human life."[50] Juan Maldonado took this idea further in stating that the Indians proved the Ciceronian notion that men without laws and letters were deprived of their humanity.[51] Here we are not far from Quirini's assessment of the Turks in 1453 as "a barbaric, uncultivated race, without established customs, or laws, living a careless, vagrant, arbitrary life. . . ."[52] Humanist Juan Ginés de Sepúlveda of Cordoba echoed these humanist views on barbarism and civility, but, more intriguing, he appears to have seen the use of force against Indians as related to crusade against the Turks. His *Democrates secundus sive de justis causis belli apud indos* (c. 1544) was part of a trilogy that he began in 1529 with an exhortation to Charles V to battle the Turks. Pagden is right in describing Sepúlveda as "far from . . . the enlightened humanist many historians have tried to make him,"[53] but perhaps Pagden's definition of Renaissance humanism is overly sanguine to begin with. Sepúlveda fits right in with the humanist traditions he learned in Italy, applying them to both Turks and Native Americans.

In his study of intellectual approaches to the New World encounter, Stephen Greenblatt speaks of the innate sense of superiority exhibited by Europeans. The origins of this view, he states, are hard to determine, but Western definitions of literacy seem key to the development of this perception.[54] Samuel Purchas described it as the "literall advantage" in the early seventeenth century—a grace given by God in addition to the senses, so that men may excel beasts and one another. Men who possess the use of letters and writing "are accounted Civill and more both Sociable and Religious," while those who lack it "are esteemed Brutish, Savage, Barbarous."[55] This emphasis on literacy and learning bears a strong resemblance to humanist attacks on the Turks as brutes who savagely destroyed books and scattered scholars, impoverishing the classical heritage of the Greek East. While the Ottomans were far from illiterate, humanists—who were well aware of this—nonetheless built a case against the Turks as barbarians opposed to higher culture and the arts, men who in Ficino's words "trample with filthy feet on the disciplines of all laws and liberal arts and . . . on Holy Religion" attempting to obliterate them from memory.[56]

My argument is that European assertions of intellectual superiority over Native Americans did not spontaneously arise on the first contacts between the two cultures. In many ways the Turkish advance provided compelling conditions under which humanists constructed a coherent vision of Western culture and its inherent superiority to other societies. Ironically, the colonial power dynamic that Said sees as integral to Western assertions of cultural supremacy was wholly absent when the humanists wrote about the Ottomans—a seemingly invincible empire capable of overrunning Europe.[57] Nevertheless, through their writings on the Turks, humanists manufactured a definition of Western culture that would ideologically support later generations when the power dynamic was reversed. By the late fifteenth century theorists of imperialism and conquerors had a ready arsenal of justifications for European hegemony.

Columbus believed that he had every right to rename and take possession of the lands he encountered in the West; his confidence stems from natural law but also from a sense of cultural superiority in keeping with humanistic definitions.[58] Hence, Columbus's cultural chauvinism was born in Europe, not in the Americas after careful observation of the Indians he encountered. The classical tradition, as interpreted and shaped by humanists into an even broader and more powerful notion than the Greeks or Romans knew, became one of the most important modes for assessing, and usually dismissing, other cultures.[59] Walter Mignolo has documented how, even well into the colonial period, the fresh and creative writings by persons of mixed ancestry and intellectual traditions went ignored by the larger reading public because they did not mimic the classical style or language of the Renaissance canon.[60] When Native Americans did not fit into a specific, humanist model of civilization they were classified as somehow beneath or behind European standards—much as the Turks were labeled before them. Perhaps Renaissance thinkers noticed the Muslim world's lack of interest in the modern or ancient West—apart from Greek philosophy and science—and judged this to be a sign of backwardness.[61]

This is not to say that other circumstances did not contribute to the continuing Western discourse of superiority. Every part of the world and every actor involved brought a unique set of conditions to the situation; context cannot be ignored. To suggest that there was a straight and recognizable line between Renaissance humanism and every assertion of Western primacy is to deny the roles that political power, economic forces, religion, and scholasticism would all play. But the role of humanities and the chauvinistic mindset established by humanists were important parts of this complex picture. One cannot argue that a people are subhuman or savage without having a clear notion of what it means to be human and civilized. Renaissance thinkers created an enduring and cogent definition of both ideas. We may disagree with the Eurocentric worldview today, but Burckhardt was right in asserting the importance of the Renaissance in creating the canon.[62] A crucial aspect of the formation of the concept of "Western civilization" that he does not address, however, is the ideological struggle against the Ottoman East.

Where, then, do these important developments leave us in regard to modern Western perceptions of the Turks and the Muslim world? I would like to suggest a few ways in which the humanist legacy may have made an impact. First, the rhetoric of the Turks as barbarians who ravaged Greece and abhorred higher culture and civility remained strong through the nineteenth century.[63] Sultans were readily described as oriental despots and the Turks as bloodthirsty and anti-Christian. What is striking is the way so many Western writers took for granted that violent events in the Ottoman East arose from some ingrained national tendency toward cruelty and barbarity.[64] In 1876 William Gladstone, who served four terms as prime minister of Britain, wrote one of the most popular and bombastic reactions to Ottoman violence against Bulgarian Christians—emotionally entitled *Bulgarian Horrors*. In this pamphlet are venomous descriptions of the Turks, such as: "They are not the mild Mohametans of India, nor the chivalrous Saladins of Syria, nor the cultured Moors of Spain. They were, upon the whole, from the black day when they first entered Europe, the one great anti-human specimen of humanity. Wherever they went, a broad line of blood marked the trail behind them; and as far as their dominion reached, civilisation disappeared from view."[65] Gladstone's pamphlet, while criticized by Benjamin Disraeli, quickly became a best-seller in England.[66] Thousands of readers were treated to the spectacle of a nation that purportedly wiped out all who opposed it and destroyed the fruits of civilization in the process. Such rhetoric is not far from the negative strand of humanist depictions of the Turks as barbarians.

The Turks today still occupy a tenuous position in Western thought as they struggle for acceptance into the European Union.[67] Their history is misunderstood, sensationalized, and oversimplified.[68] The Ottoman past continues to be associated with not only the modern Turks but also Eastern European Muslims. The most tragic manifestation of lingering prejudice against the Turks and the discourse of East versus West, Christianity versus Islam, and Europe versus the Turks are the numerous conflicts in the Balkans. The Serbs began their war against Bosnian Muslims by resurrecting supposedly "ancient hatreds" between Turks and Serbs. One heavy-handed use of such propaganda was a speech calling for Serbian resurgence, which was delivered in 1987 on the yearly anniversary of the fourteenth-century battle of Kosovo by Slobodan Milosevic. The coffin of Knez Lazar, the Serbian hero who was executed after the famous battle, had for the previous year been touring every town in Serbia, where it was greeted by black-clad, wailing mourners.[69] In addition to such symbolic misuses of history, Serbs and sometimes Croats have used the term "Turk" to refer to Bosnian Muslims.[70] The Bosnian Muslims are no more ethnically Turkish than the Serbs are, but they were subjected to the horrors of ethnic cleansing while Europeans and Americans looked on.[71] How much were participants and bystanders influenced by stereotypes of ethnic hatred and religious extremism attributed to the highly Europeanized Bosnian Muslims? How could stories of centuries of conflict, based on nineteenth-century nationalist and revisionist history and not on fact, have been used as an excuse for the violence that was taking place? While the reasons for this violence are complex and rooted in more-recent events and ideologies, the humanist discourse of barbaric Turks seems an important part of the equation.

Whether or not Renaissance rhetoric of Turkish barbarism carries over to the Muslim East at large is a more difficult question to answer, but a few possible connections may be posited. First, recall that humanists started to blur the boundaries between the Turks and other Muslims when they began to describe all believers in Islam as barbaric. This may have arisen from a lazy use of terminology, which was inaccurate to begin with. Perhaps, however, it is bound up with parochial humanist notions of (Western) civilization. They defined their own culture as advanced—among other reasons—for its replication of classical values and learning. Part of a very religious society themselves, they nevertheless took pride in their secular values inherited from Greco-Roman civilization. When humanists looked at the Islamic world, even beyond the Ottoman Empire, they saw no equal appreciation of classical culture or especially secular learning and arts. Were the humanists, perhaps, already generating the Western stereotype of Muslims as backward religious zealots?

If we look ahead to modern scholarship on Islam, the same sense of cultural superiority and authority to judge the East displayed by humanists marks the work of many orientalist scholars of more recent times. Orientalists, of course, were more familiar with their subject, traveling to the East and learning its languages, which is something few humanists accomplished. Still, their sense of Western civilization as the marker against which they judged and neatly defined the East seems as much a product of Renaissance humanist concepts as it was an outgrowth of the power relations inherent in colonialism, not to mention wide differences in technology and political practice. Another intriguing connection between humanism and orientalism may be the latter's preference for the *ancient* Near East as a topic for study until the late nineteenth century—a classicist leaning that further distanced Western scholars from both contemporary and historical Islamic culture.[72] The tendency of modern Muslims to avoid the ancient period, while simultaneously shying away from Western technology and practices in preference for Islamic tradition, may have further ingrained the orientalists' sense of Muslims as an uncultured folk opposed to progress.[73]

I raise these questions to show the connections that I see between humanist discourse on the Turks and modern Western concepts of Turkey, the East, and Islam. Indeed, the discourse was all too easily revived in the aftermath of September 11, 2001, with comments from leaders such as Silvio Berlusconi regarding the "superiority of Western civilization." Humanists, then, set into motion concepts that would influence the way Westerners conceptualize and discuss these issues. Some humanists initiated a trend toward relativism by admiring the Turks as a culture and a nation despite their religious differences. Other humanists called for greater acceptance and understanding of the Turks and all Muslims as believers in God who were not so different from Christians in their morality and practices. Yet another, substantially larger, group of humanists initiated a trend in negative attitudes toward the Turks as a culture with images of backwardness, ignorance, cruelty, inhumanity, and barbarity. Edward Said has illuminated the ways in which Western society still holds harsh judgments of Eastern Islamic societies as a whole.[74] Perhaps a better understanding of Renaissance humanist discourse on the Turks and Islam will reveal both how false and how long-lived some of these negative attitudes are, and will shed some light on the more positive moments in humanism that paved the way for attitudes of cultural openness.

In the final analysis, what I am arguing is the centrality of Renaissance humanism to the development of modern Western perceptions of its own culture and other cultures. We have seen how humanists created a discourse of European, Christian cultural superiority versus Eastern barbarity—an ideology that compromises humanism's shining invention of the dignity of man. This sad tradition is as much a part of our inheritance from the Renaissance as is republican thought or the celebration of individuality and free will. Humanist rhetoric, then, in many ways contains the seeds of cultural chauvinism in its very celebration of Western civilization. And yet, as we have also seen, does it not also contain the opposite tendencies as well? By creating a secular discourse on the Turks, humanists also found themselves able to discuss their longtime adversaries without the bite of religious hostility. Like Greek and Roman ethnographers, they could begin to analyze the Turks as a people whose practices had their own logic, with visibly successful results. Renaissance cultural attitudes, in short, have left us with a complex set of notions with which we continue to wrestle but cannot afford to ignore.

Notes

Introduction

1. For a detailed account of the siege, see Kenneth Setton, *The Papacy and the Levant (1205–1571)* (Philadelphia: American Philosophical Society, 1978), 2: chap. 4. A highly readable, if somewhat less accurate, account of the siege is told by Sir Steven Runciman, *The Fall of Constantinople 1453* (Cambridge: Cambridge University Press, 1965). See also Colin Imber, *The Ottoman Empire 1300–1481* (Istanbul: Isis Press, 1990), chap. 7; Franz Babinger, *Mehmed the Conqueror and his Time*, tr. Ralph Manheim (1953; rev. ed., Princeton, N.J.: Princeton University Press, 1978), chap. 2. More recently Marios Philippides has challenged some classic views of the siege in "Urban's Bombard(s), Gunpowder, and the Siege of Constantinople (1453)," *Byzantine Studies*, n.s., 4 (1999): 1–67. An excellent, although pronouncedly anti-Greek, primary source is Leonard of Chios's eyewitness account, found in J. R. Melville Jones, tr. and ed. *The Siege of Constantinople 1453: Seven Contemporary Accounts* (Amsterdam: Adolf M. Hakkert, 1972).

2. According to Muslim law, any city that did not surrender to its attackers had no rights once taken by storm and was subject to three days of unrestricted pillage. See Runciman, *Fall of Constantinople*, 145; Norman Itzkowitz, *The Ottoman Empire and Islamic Tradition* (Chicago: University of Chicago Press, 1972), 25.

3. Robert Schwoebel provides the best account of Western sources for and reactions to the fall of Constantinople; see *The Shadow of the Crescent: The Renaissance Image of the Turk (1453–1517)* (New York: St. Martin's Press, 1967), chap. 1. For the reaction in Rome see Stefano Infessura, *Diario della città di Roma*, ed. Oreste Tommasini (Rome: Forzani. E. C. Tipografi del Senato, 1890), 57–58.

4. The Venetian Senate's letter to the pope was read aloud in Bologna and probably other courts as it made its way south. See Agostino Pertusi, ed., *La caduta di Costantinopoli* (Milan: Arnoldo Mondadori Editore, 1976), 2:21. On laments see ibid., vol. 2; Lauro Martines, *Strong Words: Writing and Social Strain in the Italian Renaissance* (Baltimore: Johns Hopkins University Press, 2001), 244–48. For predictions of a Turkish attack on Rome, see Schwoebel, *Shadow of the Crescent*, 2.

5. Letter to the Doge of Venice (13 July 1453): "Viri instar pecudum trucidati; abductae mulieres; raptae virgines: Infantes e parentum complexibus sublati. Si qui ex tanta clade superfuerunt, vel in vinculis ut aere redimerentur servati, vel omni genere cruciatus affecti, vel ad turpissimam servitutem reducti"; see Henri Vast, ed., *Le Cardinal Bessarion* (Paris: Librairie Hachette et Companie, 1878), 455;

English tr., Mary M. McLaughlin, "Letter to Francesco Foscari, Doge of Venice," in *The Portable Renaissance Reader*, ed. James Bruce Ross and Mary M. Mc-Laughlin (New York: Penguin Books, 1953), 71.

6. "secunda mors ista Homero est, secundus Platoni obitus" (Letter to Nicholas V, in *Der Briefwechsel des Eneas Silvius Piccolomini*, Abt. 3, ed. Rudolf Wolkan, in *Fontes rerum austriacarum*, Bd. 68 (Vienna: Alfred Holder, 1918), 200; Pertusi, *Caduta di Costantinopoli*, 2:46. See Chapter 2 below for more humanist reactions to 1453.

7. See Edward W. Said, "East Isn't East: The Impending End of the Age of Orientalism," *Times Literary Supplement* (3 February 1995): 5–6; idem, *Orientalism* (New York: Vintage Books, 1978), 28; Homi Bhabha, *The Location of Culture* (London: Routledge, 1994), 1–9.

8. See Samuel Huntington, *The Clash of Civilizations and the Remaking of World Order* (New York: Touchstone Books, 1998).

9. It may be more precise to say that the Greeks introduced the ideas of East and Asia; the opposite of these poles varied from Greece to Europe to the West. For more on ancient perceptions of geographical and cultural poles, see Chapter 2.

10. Medieval perceptions of Islam are discussed in Chapter 1.

11. Key moments in the Ottoman advance will be discussed at greater length in the following chapters. For further reading, see Imber, *Ottoman Empire 1300–1481*; Cemal Kafadar, *Between Two Worlds: The Construction of the Ottoman State* (Berkeley: University of California Press, 1995); Itzkowitz, *Ottoman Empire*; L. Carl Brown, ed., *Imperial Legacy: The Ottoman Imprint on the Balkans and the Middle East* (New York: Columbia University Press, 1996). A classic standard of early Ottoman history is Halil Inalcik, *The Ottoman Empire*, tr. Norman Itzkowitz and Colin Imber (London: Weidenfeld and Nicolson, 1973). Also useful is John V. A. Fine, *The Late Medieval Balkans* (Ann Arbor: University of Michigan Press, 1987).

12. See Setton, *Papacy and the Levant*; Norman Housley, *The Later Crusades: From Lyons to Alcazar 1274–1580* (Oxford: Oxford University Press, 1992). Schwoebel presents an overview of European responses on a variety of levels in *Shadow of the Crescent*; see also Kate Fleet, "Italian Perceptions of the Turks in the Fourteenth and Fifteenth Centuries," *Journal of Mediterranean Studies* 5, no. 2 (1995): 159–72. See also my article "The Early Ottoman Empire," in *Trade, Travel, and Exploration in the Middle Ages: An Encyclopedia*, ed. John Block Friedman and Kristen Mossler Figg (New York: Garland Press, 2000). Two other studies that present useful overviews of the Ottoman advance in Europe but overestimate conciliatory attitudes toward the Ottomans, especially in Eastern Europe, are Paul Coles, *The Ottoman Impact on Europe* (London: Harcourt, Brace, and World, 1968); and Dorothy Vaughn, *Europe and the Turk: A Pattern of Alliances 1350–1700* (Liverpool: University Press, 1954).

13. Lisa Jardine and Jerry Brotton have depicted these relations as a sign of cultural openness and respectful exchange between East and West. But such claims are minimized by their heavy reliance on material goods and artwork and their superficial treatment of written sources. See Jardine, *Worldly Goods: A New History*

of the Renaissance (New York: W. W. Norton, 1996); Jardine and Brotton, *Global Interests: Renaissance Art between East and West* (Ithaca, N.Y.: Cornell University Press, 2000); Brotton, *The Renaissance Bazaar* (Oxford: Oxford University Press, 2002).

14. R. W. Southern, *Western Views of Islam in the Middle Ages* (Cambridge: Harvard University Press, 1962).

15. In contrast, much work has been written on cultural responses to the Turks in the later Renaissance, mostly in northern Europe. See Samuel Chew, *The Crescent and the Rose: Islam and England during the Renaissance* (1937; repr., New York: Octagon Books, 1965); Charles Issawi, *Cross-Cultural Encounters and Conflicts* (Oxford: Oxford University Press, 1998); Nabil Matar, *Turks, Moors, and Englishmen in the Age of Discovery* (New York: Columbia University Press, 1999); Clarence Dana Rouillard, *The Turk in French History, Thought, and Literature* (Paris: Boivin et Companie Editeurs, 1941); Daniel Vitkus, "Early Modern Orientalism: Representations of Islam in Sixteenth- and Seventeenth-Century Europe," in *Western Views of Islam in Medieval and Early Modern Europe: Perception of Other*, ed. David Blanks and Michael Frassetto (New York: St. Martin's Press, 1999); Andrew Wheatcroft, *The Ottomans* (London: Viking Press, 1993); Eric Dursteler, "Identity and Coexistence in the Eastern Mediterranean, ca. 1600," *New Perspectives on Turkey* 18 (spring 1998): 113–30.

16. James Hankins provides an indication of the size of this literature in stating that he collected more than four hundred texts written by more than fifty humanists; this number, he adds, is not complete. See Hankins, "Renaissance Crusaders: Humanist Crusade Literature in the Age of Mehmed II," *Dumbarton Oaks Papers* 49 (1995): 112 n. 3. I would like to thank Prof. Hankins for sharing his manuscript of this article with me before its publication.

17. Hankins has also noted this perceived incongruity; see his "Renaissance Crusaders," 111.

18. Myron P. Gilmore, *The World of Humanism: 1453–1517* (New York: Harper and Row, 1952), 21; cf. Robert Schwoebel, "Coexistence, Conversion, and the Crusade against the Turks," *Studies in the Renaissance* 12 (1965): 165 n. 4.

19. Babinger, *Mehmed the Conqueror*, 198.

20. Petrarch, Pius II, Benedetto Accolti, Bernardo Giustiniani, Lauro Quirini, George of Trebizond, and Cardinal Bessarion, among others, publicly and laboriously supported crusade. The letters of humanists such as Donato Acciaiuoli and Poggio Bracciolini reveal a personal concern over the Turkish advance. See also the letters of Marco Parenti, who has been described as a Florentine humanist, or at least a citizen with strong ties to the movement: *Lettere*, ed. Maria Marrese (Florence: Leo S. Olschki Editore, 1996), 68, 216, 220, 225, 228.

21. Housley, *Later Crusades*, 387. As far as the sincerity of the humanists is concerned, Housley has also argued that "a polished Latin prose style and genuine enthusiasm were not mutually exclusive attributes" (ibid.). Michael J. Heath provides a sense of readership and the dissemination of humanist works in *Crusading Commonplaces: La Noue, Lucinge and Rhetoric Against the Turks* (Geneva: Librairie Droz, 1986).

22. To quote Norman Daniel, "[following the mid fourteenth century] it

would be monotonous to read mere variations on recognized themes, in which new elements would be only slowly perceptible"; see his *Islam and the West: The Making of an Image* (1960. rev. ed. Oxford: Oneworld Publications, 1993), 306–7.

23. Robert Black, *Benedetto Accolti and the Florentine Renaissance* (Cambridge: Cambridge University Press, 1985), see also idem, "La storia della prima crociata di Benedetto Accolti e la diplomazia fiorentina rispetto all'Oriente," *Archivio storico italiano* 131 (1973): 3–25.

24. Hankins, "Renaissance Crusaders."

25. For selections from edited texts, see Pertusi, *Caduta di Costantinopoli*; idem, ed., *Testi inediti e poco noti sulla caduta di Costantinopoli* (Bologna: Pàtron Editore, 1983); Lucia Gualdo Rosa, Isabella Nuovo, and Domenico Defilippis, eds., *Gli umanisti e la guerra otrantina* (Bari: Dedalo, 1982); Norman Housley, ed. and tr., *Documents on the Later Crusades 1274–1580* (New York: St. Martin's Press, 1996). For studies, see Agostino Pertusi, "I primi studi in occidente sull' origine e la potenza dei Turchi," *Studi veneziani* 12 (1970): 465–522; Francesco Tateo, "L'ideologia umanistica e il simbolo 'immane' di Otranto," in *Otranto 1480*, ed. Cosimo Damiano Fonseca (Lecce: Galatina Congedo Editore, 1986), 1:153–80; Schmügge, *Die Kreuzzüge aus der Sicht humanisticher Geschichtsschreiber* (Basel: Verlag Helbing & Lichtenhahn, 1987); Heath, *Crusading Commonplaces*; John Monfasani, *George of Trebizond: A Biography and a Study of His Rhetoric and Logic* (Leiden: E. J. Brill, 1976); Margaret Meserve, "Medieval Sources for Renaissance Theories on the Origins of the Ottoman Turks," in *Europa und die Türken in der Renaissance*, ed. Bodo Guthmüller and Wilhelm Kühlmann (Tübingen: Max Niemeyer Verlag, 2000), 409–36;

26. Schwoebel, *Shadow of the Crescent*, see especially chap. 6; idem, "Coexistence, Conversion, and the Crusade"; Housley, *Later Crusades*, see especially 384–89. See also Eric Cochrane, *Historians and Historiography in the Italian Renaissance* (Chicago: University of Chicago Press, 1980), 324–37; Franco Cardini, "La crociata mito politico," *Il pensiero politico* (1975): 3–32 (also in *Studi sulla storia e sull'idea di crociata*, ed. Franco Cardini [Rome: Jouvence, 1993], 181–212); idem, *Europa e Islam: storia di un malinteso* (Rome: Laterza, 1999), chaps. 8–9; Charles L. Stinger, *The Renaissance in Rome* (Bloomington: Indiana University Press, 1985), 106–23.

27. A growing number of medieval, Renaissance, and early modern scholars have begun to incorporate postmodern theory into their work on perceptions of Islam. See the collected essays in *Western Views of Islam in Medieval and Early Modern Europe*, ed. Blanks and Frassetto, and *The Postcolonial Middle Ages*, ed. Jeffrey Jerome Cohen (New York: St. Martin's Press, 2000). See also the special issue on race and ethnicity in the Middle Ages in *The Journal of Medieval and Early Modern Studies* 31, no. 1 (winter 2001).

28. Said, *Orientalism*, 1–28. For a recent and condensed statement of these theories and a response to some of his critics, see Said, "East Isn't East," 3–6.

29. This is what Said means when he says that orientalists *create* the East as much as they *represent* it (*Orientalism*, 40–42).

30. For all the dreams and elaborate plans of several Renaissance princes, no European power managed to establish an imperialist presence in the Muslim East

before the modern era. Portugal's conquests in North Africa and India, however, did present serious challenges to local Muslim rulers.

31. See Chapter 2 for specific references.

32. Said's tendency to generalize about the rich and diverse fields of Eastern studies and the vast number of scholars who comprise these fields has been noted by several scholars who have criticized his one-sided depiction of orientalism as complicitous in the Western quest for cultural hegemony. Among them are Emmanuel Sivan, "Edward Said and His Arab Reviewers," *Jerusalem Quarterly* 35 (spring 1985): 11–23; Aijaz Ahmad, "Orientalism and After: Ambivalence and Metropolitan Location in the Work of Edward Said," in *In Theory: Classes, Nations, Literatures*, ed. Aijaz Ahmad (London: Verso, 1992), 159–219, especially 183; Maxime Rodinson, *Europe and the Mystique of Islam*, tr. Roger Veinus (Seattle: University of Washington Press, 1987), 130–31. Said responds in "East Isn't East," 4.

33. Indeed, Said's own ambivalence regarding modern humanism has been noted as problematic. On the one hand, as Aijaz Ahmad argues, Said charges Western humanism with complicity in colonialism and the cultural subjugation of the East. Yet, even as he censures the history of humanism, he invokes the ideals of liberal humanism—tolerance, accommodation, cultural pluralism, and relativism—as a means toward undoing the damage of orientalism. See Ahmad, "Orientalism," 163–64.

34. Stephen Greenblatt, *Marvelous Possessions: The Wonder of the New World* (Chicago: University of Chicago Press, 1991), 12–13.

35. Said's model of the orientalists' "textual universe" also offers a useful comparison; see his *Orientalism*, 52.

36. John W. Dower, *War without Mercy: Race and Power in the Pacific War* (New York: Pantheon Books, 1986), 302–3. Other useful comparative studies include Bernard Sheehan, *Savagism and Civility: Indians and Englishmen in Colonial Virginia* (Cambridge: Cambridge University Press, 1980); Urs Bitterly, *Cultures in Conflict: Encounters between European and Non-European Cultures, 1492–1800*, tr. Ritchie Robertson (Stanford, Calif.: Stanford University Press, 1989).

37. Denys Hay, *Europe: The Emergence of an Idea* (Edinburgh: Edinburgh University Press, 1957).

38. Paul Oskar Kristeller, *Renaissance Thought: The Classic, Scholastic and Humanist Strains* (1955; repr., New York: Harper and Row, 1961), 9–10. For a brief overview of the rise and development of humanism see Ronald Witt, "The Humanist Movement," in *The Handbook of European History 1400–1600*, ed. Thomas A. Brady, Jr., Heiko Oberman, and James D. Tracy (Grand Rapids, Mich.: William B. Eerdmans Publishing Co., 1995), 2:93–125.

39. For more information on this subject, see Paul F. Grendler's *Schooling in Renaissance Italy* (Baltimore: Johns Hopkins University Press, 1989).

40. Primary rhetoric was regarded by the ancient Greeks and Romans as the highest use of persuasion—as an act intended for the public good. Burgeoning civic life in Italy as well as the resurgence of classical studies made primary rhetoric a dominant form until around 1500 when the political climate began to change. See George A. Kennedy, *Classical Rhetoric and its Christian and Secular Tradition*

from Ancient to Modern Times, 2d ed. (Chapel Hill: University of North Carolina Press, 1999), 2–3, 228, 237.

41. Jules Michelet, Georg Voigt, and Grendler posited the former view; see Grendler, *Schooling in Renaissance Italy*; Zachary Schiffman, *Humanism and the Renaissance* (Boston: Houghton Mifflin, 2002), 1–5, Albert Rabil Jr., ed., *Renaissance Humanism: Foundations, Forms, and Legacy* (Philadelphia: University of Pennsylvania Press, 1988), 1:xi–xii. On the latter view, see Kristeller, *Renaissance Thought: The Classic, Scholastic, and Humanistic Strains*, 100–111; Schiffman, *Humanism and the Renaissance*, 3–4; Ronald G. Witt, *'In the Footsteps of the Ancients': The Origins of Humanism from Lovato to Bruni* (Leiden: Brill, 2000); Robert Black, "Italian Renaissance Education: Changing Perspectives and Continuing Controversies," *Journal of the History of Ideas* 52, no. 2 (1991): 315–34; idem., "The Donation of Constantine: A New Source for the Concept of the Renaissance?," in *Language and Images of Renaissance Italy*, ed. Alison Brown (Oxford: Clarendon Press, 1995), 51–85; idem, *Benedetto Accolti and the Florentine Renaissance*, xi, 317 29.

42. On the former view, see the work of Ernst Cassirer; Schiffman, *Humanism and the Renaissance*, 1–5. On the latter view, see Charles Trinkaus, *In Our Image and Likeness: Humanity and Divinity in Italian Humanist Thought* (London: Constable, 1970).

43. On the former view, again see Cassirer and also Eugenio Garin, *Italian Humanism: Philosophy and Civic Life in the Renaissance*, tr. Peter Munz (New York: Harper and Row, 1965); Hans Baron, *The Crisis of the Early Italian Renaissance* (Princeton, N.J.: Princeton University Press, 1966); Hanna H. Gray, "Renaissance Humanism: The Pursuit of Eloquence," in *Renaissance Essays from the Journal of the History of Ideas*, ed. P. O. Kristeller and Philip P. Wiener (New York: Harper and Row, 1968), 199–216; Arthur Field, *The Origins of the Platonic Academy of Florence* (Princeton, N.J.: Princeton University Press, 1988); Kenneth Gouwens, "Perceiving the Past: Renaissance Humanism after the 'Cognitive Turn,'" *American Historical Review* 103, no. 1 (1998): 55–82. On the latter view, see Anthony Grafton and Lisa Jardine, *From Humanism to the Humanities: Education and the Liberal Arts in Fifteenth- and Sixteenth-Century Europe* (Cambridge: Harvard University Press, 1986), especially 22–26, 122; Black, "Italian Renaissance Education."

44. For a brief discussion of this polarity, see my article "New Barbarian or Worthy Adversary? Humanist Constructs of the Ottoman Turks in Fifteenth-Century Italy," in *Western Views of Islam in Medieval and Early Modern Europe: Perception of Other*, ed. David Blanks and Michael Frassetto (New York: St. Martin's Press, 1999), 185–205. Other scholars have noted the dichotomy of civilization versus barbarism inherent in humanist works. See Schwoebel, *Shadow of the Crescent*, 152; Housley, *Later Crusades*, 385; Hankins, "Renaissance Crusaders," 145.

45. See the epilogue for more discussion of these tendencies. Norman Daniel has argued that modern notions of colonialism originated in the Crusades with propaganda touting Christian superiority; see Daniel, "Crusade Propaganda," in *A History of the Crusades*, ed. Kenneth M. Setton, vol. 6, ed. Harry W. Hazard and Norman P. Zacour (Madison: University of Wisconsin Press, 1989), 88–89,

94–95. Despite the merits of Daniel's argument, I would argue that humanist biases toward secular culture were equally or perhaps more important. Not all modern imperial programs sought to convert native populations, but cultural "progress" was almost always a goal.

46. Gouwens, "Perceiving the Past," 55–56, 62–63, 65, 77, 80–82. Carol Everhardt Quillen has discussed the transformative aspect of humanist readings of classical texts in Petrarch's encounter with Saint Augustine; see her *Rereading the Renaissance: Petrarch, Augustine, and the Language of Humanism* (Ann Arbor: University of Michigan Press, 1998), 106–47, especially 133. While Anthony Grafton still opines that relatively few humanists could have been so deeply affected by the past, in later works he too has underscored the creative, complex, and even scientific aspects of humanist readings of ancient texts; see his *Defenders of the Text: The Traditions of Scholarship in the Age of Science 1450–1800* (Cambridge: Harvard University Press, 1991); see also his *Commerce with the Classics: Ancient Books and Renaissance Readers* (Ann Arbor: University of Michigan Press, 1997).

47. On the originality of humanists in general, see Hanna Gray, "Renaissance Humanism," 200; Field, *Origins of the Platonic Academy*, 26, 105, 274, and passim.

48. Peter Burke discusses the importance of networks or circles as channels through which the process of cultural reception took place; see his *The European Renaissance: Centres and Peripheries* (Oxford: Blackwell Publishers, 1998), 10–12. Regarding the scholarly circle that formed around Donato Acciaiuoli in Florence, see Field, *Origins of the Platonic Academy*, 74–76. More closely related to our subject is Robert Black's mention of a "circle of ardent crusading enthusiasts" in Florence, which included Benedetto Accolti and Agnolo and Donato Acciaiuoli; see Black, *Benedetto Accolti*, x.

49. For many scholars, the history of ideas and the discourse of the Other imply a sense of timelessness and a lack of determination. That is to say, ideas are transmitted unbroken over both time and space and are absorbed and used unconsciously. As David Nirenberg argues in his study on fourteenth-century persecution of minorities, such a model ignores differences in historical context and denies agency to the people who adopted such views; see his *Communities of Violence: Persecution of Minorities in the Middle Ages* (Princeton, N.J.: Princeton University Press, 1996), 5–6.

50. When I speak of a humanist discourse, it is with the knowledge that more than one discourse was spoken at the time, although one type seemed to dominate. Moreover, the importance of authorial choice and individuality is addressed in this study. Groups of humanists helped to create this discourse, in some ways almost organically, but individuals certainly made their mark.

51. The dhimmi, literally "the protected," were Jews, Christians, and Zoroastrians who chose to continue in their own faith after Muslim conquest but paid for the privilege with high taxes, exclusion from political office and certain juridical rights, and a host of practices designed to reflect their humbled status. See Bat Ye'or, *The Decline of Eastern Christianity under Islam: From Jihad to Dhimmitude Seventh–Twentieth Century*, tr. Miriam Kochan and David Littman (Cranbury,

N.J.: Associated University Presses, 1996). Thanks to John Monfasani for this reference.

52. See Amin Maalouf, *The Crusades through Arab Eyes*, tr. Jon Rothschild (New York: Schocken Books, 1985); Carole Hillenbrand, *The Crusades: Islamic Perspectives* (New York: Routledge, 2000). For primary sources, see Francesco Gabrieli, ed. and tr., *Arab Historians of the Crusades*, tr. from Italian by E. J. Costello (Berkeley: University of California Press, 1969). Western writers, it should be noted, displayed the same tendency to mislabel Muslims from different cultures and countries.

53. See Bernard Lewis, *The Muslim Discovery of Europe* (New York: W. W. Norton and Co., 1982); Maalouf, *Crusades through Arab Eyes*, 262–66.

54. See Chapter 2 for a discussion of Mehmed II's cultural interests and attitudes of the Ottoman court.

Chapter 1

1. See Chapter 4 for a fuller discussion of religious works such as sermons and theological treatises.

2. See Wallace K. Ferguson, *The Renaissance* (New York: Holt, Rinehart and Winston, Inc., 1940). See also Kristeller, *Renaissance Thought*, 100–111; Black, "Donation of Constantine"; Burke, *European Renaissance*, 20–22.

3. Black, *Benedetto Accolti*, 317–29.

4. Grafton, *Defenders of the Text*, 37. Grafton uses the term "allegorical" where I have substituted "ahistorical." "Ahistorical" seems more appropriate, given James Hankins's explanation of the symbolic, and even religious and philosophical, aspects of an allegorical reading. Hankins uses the term "scholastic reading" for largely ahistorical interpretations and the term "critical reading" for a more rigorous historical approach to texts, but the latter practice did not fully evolve until the later fifteenth century. See James Hankins, *Plato in the Italian Renaissance* (Leiden: E. J. Brill, 1990), 1:23–25.

5. Both Norman Daniel and R. W. Southern have written rich studies on Western views of Islam that attempt to impose some structure on the mass of medieval and Renaissance primary sources. See Daniel, *Islam and the West*; Southern, *Western Views of Islam*. Benjamin Z. Kedar's *Crusade and Mission: European Approaches toward the Muslims* (Princeton, N.J.: Princeton University Press, 1984) takes a more critical approach to a wide range of sources within the context of their time. See his introductory remarks for an overview of the challenges of this field and interpretive pitfalls. Two more-recent collections of essays deal with medieval to early modern perceptions: John Victor Tolan, ed., *Medieval Christian Perceptions of Islam* (New York: Garland Press, 1996); and Blanks and Frassetto, ed. *Western Views of Islam*. David Blanks's article "Western Views of Islam in the Premodern Period: A Brief History of Past Approaches," in *Western Views of Islam*, provides a lucid overview of scholarship on this topic. Another recent survey of attitudes ranging from the Middle Ages to the modern period is Cardini's *Europa e Islam*.

6. Southern, *Western Views of Islam*, 14.

7. Kedar, *Crusade and Mission*, chap. 1.

8. See Hans Eberhard Mayer, *The Crusades*, tr. John Gillingham (1972; repr., Oxford: Oxford University Press, 1989); Jonathan Riley-Smith, *The Crusades: A Short History* (New Haven, Conn.: Yale University Press, 1987); Steven Runciman, *History of the Crusades*, vol. 1, *The First Crusade* (Cambridge: Cambridge University Press, 1951); P. M. Holt, *The Age of the Crusades from the Eleventh Century to 1517* (New York: Longman, 1986); Maalouf, *Crusades through Arab Eyes*. On the development of the concepts, terminology, theology, and legal issues of crusading, see Christopher Tyerman, *The Invention of the Crusades* (Toronto: University of Toronto Press, 1998).

9. Given their generally "un-Christian" actions, Steven Runciman argued that crusaders were driven in large part by worldly motives; see his *History of the Crusades*, vols. 1–3 (Cambridge: Cambridge University Press, 1951–54), passim. Jonathan Riley-Smith has provided a corrective in examining the great role spirituality—according to the context of their times—played in the decisions and actions of crusaders; see his *The First Crusade and the Idea of Crusading* (Philadelphia: University of Pennsylvania Press, 1986), especially chaps. 2 and 4.

10. Dana C. Munro, "The Western Attitude toward Islam during the Period of the Crusades," *Speculum* 6 (1931): 330.

11. As Marcus Bull asserts, the call for an armed pilgrimage was so successful precisely because it was such a novelty; see his "Origins," in *The Oxford Illustrated History of the Crusades*, ed. Jonathan Riley-Smith (Oxford: Oxford University Press, 1995), 17. There were earlier developments, however, such as Adhemar of Chabannes's sermons (1030s) on the "mad" Caliph al-Hakim's destruction of the Church of the Holy Sepulcher in Jerusalem in 1010; see Michael Frassetto, "The Image of the Saracen as Heretic in the Sermons of Adhemar of Chabannes," in *Western Views of Islam*, ed. Blanks and Frassetto, 83–96. Also before 1095 fighters in Sicily and Spain were slowly developing a sense of pro-Christian ideology as they fought largely Muslim armies.

12. According to Norman Daniel, "In Urban's preaching we find new notions, more especially new sentiments, that correspond to ideas immediately and thenceforward in general use"; see his "Crusade Propaganda," 40.

13. Version of Robert the Monk, *Historia Hierosolymitana*, in *The First Crusade*, 2d ed., ed. Edward Peters (Philadelphia: University of Pennsylvania Press, 1998), 27.

14. By Islamic law, Christians as well as Jews who submitted to Muslim overlordship and paid a poll tax were to be protected and allowed freedom of worship. Apart from radicals such as al-Hakim, who persecuted both Christians and Jews and destroyed the Holy Sepulcher, Muslim leaders tended to respect this law. See Mayer, *Crusades*, 5–6; Bernard Lewis, *Islam and the West* (Oxford: Oxford University Press, 1993), 6. Urban may have been responding to reports of raids by brigands, which increasingly affected pilgrims around this time.

15. The *Gesta Francorum* speaks of the crusaders shedding so much blood that they waded in it up to their ankles; Raymond d'Aguilers describes horses wading in blood up to their knees. See Edward Peters, ed., *The First Crusade: The*

Chronicle of Fulcher of Chartres and Other Source Materials, 2d ed. (Philadelphia: University of Pennsylvania Press, 1998), 255, 266.

16. Tyerman argues that the Crusades should not be viewed as a discrete entity that affected other aspects of medieval life, but rather as an undertaking that answered the various needs and desires of the culture that created it; see his *Invention of the Crusades*, 6. Robert Bartlett has identified sources of this unity in the replication of cultural units (towns, churches, monasteries, estates) in the process of colonialism within Europe. R. I. Moore and Jeffrey Richards point to the rising persecution of European minorities such as Jews, heretics, lepers, homosexuals, and prostitutes in this period as crucial to the formation of the perception of social homogeneity or purity, and in Moore's view, centralization of secular and clerical power. See Bartlett, *The Making of Europe: Conquest, Colonization and Cultural Change 950–1350* (Princeton, N.J.: Princeton University Press, 1993); Moore, *The Formation of a Persecuting Society* (Cambridge, Mass.: Blackwell, 1987); Richards, *Sex, Dissidence, and Damnation: Minority Groups in the Middle Ages* (London: Routledge, 1991).

17. At Clermont, Urban reportedly urged his audience to take up the cross with the words "Oh race of Franks, race from across the mountains, race chosen and beloved by God—as shines forth in very many of your works—set apart from all nations by the situation of your country, as well as by your catholic faith and the honor of the holy church! . . . Let the deeds of your ancestors move you and incite your minds to manly achievements"; see Peters, *First Crusade*, 27.

18. Said, *Orientalism*, 7.

19. Daniel, "Crusade Propaganda," 54–55, 41.

20. As Maxime Rodinson has argued, the image of Islam "was not drawn simply from the Crusades, as some have maintained, but rather from the Latin Christian world's gradually developing ideological unity. This produced a sharper image of the enemy's features and focused the energies of the West on the Crusades"; see his *Europe and the Mystique of Islam*, 7.

21. Southern, *Western Views of Islam*, 28.

22. John V. Tolan, "Muslims as Pagan Idolaters in Chronicles of the First Crusade," in *Western Views of Islam*, ed. Blanks and Frassetto, 97–117.

23. On crusade apologetics, see James Turner Johnson, "Historical Roots and Sources of the Just War Tradition in Western Culture," in *Just War and Jihad*, ed. John Kelsay and James Turner Johnson (New York: Greenwood Press, 1991), 3–30. On the widespread support for crusade, despite some opposition following losses in the Holy Land, see Elizabeth Siberry, *Criticism of Crusading 1095–1274* (Oxford: Clarendon Press, 1985).

24. Nirenberg, *Communities of Violence*, 8–10.

25. Rodinson, *Mystique of Islam*, 9–10.

26. Bernard Hamilton, for example, has challenged the long-held notion that local Franks and Muslim rulers would have gotten along perfectly well had it not been for the oafish aggression of new waves of crusaders; see his *The Leper King and His Heirs: Baldwin IV and the Crusader Kingdom of Jerusalem* (Cambridge: Cambridge University Press, 2000).

27. Usamah, the amir of Shaizar, wrote during the middle of the twelfth

century. Selections from his memoirs are available in translation in Gabrieli, *Arab Historians of the Crusades*, chap. 9. For useful cautions on reading Usamah, see Hillenbrand, *Crusades*, 259–62. See also Daniel, "Crusade Propaganda," 74–75. For a Christian perspective on Frankish acculturation, see Fulcher of Chartres in Peters, *First Crusade*, 281. This process of acculturation often rankled new arrivals from France and other parts of Europe, who derided the local *pullani* as morally deficient or unmanly. See Joshua Prawer *The World of the Crusaders* (New York: Quadrangle Books, 1972), 91.

28. See David Abulafia, *Frederick II: A Medieval Emperor* (Oxford: Oxford University Press, 1992); Richard Fletcher, *Moorish Spain* (Berkeley: University of California Press, 1992); idem, *The Quest for El Cid* (New York: Knopf, 1990).

29. Arab philosophy reached its height under Avicenna (Ibn Sinna, d. 1037) and Averroes (Ibn Rushd, d. 1198). Following Alfonso VI's conquest of Toledo (1085), numerous translations from Arabic were commissioned; both ancient Greek texts and Arab commentaries were now available in their entirety to Latin audiences for the first time. See W. Montgomery Watt, *The Influence of Islam on Medieval Europe* (Edinburgh: Edinburgh University Press, 1972), 40–43, 60–62; Irfan Shahid, "Byzantium and the Islamic World," in *Byzantium a World Civilization*, ed. Angeliki Laiou and Henry Maguire (Washington, D.C.: Dumbarton Oaks, 1992), 49–60. See also Bernard Lewis, *The Arabs in History* (New York: Harper and Row, 1966), 115–30.

30. Rodinson, *Mystique of Islam*, 16.

31. See Alauddin Samarrai, "Arabs and Latins in the Middle Ages: Enemies, Partners, and Scholars," in *Western Views of Islam*, ed. Blanks and Frassetto, 142. See also Kedar, *Crusade and Mission*, 90–91, for a discussion of Christian translators' unwillingness to credit "Arab" sources as also being "Saracen" or Muslim. Kedar takes a more optimistic view of the effect that Pedro Alfonsi's work of ethical philosophy, *Disciplina clericalis*, may have had on its audience owing to the favorable depiction of Saracens in its fables or exempla. See Kedar, *Crusade and Mission*, 91–92, and especially John V. Tolan, *Petrus Alfonsi and His Medieval Readers* (Gainesville: University Press of Florida, 1993).

32. See Chapter 4 for a discussion of humanist attitudes toward the tradition of learning within medieval Islam. On the various meanings of Eastern-inspired headgear, see Charlotte Jirousek, "More than Oriental Splendor: European and Ottoman Headgear; 1380–1580," *Dress* 22 (1995): 22–33.

33. See Jo Ann Hoeppner Moran Cruz, "Popular Attitudes towards Islam in Medieval Europe," in *Western Views of Islam*, ed. Blanks and Frassetto. For a slightly different perspective, see Michael Routledge, "Songs," in *Oxford Illustrated History of the Crusades*, ed. Riley-Smith.

34. *The Song of Roland*, tr. Glyn Burgess (London: Penguin Books, 1990), 8.

35. In the first *laisse* of the poem King Marsile, Charlemagne's Saracen foil, is introduced as "King Marsile who does not love God. He serves Mohammed and calls upon Apollo"; see *Song of Roland*, 29. Muslims too are depicted as worshipping a trinity of gods: Muhammad, Apollo, and Tervagant and their idols; see ibid., 114, *laisse* 194; 111, *laisse* 187. Still another episode describes Satan carrying off the soul of "the pagan" Malprimis of Brigal; see ibid., 69, *laisse* 96.

36. Munro, "Western Attitude," 331; Tolan, "Muslims as Pagan Idolaters," 97–117.

37. Routledge, "Songs," 111; Daniel, "Crusade Propaganda," 63–73. On the attribution of polytheism to Islam, which Daniel interprets as a conscious fiction employed for dramatic purposes, see Norman Daniel, *Heroes and Saracens: An Interpretation of the Chansons de Geste* (Edinburgh: Edinburgh University Press, 1984), chap. 6.

38. Cruz, "Popular Attitudes," 55–61.

39. *Song of Roland*, 129, *laisse* 231, for example, states, "Oh God, what a noble baron," but with the usual caveat "if only he were a Christian!"

40. On Pedro Alfonsi's moral tales *Disciplina clericalis*, which were widely copied in Latin and translated into other languages, see Tolan, *Petrus Alfonsi*. Boccaccio appears to have used some of Alfonsi's stories.

41. Giovanni Villani's *Cronica* also includes a long digression on the rise of Islam, which will be discussed in Chapter 4 in the context of religious polemic. Marco Polo's *Travels* and other travel accounts available in the vernacular also contained some information on Islamic areas.

42. For further reading on Dante's views on Islam and crusades, see R. W. Southern, "Dante and Islam" in *Relations between East and West in the Middle Ages*, ed. Derek Baker (Edinburgh: Edinburgh University Press, 1973), 133–45; Brenda Deen Schildgen, "Dante and the Crusades," *Dante Studies* 116 (1998): 95–125. Both Southern and Schildgen argue that Dante was only interested in crusade as a mirror for problems in the Latin West. While this argument has some merit, it seems a bit overstated. It may be argued that Dante's attempt to bring Islam into his own frame of reference shows an even greater attempt to conceptualize it; he reduces the subject but still shows a strong desire to comprehend it.

43. Dante, *The Divine Comedy (Inferno)*, tr. Charles S. Singleton (Princeton, N.J.: Princeton University Press, 1970), 37.

44. It should be noted here that although Dante appears to accept the Christian doctrine on baptism and salvation—albeit sorrowfully—some of Dante's contemporaries thought damnation of the unbaptized to be an unlikely action for a just and merciful God. See Cruz, "Popular Attitudes toward Islam," 61–62.

45. He presented Islam as a schismatic religion, presumably an offshoot of Christianity, as many of Dante's contemporaries still believed. This is made clear in canto 28; *Inferno*, 295. It is interesting that Muhammad's crime, as viewed by Dante, is not blasphemy but rather discord, reflecting Dante's own troubles with political disunity. See John M. Najemy, "Dante and Florence," in *The Cambridge Companion to Dante*, ed. Rachel Jacoff (Cambridge: Cambridge University Press, 1993). Dante's antipathy for Islam is also apparent in canto 15 of the *Paradiso* where his ancestor Cacciaguida describes how he went on crusade to battle against the "iniquity of that law [Islam]" and died at the hands of "that foul folk"; see Dante, *Divine Comedy (Paradiso)*, tr. Singleton, 173.

46. My thanks to John Ahern for his suggestions on the *Decameron*.

47. See, for example, Giovanni Boccaccio, *Decameron*, ed. Charles Singleton (Bari: Giuseppe Laterza e Figli, 1955), 1. 3, 2. 7, 2. 9, 5. 2, 10. 9.

48. For more information on this work, which most scholars now agree was

penned by an armchair traveler posing as a fictitious knight, see M. C. Seymour, *Sir John Mandeville* (Aldershot: Variorum, 1993). See also Greenblatt, *Marvelous Possessions*, 26–51.

49. "... io vado in questo passagio sí per onor del corpo e sí per salute dell'anima" (Boccaccio, *Decameron*, 2. 298).

50. For further reading on Petrarch, see E. H. Wilkins, *The Life of Petrarch* (Chicago: University of Chicago Press, 1961); idem, *Studies in the Life and Works of Petrarch* (Cambridge, Mass.: Medieval Academy of America, 1955); Giuseppe Mazzotta, *The Worlds of Petrarch* (Durham, N.C.: Duke University Press, 1993); Giuseppe Billanovich, *Petrarca Letterato* (Rome: Edizioni di Storia e Letteratura, 1947); Hans Baron, *From Petrarch to Leonardo Bruni* (Chicago: University of Chicago Press, 1968); Quillen, *Rereading the Renaissance*; Marjorie O'Rourke Boyle, *Petrarch's Genius* (Berkeley: University of California Press, 1991).

51. Setton, *Papacy and the Levant*, vol. 1.

52. On Philip's planned crusade, see Housley, *Later Crusades*, 34–35; see also Christopher Tyerman, "Philip VI and the Recovery of the Holy Land," *English Historical Review* 100 (1985): 25–52.

53. For a fuller discussion of Petrarch's views of crusading, Islam, and Byzantium, see my article "Petrarch's Vision of the Muslim and Byzantine East," *Speculum* 76, no. 2 (April 2001): 284–314.

54. *Petrarch's Lyric Poems*, ed. and tr. Robert M. Durling (Cambridge: Harvard University Press, 1976), 76–77. Petrarch's poem 27, incidentally, also celebrated Philip's planned crusade.

55. Both popular legend and histories by William of Tyre and Anna Comnena place Peter in a position of greater initiative and leadership than even Urban II or the lay nobility. See Mayer, *Crusades*, 39; Petrarch, *De vita solitaria*, ed. and tr. Marco Noce (Milan: Arnoldo Mondadori Editore, 1992), 381–82 n. 1.

56. "Is est Petrus heremita, qui olim in territorio Ambianensi solitariam vitam duxit, qualem sane non latuit. Dum enim indignari et irasci iam Cristus inciperet hereditatem propriam tam diu suis et nostris ab hostibus conculcari, non ulli regum cristianorum pingues somnos in plumis purpuraque captantium, non romano pontifici Urbano, gravi licet ornatoque viro occupato tamen, sed Petro inopi, otioso, solitario et humiliore grabatulo quiescenti, quid fieri vellet aperuit ..." (Petrarch, *Vita solitaria*, ed. Noce, 226; English tr., *The Life of Solitude*, ed. and tr. Jacob Zeitlin [Urbana: University of Illinois Press, 1924], 237).

57. For a particularly potent use of this image of Christ calling for vengeance (in this case actually from the cross), see *La Chanson d'Antioche*, a portion of which may be found in translation in Peters, *First Crusade*, 302–6.

58. "terram maioribus nostris promissam, nobis ereptam, nobis debitam si viri essemus, spei nostre sedem, arram patrie eterne, nunc egiptiacus canis tenet!" (Petrarch, *Vita solitaria*, ed. Noce, 228; English tr. *Life of Solitude*, 238–39).

59. Peters, *First Crusade*, 32 (Baldric of Dol's version), 28 (Robert the Monk's version).

60. Virginia Berry, "Peter the Venerable and the Crusades," in *Petrus Venerabilis 1156–1956*, ed. Giles Constable and James Kritzeck (Rome: Herder, 1956), 160. See Chapter 4 below for more on Peter the Venerable.

61. See Chapter 2 on Petrarch's use of Caesar as protocrusader.

62. Both Fine and Imber see the battle as a draw. See Fine, *Late Medieval Balkans*, 410; Imber, *Ottoman Empire*, 36. In the war between Serbia and Bosnia in the early 1990s, Kosovo would be used as Serbian propaganda, calling for vengeance against the Bosnian "Turks"; see Epilogue below.

63. See Chapter 2 for a fuller discussion of Salutati.

64. "nobisque notissimum foret . . . collapsi superbam temeritatem, temerariamque superbiam maomecthicole Lamoratti qui frigum sive turchorum imperio violenter adepto christianitatem et salvatoris nostri nomen ex orbis facie tollere cogitabat et si potuisset de libro viventum abolere . . ." (Latin: Archivio di Stato Firenze, *Signori, Missive Prima Cancelleria* 21, fol. 139r; English tr. from Thomas A. Emmert, *Serbian Golgotha: Kosovo, 1389* [New York: East European Monographs, 1990], 45–46).

65. For a description of the raids of the early 1370s and Schiltberger's account of executions and attacks on Hungary following the Crusade of Nicopolis, see Imber, *Ottoman Empire*, 29, 46–47.

66. See Housley, *Later Crusades*, 71; Inalcik, *Ottoman Empire*, 13–14.

67. Robert J. Donia and John V. A. Fine, *Bosnia and Hercegovina: A Tradition Betrayed* (New York: Columbia University Press, 1994), 64–66. Catholics were given less autonomy since they were viewed as a dangerous link to crusading powers to the west. Bat Ye'or notes how Balkan peasants both suffered and prospered under the system; the practice of *devshirme*, which will be discussed in Chapter 2, violated principles of dhimmitude; see Ye'or, *Decline of Eastern Christianity*, 76–77.

68. Salutati projects a very different attitude toward the Turks in a letter of 1397, which will be discussed in Chapter 2.

69. For further reading on Poggio, see Ernst Walser, *Poggius Florentinus Leben und Werke* (Berlin: B. G. Teubner, 1914); Phyllis Walter Goodhart Gordan, *Two Renaissance Book Hunters: The Letters of Poggius Bracciolini to Nicolaus de Niccolis* (New York: Columbia University Press, 1974); George Holmes, *The Florentine Enlightenment* (Oxford: Clarendon Press, 1969).

70. For further information on Hunyadi, see Joseph Held, *Hunyadi: Legend and Reality* (Boulder, Colo.: East European Monographs, 1985).

71. Riley-Smith, *Crusades*, 234.

72. Fine, *Late Medieval Balkans*, 548–50; Setton, *Papacy and the Levant*, 2:67–107; Imber, *Ottoman Empire*, 122–36; Housley, *Later Crusades*, 83–89; Itzkowitz, *Ottoman Empire*, 22–24; Inalcik, *Ottoman Empire*, 19–21; Held, *Hunyadi*, 91–112; Oscar Halecki, *From Florence to Brest (1439–1596)* (Rome: Sacrum Poloniae Millenium, 1958), 66–76.

73. Setton, *Papacy and the Levant*, 2:91.

74. John M. McManamon, S.J., *Funeral Oratory and the Cultural Ideals of Italian Humanism* (Chapel Hill: University of North Carolina Press, 1989), 2.

75. "Fuere quondam infiniti paene martyres, qui fidei Salvatoris nostri suo sanguine testimonium attulerunt. Sed culpa temporum iam multis saeculis cessavit id sanctitatis genus, ut iam desuetum esset sanguinem quemque velle suum pro Christi fide profundere. At hic vir egregius iam oblitteratam consuetudinem reno-

vavit" (Poggio Bracciolini, "Oratio in funere reverendissimi Cardinalis D. Iuliani de Caesarinis Romani," in *Spicilegium Romanum*, vol. 10, ed. Angelo Mai [Rome: Typis Collegii Urbani, 1844], 381, 375).

76. "Quid enim gloriosius esse potest quam bellum suscipere adversus hostes fidei pro fidelium defensione?" (Poggio Bracciolini, *Lettere*, vol. 3, ed. Helene Harth [Florence: Leo S. Olschki Editore, 1984], 66).

77. On the concept of engaged representations, see Greenblatt, *Marvelous Possessions*, 12–13.

78. Bracciolini, *Lettere*, 3:67. This and other humanist accusations of Satanism will be discussed in Chapter 4.

79. Bracciolini, "Oratio," 375. See Chapter 2 for a full discussion of the popular humanist practice of describing the Turks as barbarians.

80. Both notions will be discussed at length in the following chapter.

81. "cum antiquorum ducum atque imperatorum, quos prisci scriptores commendant, virtutibus et rebus gestis debeant comparari" (Bracciolini, *Lettere*, 3:66).

82. Denys Hay, "Flavio Biondo and the Middle Ages," *Proceedings of the British Academy* 45 (1959): 106–7. The *Decades* were very influential in the study of the Middle Ages, but they were cumbersome and lengthy. Aeneas Silvius Piccolomini prepared an epitome, or an abridged version, of them. See Cochrane, *Historians and Historiography*, 37.

83. On the genre of deliberative rhetoric, see Kennedy, *Classical Rhetoric*, 7–8, 228, 237. On the rhetoric of crusade orations, see Heath, *Crusading Commonplaces*, 10–11, and passim; see also Hankins, *Renaissance Crusaders*, 116.

84. Flavio Biondo, *Scritti inediti e rari di Biondo Flavio (Studi e Testi*, vol. 48), ed. Bartolomeo Nogara (Rome: Tipografia Poliglotta Vaticana, 1927), cxxxiv–cxxxv.

85. "Sic nostri postea Christiani per tempora Urbani secundi pontificis Romani, ducibus Hugone Magno regis Franciae germano, Gottifredo Boliono et Boemundo Roberti Guiscardi filio illius qui tuum Italicense regnum primus instituit: sic plerique postea alii, quos non est huius temporis et voluminis referre, Bosporo transmisso, de infidelibus triumpharunt" (ibid., 46).

86. Ibid., 64.

87. See Chapter 2 for a fuller discussion of Manetti and this oration.

88. Manetti seems to be referring to King Louis of France, who went on the Second Crusade, called by Pope Eugenius III in 1444.

89. "Si Joannes Heraclio, si Gelasius Godefrido pro recuperatione terre sancte, si rursus Eugenius Lodovico pro subsidio constantinopolis obsesse devotos crucis sancte caracteres reiectis iuris apicibus ut scriptum est liberaliter ac magnifice concessere profecto tu Caliste optime Alfonso regi pariter quin immo liberalius ac magnificentius idem sacro sancte crucis signum iure concedere posse videris, cum non recuperatione terre sancte ut predicti Heraclius et Godifredus non pro constantinopolis opitulatione ut commemoratus Ludovicus adversus turcos moveret. Sed recte pro cristiane fidei defensione . . ." (Giannozzo Manetti, *Oratio ad Calixtum summum pontificem*, Biblioteca Laurenziana, Florence, San Marco 456, fol. 59r).

90. Ernst Curtius, *European Literature and the Latin Middle Ages*, tr. Willard R. Trask (1953; repr., with afterword by Peter Godman, Princeton, N.J.: Princeton University Press, 1990), 70.

91. Aeneas Silvius Piccolomini also spoke of Pope Urban II and Godfrey of Bouillon in an oration to Pope Nicholas V on behalf of the Holy Roman Emperor Frederick III (1452). See Black, *Benedetto Accolti*, 239.

92. Black, *Benedetto Accolti*, x–xi, 259–60; on Florence's support of crusade, see ibid., chap. 9.

93. Printed in *Recueil des historiens des croisades (historiens occidentaux)*, tom. 5, part 2 (Paris: Imprimerie Nationale, 1895).

94. Black, *Benedetto Accolti*, 269.

95. "[the first crusaders] quorum si extaret memoria, si virtus eorum, laus, nomen per ora hominum volitaret et saepe in libris legeretur, plurimi forsan cupidine laudis vel pudore adducti, vel ob spem celestis felicitatis ad eamdem virtutem excitarentur delerentque communem labem, nostra etate maxime auctam, quod scilicet hostes Christi religionis non modo sepulchrum eius tenent sed longe ac late suum imperium extenderunt" (Latin and English tr., Black, *Benedetto Accolti*, 237; Accolti, *De bello a christianis*, 530).

96. "Nil acerbius fuit bonis omnibus quam capi ab his Iudeam provinciam, templa locaque omnia profanari per que versatus Christus fuerat, in quibus fecit prodigia maxima, verbis edocuit veritatem. . . . Auxit quoque indignitatem rei barbarorum sevitia, per quos in ea provincia christianum genus pene ad internitionem est redactum, ita omnis crudelitatis, libidinis et inhumane superbie in eiusmodi homines editum et exemplum" (Latin and English tr., Black, *Benedetto Accolti*, 265–66; Accolti, *De bello a christianis*, 533).

97. Black, *Benedetto Accolti*, 266.

98. "Christi hostes continuo in illum blasfemias evocarunt, eiusdem cultores immani sevitia persecuntur, sacras suas hedes et sacrorum omnium evertunt, vel, quod deterius est, pro deo in illis nefandos ac scelestos demones venerantur qui, pecudum more ducentes vitam, nullam unquam virtutem inter vitia discrimen habuerint" (Latin and English tr. Black, *Benedetto Accolti*, 263).

99. Black, *Benedetto Accolti*, 267; Accolti, *De bello a christianis*, 536–37.

100. Elements in the above passage, as in Urban's sermon, may also be traced to popular medieval legends about Islam. These legends will be discussed in Chapter 4 below. See Daniel, *Islam and the West*.

101. Black, *Benedetto Accolti*, 299. Robert of St. Remy's work is entitled *Historia hierosolymitana*; Sanuto's is *Liber secretorum fidelium crucis*.

102. Black, *Benedetto Accolti*, 302.

103. Ibid., 299.

104. W. R. Jones, "The Image of the Barbarian in Medieval Europe," *Comparative Studies in Society and History* 13 (1971): 392.

105. Ibid., 395. The anonymous author of the *Gesta francorum* does occasionally refer to Muslims as "barbarians."

106. Black, *Benedetto Accolti*, 306.

107. As Black argues, Accolti did not view history as a discipline distinct from rhetoric; see ibid., 292.

108. Petrarch, "On His Own Ignorance and That of Many Others," tr. Hans Nachod, in *The Renaissance Philosophy of Man*, ed. Ernst Cassirer et al. (Chicago: University of Chicago Press, 1971), 103. On humanist rhetoric and oratory, see Gray, "Renaissance Humanism," 199–216, especially 203.

109. See Chapter 2 for a fuller discussion of the significance of the term *barbarus* and its uses among humanists; see also Chapter 4 for discussion of Accolti's *De bello* and the concept of barbarism vs. civilization within a religious context.

110. Black, *Benedetto Accolti*, 263.

111. Cochrane, *Historians and Historiography*, 27.

112. Franco Cardini, "Risuona ancora per l'Europa l'olifante," in *Studi sulla storia*, ed. Cardini, 220–21; see also Daniela Delcorno Branca, *Il romanzo cavalleresco medievale* (Florence: G. C. Sansoni, 1974).

113. Gloria Allaire, *Andrea Barberino and the Language of Chivalry* (Gainesville: University Press of Florida, 1997), 1.

114. Branca, *Romanzo cavalleresco*, 14.

115. Tullia d'Aragona wrote a version of Guerrino il Meschino in the sixteenth century. Thanks to Julia Hairston for this reference.

116. Allaire, *Andrea Barberino*, 1–4, 6. For more on geographical portrayals of the East in chivalric literature, see Reto R. Bezzola, "L'Oriente nel poema cavalleresco del primo Rinascimento," in *Venezia e l'Oriente fra tardo medioevo e rinascimento*, ed. Agostino Pertusi (Venice: G. C. Sansoni, 1966), 495–510.

117. Gerardo C. A. Ciarambino, *Carlomagno, Gano e Orlando in alcuni romanzi italiani del XIV e XV secolo* (Pisa: Giardini Editori e Stampatori, 1976), 40, 48.

118. This work is currently being edited by Gloria Allaire; see her "Portrayal of Muslims in Andrea da Barberino's *Guerrino il Meschino*," in *Medieval Christian Perceptions of Islam*, ed. Tolan, 243–69.

119. Allaire, "Portrayal of Muslims," 259–60.

120. Ciarambino, *Carlomagno*, 60–62.

121. Ibid., 63.

122. See the introduction to the *Song of Roland*, tr. Burgess, 9.

123. See Robert Harrison, introduction to *Song of Roland*, tr. Robert Harrison (New York: Mentor, 1970), 8–10.

124. Version of Robert of Rheims, in Peters, *First Crusade*, 27. "Pagans" here may also be a reference to Charlemagne's campaigns against the Saxons.

125. Giovanni Villani, *Nuova Cronica*, ed. Giuseppe Porta (Parma: Fondazione Pietro Bembo, 1990), 1:128 (bk. 3, chap. 13).

126. George of Trebizond referred to the legend of Charlemagne's exploits in Spain in a letter to Alfonso of Aragon (1442). He appeals to Alfonso to follow the example of the Frankish king, who centuries earlier saved Europe from the *Africani*. See Monfasani, *George of Trebizond*, 50–52; George of Trebizond, *Collectanea Trapezuntiana: Texts, Documents, and Bibliographies of George of Trebizond*, ed. John Monfasani (Binghamton, N.Y.: Medieval and Renaissance Texts and Studies, 1984), 429.

127. See Margery Ganz, "The Humanist as Citizen: Donato di Neri Acciaiuoli, 1428–1473" (Ph.D. thesis, Syracuse University, 1979). See also Lauro Martines,

The Social World of Florentine Humanists 1390–1460 (Princeton, N.J.: Princeton University Press, 1963), 348–49; Field, *Origins of the Platonic Academy*, 60–62; Eugenio Garin, *Portraits from the Quattrocento*, tr. Victor A. and Elizabeth Velen (New York: Harper and Row, 1972). On the Acciaiuoli family in Greece, see Curzio Ugurgieri della Berardenga, *Gli Acciaiuoli di Firenze nella luce del loro tempo (1160–1834)* (Florence: Leo S. Olschki Editore, 1962), 1:chap. 9. Many of Donato's letters may be found in the Biblioteca Nazionale Centrale, Firenze, Magliabecchiano VIII, 1390; see Ganz, op. cit., for references to his works and letters.

128. Black, *Benedetto Accolti*, x.

129. Yet, Donato freely questioned other legends, such as the involvement of Roland in the Spanish campaign. See J. Monfrin, "La figure de Charlemagne dans l'historiographie du xvᵉ siècle," *Annuaire du bulletin de la Société de l'Histoire de France* (1964–65): 75.

130. Ugurgieri della Berardenga, *Gli Acciaioli*, 2:553.

131. "Cum vero ea tempestate barbarae gentes, quae nostrae religioni perpetuum bellum indixerant, Hispaniam gravi servitute oppressam tenerent, Carolus rei indignitate commotus, ad eam liberandam mentem convertit" (Donato Acciaiuoli, *La Vita Caroli di Donato Acciaiuoli*, ed. Daniela Gatti [Bologna: Pàtron Editore, 1981], 109).

132. *Two Lives of Charlemagne*, ed. and tr. Lewis Thorpe (Middlesex: Penguin Books, 1969), 64–65 (bk. 2, chap. 9).

133. "Sic igitur Hispania pene omnis in Francorum potestatem devenit. Victis praecipue imperatum ut falsis relictis diis Christianae fidei legem acciperent a Carolo . . ." (Acciaiuoli, *Vita Caroli*, 110).

134. *Song of Roland*, 32, 146; *laisses* 8, 272.

135. Acciaiuoli, *Vita Caroli*, 72.

136. A member of the patrician class, an active statesman, and a longtime proponent of war against the Turks, Giustiniani also seized opportunities to recruit support for a crusade on diplomatic missions to Germany and Rome. See Patricia Labalme, *Bernardo Giustiniani: A Venetian of the Quattrocento* (Rome: Edizioni di Storia e Letteratura, 1969), 139–41, 160–67, 180. For a brief biographical sketch of Giustiniani, see Margaret L. King, *Venetian Humanism in an Age of Patrician Dominance* (Princeton, N.J.: Princeton University Press, 1986), 381–83.

137. See Villani, *Nuova Cronica*, 1:143–52; Leonardo Bruni, *Historiarum florentini populi*, ed. Emilio Santini and Carmina di Pierro, in *Rerum Italicarum Scriptores*, vol. 19, part 3, no. 1–3:24; English translation available in *History of the Florentine People*, ed. and tr. James Hankins (Cambridge, Mass.: I Tatti Renaissance Library, 2001), 94, 96; Acciaiuoli, *Vita Caroli*, 61, 63. Acciaiuoli also credits Charlemagne with the building of temples in the city; this may be a reference to Santi Apostoli, perhaps the oldest standing church in Florence, which was connected to the Acciaiuoli family and names Charlemagne as its donor.

138. Acciaiuoli, *Vita Caroli*, 117.

139. Monfrin, "Figure de Charlemagne," 71.

140. The impetus for such a long fund-raising trip may have come from the local clergy's meeting with Frankish envoys who passed through Jerusalem on their

way to Harun al-Rashid's court in 797. See Steven Runciman, "Charlemagne and Palestine," *English Historical Review* 50 (1935): 608–9.

141. Jules Coulet, *Etudes sur l'ancien poème français du voyage de Charlemagne in Orient* (Montpellier: Coulet et Fils Editeurs, 1907), 74–75.

142. Charlemagne may have been seeking an alliance with Harun al-Rashid as a counterweight to Byzantium, which was an obstacle to the emperor's claims in Italy and to his title as Roman emperor. The caliph stood to gain from having a partner on the borders of his political rivals in Spain, the Umayyads. See Runciman, "Charlemagne and Palestine," 608.

143. Runciman, "Charlemagne and Palestine," 612–15; Acciaiuoli, *Vita Caroli*, 69 n. 95. See also Francisque Michel, *Charlemagne: An Anglo-Norman Poem of the Twelfth Century* (London: William Pickering, 1836), xiii.

144. The Annals of Lorsch, which do not exhibit Einhard's tendency to inflate Charlemagne's deeds, mention no such protectorate. The Annals, however, were not well read. See *Two Lives of Charlemagne*, 70 (bk. 2, chap. 16); Runciman, "Charlemagne and Palestine," 611–12.

145. Michel, *Charlemagne*, xiv.

146. The earliest account physically placing Charlemagne in the East was written by a monk named Benedetto (c. 1000). It describes Charlemagne's visit to Jerusalem and the Byzantine court, whence he brought back relics that he donated to Benedetto's monastery Sant'Andrea del Soratte. See Acciaiuoli, *Vita Caroli*, 70–71; Coulet, *Etudes sur l'ancien poème*, chap. 2.

147. A claim made by a certain "Primat" from the abbey of Saint Denis in his thirteenth-century French translation of *The Chronicles of St. Denis*, a compilation of Latin chronicles, biographies, and hagiographies. See *A Thirteenth Century Life of Charlemagne*, ed. and tr. Robert Levine (New York: Garland Publishing, 1991), vii, et infra.

148. Mayer, *Crusades*, 56.

149. "con la forza de' suoi dodici baroni, e peri di Francia chiamati paladini . . . passò oltremare a richiesta dello 'mperadore Michele di Gostantinopoli, e del patriarca di Gerusalem, e conquistò la Terrasanta e Gerusalem, chell'occupavano i Saracini, e acquistò a lo 'mperadore di Gostantinopoli tutto lo'mperio di levante quale aveano occupato i Saracini e' Turchi. E tornando in Gostantinopoli, lo imperadore Michele gli volle donare molte ricchissimi tesori, nulla volle prendere, se non il legno de la santa croce, e 'l chiovo di Cristo . . ." (Villani, *Nuova Cronica*, 1:128 [bk. 3, chap. 13].

150. *The Journey of Charlemagne*, ed. Jean-Louis G. Picherit (Birmingham: Summa Publications, 1984), iii.

151. In the Church of the Holy Sepulcher a Jew, beholding Charlemagne seated on the altar, claims that he has seen God. In another episode the Byzantine emperor overhears boasts made by the paladins, which he later forces them to fulfill—they manage to do so, with God's aid. Oliver, for example, claims that he can take the emperor's daughter no fewer than one hundred times in one night.

152. "nel petto al novo Carlo spira / la vendetta ch'a noi tardata noce, / sì che molt'anni Europa ne sospira" (Italian text and English translation: *Petrarch's*

Lyric Poems, tr. and ed. Robert M. Durling [Cambridge: Harvard University Press, 1976], 74–75).

153. Biondo discusses Charlemagne at some length and praises his deeds, but he mentions nothing about Charlemagne spending any time in the Holy Land. In fact, when Biondo discusses the Christian conquest of Jerusalem in 1099, he says that the city had been in Muslim hands for 449 years. While Biondo's calculations fall short by twelve years, his estimate certainly precludes any belief on his part that Charlemagne captured the city. See Flavio Biondo, *Historiarum ab inclinatione Romani imperii decades* (Venice, 1544), fol. 126r.

154. "Carolus magnus multo sudore primo terram illam vendicavit, deinde perditam recuperavit Gotifridus" (Piccolomini, in *Briefwechsel,* Abt. 3, 211). For more on Aeneas, Sienese humanist, diplomat, and pope (Pius II), see Chapter 2 below.

155. "addunt scriptores nonnuli [*sic*] rem maximo memoratu dignam, quam ego ut certam affirmare, quia nulla apud alios auctores eius rei mentio est, nec ut incertam relinquere ausim. Tradunt, enim, cum Hierosolima gravi barbarorum dominatu oppressa teneretur, Carolum Constantini Imperatoris praecibus evocatum, simul et rei indignitate commotum, ad liberandum sanctissimum locum, ubi omnium gentium salus est orta, cum ingenti exercitu accessisse, profligatisque barbaris, ac ex omni provincia pulsis, Christianos in urbem restituisse, firmisque praesidiis munitam reliquisse . . ." (Acciaiuoli, *Vita Caroli,* 118).

156. Acciaiuoli, *Vita Caroli,* 101.

157. George will be discussed at greater length in Chapters 3 and, especially, 4. Only briefly in this oration does George mention the Ottoman Turks as a target. Regarding this oration and George's roundabout method in dealing with the Ottoman problem, see Monfasani, *George of Trebizond,* 51–52, 129.

158. "Veniat, queso, in mentem qua ex re Carolus ille magnus ad hec usque tempora tantus fertur. Ille, inquam, Carolus, qui primus Romanorum imperium ex Grecia in Gallias transtulit, qui totius fere Europe dominus factus, Africam etiam vehementius vexavit. Undique igitur ille magnus factus est. Nonne Hierusalem liberata et Egypto ac Syria perdomita? Nam cum Arabes sanctissima illa loca occupassent, intellexit illico prudentissimus rex inde sibi non [solum regna] Christianorumque imperium sponte sua venturum, sed laudem quoque eternam, tam in terris quam etiam in celis, affuturam" (George of Trebizond, *Collectanea Trapezuntiana,* 429).

159. Verino was employed as a notary by various committees in the Florentine government, in positions he often found undignified. He also tutored children of noble families such as Giovanni de' Medici (later Pope Leo X). See Alfonso Lazzari, *Ugolino e Michele Verino: Studi biografici e critici* (Turin: Libreria Carlo Clausen, 1897), chaps. 3–4.

160. For a discussion of the *Carlias* and Verino's other works, see Lazzari, *Ugolino e Michele Verino.* A recent edition of the work is Niklaus Thurn's *Ugolino Verino: Carlias* (Munich: Wilhelm Fink Verlag, 1995). Thurn argues for the earlier date of composition cited above, see ibid., 16; Lazzari dates the work between 1486 and 1487.

161. Lazzari, *Ugolino e Michele Verino*, 154; J. B. Hainsworth, *The Idea of Epic* (Berkeley: University of California Press, 1991), 92.

162. Lazzari, *Ugolino e Michele Verino*, 100.

163. Biblioteca Riccardiana, Florence, Riccardiano 838, fol. 13v (hereafter referred to as "Ricc. 838"). See Chapter 4 for a fuller discussion of humanist examples of religious polemic.

164. A mountain range in the most northern part of Scythia.

165. "Nos ergo humanae miserati incommoda gentis ,/ turpe putabamus gelido pugnare subaxe; / nostraque ripheis extendere montibus arma / neglecta tellure dei quam barbarus hostis / servitio pressam longos impune per annos / foedarat christi convulsa funditus arce; / Proque sacris illic aderant presepia templis / quin etiam ipse dei caelo demissus ab alto / saepe mihi occurens haec bella capessere iussit / interpres raphael cum nox involueret umbra / tellurem tum saepe dei sum voce monentis / visus in arma rapi; cessas nostra opida cessas / extorquere feris tandem subrepta tyrannis" (Ricc. 838, fol. 13v–14r).

166. Lazzari, *Ugolino e Michele Verino*, 159–60.

167. Ugolino Verino, *Panegyricon ad Ferdinandum regem et Isabellam reginam hispaniarum de saracenae baetidos gloriosa expugnatione*, ed. Joseph Fogel and Ladislaus Juhasz (Leipzig: Teubner, 1933).

168. Louis XI may have encouraged Verino to write the work; Charles VIII's near worship of Charlemagne was well known, as can be seen in his orders that the canonized Charlemagne's feast day be duly celebrated. See Lazzari, *Ugolino e Michele Verino*, 154.

169. Labalme, *Bernardo Giustiniani*, 162; Housley, *Later Crusades*, 390.

170. For a discussion of the Second Charlemagne prophecy, see Bernard McGinn, *Visions of the End: Apocalyptic Traditions of the Middle Ages* (New York: Columbia University Press, 1979), 172, 247–48, 278, 250. See also Marjorie Reeves, *The Influence of Prophecy in the Later Middle Ages* (Oxford: Clarendon Press, 1969), 301–2, 320–31; Richard Emmerson, *Antichrist in the Middle Ages* (Seattle: University of Washington Press, 1981), 68–69.

171. See Donald Weinstein, *Savonarola and Florence* (Princeton, N.J.: Princeton University Press, 1970), 166, 113; Reeves, *Influence of Prophecy*, 324–29.

172. For the dissemination of the prophecy in fourteenth-century France, see Reeves, *Influence of Prophecy*, 320–21. For the relevant section of Christine de Pizan's *Ditié de Jehanne d'Arc* (1429), see Housley, *Documents on the Later Crusades*, 132–33. On Dubois's tract, see Housley, *Later Crusades*, 26.

173. "Idque potissimum tibi Rex Carole destinavi, non solum quia nomen et genus ab illo deducis. Verum mores et facta emularis. Ut te speremus auctore hierosolimam rursus cum omni regione depulso immo sublato maumetti foetore indui sacrosanctam christi veritatem augustalemque iterum dignitatem" (Ricc. 838, fol. 1r).

174. See Marcia B. Hall, "Savonarola's Preaching and the Patronage of Art," in *Christianity and the Renaissance: Image and Religious Imagination in the Quattrocento*, ed. Timothy Verdon and John Henderson (Syracuse, N.Y.: Syracuse University Press, 1990), 497–99.

175. See Weinstein, *Savonarola and Florence*, for details on Savonarola's rise and fall.

176. Ibid., 100, 239; see also Garin, *Portraits of the Quattrocento*, 224, 226.

177. Weinstein, *Savonarola and Florence*, 166–67.

178. It has also been suggested that, from the late fourteenth century on, some Florentines consciously portrayed Charlemagne as the city's founder so as to link their hometown to the Second Charlemagne's glorious coming. See Weinstein, *Savonarola and Florence*, 39. Verino describes Charlemagne as Florence's second founder in his *De illustratione urbis florentiae: Libri tres* (Florence, 1636), 11.

179. Lazzari, *Ugolino e Michele Verino*, 164–66; Monfrin, "Figure de Charlemagne," 77–78. According to Marjorie Reeves, another late quattrocento humanist who may have drawn on the Second Charlemagne prophecy was the Byzantine Michael Tarcaniota Marullus; see Reeves, *Influence of Prophecy*, 355. See also *Michaelis Marulli Carmina*, ed. Alessandro Perosa (Turici: Societas Thesauri Mundi, 1951), 98–100.

180. It is not known whether Ficino actually delivered the oration; see Weinstein, *Savonarola and Florence*, 187.

181. Eschatological approaches to the crusade and the Turks will be discussed at length in Chapter 4.

182. Norman Daniel focuses on the negative aspects of this continuity; see his *Islam and the West*, 306–8.

Chapter 2

1. See Gouwens, "Perceiving the Past." One of the most avid collectors of the fifteenth century was Niccolò Niccoli, who amassed a great library of classical texts as well as ancient medals and sculptures. See Vespasiano da Bisticci's life of Niccoli in *Le Vite*, ed. Aulo Greco (Florence: Istituto Nazionale di Studi sul Rinascimento, 1970).

2. Petrarch, Letter 24.3 in *Letters on Familiar Matters*, vol. 3, tr. Aldo S. Bernardo (Baltimore: Johns Hopkins University Press, 1985). Machiavelli, letter to Vettori (10 December 1513) in *Letters of Machiavelli*, ed. and tr. Allan Gilbert (Chicago: University of Chicago Press, 1961), 139–44. For more on this letter and Machiavelli's relationship to humanism, see John M. Najemy, *Between Friends: Discourses of Power and Desire in the Machiavelli-Vettori Letters of 1513–1515* (Princeton, N.J.: Princeton University Press, 1993).

3. Gouwens, "Perceiving the Past," 80.

4. Quillen, *Rereading the Renaissance*, 133; Hankins, *Plato in the Italian Renaissance*, 1:23–25; Grafton, *Defenders of the Text*, 25–37.

5. It should be noted that Burckhardt, despite his grand claims for the Renaissance as a cultural efflorescence heralding the modern period, saw neither humanism nor the classical revival as crucial to the Renaissance; humanism, he argued, was more a product than a cause of the Renaissance. See Jacob Burckhardt,

The Civilization of the Renaissance in Italy, tr. S. G. C. Middlemore (New York: Modern Library, 1954), 201; Schiffman, *Humanism and the Renaissance*, 2. Hankins too has commented on the connection between classical, if not necessarily secular, ideals and Europe's growing sense of itself as a "civilized" culture with a mission to oppose barbarism; see his "Renaissance Crusaders," 145–46.

6. The role of Greek perceptions and rhetoric regarding the Turks will be further explored in the following chapter.

7. A few scholars have noted the influence of the classics in humanist approaches to the Turks. See Hankins, "Renaissance Crusaders"; Black, *Benedetto Accolti*, 237; Schwoebel, *Shadow of the Crescent*, 147–48.

8. See Daniel, *Islam and the West*, 306–7.

9. Anthony Grafton, April Shelford, and Nancy Siraisi, *New Worlds, Ancient Texts: The Power of Tradition and the Shock of Discovery* (Cambridge, Mass.: Belknap Press, 1992), 6. See the Epilogue below for further discussion of this topic.

10. Paul Cartledge, *The Greeks: A Portrait of Self and Others* (Oxford: Oxford University Press, 1993), 37–38. The following discussion will focus on texts; for further reading on Greek views of cultural and social outsiders as depicted in art, see Beth Cohen, ed., *Not the Classical Ideal: Athens and the Construction of the Other in Greek Art* (Leiden: Brill, 2003).

11. Edith Hall, *Inventing the Barbarian* (Oxford: Clarendon Press, 1989), 9; Cartledge, *Greeks*, 39.

12. Cartledge, *Greeks*, 39.

13. Aeschylus has the Persians refer to themselves as "barbarians" on several occasions, among them lines 187 and 255.

14. Hall, *Inventing the Barbarian*, 79–81.

15. Dionysos comes to punish his aunts (i.e., the royal family) for their abuse of his mother. He accomplishes this by stirring the king's mother, her sisters, and all the women of Thebes into a frenzy of orgiastic raving that culminates in the murder of the young king at his mother's hand, suggesting the primal excesses associated with the barbarian East. See Hall, *Inventing the Barbarian*, 151–54; Said, *Orientalism*, 56–57.

16. Euripides also seems critical of blind cultural chauvinism in his caricature of Dionysos's truculent antagonist King Pentheus, who aggressively opines, "Asians aren't Greeks—what do they know?" See Euripides, *Bakkhai*, tr. Robert Bagg (Amherst: University of Massachusetts Press, 1978), 35, line 661. Moreover, several characters of barbarian ethnicity in Euripides' other plays embody "Greek" virtues such as courage or restraint, making it difficult to discern his opinion of the barbarian; see Hall, *Inventing the Barbarian*, 211–13, 221.

17. Hall, *Inventing the Barbarian*, 1.

18. Charles Rowan Beye, *Ancient Greek Literature and Society*, 2d. ed. (Ithaca, N.Y.: Cornell University Press, 1987), 127.

19. Josiah Ober and Barry Strauss, "Drama, Political Rhetoric, and the Discourse of Athenian Democracy," in *Nothing to do with Dionysos?: Athenian Drama in Its Social Context*, ed. John J. Winkler and Froma Zeitlin (Princeton, N.J.: Princeton University Press, 1989), 237–70, especially 239.

20. Cartledge, *Greeks*, 59.

21. Herodotus, *The Histories*, tr. Aubrey de Sélincourt, ed. A. R. Burn (London: Penguin Books, 1972), bk. 4, particularly 271–98.

22. On his condemnation of despotic tyranny, particularly among the Persians, see Cartledge, *Greeks*, 61. On the rhetoric of Self and Other, see François Hartog, *The Mirror of Herodotus*, tr. Janet Lloyd (Berkeley: University of California Press, 1988).

23. Arnaldo Momigliano, "The Place of Herodotus in the History of Historiography," in *Studies in Historiography*, ed. A. Momigliano (London: Weidenfeld and Nicolson, 1966), 133, 138–39.

24. This idea springs from a notion of "the natural slave," which he qualifies by saying, "there are some [i.e., the barbarians] who are everywhere and inherently slaves, and others [i.e., the Greeks] who are everywhere and inherently free"; see Aristotle, *The Politics*, ed. and tr. Ernest Barker (London: Oxford University Press, 1970), 16.

25. Cartledge, *Greeks*, 40.

26. Arno Borst, *Medieval Worlds: Barbarians, Heretics and Artists in the Middle Ages* (Chicago: University of Chicago Press, 1992), 4–5.

27. F. W. Wallbank, *The Hellenistic World* (Cambridge: Harvard University Press, 1981), 64–66, 78; see also Arnaldo Momigliano, *Alien Wisdom: The Limits of Hellenization* (Cambridge: Cambridge University Press, 1975). More-recent research has demonstrated that the Greeks and the Macedonians relied, often heavily, on local infrastructures and learning. See the collection of essays edited by Amelie Kuhrt and Susan Sherwin-White in *Hellenism in the East* (Berkeley: University of California Press, 1987). These findings, however, do not invalidate Momigliano's arguments about the closed nature of Greek cultural perceptions of superiority and a lack of interest in learning other peoples' languages.

28. Borst, *Medieval Worlds*, 5.

29. Ibid., 4–5.

30. Tenney Frank, "Race Mixture in the Roman Empire," in *The Fall of Rome*, ed. Mortimer Chambers (New York: Holt, Rinehart and Winston, 1963), 49. Juvenal's *Satire* 3 also points, albeit cynically, to the high proportion of Greeks and Syrians in Rome.

31. Erich S. Gruen, *Culture and National Identity in Republican Rome* (Ithaca, N.Y.: Cornell University Press, 1992), 52, 80–83.

32. A. N. Sherwin-White, *Racial Prejudice in Imperial Rome* (Cambridge: Cambridge University Press, 1967), 73–74, 101.

33. See Cicero's oration *Pro Flacco* in *Cicero in Twenty-eight Volumes*, ed. and tr. C. Macdonald (Cambridge: Harvard University Press, 1976), 10:450–54.

34. Sherwin-White, *Racial Prejudice*, 60–61, 74.

35. Momigliano, *Alien Wisdom*, 71–72.

36. Sherwin-White, *Racial Prejudice*, 13–20.

37. Cicero, *The Speeches*, ed. and tr. N. H. Watts (Cambridge: Harvard University Press, 1958), 312–13, 328–29, 334–39.

38. Ibid., 340–41.

39. Cicero never seriously returned to the subject of the Gauls in later works. See Momigliano, *Alien Wisdom*, 71. Cicero's goal in this work was the same as in

Pro Flacco: to defend a Roman against foreign accusers. Hence he resorts to cultural stereotypes in each work.

40. Bernard Sheehan describes a similar shift in English attitudes toward the Indians of Virginia, who were initially depicted as "noble savages" and later as ignoble, even Satanic, savages when they began resisting territorial encroachment; see Sheehan, *Savagism and Civility*.

41. Gerhart B. Ladner, "On Roman Attitudes toward Barbarians in Late Antiquity," *Viator* 7 (1976): 21. Thanks to Vicki Szabo for this reference.

42. Sherwin-White, *Racial Prejudice*, 3–12.

43. J. P. V. D. Balsdon, *Romans and Aliens* (London: Duckworth and Co., 1979), 59–60.

44. See Victor Davis Hanson, *The Western Way of War* (New York: Alfred A. Knopf, 1989), 15–16.

45. Balsdon, *Romans and Aliens*, 61–62.

46. Tacitus, *The Complete Works of Tacitus*, ed. Moses Hadas (New York: The Modern Library, 1942), 716.

47. Tacitus's positive views of the Britons as freedom fighters may be complicated by his own ambivalence about Rome and its rulers, particularly his resentment of Domitian's cruel and arbitrary rule. See Ronald Martin, *Tacitus* (London: Batsford Academic and Educational Ltd., 1981), 39–49. On the ethnographic intent of the *Germania*, see ibid., 49–50. See also Sherwin-White, *Racial Prejudice*, 24.

48. Ammianus Marcellinus, *The Histories*, ed. and tr. John Rolfe (Cambridge: Harvard University Press, 1964), 3:380–95 (bk. 31, 2).

49. Ibid., 1:27 (bk. 14, 4).

50. See Alan Cameron, *Claudian: Poetry and Propaganda at the Court of Honorius* (Oxford: Clarendon Press, 1970), chap. 7.

51. Momigliano, *Alien Wisdom*, 8, 16–19, 149, 7.

52. Jerry H. Bentley, *Old World Encounters* (New York: Oxford University Press, 1993), 59–60.

53. Cf. Borst, *Medieval Worlds*, 5.

54. George Boas, *Essays on Primitivism and Related Ideas in the Middle Ages* (Baltimore: Johns Hopkins University Press, 1948), 132.

55. Ibid., 136.

56. Letter to Principia (127.12); see Saint Jerome, *Selected Letters*, ed. and tr. F. A. Wright (London: William Heinemann, 1933), 462–63.

57. Walter Goffart, *Barbarians and Romans A.D. 418–584: The Techniques of Accommodation* (Princeton, N.J.: Princeton University Press, 1980), 34–35.

58. What follows is a brief discussion of Petrarch's use of classical motifs. For a fuller treatment of this topic and related issues, see my article "Petrarch's Vision."

59. "Siamo con ciò nell'ambito d'uno scontro fra 'civiltà' e 'barbarie' che non è più tanto né più solo quello fra Cristianità ed Islam, ma ch'è piuttosto quello, erodoteo, fra Europa ed Asia." See Cardini, "La crociata mito politico." For a discussion of medieval references in this poem, see Chapter 1 above.

60. Italian and English translation: Petrarch's *Lyric Poems*, ed. and tr. Durling, 80–81.

61. "la vendetta ch' a noi tardata noce / sì che molt'anni Europa ne sospira"; "popolo infelice d'oriente" (ibid., 74–75, 80–81).

62. "sempre in ghiaccio et in gelate nevi, / tutta lontana dal camin del sole"; "Turchi Arabi et Caldei . . . popolo ignudo, paventoso et lento, / che ferro mai non strigne, / ma tutt' i colpi suoi commette al vento" (ibid., 76–77).

63. See Balsdon, *Romans and Aliens*, 1; Hanson, *Western Way of War*, 15–16. Incidentally, William of Malmesbury launches a similar attack on Eastern archery; see Munro, "Western Attitude," 334.

64. On Petrarch's ambivalence toward the Germans in this poem, see Petrarch, *Canzoniere or Rerum vulgarium fragmenta*, ed. Mark Musa (Bloomington: University of Indiana Press, 1996), 539 nn. 47–50; Mazzotta discusses the deliberate inconsistencies of poem 28 in his *Worlds of Petrarch*, 129–34. See also Petrarch's "Italia mia" for harsh views of northern Europeans.

65. *Petrarch's Lyric Poems*, ed. and tr. Durling, 78–79.

66. "dic pater, libet equidem percuntari: si hodie Iulius Cesar ab inferis remearet animum illum potentiamque suam referens, et Rome, hoc est in patria sua vivens, ut hauddubie faceret, Cristi nomen agnosceret, diutius ne passurum credimus, quod egiptius latro . . . non dicam Ierosolimam et Iudeam et Syriam, sed ipsam Egiptum atque Alexandriam possideret . . ?" (Petrarch, *Vita solitaria*, 240; English tr., *Life of Solitude*, 246).

67. Apart from Julius Caesar, one might consider Petrarch's adoption of Cicero as an honorary Christian in letter 21.10 in Petrarch, *Letters on Familiar Matters*, 21:10.

68. "Non quero quam id iuste egerit, sed animi vim et acrimoniam illam miror ac necessariam temporibus nostris dico" (Petrarch, *Vita solitaria*, 240; English tr., *Life of Solitude*, 246).

69. See Augustine's *Confessions* 1:13.

70. "puto nullum ibi reperies qui literas nostras norit aut diligat, nisi peregrinus forte vel mercator vel captivus sit" (Petrarch, *Vita solitaria*, 234, 236; English tr., *Life of Solitude*, 243).

71. "But why say more? I shall scarcely be persuaded that anything good can come from Arabia" (Petrarch, *Letters of Old Age*, tr. Aldo S. Bernardo et al. (Baltimore: Johns Hopkins University Press, 1992), 2:472.

72. Petrarch, *Vita solitaria*, 236; *Life of Solitude*, 243.

73. Petrarch had a much stronger sense of northern Europeans as barbarians, as seen in his "Italia mia"; Denys Hay discusses this as well as views of other Italians in "Italy and Barbarian Europe," in *Italian Renaissance Studies: A Tribute to the Late Cecilia M. Ady*, ed. E. F. Jacob (London: Faber and Faber, 1960), 48–68. A more balanced discussion of barbarism is presented by Francesco Tateo, who argues that Italians perceived themselves as caught between Eastern and Western barbarians, thereby giving weight to the humanist rhetoric of the Turkish advance; see Tateo, "Gli stereotipi letterari," in *Europa e Mediterraneo tra medioevo e prima età moderna l'osservatorio italiano*, ed. Sergio Gensini (Commune San Miniato: Pacini Editore, 1992), 26–32.

74. Petrarch, letters 12.1, 23.2, in *Letters on Familiar Matters* and in *Letters of Old Age*, letters 7.1 and 9.1.

75. See Bisaha, "Petrarch's Vision," 298, 301–3, 313. Petrarch's views on Byzantium are also discussed in my article and below in Chapter 3.

76. See Berthold L. Ullman, *The Humanism of Coluccio Salutati* (Padua: Editrice Antenore, 1963); Ronald Witt, *Hercules at the Crossroads: The Life, Works and Thought of Coluccio Salutati* (Durham, N.C.: Duke University Press, 1983).

77. Baron, *Crisis of the Early Italian Renaissance*; see also Witt, *Hercules at the Crossroads*; Ullman, *Humanism of Coluccio Salutati*, 26–30.

78. See Chapter 1 for Salutati's letter to King Tvrtko of Bosnia.

79. Imber, *Ottoman Empire*, 33–34, 44–47; Setton, *Papacy and the Levant*, 1:341–56; Housley, *Later Crusades*, 75–77.

80. For more information on this period, see Fine, *Late Medieval Balkans*.

81. Housley, *Later Crusades*, 77–78.

82. In this work (written in 1400) Christine relates the sorrows of a young woman whose lover was captured at the battle and remained a prisoner of the Turks. Thanks to Charity Cannon Willard for this reference.

83. Fellow humanist Pier Paolo Vergerio also commented on Turkish unity versus Christian disunity in 1398/99; see his *Epistolario*, ed. Leonardo Smith (Rome: Tipografia del Senato, 1934), 230 (letter 89).

84. On humanist letter writing, see Cecil H. Clough, "The Cult of Antiquity: Letters and Letter Collections," in *Cultural Aspects of the Italian Renaissance: Essays in Honor of Paul Oskar Kristeller*, ed. Cecil H. Clough (Manchester: Manchester University Press, 1976), 33–67; Najemy, *Between Friends*, 30–42; Hankins, "Renaissance Crusaders," 116. Salutati hoped that this particular letter would be circulated among the other princes attending the Diet. The letter became quite well known; even Charles VI of France refers to it in a missive to Florence in 1399. See Ullman, *Humanism of Coluccio Salutati*, 79–80; Coluccio Salutati, *Epistolario di Coluccio Salutati*, ed. Francesco Novati (Rome: Forzani E. C. Tipografi del Senato, 1896), 3:197 n. 1.

85. Salutati warns, "do not leave yourselves exposed to the Gentiles and Saracens who are so gripped in error by their Muhammad, and are always hostile to the Christians . . ." (Nolite pati Gentilibus et Saracenis, qui tanto de suo Maumetto tenentur errore semperque Christianis infesti sunt) (Salutati, *Epistolario*, 3:207–8).

86. "Videtis Teucros; sic enim appellare potius libet quam Turchos, postquam apud Teucriam dominantur, licet fama sit ipsos a monte Caucaso descendisse" (ibid., 208). Similarly in his letter to the king of Bosnia (1389), he referred to the Turkish troops as *milia Troianorum infidelium*. See Emmert, *Serbian Golgotha*, 46; Salutati, *Epistolario*, 3:208 n. 1.; ASF *Signori Missive, Prima Cancelleria* 21, fol. 139r.

87. Medieval thinkers derived this theory from a seventh-century amalgam of chronicles attributed to a certain "Fredegarius." According to this source, after the legendary fall of Troy some refugees under "Friga" fled to Macedonia, others under "Francio" found their way to the Rhine—the French claimed ancestry from this group—and the last group under "Turchot" remained in the area. See Michael

J. Heath, "Renaissance Scholars and the Origins of the Turks," *Bibliothèque d'humanisme et renaissance* 41 (1979): 456. As a result of this legend, when Europeans first heard of the Seljuk Turks and the Ottoman Turks, some began to suppose that they were the descendants of Turchot. It became fashionable to refer to the Turks as *Teucri*, a byname for the Trojans used by Virgil and Ovid, among others. See Terence Spencer, "Turks and Trojans in the Renaissance," *Modern Language Review* 47 (1952): 331; see Virgil's *Aeneid*, bk. 1, verses 38 and 248; bk. 2, verse 252.

88. "videtis, inquam Teucros, ferocissimum genus hominum, quam alte presumant. nolite quod tango negligere. confidunt et credunt Christi nomen per universum orbem delere esseque dicunt in fatis suis ut Italiam vastent et usque civitatem divisam flumine, quam Romam interpretantur, venientes, omnia ferro igneque consument" (Salutati, *Epistolario*, 3: 208).

89. "Mirum in modum principes ipsorum gentes suas ad bella nutriunt; decem vel duodecim annorum pueros ad militiam rapiunt, venationibus et laboribus assuefaciunt atque durant, ad currendum exsiliendumque quotidiana doctrina et experientia strenuos reddunt. cibis grossissimis paneque solido, nigro, multisque permixto frugibus pascuntur; quod delicatius comedunt sudore venationis acquirunt; denique taliter instituti sunt, quod unica veste soloque pane contenti vivant. mirum in modum patientes frigoris et caloris; imbres et nives . . . sine querela suscipiunt" (ibid., 208–9).

90. Kafadar, *Between Two Worlds*, 17.

91. Itzkowitz, *Ottoman Empire*, 49–51; Inalcik, *Ottoman Empire*, 78–79. See also V. L. Menage, "Devshirme," in *Encyclopedia of Islam* (London: E. J. Brill, 1965), 2:210–13; idem., "Some Notes on the Devshirme," *Bulletin of the School of Oriental and African Studies* 29 (1966): 64–78.

92. The case of Mehmed Sokollu, who rose to the rank of grand vizier, is illustrative but exceptional in many ways. See Donia and Fine, *Bosnia and Hercegovina*, 45–48. Poggio Bracciolini reflected popular condemnation of this practice in a sermon before the battle of Varna attributed to Cesarini. Here Poggio/Cesarini laments the devshirme as a stirring battle cry for Christians. See Bracciolini, "Oratio in funere," 381. Sixteenth-century writer Teodoro Spandugino, a Greek-Italian who spent time in Greece and wrote a book about the Ottomans, noted the low age of marriage among Christian subjects as a means to evade the levy. See Theodore Spandounes, *On the Origin of the Ottoman Emperors*, ed. and tr. Donald M. Nicol (Cambridge: Cambridge University Press, 1997), 124; Schwoebel, *Shadow of the Crescent*, 210–11.

93. Apart from this one, tempting similarity to the *Germania*, there is little reason to suspect that Salutati came in contact with Tacitus before c. 1403; see Witt, *Hercules at the Crossroads*, 167. The *Germania* was probably not known in Florence until Poggio's discovery of the text in 1425. See L. D. Reynolds, ed., *Texts and Transmission: A Survey of the Latin Classics* (Oxford: Clarendon Press, 1983), 410; Robert Ulery, "Tacitus," in *Catologus Translationum et commentariorum: Medieval and Renaissance Latin Translations and Commentaries*, ed. F. E. Cranz and P. O. Kristeller (Washington, D.C.: Catholic University of America Press, 1986): 6:91–93. On Caesar and Seneca's views of the Germans and Scythians, see

George Boas and Arthur Lovejoy, *Primitivism and Related Ideas in Antiquity* (Baltimore: Johns Hopkins University Press, 1935), 362–66.

94. "Non enim usque adeo barbari sunt, quod Deum esse non credant, quod aliam esse vitam et gloriam non arbitrentur; sed certum habent fore quod pugnantes pro Domino suo vel lege sua perpetua recipiantur in gloria. quod tanto firmius credunt quanto simplicius et ineruditius vivunt" (Salutati, *Epistolario*, 3:209).

95. One should perhaps not put too much stock in this seeming praise of simplicity and ignorance, however, given Salutati's view that nature inclines an individual toward virtue but that learning must be present if one is to understand and achieve virtue. See Witt, *Hercules at the Crossroads*, 69–70.

96. "Credite michi: genus hoc hominum, quorum cum mores, vitam et instituta percipio, fortissimorum Romanorum ritum consuetudinesque recordor . . ." (Salutati, *Epistolario*, 3:209).

97. After expounding on Turkish virtues he contrasts them to Christian customs: "we Christians, however, are devoted to excess and laziness; we are zealous in luxury and appetite" (Nos autem Christiani traditi luxui et inertie, luxurie et gule intendimus . . .) (ibid., 209). Following a lengthy tirade about the pitiable state of the Church, he once again raises the specter of the Turkish menace, asking if the Schism will only be ended by internal war or an invasion of the Turks (ibid., 211).

98. Witt, *Hercules at the Crossroads*, 246–52.

99. Filelfo's *Amyris* is discussed at the end of this chapter. For *bailo* comparisons of the Turks to ancient Romans, see Lucette Valensi, *The Birth of the Despot: Venice and the Sublime Porte,* tr. Arthur Denner (Ithaca, N.Y.: Cornell University Press, 1993).

100. See Baron, *Crisis of the Early Italian Renaissance*; Paolo Viti, *Leonardo Bruni e Firenze: Studi sulle lettere pubbliche e private* (Rome: Bulzoni Editore, 1992); Gordon Griffiths, James Hankins, and David Thompson, *The Humanism of Leonardo Bruni: Selected Texts* (Binghamton, N.Y.: Medieval and Renaissance Texts and Studies, 1987); Martines, *Social World of Florentine Humanists*, 117–23, 165–76.

101. Francesco Paolo Luiso, *Studi sull'epistolario di Leonardo Bruni*, ed. Lucia Gualdo Rosa (Rome: Istituto Storico Italiano per il Medioevo, 1980), 160. On the growing importance of letter writing as a rhetorical device and Bruni's collection of his letters with an eye toward publication, see Clough, "Cult of Antiquity," 38–39.

102. "Causa vero amissionis, ut ad tuum quaesitum veniamus, illa puto, quod afflicta quondam Italia Gothorum, et Longobardorum longa invasione tanta calamitate nostros homines oppressere, ut omnino librorum, studiorumque obliviscerentur" (Leonardo Bruni, *Leonardi Bruni Arretini Epistolarum Libri VIII* [bk. 10, letter 22], ed. Lorenzo Mehus [Florence, 1741], 193).

103. "tam longa servitute vastatis, atque incensis pluribus urbibus, quasi desperatis rebus studia librique interiere" (ibid.).

104. Theodor E. Mommsen, "Petrarch's Conception of the 'Dark Ages,'" *Speculum* 17 (1942): 226–42. See also Black, "Donation of Constantine," 83–84;

Frate Guido da Pisa used this idea earlier (1330) to emphasize Dante's achievement. Black points out that some writers, such as Filippo Villani, Albrecht Dürer, Machiavelli, and Montaigne, blamed early Christian fanaticism for the destruction or decline of pagan works of literature and art; see ibid., 78–79.

105. Leonardo Bruni, "Dialogi ad Petrum Histrum," tr. David Thompson, in *The Humanism of Leonardo Bruni: Selected Texts*, ed. Gordon Griffiths et al. (Binghamton, N.Y.: Medieval and Renaissance Texts and Studies, 1987), 70.

106. Bruni presents such a vision in the context of Petrarch's achievement for restoring the elegance of ancient rhetoric after centuries of loss and degradation. See his "Life of Petrarch" in *The Three Crowns of Florence: Humanist Assessments of Dante, Petrarch, and Boccaccio*, ed. and tr. David Thompson and Alan F. Nagel (New York: Harper and Row, 1972), 76–77.

107. Bruni, *Humanism of Bruni*, ed. and tr. Griffiths et al., 183. Bruni also dedicated his paraphrase of Procopius to Giuliano Cesarini in 1441, perhaps intending to draw attention to the Turkish advance and the need for Western assistance in the crusade of Varna. See Hankins, "Renaissance Crusaders," 116–17. More recently Hankins expressed some doubts on the crusade connection in the dedication in his "Chrysoloras and the Greek Studies of Leonardo Bruni," in *Manuele Crisolora e il ritorno del greco in occidente*, ed. Riccardo Maisano and Antonio Rollo (Naples: Istituto Universitario Orientale, 2002), 190–91.

108. Bruni, *Leonardo Bruni Arretini Epistolarum*, 196.

109. "Id tale aliquid fuit tunc in Italia, quale nunc est in Graecia a Turcis occupata. Sic enim nunc afflicta est gens Graecorum, ut qui dudum magistri, et principes studiorum erant, vix nunc reperiantur ex eis, qui primas literas sciant" (ibid.).

110. Bruni appears to be describing barbarians in accordance with Hellenistic and Roman Republican definitions—as an inferior, uncultivated, and stupid people. See Borst, *Medieval Worlds*, 4–5.

111. See Chapter 3 for Salutati's ambivalent views on Byzantine learning.

112. Ciriaco will be discussed in the following chapter; on his friendship with Bruni, see Jean Colin, *Cyriaque d'Ancône: le voyager, le marchand, l'humaniste* (Paris: Maloine Éditeur, 1981), 402–3. See also Ciriaco d'Ancona, *Later Travels*, ed. Edward W. Bodnar (Cambridge: Harvard University Press, forthcoming). Thanks to James Hankins for this reference. Ciriaco and perhaps Bruni himself may have taken cues from the Greek scholar George Gemistos Plethon, who met Ciriaco in 1437 and attended the Council of Florence in 1439. See C. M. Woodhouse, *George Gemistos Plethon: The Last of the Hellenes* (Oxford: Clarendon Press, 1986), 165. Plethon will be discussed in Chapter 3 below.

113. Schwoebel, *Shadow of the Crescent*, 152.

114. The Sicilian humanist Aurispa (1376–1459) significantly enlarged the circulation of Greek texts in Italy when he brought hundreds of manuscripts to Italy in 1423 after his second trip to Greece; 238 of these manuscripts were pagan texts, and an unknown number were Christian texts. See N. G. Wilson, *From Byzantium to Italy: Greek Studies in the Italian Renaissance* (Baltimore: Johns Hopkins University Press, 1992), 25–26. On Poggio's efforts, see Gordan, *Two Renaissance Book Hunters*.

115. Labalme, *Bernardo Giustiniani*, 139–40.

116. A description of the siege may be found in the Introduction above.

117. Turkish eyewitness Tursun Beg's description contains little indication of gratuitous slaughter or rape; see Pertusi, *Caduta di Costantinopoli*, 1:305–31. For a paraphrase of the work in English as well as the original Turkish text, see Halil Inalcik, ed., *The History of Mehmed the Conqueror* (Minneapolis: Bibliotheca Islamica, 1978). For a discussion of contemporary Turkish sources, or the lack thereof, see Babinger, *Mehmed the Conqueror*, 470–71. Greek writers seem less horrified by the "otherness" of their attackers and show less tendency to exaggerate their actions than do Western chroniclers. This is probably due to the close contact Greeks had with the Turks over the centuries; some writers such as Kritoboulos served as officials in Mehmed's government. See Kritoboulos, *The History of Mehmed the Conqueror*, ed. and tr. Charles T. Riggs (Princeton, N.J.: Princeton University Press, 1954), 75. Doukas incorporated reports of Turkish soldiers who had stormed the city, saying that the initial slaughter arose from their incorrect assumption that at least fifty thousand men were defending the walls. Had they known the true number of defenders, they "would have sold them like sheep"; see Doukas, *Decline and Fall of Byzantium to the Ottoman Turks*, ed. and tr. Harry J. Magoulias (Detroit: Wayne State University Press, 1975), 224–25. See also Setton, *Papacy and the Levant*, 2:132–33; Runciman, *Fall of Constantinople*, 145. Paul Coles notes that "as one moved westwards into the heartlands of European society, the Ottomans became increasingly the object of loathing and fear," but he probably overstates his case in claiming that Eastern Europeans gave their Ottoman "liberators" a warm welcome; see Coles, *Ottoman Impact on Europe*, 145.

118. Leslie F. Smith has commented on the similarities in Western accounts in "Pope Pius II's Use of Turkish Atrocities," *Southwestern Social Science Quarterly* 46 (1966): 408–15.

119. See Pertusi, *Caduta di Costantinopoli*, vol. 1; see also Jones, *Siege of Constantinople*, for Leonard's full account; the Latin text, *Historia Constantinopolitanae*, is in *Patrologia Graeca*, ed. J. P. Migne, 1866, vol. 159. On the importance of Leonard's account as a source for Western readers and historians, see Marios Philippides, "The Fall of Constantinople 1453: Bishop Leonardo Giustiniani and His Italian Followers," *Viator* 29 (1998): 189–225.

120. Arguably, the pillage was no worse than that of 1204 at the hands of Christian crusaders.

121. Robert Schwoebel provides the best account of Western sources for and reactions to the fall of Constantinople; see his *Shadow of the Crescent*, chap. 1.

122. Other considerations, such as French aggression and a desire for internal stability, made a general peace desirable. See Riccardo Fubini, "The Italian League and the Policy of the Balance of Power at the Accession of Lorenzo de' Medici," *Journal of Modern History* 67 supplement (December 1995): 166–86. See also Garrett Mattingly, *Renaissance Diplomacy* (1955; rep., New York: Dover Publications, 1988), 75. Still, historians have tended to downplay fears of the Turkish threat as a key factor in the success of negotiations, which had been attempted and abandoned before.

123. As Schwoebel argues, we must not overlook the concern or sincerity on

the part of individual princes. Housley too has defeated the notion that the crusading spirit had died; he reveals a vast assortment of efforts to organize crusades and the many smaller-scale efforts that produced tangible results. Only the fragmenting of the ideal of Christendom itself with the coming of the Protestant Reformation seems to have brought crusading interests to a sharp decline. See Schwoebel, *Shadow of the Crescent*, 33; Housley, *Later Crusades*, 379–80 and passim.

124. Martines, *Strong Words*, 244–48. For the texts of several surviving laments on the fall of Constantinople, see Pertusi, *Caduta di Costantinopoli*, vol. 2.

125. Michael Ben Shabbetai Cohen Balbo, "A Hebrew Lament from Venetian Crete on the Fall of Constantinople," tr. Avi Sharon, *Dialogos: Hellenic Studies Review* 6 (1999): 43–46.

126. Setton, *Papacy and the Levant*, 2:159; Housley, *Later Crusades*, 404–18. See Black, *Benedetto Accolti*, chap. 9, for in-depth discussion of fund-raising for Pius II's crusade.

127. Aeneas Silvius Piccolomini (Pope Pius II), *De captione urbis Constantinopolitanae Tractaculus* (Rome: Johannes Gensberg, c. 1474). This pamphlet, as compared to Pius's more eloquent letters on 1453, is a less embellished account of the siege.

128. On indulgences, see Setton, *Papacy and the Levant*, 2:158–59; Housley, *Later Crusades*, 387–88. On calendars and lunation tracts, see Eckehard Simon, *The Türkenkalender (1454) Attributed to Gutenberg and the Strasbourg Lunation Tracts* (Cambridge, Mass.: The Medieval Academy of America, 1988).

129. Others have noted this as well. See Black, *Benedetto Accolti*, 230; Hankins, *Renaissance Humanists*, 112.

130. Michael Heath has attributed the development of several humanist crusading commonplaces to the authorship of Aeneas Silvius Piccolomini (Pius II); see Heath, *Crusading Commonplaces*, 27. He had much influence in this area, but as I have shown above, other humanists before him had begun to develop common humanistic themes, albeit tentatively. I tend to view the development of a post-1453 discourse on the Turks as more of an organic group effort than the creation of one or two individuals.

131. Gouwens, "Perceiving the Past," 80.

132. Here I quote Schwoebel's term; see his *Shadow of the Crescent*, 147.

133. See Introduction above for the quotation. (Vast, *Cardinal Bessarion*, 455; English tr., *Portable Renaissance Reader*, 71).

134. "non teucri sunt . . . sed potius truces sunt appelandi" (Niccolò Tignosi, *Expugnatio Constantinopolitana*, ed. Mario Sensi, in Sensi, "Niccolò Tignosi da Foligno opera e il pensiero," *Annali della facoltà di lettere e filosofia della Università degli Studi di Perugia* 9 (1971–72): 430). David Lines has recently challenged the long-held assumption that Tignosi taught Ficino. See *Aristotle's Ethics in the Italian Renaissance (ca. 1300–1650)* (Leiden: E. J. Brill, 2002), 192. Thanks to James Hankins for this reference.

135. "Tanta sanguinis effusio facta, ut rivi cruoris per urbem currerent" (Pertusi, *Caduta di Costantinopoli*, 2:52; Piccolomini, *Briefwechsel*, ed. Wolkan, 207).

136. "Constantinopolitane urbis et miserimae captivitatis, conquerentibus tam asperam atque immanem Barbarorum crudelitatem in caede et sanguine fide-

lium debacchatam" (Poggio Bracciolini, *De miseria conditionis humanae* (1455) *Opera Omnia* [1538; repr., Turin: Bottega d'Erasmo, 1964], 1:88).

137. A discussion of rape as a wartime problem in Renaissance Italy may be found in Diana Robin, *Filelfo in Milan* (Princeton, N.J.: Princeton University Press, 1991), 65–81.

138. Aeneas's letters attracted a wide audience for their political content and gossipy, racy style. No fewer than ten different collections of his letters were printed before 1500. See Clough, "Cult of Antiquity," 44–45.

139. Aeneas called for a crusade as early as 1436 at the Council of Basel, years before he entered the Church. See Black, *Benedetto Accolti*, 228.

140. "Quid caedes in regia urbe factas referam, prostitutas virgines, ephebos muliebria passos, violatas sanctimoniales, omne monachorum feminarumque genus turpiter habitum? . . . Aiunt, qui praesentes fuere, spurcissimum illum Turchorum ducem, sive ut aptius loquar, teterrimam bestiam apud summam aram sanctae Sophiae propalam videntibus omnibus nobilissimam virginem ac fratrem eius adolescentem regalis sanguinis construprasse ac deinde necari iussisse" (Letter to Leonardo Benvoglienti, in Pertusi, *Caduta di Costantinopoli*, 2:62, 64.

141. Pertusi, *Caduta di Costantinopoli*, 1:431 n. 20. The story, despite its falsity, enjoyed some popularity in Germany and France and appeared in at least two other versions of the siege. See Schwoebel, *Shadow of the Crescent*, 12–13. Thanks to Marios Philippides for his insights on this question.

142. Sources supporting this version include Doukas, Chalcocondylas, Leonard of Chios, and Adam of Montaldo. See also Runciman, *Fall of Constantinople*, 151.

143. Smith, "Pope Pius II's Use of Turkish Atrocities," 408–15.

144. An attention to style need not connote a lack of feeling. In a similar vein, Ronald Witt has answered critics of Salutati, who saw a lack of grief in letters regarding the deaths of his wife and son because they contained studied language and citations; see Witt, *Hercules at the Crossroads*, 420. See also Gouwens, "Perceiving the Past."

145. See Andrew Wheatcroft's discussion of these early modern cultural designations in chaps. 7–8 of *Ottomans*. Minimizing the image of the Turks as cruel, C. A. Patrides has argued that reports of Turkish atrocities may have been understood by many in a more religious vein—as God's just wrath in which the Turks were merely his tools; see Patrides, " 'The Bloody and Cruell Turke': The Background of a Renaissance Commonplace," *Studies in the Renaissance* 10 (1963): 126–35. The humanists' delight in stressing the barbarity of the Turks and, as we will shortly see, their characterization of their culture would seem to suggest otherwise.

146. It must be mentioned here that Western European laments on 1453 were complicated by the commonly held perception of the Greeks as "schismatics." See Chapter 3 for a discussion of these tensions.

147. See, for instance, George of Trebizond's *Exhortatio* to Nicholas V (1452) and Poggio Bracciolini's *De miseria humanae conditionis* (1455), both of which are discussed later in this chapter.

148. Leonard of Chios, Letter to Nicholas V, in *Siege of Constantinople*, ed. and tr. Jones, 38–39.

149. "gaudet si quis infantes innuptasque puellas altaria iuxta sacrisque in locis exenterat, aut reliquias sanctorum, quibus civitas referta est, pedibus et sanguine calcat, cenosunoque de turpe et blasfemnias etiam ecclesias concremat igni" (Pertusi, *Testi inediti*, 118). See also Sensi, "Niccolò Tignosi," 430.

150. "I suffer at the thought that Hagia Sophia, very famous throughout the world, is destroyed or profaned, that the infinite number of basilicas dedicated to the saints, true works of art, are ruined or contaminated by the filth of Muhammad" (*Doleo templum illud toto terrarum orbe famosissimum Sophiae vel destrui vel pollui; doleo infinitas sanctorum basilicas opere mirando constructas vel ruinae vel spurcitiae Maumethi subiacere*) (Pertusi, *Caduta di Costantinopoli*, 2:46; Piccolomini, *Briefwechsel*, ed. Wolkan, 200).

151. "Mansit usque in hanc diem vetustae sapientiae apud Constantinopolim monumentum, ac velut ibi domicilium litterarum esset, nemo Latinorum satis videri doctus poterat, nisi Constantinopoli per tempus studuisset. Quoque florente Roma doctrinarum nomen habuerunt Athenae, id nostra tempestate videbatur Constantinopolis obtinere" (Pertusi, *Caduta di Costantinopoli*, 2:52; Piccolomini, *Briefwechsel*, ed. Wolkan, 208.

152. See Chapter 3 for a discussion of Italian visitors to Constantinople and the impressions Greek visitors made on Italians.

153. Primary sources are discussed below. Runciman states that most of the books were burned but some were sold off; see his *Fall of Constantinople*, 148. Setton gives a similar account of the fate of these books in *Papacy and the Levant*, 2:130–31. Even Paul Wittek, in a somewhat sanguine attempt to downplay this aspect of the sack, can only say that "the heritage of Greek literature assembled there [did not] perish entirely" and that many of these books found their way west through traders; see Wittek, "An Eloquent Conquest," in *The Fall of Constantinople* (London: School of Oriental and African Studies, 1955), 36.

154. Pertusi, *Testi inediti*, 74; a full version of the letter may be found in Konrad Krautter et al., eds., *Lauro Quirini umanista* (Florence: Leo S. Olschki Editore, 1977), 223–33. See also Setton, *Papacy and the Levant*, 2:130–31.

155. Kritoboulos, *History of Mehmed*, 74

156. Doukas, *Decline and Fall of Byzantium*, 240.

157. Julian Raby, "East and West in Mehmed the Conqueror's Library," *Bulletin du bibliophile* (1987): 297–321, especially 299.

158. See Runciman, *Fall of Constantinople*, 148–49, 153; Babinger, *Mehmed the Conqueror*, 94.

159. Paula Findlen presents an illuminating deconstruction of Renaissance possession of the past, with book ownership as a profound means of intellectual ownership; see her "Possessing the Past: The Material World of the Italian Renaissance," *American Historical Review* 103, no. 1 (February 1998): 84–114, especially 91–93. See also Gordan, *Two Renaissance Book Hunters*.

160. Gordan, *Two Renaissance Book Hunters*, 15.

161. Lotte Labowsky, "Il Cardinale Bessarione e gli inizi della Biblioteca Marciana," in *Venezia e l'Oriente fra tardo medioevo e rinascimento*, ed. Agostino Per-

tusi (Venice: Sansoni, 1966), 159–82; see Chapter 3 below for a discussion of Bessarion's work in this regard, as well as his dedicatory letter describing the threat the Turks posed to Greek learning.

162. King, *Venetian Humanism*, 419; Vittore Branca, "Lauro Quirini e il commercio librario a Venezia e Firenze," in *Venezia centro di mediazione tra oriente e occidente (secoli XV–XVI) aspetti e problemi*, ed. Hans-Georg Beck, Manoussos Manoussacas, and Agostino Pertusi (Florence: Leo S. Olschki Editore, 1977), 371–73; Carlo Seno and Giorgio Ravegnani, "Cronologia della vita e delle opere di Lauro Quirini," in *Lauro Quirini umanista*, ed. Krautter et al., 11–18.

163. "sed eversio totius gentis facta est—, nomen Graecorum deletum. [Ultra centum et viginti milia librorum volumina, ut a reverendissimo cardinali Rutheno (Isidore of Kiev) accepi, devastata.] Ergo et lingua et litteratura Graecorum tanto tempore, tanto labore, tanta industria inventa, aucta, perfecta peribit, heu peribit!" (Pertusi, *Testi inediti*, 74).

164. "Gens barbara, gens inculta, nullis certis moribus, nullis legibus, sed fusa, vaga, arbitraria vivens. . . ." (ibid., 76).

165. Brent D. Shaw, " 'Eaters of Flesh, Drinkers of Milk': The Ancient Mediterranean Ideology of the Pastoral Nomad," *Ancient Society* 13/14 (1982–83): 19–20, 30. (Thanks to Alex Schubert for this reference.) William of Tyre presents a similar picture of the Seljuk Turks in his history of the Crusades. Whether William used the same ancient sources that influenced Quirini or Quirini used William's account is hard to say. We do know that William was well trained in the Latin classics. See William of Tyre, *A History of Deeds Done beyond the Sea*, ed. and tr. Emily Atwater Babcock and A. C. Krey (New York: Columbia University Press, 1943), 1:34, 72.

166. "Constantinopolis in manus hostium venerit . . . nunquam illa urbe Christiani nominis hostes potiti sunt neque basilice sanctorum destructe sunt neque bibliothece combuste neque despoliata penitus monasteria" (Piccolomini, *Briefwechsel*, ed. Wolkan, 208). Of course, such a claim does not account for the destruction wrought by Christian soldiers in 1204.

167. "Xerxes et Darius, qui quondam magnis cladibus Greciam afflixere, bellum viris, non litteris intulerunt. Romani, quamvis Greciam in potestatem suam redegissent, non solum Grecas litteras aspernati non sunt, sed ultro amplexi veneratique referuntur, adeo, ut tunc quisque doctissimus haberetur, cum Greci sermonis videretur peritissimus esse" (ibid., 209).

168. "nunc sub Turchorum imperio secus eveniet, sevissimorum hominum, bonorum morum atque litterarum hostium" (ibid., 209).

169. "in libidinem provoluti sunt, litterarum studi parvi faciunt, incredibili fastu superbiunt. in quorum manus venisse Grecam eloquentiam non scio, quis bone mentis non doleat . . ." (ibid., 209–10).

170. "Neque enim, ut plerique arbitrantur, Asiani sunt ab origine Turci, quos vocant Teucros, ex quibus est Romanorum origo, quibus literae non essent odio" (Piccolomini, "Oratio Aeneae de Constantinopolitana Clade et bello contra Turcos congregando, Epist. CXXX," in idem *Opera quae extant Omnia* (Frankfurt: Minerva, 1967), 681. See Heath, "Renaissance Scholars," 461.

171. "secunda mors ista Homero est, secundus Platoni obitus" (Letter to

Nicholas V, in Piccolomini, *Briefwechsel,* ed. Wolkan, 200; Pertusi, *Caduta di Costantinopoli,* 2:47).

172. Humanists, it should be noted, were apt to regard anyone perceived to be an enemy of literature as a barbarian. Poggio Bracciolini describes monks, whose monasteries "imprison" valuable ancient texts, as such. See Gordan, *Two Renaissance Book Hunters,* 99–100, 195; Black, "Donation of Constantine," 78–79.

173. See Schwoebel, *Shadow of the Crescent,* 20–21; Martines, *Strong Words;* Heath, *Crusading Commonplaces,* 30–31.

174. There was some debate over authorship, Bernardino da Cingoli often being credited with the work, but Pertusi presents evidence that Pisano wrote it. Pertusi has edited a large part of Pisano's lament as well as several other laments from Italy, Germany, and Eastern Europe. See Pertusi, *Testi inediti,* 297–98.

175. "Et era sì gran numero adunato / Di tanti libri e d'ogni gran valore / Ben sessanta miglaia era i[l] volume; / Tucti fur[no] arsi e butati nel fiume / Piangete omai, filosofi e doctori, / Piangete, greci, piangete, latini, / piangete voi, o grandi studiatori, / Piangete sempre, poi ch'e Siracini, / Piangete, chè v'àn tolti e vostri onori" (Pertusi, *Testi inediti,* 303).

176. This will be addressed in the Epilogue. See Heath, *Crusading Commonplaces,* 30–31, for a discussion of French writers on this theme.

177. "Video orbem terrarum semper variis tempestatum fluctibus agitatum. Vereor ne Vandalorum aut Gothorum tempora redeant" (Letter to Pietro Da Noceto (25 July 1453), in Bracciolini, *Lettere,* ed. Harth, 3:158).

178. "Gotos evertisse Romam insevissime adversus cives et populum et pene fuditus effudisse, clara narrat historia. Verum si nuper acta sunt que vulgo de Constantina urbe predicantur, profecto clades illa quam tunc romani pepersi sunt huic que nunc grecis illata est minime comparetur. Superfuerunt etenim qui potuerunt urbem illam de novo construere, rehedificatumque custodire, quamquam extores profugi multis mensibus vagarentur. Huic vero non modo cives, neque accole superfuerunt. Nam vel omnes cesi sunt, aut cum in naves se precipitant marinis fluctibus submerguntur" (Tignosi, *Expugnatio,* ed. Sensi, 423).

179. Piccolomini, *Briefwechsel,* ed. Wolkan, 207; for a similar reference see his Letter to Nicholas V, in Pertusi, *Caduta di Costantinopoli,* 2:46.

180. According to Augustine, anyone, pagan or Christian, who sought refuge in Christian basilicas or shrines was spared by the invading Goths; see Augustine, *City of God,* bk. 1, chaps. 1 and 7.

181. "Hanc italie vastitatem: pernitiem populorum, eversionem totius europe, nonne maiores nostri sepe senserunt? Cum ghoti, vandoli aliique populi barbarorum italiam devastarunt, quorum ego immanitatem cum ex antiquorum monimentis [*sic*] percipio, similem calamitatem formidandam fuisse censeo, nisi Voida obstitisset, qui ad reprimendam turcorum audaciam non tam natus, quam divino benificio christiane rei publice donatus esse videatur" (Donato Acciaiuoli, *Oratio funebris Joannis Vaivode,* in Biblioteca Nazionale Centrale, Florence, Magliabecchiano IX, 123, fol. 85r).

182. Given the similarity of Donato's tone to Bruni's, Procopius seems a likely choice, especially since Bruni had helped to popularize the source.

183. In a letter of 1463 to Pope Pius II, Donato repeats this theme, specifically

saying that they must learn from history to prepare for the future. See Garin, *Portraits*, 89. See Donato Acciaiuoli, (Letters), BNCF, Magliabecchiano VIII, 1390, fols. 47r–v. Cardinal Bessarion compares the Turkish threat to Italy to the destruction brought on Rome by the Goths and the Gauls; see Bessarion, *Oratione III*, in *Patrologia Graeca*, 161:658.

184. Greenblatt, *Marvelous Possessions*, 12–13.

185. See Garin, *Portraits*, 85–89.

186. The Greek historian Kritoboulos compares the siege to that of many other cities, including Rome, but concludes that 1453 was far worse than any of them; see his *History of Mehmed*, 77–79.

187. The city of Rome was no longer a major political center by this time. The sack of 410 was one in a chain of events and developments that led to—among other shifts—the localization of power, the decline of the great cities, the breakdown of communications, and the privatization of education. See Peter Brown, *The World of Late Antiquity* (London: W. W. Norton and Co., 1971). Flavio Biondo viewed the sack of Rome as the beginning of the end of the Roman Empire; see Cochrane, *Historians and Historiography*, 36. Uberto Decembrio viewed the Middle Ages as a period of cultural sterility; see Albert Rabil Jr., "Humanism in Milan," in *Renaissance Humanism*, ed. Rabil, 1:240. Bruni, as mentioned earlier, saw the fifth-century sacks of Rome as a main causes of its cultural decline.

188. Alison Brown, *Bartolomeo Scala 1430–1497, Chancellor of Florence* (Princeton, N.J.: Princeton University Press, 1979), 304–5.

189. C. P. Cavafy, "Waiting for the Barbarians," in *Collected Poems*, tr. Edmund Keeley and Philip Sherrard, ed. George Savidis, rev. ed. (Princeton, N.J.: Princeton University Press, 1992), 19.

190. One of the most ardent explications of such a view may be found in Pius II's Letter to Mehmed II, which will be discussed at length in Chapter 4. See Piccolomini, *Epistola ad Mahomatem II (Epistle to Mohammed II)*, ed. and tr. Albert R. Baca (New York: Peter Lang, 1990), especially bks. 1, 2, 16–18.

191. "ut mea urbe vivere velis, in qua non barbari, non insolentes viri, sed humani domestici, beneque morati homines vitam ducunt" (Acciaiuoli, [Letters] BNCF, Magliabecchiano VIII, 1390, fol. 86r). For further information on Donato's correspondence with Argyropoulos, see Field, *Origins*, 82ff.

192. Poggio's *De miseria humanae conditionis*, a dialogue on coping with life's sorrows, featuring Cosimo de' Medici and Matteo Palmieri, opens and takes its theme from Cosimo's remarks on the horrors of 1453. In the voice of Cosimo, Poggio calls to mind the "harsh and savage cruelty of the barbarians" (*asperam atque immanem Barbarorum crudelitatem*). See Bracciolini, *Opera Omnia*, 88. See also Donato's funeral oration on John Hunyadi (1456), which will be discussed below.

193. An example of this rhetoric appears in the oration Accolti composed for Florentine ambassadors at the Congress of Mantua (1459); see Black, *Benedetto Accolti*, 262–63.

194. For example, see ASF, *Missive, Prima Cancelleria* 42, fol. 130r–v (letter to the Grand Master of Rhodes), and *Missive* 44, fol. 140v–41r (letter to Pius II).

195. See Black, *Benedetto Accolti*, 326, 290.

196. See, for example, in Accolti's *Dialogue* his discussion of the decline in learning and especially history in Italy and Greece following the arrival of the "barbarians" (ibid., 290).

197. Jones, "Image of the Barbarian," 376–407, especially 392.

198. See Ulrich W. Haarmann, "Ideology and History, Identity and Alterity: The Arab Image of the Turk from the 'Abbasids to Modern Egypt," *International Journal of Middle East Studies* 20 (1988): 175–96. My thanks to William C. Jordan for this reference.

199. Kritoboulos's contemporary portrayal of Mehmed's efforts may be a bit exaggerated, but it does point to a systematic approach to rehabilitating the city; see his *History of Mehmed the Conqueror*, 93–94.

200. Charles Issawi, "Europe, Economics, and War," in *Imperial Legacy*, ed. Brown, 229. See also Inalcik, *Ottoman Empire*, 165–72; Babinger, *Mehmed the Conqueror*, 462–94.

201. See Raby's study of Mehmed's library, reflective of his eclectic tastes, Raby, "East and West"; Babinger discusses the library's limits in *Mehmed the Conqueror*, 500–501.

202. See Babinger, *Mehmed the Conqueror*, 378–80.

203. One view lumps Mehmed with Matthias Corvinus as examples of the peripheries of Renaissance culture and patronage; see Burke, *European Renaissance*, 58. See also Setton, *Papacy and the Levant*, 2:142 n. 12, for a discussion of this view and its proponents. On a related note, in *Global Interests*, Jardine and Brotton have argued—based on such exchanges between Mehmed's court and Western Europe, as well as the presence of Ottoman goods in Western art and common images in both Ottoman and European art—that there was little East-West antagonism and much cultural openness and exchange. While these views are interesting, Burke, Jardine, and Brotton present no new or compelling evidence to support their expansive interpretations.

204. Raby has shown, however, that Mehmed did commission fine Islamic manuscripts and assemble Greek and Latin works in his library; see his "East and West."

205. Mehmed built on a rather small scale compared to the projects of his son and grandson, and the buildings were less interesting and unique than those of his successors; see Babinger, *Mehmed the Conqueror*, 462–66. A recent study has argued that the Ottomans' lack of originality in architecture for several decades following the fall of Constantinople may be attributed to a sense of awe before such great structures as Hagia Sophia; only after an adjustment or "mourning" period of many years in which the Turks dealt with this sense of inferiority did they begin to produce great works of their own, beginning with Koca Mimar Sinan (1490–1588). See Vamik D. Volkan and Norman Itzkowitz, *Turks and Greeks: Neighbors in Conflict* (Huntingdon: Eothen Press, 1994), 48–49.

206. See Babinger, *Mehmed the Conqueror*, 462–82, 501–2; Inalcik, *Ottoman Empire*, 181; Setton, *Papacy and the Levant*, 2:142 n. 12.

207. Bernard Lewis, *Istanbul and the Civilization of the Ottoman Empire* (Norman: University of Oklahoma Press, 1963), 9.

208. See Lewis, *Muslim Discovery of Europe*.

209. The relations between the Ottoman court and Francesco Filelfo and his son Giovanni Mario are discussed in Chapter 3. Lorenzo de' Medici too had cultural contacts with the Ottoman court. See Franz Babinger, "Lorenzo de' Medici e la corte ottomana," *Archivio storico italiano* 121 (1963): 305–61.

210. As Anthony Grafton and Walter Mignolo have argued in separate works, the classical tradition acted as a barrier to understanding Native Americans on their own terms during the age of exploration and colonization. See Grafton, Shelford, and Siraisi, *New Worlds, Ancient Texts*, 1–10; Mignolo, "The Darker Side of the Renaissance: Colonization and the Discontinuity of the Classical Tradition," *Renaissance Quarterly* 45, no. 4 (1992): 808–28; see also Mignolo's book *The Darker Side of the Renaissance: Literacy, Territoriality, and Colonization* (Ann Arbor: University of Michigan Press, 1994). For further discussion of Grafton and Mignolo's theories as well as the link between humanist views of the Turks and cultural chauvinism in the New World, see the Epilogue below.

211. See Chapter 4 for further details on the siege of Otranto.

212. Perhaps Ficino skirts the issue given Florence's current war with Naples at the time. As will be discussed in Chapter 4, some Florentines openly rejoiced at the Turkish attack as it diverted Neapolitan forces from hostilities toward Siena and Florence.

213. "tandem post multa lucis secula in tenebras sub saevis Turcis, proh dolor, stellae, inquam, sub truculentis feris in tenebras corruunt. Iacent heu coelestia liberalium doctrinarum artiumque lumina iamdiu in lymbo" (Ficino, *Opera Omnia*, vol. 1, [Turin: Bottega D'Erasmo, 1962], 721; English tr., *The Letters of Marsilio Ficino*, vol. 2 [London: Shepheard-Walwyn, 1978], 4).

214. "dira haec, et immania monstra. Quae tam nefarie depopulantur agros, oppida diruunt, devorant homines" (ibid., 722 and 5, respectively).

215. "legum omnium liberaliumque artium disciplinas, atque . . . religionem sanctam . . . sordissimis pedibus impie calcant. . . . quantum in eis est, ex omni hominum memoria delent" (ibid).

216. See Valery Rees, "Hungary's Philosopher King: Mattias Corvinus 1458–90," *History Today* 44, no. 4 (March 1994): 18–24; Ficino *Letters*, 2:87.

217. A later example of such imagery appears in Ugolino Verino's 1492 panegyric to Ferdinand and Isabella of Spain. In the prologue to this work he mentions the plight of the Greek East under the Turkish advance and the destruction of learning; see Verino, *Panegyricon ad Ferdinandum regem et Isabellam reginam*, 1. See also the Epilogue below for sixteenth-century examples.

218. Rees, "Philosopher King," 19; Babinger, *Mehmed the Conqueror*, 394. Mehmed's death a few months before this conquest and the struggle between his sons for the throne also probably weakened the troops' resolve to put up much resistance.

219. On Biondo's view of the Scythians, see Meserve, "Medieval Sources," 114.

220. Namely his letter to Nicholas of Cusa on the fall of Constantinople in 1453 and his *De Constantinopolitana clade*. See Pertusi, *Caduta di Costantinopoli*, 2:54, Piccolomini, *Briefwechsel*, ed. Wolkan, 209; and idem, *Opera Omnia*, 681, respectively.

221. Pertusi, "I primi studi," 471, 475.

222. Ibid., 477.

223. Jones, "Image of the Barbarian," 400.

224. Heath, "Renaissance Scholars," 456–67.

225. Meserve, "Medieval Sources," 413–14, 422, 435–36.

226. Texts of Herodotus were available in Italy by this time, including a translation into Latin by Lorenzo Valla (c. 1450). See Remigio Sabbadini, *Le scoperte dei codici latini e greci ne' secoli XIV e XV* (Florence: G. C. Sansoni Editore, 1967), 1:49, 63.

227. Aeneas seems to have drawn on Herodotus in writing his letter to Mehmed II in 1461; this will be discussed in Chapter 4.

228. Momigliano, "Place of Herodotus," in Momigliano, *Studies in Historiography*, 130, 133, 139.

229. Boas and Lovejoy, *Primitivism in Antiquity*, 129–37.

230. "feroces populi, quos Iordanus, et alii nonnulli, ex mulieribus magis et daemonum semine natos crediderunt" (Piccolomini, *Opera Omnia*, 307).

231. "Natio truculenta et ignominiosa in cunctis stupris ac lupanaribus fornicaria: comedit quae caeteri abominantur, iumentorum, luporum, ac vulturum carnes, et quod magis horreas, hominum abortiva . . ." (ibid.). See Aethicus, *Die Kosmographie des Aethicus*, ed. Otto Prinz (Munich: Monumenta Germaniae Historica, 1993), 120.

232. See Shaw, "Eaters of Flesh, Drinkers of Milk," 5–31.

233. Biographical information on Filelfo will appear in Chapter 3.

234. See Gaza's *De Origine Turcarum* in *Patrologia Graeca* 161: 997–1006. See also Pertusi, "I primi studi," 470; Schwoebel, *Shadow of the Crescent*, 148. Pertusi states that the dates of Gaza's works are uncertain, but we do know that Filelfo probably received them after 1451.

235. Schwoebel, *Shadow of the Crescent*, 151.

236. "Quis unus omnium Turcos ignoret fugitivos esse Scytharum servos eosque pastores: qui ex ergastulis illius vasti et inhospitabilis montis Caucasi cum in Persida ac Mediam latrocinatum descendissent: nullumque certum incolerent domicilium praeter obsoleta lustra et horrentes sylvarum latebras . . ." (Francesco Filelfo, *Orationes cum quibusdam aliis eiusdem operibus* [Basel, 1498], n. pag.).

237. Heath argues that from Aeneas's time onward a decisive shift toward the Scythian school of thought took place among European scholarship. Erasmus, among other humanists, accepted it without question. Only in the late nineteenth century did the real origins of the Turks become clear. See Heath, "Renaissance Scholars," 461–63.

238. See Accolti's history of the First Crusade (*De bello*) and political writings; cf. Cochrane, *Historians and Historiography*, 27. For Donato, see *Vita Caroli*, 109. For Aeneas see his Letter to Nicholas of Cusa (1453), *Briefwechsel*, ed. Wolkan, 215; see also his *Commentaries*, bk. 7, *Commentaries of Pius II*, tr. Florence Alden Gragg, ed. Leona C. Gabel (Northampton, Mass.: Smith College, 1951), 4:478. Francesco Filelfo, incidentally, appears to have had a much more complex view of Muslims, eschewing the temptation to treat them as one monolithic culture; his source base was more extensive than those of most humanist historians. Margaret

Meserve argued these points in her conference talk "Francesco Filelfo and the Turks" delivered at the nineteenth International Congress of Historical Sciences (Oslo, 2000).

239. Verino, *Panegyricon*, 1.

240. Karl H. Dannenfeldt, "The Renaissance Humanists and the Knowledge of Arabic," *Studies in the Renaissance* 2 (1955): 105. Another example is Johannes Michael Nagonius's Latin poem to Julius II (1506) urging him to emulate ancients such as Julius Caesar and seize Antioch, Egypt, and Jerusalem from the teeth of the "barbarians"; see Stinger, *Renaissance in Rome*, 109.

241. This development has been blamed on the Crusades, but Maalouf argues that Arab leadership and culture was being eclipsed by internal shifts in power that preceded the arrival of the Franks; see his *Crusades through Arab Eyes*, 261–64.

242. The connection between Western perceptions of Arab learning and Islam is discussed in Chapter 4.

243. See Biondo, *Scritti inediti*, ed. Nogara, cli–cliv, for an overview of this work.

244. "Tuque interea dum priscae urbis Romae triumphos lectitabis: clarissimum quem pio tibi optimus pientissimusque Deus noster ex deletis inanitis Turcorum opibus ex liberataque primum omnium Europa, post Hierosolyma et terra illi adiacente sancta daturus est triumphum expectabis brevi, ut auguror et confido, cum summo applausu summa omnium gloria ducendum" (Flavio Biondo, "Roma Triumphans," in his *Opera Historica* [Basel, 1531], 1).

245. This comparison of crusade and ancient Roman imperialism, incidentally, had been made before by Biondo. In his oration of 1453 to Alfonso of Naples, Biondo compared his anticipated crusade victories not only to those of Godfrey and Bohemond but also to the campaigns of Scipio Asiaticus and Pompey. See Chapter 1.

246. It was not until 380 that Theodosius declared Christianity the official religion of Rome.

247. Stinger, *Renaissance in Rome*, 184.

248. Although born and educated in Greece, Bessarion went over to the Roman rite and was an accomplished Latin scholar as well as a Platonist. He spent most of his adult years in Italy, where he labored hard in the cause of crusade for his homeland. For more details on his life and career, see Chapter 3.

249. Demosthenes, "First Olynthiac" in his *Orations*, tr. J. H. Vince (New York: G. P. Putnam, 1930), 4–21. See also J. R. Ellis and R. D. Milns, *The Spectre of Philip: Demosthenes' First Philippic, Olynthiacs and Speech on the Peace* (Sydney: Sydney University Press, 1970), 34–64.

250. See Chapter 3 for a discussion of the fall of Negroponte.

251. See, for example, Biblioteca Riccardiana, Florence, Riccardiano 365, fols. 33r–42v.

252. "Audite, Christiani principes, Demosthenem philosophum et oratorem, iam tot secula mortuum, de statu hostis vestri nunc disserentem eloquentissime, et sapientissime monstrantem quid vos facere oporteat, ne in graviora dilabamini" (Ricc. 365, fol. 33r; Cardinal Bessarion, *Epistolae et orationes* [1471], 30v).

253. "Itaque cum huius et auctoritatem graviorem, et orationem magis appos

itam ad persuadendum existimarem quam verba mea, constitui ut ipse dicat sententiam" (Cardinal Bessarion, "Orationes contra Turcas," in *Patrologia Graeca*, 161:670).

254. "Ita enim tunc Graeciae Philippus imminebat, ut nunc Turcus Italiae. Sustineat igitur Philippus Turci personam, Itali, Atheniensium, nos Demosthenis. Jam facile intelliges totam orationem causae nostrae convenire" (ibid.).

255. "Nobis quoque non pro agri finibus sed pro libertate pro capite et patriae salute dimicandum est" (Ricc. 365, fol. 34r; Bessarion, *Epistolae et orationes*, 31r).

256. For manuscript and printing notes on this oration, as well as addenda omitted by the *Patrologia Graeca*, see John Monfasani, "Bessarion Latinus," in his *Byzantine Scholars in Renaissance Italy: Cardinal Bessarion and Other Emigres* (Aldershot: Variorum, 1995), II:180, 202–3.

257. Field, *Origins of the Platonic Academy*, 64–67. See also Martines, *Social World*, 131–38, 176–91.

258. Martines, *Social World*, 189–91.

259. Heinz Willi Wittschier, *Giannozzo Manetti: Das Corpus der Orationes* (Graz: Bohlau Verlag, 1968), 134–38. This, of course, was before Alfonso would fall from grace with the pope by using the crusade fleet to attack the Genoese. For further details of Alfonso and Calixtus's relationship, see Ludwig Pastor, *History of the Popes* (London: Kegan Paul, Trench, Trubner, and Co., 1899), 2:328–31, 359–66.

260. Wittschier, *Giannozzo Manetti*, 136–37.

261. See *Cicero: The Speeches*, ed. H. Grose Hodge (Cambridge: Harvard University Press, 1959), 2–11.

262. Manetti, *Oratio ad Calixtum*, fol. 52v. See Heath, *Crusading Commonplaces* for a fuller discussion of rhetorical themes in crusade orations.

263. Cicero, *The Speeches*, ed. Hodge, 20–21.

264. Chester G. Starr, *A History of the Ancient World*, 3d ed. (New York: Oxford University Press, 1983), 528.

265. "delenda esset a quiritibus illa macula mitridatico bello superiore suscepta que iam penitus insederat atque in populi romani nomine ob id inveteraverat" (Manetti, *Oratio*, fol. 53r).

266. Ibid.

267. Cicero, *Speeches*, ed. Hodge, 16–19.

268. "In hoc nostro sicut in illo non traditur salus sotiorum atque amicorum sed certe salubritas vel pernicies omnium cristianorum periclitatur et luditur, non de vectigalibus ut ibi sed de amplis patrimoniis agitur, non de multorum civium romanorum bonis ut illic, sed de preciosis et infinitis cunctarum fidelium gentium thesauris tractatur . . ." (Manetti, *Oratio*, fol. 53r).

269. "Mehembetus turcorum ductor etate iuvenis animo magnus potentia maximus . . ." (ibid., 54v).

270. See Anthony Pagden, "Europe: Conceptualizing a Continent," in *The Idea of Europe from Antiquity to the European Union*, ed. Anthony Pagden (Cambridge: Cambridge University Press, 2002), 33–39. See also Hay, *Europe*. Hay notes that Isocrates (d. 338 B.C.E.) used the term "Europe" to denote Greece, and "Asia" for Persia; see ibid., 3. Both Pagden and Hay agree that "Europe" is hard

to pin down in ancient Greek culture; see Hay, *Europe*, 4; Pagden, "Europe," 38. See also J. R. Hale, *The Civilization of Europe in the Renaissance* (New York: Atheneum, 1994), 38–43.

271. The Romans may have found such distinctions less tenable, given the location of Germanic "barbarians" who were as much a part of the West as they were, not to mention Carthage directly to the South. See Balsdon, *Romans and Aliens*, 60–64.

272. William C. Jordan, "'Europe' in the Middle Ages," in *Idea of Europe*, ed. Pagden, 72–90. See also Hay, *Europe*, 16–36.

273. Suzanne Conklin Akbari, "From Due East to True North: Orientalism and Orientation," in *The Postcolonial Middle Ages*, ed. Jeffrey Jerome Cohen (New York: St. Martin's Press, 2000).

274. Hay has credited the work of humanists, particularly regarding the Turkish advance, as a crucial stage in the development of "Europe"; see his *Europe*, 82–87.

275. George of Trebizond's career, this oration, and its use of Europe and Asia are discussed at length in Chapter 3 below. See Monfasani, *George of Trebizond*, 128–30; for the text of the oration see George of Trebizond, *Collectanea Trapezuntiana*, ed. Monfasani, 434–44.

276. Alfonso signed the pact in January 1455; see Mattingly, *Renaissance Diplomacy*, 76.

277. Black, *Benedetto Accolti*, 269. Actually, Naples was the last power to sign the treaty and did so "sullenly," according to Mattingly; see his *Renaissance Diplomacy*, 76.

278. Bracciolini, *Lettere*, 3:324. Alfonso was generally regarded as a natural choice to lead crusade because of his control of Sicily, which was both vulnerable to invasion and a logical place from which to launch a Christian offensive. See Biondo, *Scritti inediti*, ed. Nogara, cxxxv. Alfonso added to these expectations by twice offering to lead a crusade (1451 and 1455); see Fubini, "Italian League," 177–78.

279. "Illa vero que pro christiani nominis defensione, pro dei cultu, pro communi utilitate, pro incremento religionis et fidei agenda suscipiuntur una omnium voce, uno sermone, uno plausu celebrentur oportet" (Bracciolini, *Lettere*, 3:325).

280. Poggio wrote a letter, similar in content, to Emperor Frederick III in December 1455/January 1456. This later letter, however, is marked by a greater sense of confidence and urgency than was the earlier letter to Alfonso. Not only does he try to shame Frederick for taking no military initiative against the Turks two years after Constantinople had fallen, but he also warns him that the Turks are now eyeing his land, desiring to enslave him and his people. See ibid., 381–87.

281. "Audivi quosdam egregios pace et bello viros asserentes, nunquam Teucros Europa pelli posse dum illis mare pervium erit, dum ex Asia presidia subministrabuntur . . . Europam aiunt corpus esse, ex Asia animam ac spiritus accersiri" (ibid., 323).

282. Europe, Biondo argues, has always exceeded other parts of the world in excellence and might; to support this argument he invokes the models of Alexander and the Romans; see Biondo, "Ad Alphonsum Aragonem," in his *Scritti ine-*

diti, ed. Nogara, 32–33. Giustiniani's oration, written to congratulate the new pope on his election and incite his support for the Venetian war against the Turks, describes Mehmed as subjugating the East while also desiring to invade and conquer the West; see Labalme, *Bernardo Giustiniani*, 195, 199–200. Donato speaks of Hungary as a bulwark of Christendom and repeatedly describes Hunyadi as saving "Europe" from the Turkish advance; see Acciaiuoli, *Oratio funebris.*

283. Hay, *Europe*, 83–87.

284. "Non pugnabis contra feminas, aut Italiam, aut Hungariam, aut aliam in occidenti provinciam ingressus. Ferro hic res geritur, non Asiaticis sudibus chalybeius thorax pectora tegit" (Piccolomini, *Epistola ad Mahomatem*, ed. and tr. Baca, English tr., 13, Latin, 117). Jean-Claude Margolin sees Pius's provocative statements as a bluff; see Margolin, "Place et fonction de la rhétorique dans la lettre de Pie II à Mahomet II" in *Pio II e la cultura del suo tempo*, ed. Luisa Rotondi Secchi Tarugi (Milan: Guerini e Associati, 1991), 253–54.

285. Piccolomini, *Epistola ad Mahomatem*, 91, 199. Aeneas's views on Muslim learning will be discussed at greater length in Chapter 4.

286. See my article "Pius II's Letter to Sultan Mehmed II: A Reexamination," *Crusades* 1 (2002), for an extended discussion of this issue as well as the problems I find in accepting it as a genuine conversion piece intended for Mehmed's eyes. See also Chapter 4 below for a brief discussion of the letter.

287. Tignosi, *Expugnatio*, 426, 429.

288. "ferociam, vel potius crudelitatem ostendit, intemperiemque libidinum, quasi novus Gallicula terrorem respicientibus incutit, moribusque dicatur antiquorum studet historiis et illorum facinora cum admiratur. . . ." (ibid., 426).

289. "Tantum eorum ordinem instruendis machinis, tantam promptitudinem, tantam acierum providentiam quidam aut Scipio, aut Annibal, aut moderni belli duces admirati fuissent" (Leonard of Chios, *Historia Constantipolitanae*, 927; English tr., Jones, *Siege of Constantinople*, 15).

290. "Sed quis, obsecro, circumvallavit urbem? qui, nisi perfidi Christiani instruxere Teucros! [Testis sum, quod] Graeci, quod Latini, quod Germani, Pannones, Boetes, . . . [opera eorum fidemque didicerunt]" (Leonard of Chios, *Historia Constantinopolitanae*, 927; English tr., *Siege of Constantinople*, 15–16).

291. "imitatus Xerxis potentiam, qui ex Asia in Thraciam Bosphoro exercitum traduxit" (Leonard of Chios, *Historia Constantinopolitanae*, 931; English tr., *Siege of Constantinople*, 20–21).

292. "barbarus urbem, quam et situ loci, et moenibus et commeatu et omni genere praesidii munitissimam, quam omnis anni integrum pati posse obsidionem sperabant, viribus expugnaverit" (Vast, *Cardinal Bessarion*, 454; English tr., McLaughlin, *Portable Renaissance Reader*, 70–71).

293. Piccolomini, *Epistle to Mohammed II*, ed. and tr. Baca, 25, 74.

294. Here, John Dower's discussion of the malleability of American stereotypes of the Japanese in wartime and in peace is a useful analogy; see his *War without Mercy*, passim.

295. "Teucrorum tamen nomen antiquum scitis esse a Teucro ductum et ab eo Troianos *Teucros* appellatos. Post excidium vero Troie legimus nullam gentem

hoc nomen in Asia usurpasse, quod noviter et nostro seculo videtur esse excitatum" (Bracciolini, *Lettere*, ed. Harth, 3:286).

296. "Potius vero eos dixerim Turcos novo nomine, quod aliis multis nationibus contigit, quorum ratio nulla extat" (ibid.).

297. "Quod autem proprius sit eorum nomen viderint earum rerum curiosiores" (ibid.).

298. See, for example, his letters to Alfonso of Naples and Frederick III (1455) in ibid., 3:322–27, 381–87.

299. Spencer, "Turks and Trojans," 331. For a poetic version of this type of letter, see Hankins, "Renaissance Crusaders," 206–7.

300. Heath states that, from Aeneas's time onward, Renaissance scholars could and did more plausibly argue against the theory extending noble Trojan heritage to the Turks, see Heath, "Renaissance Scholars," 461.

301. Schwoebel, *Shadow of the Crescent*, 148, 171–72 n. 5.

302. An interesting twist on the Turk-Trojan connection was put forth in the late fifteenth century by the German cleric and pilgrim Felix Fabri. Fabri accepted the Trojan origins of the Turks but argued that after they escaped from Troy they settled in Scythia, where they abandoned civilized ways and lived like primitives or beasts. See Schwoebel, *Shadow of the Crescent*, 189.

303. Guillaume Favre, "Vie de Jean-Marius Philelfe," in *Mélanges d'histoire littéraire* (Geneva, 1856), 1:181.

304. Giovanni Mario Filelfo, *Amyris*, ed. Aldo Manetti (Bologna: Pàtron Editore, 1978), 19–20; see also Favre, "Vie de J. M. Philelfe," which contains a partial edition of the *Amyris* and commentary on the work. On Ferducci, his family, and the Anconitans in Constantinople, see Agostino Pertusi, "The Anconitan Colony in Constantinople and the Report of Its Consul, Benevento, on the Fall of the City," in *Charanis Studies: Essays in Honor of Peter Charanis*, ed. Angeliki E. Laiou-Thomadakis (New Brunswick, N.J.: Rutgers University Press, 1980), 199–218, especially 203–4.

305. Aldo Manetti, introduction to Giovanni Mario Filelfo, *Amyris*, 21; Schwoebel, *Shadow of the Crescent*, 148–49.

306. During the Middle Ages and certainly by the Renaissance pagan gods and goddesses were acceptable figures for moral didacticism. See Jean Seznec, *The Survival of the Pagan Gods*, tr. Barbara F. Sessions (New York: Harper and Row, 1953), 84–121.

307. Giovanni Mario Filelfo, *Amyris*, 69–70.

308. "Phrygia nam gente parentes / esse tuos, quis nescit adhuc? . . . / Othman gente satus, Priamique e stirpe relatus, / tu genus es Priami, teque ornamenta sequuntur / sanguinis invicti quondam, dein fraude remissi" (ibid., 70).

309. Ibid., 30–31, 82.

310. See Virgil, *Aeneid*, bk. 8; Augustine, *City of God*, 5:12.

311. "Bello / constitui hanc animam vel perdere, vel sceleratos / Mermidonas, nostro generi qui multa dederunt / olim damna, mea tandem confundere dextra" (Giovanni Mario Filelfo, *Amyris*, 89).

312. "Fuistis / denique subiecti Graeci, Phrygiaeque vetustae / imperium sub rege novo cum lege feretis" (ibid., 129).

313. Ibid., 32, 115; see Chapter 3 below for a fuller discussion of Filelfo's anti-Greek rhetoric.

314. Ibid., 25, 169–230; Schwoebel, *Shadow of the Crescent*, 149.

315. *In turcos adhortatio ad Christianos principes*, Biblioteca Apostolica Vaticana, Rome, Urb. Lat. 353. See also *Manuscripta* 4, no. 1 (February 1960): 5.

316. Jones, "Image of the Barbarian," 406.

Chapter 3

1. Schwoebel, *Shadow of the Crescent*, 153.

2. Deno John Geanakoplos, "Italian Humanism and the Byzantine Émigré Scholars," in *Renaissance Humanism*, ed. Rabil, 1:350–51, 368.

3. It held its own against the Seljuk Turks in the High Middle Ages and even reconquered some areas in Asia and Asia Minor; moreover, after a period of fifty-seven years it recaptured Constantinople from the Latins (1261). However, the Latin conquest of Constantinople and other areas, not to mention the piecemeal conquest of Anatolia by the Seljuks, took a tremendous toll on Byzantine resources, weakening the empire's ability to hold off the Turks indefinitely. For a differing view of Byzantium's downfall, which stresses commercial and economic factors, see John H. Pryor, "The Problem of Byzantium and the Mediterranean World, c. 1050–c. 1400," in *Montjoie: Studies in Crusade History in Honour of Hans Eberhard Mayer*, ed. Benjamin Z. Kedar, Jonathan Riley-Smith, and Rudolf Hiestand (Aldershot: Variorum, 1997), 199–211.

4. On the Schism, see Steven Runciman, *The Eastern Schism* (Oxford: Clarendon Press, 1955); Deno John Geanakoplos, *Constantinople and the West* (Madison: University of Wisconsin Press, 1989); Geoffrey Barraclough, *The Medieval Papacy* (London: Thames and Hudson, 1968).

5. Munro, "Western Attitude," 336.

6. For details on 1204 and the ensuing Latin presence in the Greek East, see Peter Lock, *The Franks in the Aegean 1204–1500* (London: Longman, 1995).

7. In an attempt to salvage the situation, Innocent tried to use the Latin rule of Constantinople as a means of carrying out a union of the two churches. Still, he saw from the beginning that the Greeks could hardly welcome the theft of their autonomy and the intrusions into their daily lives: "How is the Greek Church, so afflicted and persecuted, to return to ecclesiastical union and a devotion for the Apostolic See when she sees in the Latins only an example of perdition and the works of darkness, so that with reason, she already detests them more than dogs?" (Riley-Smith, *Crusades*, 130).

8. Housley, *Later Crusades*, 54–55.

9. This assimilation was facilitated by similar customs and traditions of warfare among the Turks and the Christian inhabitants of the borderlands. Cemal Kafadar discusses the problematic nature of identity of the Ottoman Turks and "Turks" in general, warning against a simplistic view of original ethnic and religious stocks maintaining an isolated and antagonistic existence over the course of

centuries; see Kafadar, *Between Two Worlds*, 23–27. The ramifications of the terms "Ottoman" and "Turk" are discussed by Norman Itzkowitz, "The Problem of Perceptions," in *Imperial Legacy*, ed. Brown, 30–32. For a more in-depth discussion of cultural influence and exchange, see Speros Vryonis Jr., "Byzantium and Islam, Seven–Seventeenth Century," in Vryonis, *Byzantium: Its Internal History and Relations with the Muslim World: Collected Studies* (London: Variorum Reprints, 1971), chap. 9.

10. The completion of the conquest of Bursa was actually carried out by Orhan; see Itzkowitz, *Ottoman Empire*, 11.

11. Fine does not see this exchange as a marriage; see his *Late Medieval Balkans*, 305.

12. Ironically, the papal crusade at Smyrna pushed John VI into a partnership that would, within a few years, produce disastrous results for both Byzantine and European security. See Itzkowitz, *Ottoman Empire*, 11–12.

13. See Housley, *Later Crusades*, 65; Inalcik, *Ottoman Empire*, 9–10, 134; Vaughn, *Europe and the Turk*, 30–31; Imber, *Ottoman Empire*, 24–25.

14. Inalcik, *Ottoman Empire*, 10. For European reactions and military responses to the Ottoman advance, see Housley, *Later Crusades*, 66 ff.

15. Imber identifies Amadeo as a cousin of John V Palaeologus; see Imber, *Ottoman Empire*, 28. See also Housley, *Later Crusades*, 67–68; Setton, *Papacy and the Levant*, 1:285–326.

16. Kafadar, *Between Two Worlds*, 142–45.

17. Inalcik, *Ottoman Empire*, and Itzkowitz, *Ottoman Empire*, date the capture of Adrianople as 1361. Housley, *Later Crusades*, and Imber, *Ottoman Empire*, say 1369.

18. Princes such as Shishman of Tarnovo were required to submit tribute and troops to the Ottomans, but they were not deprived of their right to rule. Shishman vacillated between obedience and defiance. Two Serbian princes, Ugljesa and Vukasin, despots of Macedonia, opposed the Ottoman advance and lost their lives attempting to win back Edirne in 1371. See Imber, *Ottoman Empire*, 29–31, 43, 45.

19. See Housley, *Later Crusades*, 69–70; Imber, *Ottoman Empire*, 29. On Catherine of Siena and crusade, see Franco Cardini, "L'idea di crociata in Sancta Caterina," in *Studi sulla storia,* ed. Cardini, 423–56.

20. See Inalcik, *Ottoman Empire*, 11–12. Inalcik argues that Pope Gregory XI's failure to launch a crusade may have made local rulers more inclined to submit to Ottoman suzerainty, but other studies do not support this.

21. See Chapter 1 for a discussion of Ottoman suzerainty in the Balkans during these years.

22. Tvrtko sent troops but was not present at the battle. See Imber, *Ottoman Empire*, 35–36.

23. Itzkowitz, *Ottoman Empire*, 13–16.

24. Imber, *Ottoman Empire*, 42–44; Inalcik, *Ottoman Empire*, 15–16.

25. Manuel II had thrown off Ottoman overlordship in 1382. He won some victories at Thessaloniki before the Ottomans besieged him in the city in 1383; this combined with a lack of aid from his brother Theodore, despot of the Peloponnesus, as well as Venice and the pope, forced him to capitulate for a few years. See

Chapter 2 for a discussion of Nicopolis. On Manuel II, see John W. Barker, *Manuel II Palaeologus (1391–1425): A Study in Late Byzantine Statesmanship* (New Brunswick, N.J.: Rutgers University Press, 1969).

26. Ottoman institutions in land holding, administration, and the *devshirme* system had managed to survive the turbulent decade, but Mehmed I (r. 1413–21) spent his hard reign almost constantly campaigning in both the Balkans and Anatolia to recover what had been lost. For developments in the civil war years, see Inalcik, *Ottoman Empire*, 17–18; Housley, *Later Crusades*, 80–82; Imber, *Ottoman Empire,* chap. 3.

27. Manuel had been ordered by Murad to imprison Mustafa, Murad's brother, in order to protect his throne, but Manuel collaborated with Mustafa against the sultan. After winning a good deal of Turkish support and some heartening victories, in January 1422 Mustafa was defeated, captured by his brother, and publicly hanged. With Mustafa dead, Murad besieged Constantinople, determined to punish Manuel's deceit. The siege lasted from 10 June until 6 September. Luckily for the Greeks, another of Murad's brothers (ironically also named Mustafa) had begun to rebel against him in Anatolia, necessitating Murad's withdrawal. By 1424, though, Byzantium was once again a vassal state of the Ottoman Empire. See Imber, *Ottoman Empire*, 91–95.

28. Inalcik holds that Murad decided to abdicate and appoint Mehmed II his heir so as to avoid another period of civil war. Imber and Itzkowitz point to Murad's reputation for piety and a desire for peaceful meditation; the recent death of his favorite son, Alaeddin, may also have affected his decision. See Inalcik, *Ottoman Empire*, 20; Imber, *Ottoman Empire*, 129; Itzkowitz, *Ottoman Empire*, 23. Setton places Murad's retirement after the battle of Varna (December 1444 or later), citing more Epicurean reasons and calling him a "fat voluptuary"; see Setton, *Papacy and the Levant*, 2:94.

29. Setton, *Papacy and the Levant*, 2:88, 96.

30. See Chapter 1 for a discussion of this crusade.

31. Inalcik, *Ottoman Empire*, 21; Setton, *Papacy and the Levant*, 2:93–94. After the battle of Varna, Murad attempted to retire again, only to be recalled to deal with rebel janissaries in 1446. He would continue to rule until his death in 1451.

32. See Chapter 2.

33. Kritoboulos, *History of Mehmed*, 158–59.

34. See Chapter 1 on the millet system. See also Volkan and Itzkowitz, *Turks and Greeks*, 154–57.

35. The following is a brief outline of Italian commercial and political involvements in the eastern Mediterranean; a fuller discussion is provided in my article "Early Ottoman Empire." See also Setton, *Papacy and the Levant*, vol. 2; Housley, *Later Crusades.*

36. See Ugurgieri Della Berardenga, *Gli Acciaioli*, 1:chap. 9. In his life of the Florentine Agnolo Acciaiuoli, Vespasiano da Bisticci recounts a run-in Agnolo had with the Turks while visiting cousins in Greece in 1433; see Vespasiano, *Vite*, 2:285–308; see also Black, *Benedetto Accolti*, 278–79.

37. Hilary Turner, "The Expanding Horizons of Cristoforo Buondelmonti,"

History Today 40 (October 1990): 40–41. See also Roberto Weiss, "Lineamenti per una storia degli studi antiquari in Italia," *Rinascimento* 9, no. 2 (1958): 179–80.

38. Turner, "Expanding Horizons," 41.

39. See Roberto Weiss, *The Renaissance Discovery of Classical Antiquity* (1969, repr., Oxford: Basil Blackwell, 1988), 135–37.

40. Roberto Weiss, "Ciriaco d'Ancona in Oriente," in *Venezia e l'Oriente*, ed. Pertusi, 324, 328.

41. Ciriaco was also in contact with Poggio, but their relations were strained at times, given Poggio's criticism of the former's Latin; see Edward W. Bodnar, S.J., *Cyriacus of Ancona and Athens* (Brussels: Latomus, 1960), 20–25. See also Babinger, *Mehmed the Conqueror*, 496; Weiss, "Ciriaco d'Ancona," 327; Colin, *Cyriaque d'Ancone*, 389–414; Weiss, *Renaissance Discovery*, 138–42; Ciriaco d'Ancona, *Later Travels*, ed. Edward W. Bodnar (Cambridge: Harvard University Press, 2003—Forthcoming).

42. See Schwoebel, *Shadow of the Crescent*, 205–6; Babinger, *Mehmed the Conqueror*, 496.

43. Julian Raby has demonstrated the errors on which this rumor was based; see his "Cyriacus of Ancona and the Ottoman Sultan Mehmed II," *Journal of the Warburg and Courtauld Institutes* 43 (1980): 242–46. Cf. Hankins, "Renaissance Crusaders," 130 n. 58. Setton also presented reasons why the story was not likely to be true; see his *Papacy and the Levant* 2:71.

44. Setton, *Papacy and the Levant*, 2:82, 87–88, 95–96.

45. A translation of this letter is available in *The Renaissance in Europe: An Anthology*, ed. Peter Elmer, Nick Webb, and Roberta Wood (New Haven: Yale University Press, 2000), 15. See chap. 1 above on Varna.

46. On the terms of the truce, see Housley, *Later Crusades*, 86–87. Historians have taken different views of the breaking of the truce. Donald Nicol chastises the Christians for breaking their oath, suggesting that Murad intended to abide by it; see his *The Last Centuries of Byzantium 1261–1453* (Cambridge: Cambridge University Press, 1993), 362–63. Setton, on the other hand, argues that neither side really felt bound by the peace and that warfare had been too fierce to let "scraps of paper" bind either side; see his *Papacy and the Levant*, 2:79–80.

47. "Sed heu! quantum ab illo deformem revisimus, quod antea bis septem iam annis exactis perspeximus; nam tunc XXX et unam columnas erectas vidimus extare, nunc vero unam de XXX manere et partim epistiliis destitutas cognovi. Sed et qui integri fere omnes incliti parietes extabant, nunc a barbaris magna quidem ex parte diminuti soloque collapsi videntur. . . . At cum civitatem undique collapsam aspexissem, et in dies a barbaris omni ex parte pessundatum iri cognovissem, indolui" (Latin: Ciriaco of Ancona, *Cyriacus of Ancona's Journeys in the Propontis and the Northern Aegean 1444–1445*, ed. Edward J. Bodnar, S.J., and Charles Mitchell (Philadelphia: American Philosophical Society, 1976), 28, 30; English translation by Chris Emlyn-Jones in *Renaissance Reader*, ed. Elmer et al., 13.

48. In 1437 Ciriaco made the acquaintance of the scholar George Gemistos Plethon, who frequently labeled the Turks "barbarians." See Woodhouse, *George Gemistos Plethon*, 26, 165. To cite some earlier examples, in 1356 Demetrios Cydones lamented the encirclement of Constantinople by the Ottomans with the phrase

"[we are] caught as if in the net of the barbarians"; see Housley, *Later Crusades*, 65. Writing in the early twelfth century, Anna Comnena freely applied the term to Persians, Turks, and other Eastern peoples. Of course, she also used "barbarian" to describe Frankish crusaders.

49. See Vergerio, *Epistolario*, 245; on the dating of this letter, see Hans Baron, *Humanistic and Political Literature in Florence and Venice at the Beginning of the Quattrocento* (Cambridge: Harvard University Press, 1955), 107–13.

50. Kenneth Setton, "The Byzantine Background to the Italian Renaissance," *Proceedings of the American Philosophical Society* 100 (1956): 72. See also *Dizionario biografico degli Italiani* (Rome: Istituto della Enciclopedia Italiana, 1997), vol. 47.

51. Paul Oskar Kristeller, *Renaissance Thought and Its Sources*, ed. Michael Mooney (New York: Columbia University Press, 1979), 143. See also Geanakoplos "Italian Humanism"; Wilson, *From Byzantium to Italy*.

52. Lisa Jardine points to the role that manuscript collecting played in this interest, citing examples from the Council of Florence (1438); see her *Worldly Goods*, 58–59. But such a view underestimates how the desire to acquire the intangible goods of knowledge and experience of the Greek world motivated humanists traveling to Greece. For a different perspective on the ownership of books, see Findlen, "Possessing the Past," 92–93.

53. On the declining Western interest in Arab learning following this shift, see W. Keith Percival, "Changes in the Approach to Language," in *Cambridge History of Later Medieval Philosophy*, ed. Norman Kretzmann et al., 817; Rodinson, *Europe and the Mystique of Islam*, 31.

54. Steven Runciman, *The Last Byzantine Renaissance* (Cambridge: Cambridge University Press, 1970), 18–23.

55. On the movement of Greek refugees in the Aegean and other areas, see Apostolos Vacalopoulos, "The Flight of the Inhabitants of Greece to the Aegean Islands, Crete, and Mane during the Turkish Invasions (Fourteenth and Fifteenth Centuries)," in *Charanis Studies*, ed. Laiou-Thomadakis, 272–83.

56. Housley, *Later Crusades*, 81; see also Runciman, *Fall of Constantinople*, 1.

57. His timing was not propitious for Western powers. France and England were experiencing renewed tensions in the Hundred Years War; Giangaleazzo Visconti of Milan was trying to bring northern Italy under his control, very nearly succeeding. The papal schism also continued to divide Europe.

58. Adam Usk, *Chronicon*, in *Byzantium*, ed. Deno John Geanakoplos (Chicago: University of Chicago Press, 1984), 38.

59. The council actually first met in Ferrara but soon had to move to Florence due to an outbreak of the plague.

60. The above discussion is based on Geanakoplos, "The Council of Florence (1438–39) and the Problem of Union between the Byzantine and Latin Churches," in Geanakoplos, *Constantinople and the West*, 224–54.

61. Joseph Gill, S.J., *The Council of Florence* (Cambridge: Cambridge University Press, 1959), 184.

62. Paolo Viti, "Il concilio Fiorentino del 1439," in Viti, *Leonardo Bruni e Firenze*, 191. Prior to this, Bruni had personally labored to bring the council from

Ferrara to Florence; see ibid., 137–88. Bruni's *Constitution of Florence*, written in Greek, seems to be another intellectual consequence of the Council of Florence. As Athanasios Moulakis argues, it was probably composed in honor of the republic's guests in order to acquaint them with the Florentine government; see his "Bruni's Constitution of Florence," *Rinascimento*, 2nd ser., 26 (1986): 143.

63. Gill, *Council of Florence*, 183.

64. See Vespasiano da Bisticci, *Renaissance Princes, Popes and Prelates*, ed. Myron Gilmore, tr. William George and Emily Waters (New York: Harper and Row, 1963), 26; cf. Geanakoplos, *Byzantium*, 310.

65. Ihor Sevcenko, quoted by Setton, "Byzantine Background," 71.

66. Setton, "Byzantine Background," 71.

67. Piero's depiction of John VIII as Pontius Pilate is far less flattering than Gozzoli's magi. Carlo Ginzburg argues that the flagellation is symbolic of the Turks' attacks on the Eastern Church, as depicted by the turbaned individual in the scene, and Byzantium's indecision and complicity in refusing to uphold the Church union; at the same time it was meant to act as a summons to crusade for its recipient, Federico da Montefeltro, the duke of Urbino. See Carlo Ginzburg, *The Enigma of Piero della Francesca*, tr. Martin Ryle and Kate Soper (London: Verso, 1985).

68. Gill, *Council of Florence*, 105–6.

69. Ibid., 114.

70. Deno John Geanakoplos, "Council of Florence," in Geanakoplos, *Constantinople and the West*, 249–50.

71. Setton, "Byzantine Background," 70. Ambrogio Traversari, for one, was greatly impressed by Bessarion and discussions of his library in Modon.

72. As Woodhouse states, however, determining who came into contact with Plethon in Florence, much less what they discussed, is a difficult task; see Woodhouse, *George Gemistos Plethon*, 26, 88–90, 155–57.

73. See John Monfasani, "Greek Renaissance Migrations," *Italian History and Culture* 8 (2002): 1–14; idem, "The Averroism of John Argyropoulos and His *Quaestio utrum intellectus humanus sit perpetuus*," *I Tatti Studies* 5 (1993): 157–208.

74. Giuseppe Cammelli, *I dotti bizantini e le origini dell'umanesimo: Manuele Crisolora* (Florence: Valecchi Editore, 1941), 1:26–31; see also Setton, "Byzantine Background," 56–57; Maisano and Rollo, *Manuele Crisolora*.

75. Holmes, *Florentine Enlightenment*, 9–15. On Bruni's translations of Greek texts, including his famous rendition of Aristotle's *Politics*, see Wilson, *From Byzantium to Italy*, 14–22, 29–31.

76. Kristeller, *Renaissance Thought and Its Sources*, 142–43.

77. Holmes, *Florentine Enlightenment*, 10.

78. Guarino da Verona (1374–1460), a student of Chrysoloras in Constantinople, taught Greek in Venice to many students including Vittorino da Feltre (1378–1446). Both Guarino and Vittorino established prestigious schools in northern Italy, the former mostly in Ferrara, the latter in Mantua, where both Greek and Latin proficiency were stressed. See Wilson, *Byzantium to Italy*, 34–47.

79. See Section 2 above for Chrysoloras's influence on Pier Paolo Vergerio.

In 1416 Andrea Giuliano, a student of Guarino da Verona, wrote a funeral oration on Chrysoloras in which he claimed that Chrysoloras's teaching helped save the Greek culture from extinction under the Turks; see McManamon, *Funeral Oratory*, 125. See also James Hankins, "Lo studio Greco nell'Occidente latino," in *I Greci: storia, cultura, arte, società*, ed. Salvatore Settis (Turin: Giulio Einaudi Editore, 2001), 3:1251.

80. Hankins, "Chrysoloras and the Greek Studies of Leonardo Bruni," 176–81.

81. Bessarion's first name was widely believed to be John, but evidence has come to light showing that it was actually Basil. See Concetta Bianca, *Da Bisanzio a Roma: Studi sul Cardinale Bessarione* (Rome: Roma nel Rinascimento, 1999), 141–49. Thanks to John Monfasani for this reference. Biographical details have largely been taken from the *Dizionario biografico degli Italiani*, 9:686–96. See also Monfasani's *Byzantine Scholars*; Ludwig Mohler, *Kardinal Bessarion als Theologe, Humanist, und Staatsmann* (1923; repr., Aalen: Scientia Verlag, 1967).

82. For most Latin compositions, however, Bessarion relied on the services of a ghostwriter, identified as Niccolò Perotti by Monfasani; see "Bessarion Latinus," in Monfasani, *Byzantine Scholars*, II:166–67. Thanks to James Hankins for this reference.

83. "Quis enim ignorat, quae etiam temporalia mala ex hac divisione nos secutura sunt? quae infortunia? quodque communem hostem et inimicum nobis Turcarum principem robustiorem contra nos ipsos efficimus? in periculoque sunt, ut omnino fere pereant quicunque ritum nostrum sequuntur Christiani, nomenque Christi illic totaliter deleatur" (Bessarion, *Oratio Dogmatica*, in *Patrologia Graeca*, ed. J. P. Migne, 1866, vol. 161:608).

84. "Quis enim nescit quod solum nobis relictum refugium erat Latinorum amicitia et unio cum eis futura, hac re sperantibus et nos ipsos tueri posse, et hostes devincere; quodque hoc solum hostem deterrebat, et eius contra nos furorem refraenabat?" (ibid., 609).

85. Bessarion was correct in stressing Ottoman fears regarding papal support, as would be later seen in Mehmed's preferential treatment of Orthodox Christian subjects over Roman Catholics.

86. Bessarion was papal governor of Bologna at the time and received the news from Venice's envoy; see Smith, "Pope Pius II's Use," 409.

87. "Urbs quae modo tali imperatore, tot illustrissimis viris, tot clarissimis antiquissimisque familiis, tanta rerum copia florebat, totius Graeciae caput, splendor et decus orientis, gymnasium optimarum artium bonorum omnium receptaculum ab immanissimis barbaris et saevissimis christianae fidei hostibus, a truculentissimis feris capta, spoliata, direpta, exhausta est. Publica pecunia dilapidata, privatae opes extinctae, Templa auro, argento, gemmis, reliquiis sanctorum aliaque pretiosissima supellectile nudata . . ." (Vast, *Cardinal Bessarion*, 454–55). English tr. (with some modifications), McLaughlin, "Letter to Francesco Foscari," in *Portable Renaissance Reader*, 71.

88. Smith, "Pope Pius II's Use," 409. On the fall of Constantinople as a chosen trauma with meaning for Western Christians as a group, see Volkan and Itzkowitz, *Turks and Greeks*, 43–44.

89. Deno John Geanakoplos, *Interaction of the "Sibling" Byzantine and Western Cultures in the Middle Ages and Italian Renaissance* (New Haven, Conn.: Yale University Press, 1976), 181.

90. Aeneas Silvius, Piccolomini (Pope Pius II), *Memoirs of a Renaissance Pope: The Commentaries of Pius II*, tr. Florence A. Gragg, ed. Leona C. Gabel (New York: Capricorn Books, 1959), 241–59; see also Schwoebel, *Shadow of the Crescent*, 68–70.

91. "(ad praedicationem Evangelii missus,) post multas diversasque nationes, quas fidei rectae christianoque nomini dedicaveram, tandem in Achaiam, Peloponnesi provinciam, multitudine hominum [cum] nobilitate tum doctrina praeditorum referctam, ita longe lateque Evangelii veritatem disseminavi ut omnem provinciam ab idolorum cultu ad veri Dei religionem converterim" (Aeneas Silvius Piccolomini [Pope Pius II], *I Commentarii*, ed. Luigi Totaro [Milan: Adelphi Edizioni, 1984], 2:1546; English tr., *Memoirs*, 255–56). Bessarion published this oration in 1467, in a revised version; Pius most likely received a copy of the oration from Bessarion and incorporated it into his *Commentaries*. See John Monfasani, "Bessarion Latinus," in Monfasani, *Byzantine Scholars*, II:166, n. 6.

92. "ego . . . profugiens, ad te . . . ita ego quoque ad te confugiens filios, quos mihi, vel potius tibi, immo vero Christo Domino nostro, genueram, impiis nunc et truculentissimis hostibus subditos, et non modo libertate corporum privatos, sed etiam de fidei integritate periclitantes, ope atque auxilio tuo ad pristinam libertatem . . . restituam . . ." (Piccolomini, *Commentarii*, 1546, 1548; English tr., *Memoirs*, 256).

93. For a discussion of the translation of this relic within the context of Rome's cult of martyrdom, see Stinger, *Renaissance in Rome*, 174–77.

94. John Julius Norwich, *A History of Venice* (New York: Vintage Books, 1989), 350–51.

95. Schwoebel, *Shadow of the Crescent*, 167.

96. See Margaret Meserve, "Cardinal Bessarion's Orations against the Turks and Their Printing History" (M.A. thesis, Warburg Institute, University of London, 1993).

97. At the same point in time Donato Acciaiuoli expressed his hope for such a development in a letter to Antonio Ivani, written shortly after the loss of Negroponte (20 July 1470); see BNCF, Magliabecchiano VIII, 1390, fol. 54v. Pope Paul II reacted by exhorting members of the Most Holy League to unite in a common assault against the Turks and calling an assembly in Rome; see Giuseppe Müller, ed., *Documenti sulle relazioni delle città toscane coll'Oriente cristiano e coi Turchi* (1879; repr., Rome: Società Multigrafica Editrice, 1966), 212–14.

98. Here Bessarion is referring to the disastrous civil wars that plagued the Byzantine Empire in the fourteenth century.

99. "Nihil aliud miseram exstinxit Graeciam, nisi discordia; nihil aliud eam orbis partem delevit, nisi bella civilia, neque solum nostra memoria, sed et priscis temporibus" (Bessarion, *Orationes contra Turcas*, in *Patrologia Graeca* vol. 161, 662.

100. See Chapter 2 for a full discussion of the work.

101. Labowsky, "Cardinale Bessarione e gli inizi della Biblioteca Marciana," 159–82.

102. For Jardine's interpretation of Bessarion's choice of Venice as approval of the republic's worldly interests, see her *Worldly Goods*, 63.

103. "Quamvis autem huic rei toto animo semper incubuerim, ardentiori tamen studio post Graeciae excidium et defleendam [*sic*] Byzantii captivitatem, in perquirendis graecis libris omnes meas vires, omnem curam, omnem operam, facultatem industriamque consumpsi. Verebar enim et vehementissime formida- bam ne cum caeteris rebus tot excellentissimi libri, tot summorum virorum sudores atque vigiliae, tot lumina orbis terrae brevi tempore periclitarentur atque perirent. . . ." (cited in Agostino Pertusi, "Le epistole storiche," in *Lauro Quirini umanista*, ed. Krautter et al., 182–83).

104. See Chapter 2.

105. This is not to minimize Bessarion's reverence for Greek Church fathers, who also represented a crowning achievement in Greek culture; see Geanakoplos, *Interaction of the "Sibling" Cultures*, 50–51, 293.

106. Chalcondyles taught Greek in Padua, Florence, and Milan; he also edited Greek texts and expended much effort trying to raise support in Italy for a crusade against the Turks. See Geanakoplos, *Interaction of the "Sibling" Cultures*, 231–53; Cammelli, *I dotti bizantini*, vol. 3.

107. "teterrimos immanissimos atque impios barbaros thurcos . . ." (Geana- koplos, *Interaction of the "Sibling" Cultures*, 300; English tr., 260).

108. "Ut quemadmodum ipsa omnes res suas preciossimas atque prestantissi- mas liberaliter et absque aliqua parsimonia iis erogaverat suaque manu ac virtute armorum Italiam olim a Gothis oppressam in suum statum restituerat. Ita nunc iacentem atque afflictam elevare et armis a manibus barbarorum liberare velint" (ibid). Ironically, the Romans were probably in little need of rescue under the Ostrogoths, who shared a good deal of power with the old Roman aristocracy and brought stability to the region. Justinian's disruptive war drove a wedge between the two groups and left the peninsula too weak to withstand the Lombard inva- sions that soon followed. See Roger Collins, *Early Medieval Europe 300–1000* (New York: St. Martin's Press, 1991), 101, 125–26.

109. The Byzantine Greeks continued to call themselves *Romioi* in recogni- tion that their empire was once the eastern half of the Roman Empire. Many West- erners such as Petrarch bristled under the word choice and what it represented, showing their possessiveness over Roman identity.

110. Background on George's life, activities, and thought may be found in Monfasani's *George of Trebizond*; Hankins, *Plato in the Italian Renaissance*, 1:pt. 3 passim.

111. Monfasani, *George of Trebizond*, 128–30.

112. "Militiades devictis Darii copiis, Themistocles pulso Xerse ingentique illo exercitu deleto triumphum de ipsis duxerunt. Alexander Magnus universam vas- tavit Asiam. Asiatici autem conati quidem sunt in Europam sepius transire, sed, Hellesponti claustris repulsi fuerunt," (George of Trebizond, *Collectanea Trapez- untiana*, ed. Monfasani, 436).

113. "Europam Parthi, qui tunc vigebant, vastarent, in Constantinopolin ab

eo conditam Romanum imperium transtulit, que urbs eos huc usque repulit" (ibid., 436).

114. As Monfasani points out, Constantinople was not on the Hellespont but the Bosporus; George most likely shifted the geographical setting to make it coincide with apocalyptic thought regarding the impending battle to hold back Gog and Magog. See ibid., 434.

115. Ibid., 437.

116. As William C. Jordan has argued, by the mid-thirteenth century "Christendom" for Western Europeans had come to exclude regions in Eastern Europe where Orthodox Christianity predominated. See Jordan, "'Europe' in the Middle Ages," in *Idea of Europe*, ed. Pagden, 75.

117. Monfasani, *George of Trebizond*, 51–52; George of Trebizond, *Collectanea*, 423–31.

118. These works will be discussed in detail in Chapter 4.

119. Born in Constantinople, Lascaris later studied at Padua, with support from Cardinal Bessarion. Like George of Trebizond and Bessarion, he mastered Latin as well as Greek. In 1475 he settled in Florence, where he would remain for twenty years as a teacher of Greek and director of the Medici Library. He went on to serve the kings of France and the papacy as a scholar and diplomat, always searching for ways to publicize and oppose the Turkish advance. See Schwoebel, *Shadow of the Crescent*, 161–66; Émile Legrand, *Bibliographie Hellenique* (Paris: Ernest Leroux Editeur, 1885), 1:131–32.

120. Lascaris communicated his findings in letters using code for such terms as the grand master of Rhodes, the Lord Turk, war, and peace. See Sebastiano Gentile, "Lorenzo e Giano Lascaris: Il fondo greco della biblioteca medicea privata," in *Lorenzo il Magnifico e il suo mondo*, ed. Gian Carlo Garfagnini (Florence: Leo S. Olschki Editore, 1994), 181–82. See also Börge Knös, *Un ambassadeur de l'hellenisme, Janus Lascaris et la tradition greco-byzantine dans l'humanisme français* (Uppsala: Almquist & Wiksells Boktryckeri AB, 1945), chap. 2; Schwoebel, *Shadow of the Crescent*, 161–66. A native Florentine, Benedetto Dei, also spied for the republic in the Ottoman East; see Benedetto Dei, *La Cronica dall'anno 1400 all'anno 1500*, ed. Roberto Barducci (Florence: Francesco Papafava Editore, 1984); Paolo Orvieto, "Un esperto orientalista del '400: Benedetto Dei," *Rinascimento*, 2d ser., 9 (1969): 205–75.

121. Lorenzo had shown some hesitation in supporting the terms of proposed anti-Turk leagues in Italy. Moreover, much has been made of Lorenzo's gift to Sultan Mehmed II in 1480 of a portrait medal in gratitude for the sultan's role in apprehending and extraditing Bernardo Bandini de' Baroncelli, a member of the Pazzi conspiracy who had fled to Constantinople; see Babinger, "Lorenzo e la corte ottomana," 318–322.

122. Schwoebel, *Shadow of the Crescent*, 162; Knös, *Ambassadeur*, 54–55.

123. On this occasion he delivered a speech, a French version of which Belleforest published fifty years later. See Heath, *Crusading Commonplaces*, 28–29; Schwoebel, *Shadow of the Crescent*, 165–66. Portions of the text of the *Harangue* are provided in Legrand, *Bibliographie Hellenique*, 1:153–56.

124. Argyropoulos will be discussed in the next section. Musurus's "Hymn to

Plato," dedicated to Pope Leo X in 1513, urges the pontiff in the voice of Plato to aid his countrymen against the barbarian Turks. Such aid would act as a reward for the great cultural gifts Greeks have brought to the West. A rather florid translation was done by William Roscoe in *The Life and Pontificate of Leo X* (1805–6; rev. ed. by Thomas Roscoe, London: Henry G. Bohn, 1846), 1.421–26; Deno John Geanakoplos discusses the work and provides a portion of Roscoe's translation in *Greek Scholars in Venice: Studies in the Dissemination of Greek Learning from Byzantium to Western Europe* (Cambridge: Harvard University Press, 1962), 150–53.

125. Babinger, *Mehmed the Conqueror*, 116–17.

126. Bessarion's beard was actually quite long. Babinger comments that the Greeks' failure to "trim their silly beards" apparently irritated Italians who wished the haughty refugees would endeavor to assimilate; see ibid., 116.

127. On the ruin of Greece as a sixteenth-century commonplace, see Heath, *Crusading Commonplaces*, 30–31; Chew, *Crescent and the Rose*, 133–37. As Chew points out, however, Greek refugees begging for assistance became identified with unscrupulous swindlers; see ibid., 137–41.

128. For a fuller discussion, see my article "Petrarch's Vision." See also Paul Piur, *Petrarcas Buch ohne Namen und die päpstliche Kurie, ein Beitrag zur Geistesgeschichte der Frührenaissance* (Halle: M. Niemeyer, 1925), 95–99; Roberto Weiss, "Petrarca e il mondo Greco," in Roberto Weiss, *Medieval and Humanist Greek: Collected Essays by Roberto Weiss* (Padua: Antenore, 1977), 166–92.

129. Setton, "Byzantine Background," 40–45.

130. Ibid., 43.

131. The Byzantine emperor John V made a similar statement to the papacy in 1358; see Elizabeth A. Zachariadou, *Trade and Crusade: Venetian Crete and the Emirates of Menteshe and Aydin (1300–1415)* (Venice: Istituto Ellenico di Studi Bizantini e Postbizantini, 1983), 65.

132. "Leo noster vere Calaber, sed ut ipse vult Thessalus, quasi nobilius sit Graecum esse quam Italum . . ." (Francesco Petrarch, *Opera Omnia* [1554; repr. Ridgewood, N.J.: Gregg Press, 1965], 2:857; English tr., *Letters of Old Age*, tr. Bernardo et al., 1:100.

133. "Graeci enim Constantinopolim alteram Romam vocant. Quam non parem modo antique, sed maiorem corporibus ac divitiis effectam, dicere ausi sunt. Quod si in utroque verum esset, sicut in utroque Sozomeni hoc scribentis, pace dixerim falsum est, certe viris, armis, ac virtutibus, et gloria parem dicere, quamvis impudens Graeculus non audebit" (ibid., 2:858 and 1:101 respectively).

134. "quisquis dixerit, dicat idem et servum nobiliorem esse quam dominum" (Franceso Petrarch, *Le familiari*, ed. Vittorio Rossi [Florence: G. C. Sansoni Editore, 1937], 1:24; English tr., *Letters on Familiar Matters*, tr. Bernardo, 1:25. On questions regarding the dating of this letter, see my article "Petrarch's Vision," 312 n. 141.

135. Zachariadou, *Trade and Crusade*, 159–63; see also Lock, *Franks in the Aegean*, 255.

136. Francesco Petrarch, *Itinerario in Terra Santa*, ed. and tr. Francesco Lo Monaco (Bergamo: Pierluigi Lubrina Editore, 1990), 68. The *Itinerarium* was recently edited and translated by Theodore J. Cachey Jr. in Francesco Petrarch,

Petrarch's Guide to the Holy Land: Itinerary to the Sepulcher of Our Lord Jesus Christ (Notre Dame, Ind.: University of Notre Dame Press, 2002).

137. Petrarch, *Familiari*, 3:278; *Letters on Familiar Matters*, 3:46. On Petrarch's warm embrace of the German Charles IV's claim as [Holy] Roman Emperor, see letter 32.6 in *Letters of Old Age*.

138. See James Harvey Robinson, *Petrarch the First Modern Man of Letters* (New York: Haskell House Publishers Ltd., 1970), 35.

139. See Bisaha, "Petrarch's Vision," 308.

140. This appears to be a reference to a joint attack on a Genoese fleet near Constantinople (13 February 1352)—Petrarch earlier in the letter mentions "three very powerful peoples" attacking the Genoese but does not name them. This could be an allusion to Aragon, Venice, and Byzantium. See Norwich, *History of Venice*, 217–18.

141. "Quinetiam de fallacibus atque inertibus Greculis et per se grande nichil ausuris non modo non doleo sed valde gaudeo, et infame illud imperium sedemque illam errorum vestris manibus eversum iri cupio, si forte vos iniuriarum suarum vindices Cristus elegit et hanc vobis ab omni plebe catholica male dilatam reposuit ultionem" Petrarch, *Familiari*, 3:120; *Letters on Familiar Matters*, 2:239.

142. On Western attempts to gather a crusade against Byzantium in the decades following 1261, see Housley, *Later Crusades*, 50–55. Ramón Lull, among others, also advocated conquest of Constantinople as a necessary step toward a successful crusade to the Holy Land in his *De aquisitione Terrae Sanctae* (1309); see Housley, *Documents on the Later Crusades*, 47–48.

143. "certe nos nostrosque hostes, a quibus nunc Hierosolyma detinetur, magnum aequor interiacct, itaque cum illis ut res nostrae, et illorum sunt, non parvus est labor . . . inter nos autem, et hos Graeculos, nihil est medium, nisi noster sopor ac nostra segnities, quibus ut odii plurimum sic nihil est virium, nilque ibi volentibus negotii est, duobus Italiae populis sponsor sim, si tu bene velle ceperis, brevi eos non iunctos modo, sed unumquemque per se, vel imbelle illud imperium eversuros, vel ad iugum matris Ecclesiae deducturos" (Petrarch, *Opera*, 2: 912; *Letters of Old Age*, 1:257).

144. Petrarch, *De vita solitaria*, ed. and tr. Noce, 234; English tr., *Life of Solitude*, ed. and tr. Zeitlin, 242.

145. ". . . cum primum Robertum amicabiliter susceperis fecerisque doceri, multorum animos ad linguam Helladum accendisti, ut iam videre videar multos fore grecarum litterarum post paucorum annorum curricula non tepide studiosos" (Salutati, *Epistolario*, 3:108; English tr. in Setton, "Byzantine Background," 57).

146. "inter deperdita penes Grecos ferme studia litterarum, cunctorum occupatis mentibus ambitione, voluptatibus et avaricia, te sentiam, veluti lumen in tenebris, emersisse" (ibid.).

147. Petrarch, Letter to Giovanni Dondi of Padua (1370); *Letters of Old Age*, 2:172. Bruni, on the other hand, attributed the decline in Greek learning to the Turkish advance, as was discussed in Chapter 2.

148. A Latinophile, Cydones was one of the few Greeks who viewed late trecento Italian scholarship as outstripping that of Byzantines. See Woodhouse, *George Gemistos Plethon*, 121, 154.

149. "Sed unum est, quo de te summe letatus sum, quod videlicet intelligam tue gentis erroribus in fide, sine qua salvari non possumus, te non teneri, ut michi tecum sermo sit non solum ut cum erudito, sed etiam cum ortodoxo" (Salutati, *Epistolario*, 3:109).

150. Monfasani, *George of Trebizond*, 134; see Chapter 4 below for a discussion of George's writings to Mehmed II.

151. George was imprisoned by the papal curia (1466) under suspicion of treason because of his letters to Mehmed. See Monfasani, *George of Trebizond*, chap. 6. Kritoboulos's views, it may be noted, are somewhat complicated by his position as a member of Mehmed's administration—governor of Imbros—and by the dedication of his history of Mehmed II to the conqueror.

152. Cochrane, *Historians and Historiography*, 328–34.

153. Robin Cormack has argued that the inhabitants of Venetian Crete freely intermingled, intermarried and often crossed over into one another's cultural and religious practices; see his "Where East Is West: Art and Its Viewers on Venetian Crete" (paper delivered at the 31st International Congress on Medieval Studies, Kalamazoo, Mich., 10 May 1996).

154. Geanakoplos, *Interaction of the "Sibling" Cultures*, chap. 9. For further discussion of the complex relationships between Venetians and Cretans, see Sally McKee, *Uncommon Dominion: Venetian Crete and the Myth of Ethnic Purity* (Philadelphia: University of Pennsylvania Press, 2000).

155. Agostino Pertusi, "Le Notizie sulla organizzazione amministrativa e militare dei Turchi nello 'Strategicon' Adversum Turcos' di Lampo Birago (c. 1453–55)," in *Studi sul medioevo cristiano: offerti a Raffaello Morghen* (Rome: Istituto Storico Italiano, 1974) 2:674–85; see also Pertusi, *Caduta di Costantinopoli*, 2:112–13.

156. Biblioteca Apostolica Vaticana, Rome, Lat. 3423, fol. 53r–v; see also Stinger, *Renaissance in Rome*, 121–22. Pertusi partially edited Birago's treatise in *Caduta di Costantinopoli*, vol. 2, and in "Notizie sulla organizzazione," 692–99.

157. See Geanakoplos, *Constantinople and the West*, 91–113; Cammelli, *I dotti bizantini*, vol. 2. See also Monfasani, "Averroism of John Argyropoulos."

158. Letter to Jacopo Lucensi: "Vir enim mihi visus est non solum eruditus ut fama audieram sed etiam sapiens gravis et vetere illa grecia dignus" (BNCF, Magliabecchiano VIII, 1390, fol. 85v.; see also Cammelli, *I dotti bizantini*, 2:48, for an edited version with slight alterations in spelling). Donato would shortly begin supporting Argyropoulos for a chair at the University of Florence; see Field, *Origins of the Platonic Academy*, chap. 4.

159. "Is igitur eversa nobilissima patria filiis in manibus barbarorum relictis omnibus bonis spoliatus ad pontificem confugere statuit quem unicum praesidium fortunis suis in tanta rerum iactura futurum esse confidit" (Acciaiuoli, [Letters] Magliabecchiano, VIII, 1390, fol. 85v; Cammelli, *I dotti bizantini*, 2:47–48).

160. See Setton, "Byzantine Background."

161. Acciaiuoli, (Letters) Magliabecchiano VIII, 1390, fol. 89v. Also, it may be noted that in his funeral oration on John Hunyadi, Donato does not seize the chance to praise Hungary as a Roman Catholic country, unlike Greece.

162. Legrand, *Bibliographie Hellenique* 1:80. See also Hankins's edition of a

Latin invective against the Greek scholar Andronicus Callistus in his "Renaissance Crusaders," 203–04.

163. Geanakoplos, *Interaction of the "Sibling" Cultures*, 281–82, 244–45.

164. "Non enim possum in communi mestitia non et ipse mestus esse" (Bracciolini, *Lettere*, ed. Harth, 3:158).

165. Cf. Schwoebel, *Shadow of the Crescent*, 17.

166. "digni mihi omni supplicio videntur" (Bracciolini, *Opera Omnia*, 89).

167. "Bis iam fidei professionem catholicae in conciliis factam abnegarunt. Tanta vero in illis tum ignavia, tum avaritia valuit, ut cum plurimo auro argentoque abundarent, ne nummum quidem impendere voluerint in eorum urbis tutelam, credo ut opulentiorem praedam Teucris reliquerent . . ." (ibid.).

168. "non casu sed divino iudicio ea calamitas accidisse videatur" (ibid.).

169. Given the multiplicity of voices in dialogues, the author's opinion may be difficult to gauge. He may express his views through several speakers or none at all.

170. For example: "Plures erant cives abundantes auro atque argento, quorum nemo ut integram predam servaret hosti in tutelam patrie nummum voluit impendere." See M. C. Davies, "Poggio Bracciolini as Rhetorician and Historian: Unpublished Pieces," *Rinascimento* 2d ser., 22 (1982): 177.

171. Runciman rejects Western accusations of hoarding; see his *Fall of Constantinople*, 80. But there are examples of parsimony, such as the Grand Duke Notaras's denial of his fabulous wealth to the struggling city; thanks to Marios Phillipides for this point.

172. Schwoebel discusses the mixed reactions of guilt and laying blame on the Greeks; see his *Shadow of the Crescent*, 14–17.

173. "Et ei Nicolao quinto christianorum summo pontifice, et Alphonso aragonum rege, regnum Sicilie possidente, ac etiam a populo Venetorum, regique Ungariae postulantibus auxilium non traduntur" (Tignosi, *Expugnatio*, ed. Sensi, 425).

174. "Quamobrem veri christicole perhibent tantam cladem Deum trinum et unum, que vere colimus, permisisse, voluisseque de hostibus suis, cum inimicis aliis vendicari. Quos, ut vides, meriti sunt in virga ferrea castigavit [*sic*]" (ibid., 428). (As the manuscript Vatican Urb. Lat. 923, fol. 36v, shows the same rendition for the last sentence, this may be a scribal error.)

175. Tignosi, *Expugnatio*, ed. Sensi, 381. See Chapter 2 for Tignosi's description of the atrocities.

176. Basile G. Spiridonakis, *Grecs, Occidentaux et Turcs de 1054 à 1453: quatre siècles d'histoire de relations internationales* (Thessaloniki: Institute for Balkan Studies, 1990), 205–6. See also Patrides, "Bloody and Cruell Turke."

177. Piccolomini, *Memoirs of a Renaissance Pope*, 65. Aeneas also openly repeated this criticism to Nicholas in his letter to him following the fall of Constantinople; see Pertusi, *Caduta de Costantinopoli* 2:48.

178. For a full discussion of this, see my article "Pius II's Letter to Sultan Mehmed"; see also Chapter 4 below.

179. "Non pugnabis contra feminas, aut Italiam, aut Hungariam, aut aliam in

occidenti provinciam ingressus" (Piccolomini, *Epistola ad Mahomatem*, ed. and tr. Baca, English, 13; Latin, 117).

180. ". . . paucissimi sub tuo imperio Christiani sunt, qui ad veritatem ambulent Evangelii. Graeci a Romanae Ecclesiae unitate aberant, cum tu Constantinopolim invasisti, neque adhuc decretum Florentinum acceperant et in errore stabant" (ibid., English, 17; Latin, 121).

181. Jean-Claude Margolin, "Place et fonction de la rhétorique," in *Pio II*, ed. Tarugi, 243–62; see especially 255.

182. For details on Filelfo's activities regarding the Greeks and the Turks, see Schwoebel, *Shadow of the Crescent*, 150–51; for the oration at Mantua, see Chapter 2 above.

183. "qui dubitasses [sic] me non litteraturam solum sed naturam etiam Graecorum adamavisse, ob idque factum omnino graecum" (from Gianvito Resta, "Filelfo tra Bisanzio e Roma," in *Francesco Filelfo nel quinto centenario della morte: atti del XVII convegno di studi maceratesi* [Padua: Editrice Antenore, 1986], 11).

184. Ibid., 48; see also his letter to Giovanni Garzoni (1468), ibid., 12–13. Many Western humanists took this view further, arguing that Greek should be learned not for its own sake but to assist in the study of Latin; see James Hankins, "Lo studio Greco nell'Occidente latino," in *I Greci*, ed. Settis, 3:1252–53.

185. *Francesco Filelfo nel quinto centenario*, 49; Cammelli, *I dotti bizantini*, 2:78. See Francesco Filelfo, *Cent-dix lettres grecques de François Filelfe*, ed. Émile Legrand (Paris: Ernest Leroux Editeur, 1892).

186. "sunt enim lachrymabilis pars Constantinopolitani naufragii qui et se et suos ab impiis Turcis redimere cupientes . . ." (Cammelli, *I dotti bizantini*, 2:78 n. 1).

187. Schwoebel, *Shadow of the Crescent*, 151.

188. Agostino Pertusi has edited the Greek text and translated it into Italian in *Testi inediti*, 264–69.

189. Francesco Filelfo, *Cent-dix lettres*, 65; see also Schwoebel, *Shadow of the Crescent*, 151; Tateo, "L'ideologia umanistica," 159.

190. Francesco Filelfo, *Cent-dix lettres*, 65.

191. Letter to Lodrisio Crivelli (August 1, 1465); ibid., 66.

192. Schwoebel, *Shadow of the Crescent*, 151–52.

193. Ibid., 152.

194. For more on the *Amyris*, see Chapter 2.

195. "Inde etiam Graeci, qui, post tot bella peracta / cum fraude atque dolis, victricia signa tulerunt / et servos duxere tuos, Mahomette, parentes, / sortiti sunt digna sua sibi praemia culpa" (Giovanni Mario Filelfo, *Amyris*, ed. Manetti, 69). Kritoboulos, it may be noted, also portrays Mehmed claiming vengeance on behalf of his Trojan ancestors; see Kritoboulos, *History of Mehmed*, 181–82.

196. Giovanni Mario Filelfo, *Amyris*, 69 n. 467; see also bk. 2, line 39.

197. Ibid., 30; see bk. 1, lines 521–96.

198. "Sed si vera licet fari, iam Graecia cunctas / mordebat sordes, iam nullis laudibus usquam / dedita, lascivo marcebat denique lecto; / non studii, ut quondam, vaenatrix Graecia, legum / non erat inventrix, nec in iis vel doctus

Homerus, / vel Plato, sive Conon. . . . Nam tot modo dogmata falsa / quae in nostram venere fidem, tot fusa venena / in Christi ecclesiam, Graecis suasoribus atque / paulatim dura structoribus arte fuerunt, / inventis composta malis, stimulantubus [*sic*] hydris / assidue Stygiis, infernique usque tyranno" (ibid., 115–16).

199. Ibid., 31, 91–98.

200. On his procrusade writings, see Chapter 2.

201. The Greeks' identification with schism and their perceived punishment by God may have played a greater role in these ambivalent attitudes than we might today imagine.

202. For example, while supporting the need for aid to Greece, Benedetto Accolti and Flavio Biondo criticized the Greeks' actions and schismatic beliefs. In his history of the First Crusade, Accolti paints the Greeks as apathetic to the advance of the Seljuk Turks circa 1095. They did not care enough about the dangers threatening the faith to ask Westerners for help; indeed the only reason a crusade took place, he argues, was through the initiative of Peter the Hermit, who witnessed the problems in the East and approached the pope. See Accolti, *De bello a christianis*, 533–34. In his exhortation to Alfonso of Aragon, Biondo insinuated that the Greeks preferred to lose their empire rather than end the schism. See Biondo, *Scritti inediti*, ed. Nogara, cxxxvi, 37.

203. Schwoebel, *Shadow of the Crescent*, 17.

204. Leonard of Chios, a Genoese papal legate, was attempting to carry out the terms of the church union when the city fell, which explains his defensiveness. See Leonard of Chios, *Historia Constantinopolitanae*: 923–41; English tr., *Siege of Constantinople*, ed. and tr. Jones, 11–41.

205. Schwoebel, *Shadow of the Crescent*, 17–18. This poem has also been partially edited by Pertusi in *Caduta di Costantinopoli*, 1:198–213.

206. See, for example, the histories of Kritoboulos and Doukas for moments of praise or ambivalence regarding their Ottoman conquerors. The Phanariots are the most prominent example of Greeks who served and benefited from their Ottoman rulers.

207. This is not to discount the resentment of Greeks who remained in the East, many of whom faced relocation, flight, poverty, and crowded settlements. See Vacalopoulos, "Flight of the Inhabitants of Greece."

208. From the fifteenth century to the seventeenth century Italy was the area most heavily colonized by Greek refugees. The cities of Venice, Padua, Naples, and Ancona were home to "communities most important for the preservation of the Greek tradition and for the ultimate establishment of a politically independent nation." See Geanakoplos, *Interaction of the "Sibling" Cultures*, 176.

209. Even after the fall of Constantinople, popes such as Calixtus III continued to push for the observance of the union in Greek areas, especially Crete, where the ruling Venetians could provide some assistance. See Monfasani, *George of Trebizond*, 137–38.

210. Geanakoplos describes a greater sense of cultural accommodation on the part of Westerners than on the part of Greek refugees, i.e., Western Europeans absorbed more from the Greeks—mostly in terms of scholarship and the arts—than vice versa; see Geanakoplos, *Interaction of the "Sibling" Cultures*, 286–89.

Monfasani argues that the Greeks absorbed more from the Latins in terms of learning and culture; see his "Greek Renaissance Migrations," 10. Regardless of who borrowed more from the other, one clearly sees a growing acceptance and enthusiasm for Greek intellectual culture in Italy and, from the sixteenth century forward, northern Europe. Ancient Greece was also clearly being incorporated into Western Europe's own heritage.

211. Volkan and Itzkowitz, *Turks and Greeks*, 87.

212. Even nonhumanists could develop a sense of ancient Greece from vernacular romances and lamented its loss. See Heath, *Crusading Commonplaces*, 29.

213. Volkan and Itzkowitz, *Turks and Greeks*, 43.

214. Just as the Greeks developed a sense of philhellenism, so did many Europeans—a phenomenon that culminated in European support of and participation in the Greek nationalist movement centuries later. Lord Byron, who died in Greece during the revolution, is the most famous representative of the European romantic movement to aid in Greek liberation; see ibid., 85–86.

Chapter 4

1. See Chapter 1, for a broader introduction to medieval positions on Islam, with particular attention to crusade sermons and propaganda, crusade histories, and literary works.

2. Munro, "Western Attitude," 337.

3. Southern, *Western Views of Islam*, 39; Munro argues, however, that Peter never decided whether Islam was a heresy or paganism; see Munro, "Western Attitude," 337.

4. Over thirty copies are still extant. See Munro, "Western Attitude," 337; Cruz, "Popular Attitudes towards Islam," 65, 78 n. 65.

5. "Aggredior, inquam, vos, non, ut nostri saepe faciunt, armis, sed verbis, non vi, sed ratione, non odio, sed amore . . . vos diligo, diligens vobis scribo, scribens ad salutem invito" (Peter the Venerable, *Liber contra sectam Saracenorum*, ed. J. P. Migne, in *Patrologia Latina*, 1890, 189:673–74; English tr., based on Southern, *Western Views*, 39). Scholars who support the optimistic interpretation of Peter the Venerable include Southern, *Western Views;* and James Kritzeck, *Peter the Venerable and Islam* (Princeton, N.J.: Princeton University Press, 1964), Chapter 2.

6. Virginia Berry, "Peter the Venerable and the Crusades," in *Petrus Venerabilis*, ed. Constable and Kritzeck, 141–62.

7. Kritzeck has argued that Peter turned to crusade after experiencing a lack of support for his earlier plan; see his "Peter the Venerable and the Toledan Collection," in *Petrus Venerabilis*, ed. Constable and Kritzeck, 186. Both Berry and Siberry argue that Peter saw crusade as a step toward facilitating conversion; see Berry, "Peter the Venerable," 153; Siberry, *Criticism of Crusading*, 17. Kedar asserts that Peter was never proconversion and that the *Liber . . . Saracenorum* was a rhetorical piece designed to persuade Christians to avoid the temptations of Islam; see Kedar, *Crusade and Mission*, 99–103.

8. According to legend, Francis succeeded in secretly converting the sultan; see *The Little Flowers of St. Francis*, no. 23, in *St. Francis of Assisi: Writings and Early Biographies*, ed. Marion A. Habig (Chicago: Franciscan Herald Press, 1972), 1353–56. See also Keith Haines, "Attitudes and Impediments to Pacifism in Medieval Europe," *Journal of Medieval History* 7 (1981): 374. It is possible that Francis's greatest motive was to achieve martyrdom, but the first unofficial rule for his order includes an appeal to "all peoples, races, tribes, and tongues, all nations and all men of all countries;" see Kedar, *Crusade and Mission*, 119–26.

9. Kedar, *Crusade and Mission*, 116–19, 126–29.

10. What he knew of Muslims in the area led him optimistically to assert in 1273, "they are near to the faith and not far from the path of salvation"; see Southern, *Western Views*, 62.

11. Ibid., 56–57. See also Roberto Weiss, "England and the Decree of the Council of Vienne on the Teaching of Greek, Arabic, Hebrew, and Syriac," in Weiss, *Medieval and Humanist Greek*, 69.

12. See Siberry, *Criticism of Crusading*, 18, 207–8; Kedar, *Crusade and Mission*, 129–31, 178–80. Lull proposed the establishment of several schools where preachers would thoroughly learn the languages of non-Christians and schismatics (Hebrew, Arabic, Tatar, and Greek). But he also fervently supported crusade and wrote on the organization of military, ruling, and social bodies that needed to be established to capture and rule the Holy Land. See Housley, *Documents on the Later Crusades*, 35–40. On Humbert of Romans, see Palmer A. Throop, *Criticism of Crusade* (Amsterdam: N. V. Swets and Zeitlinger, 1940). Humbert's *Opus tripartitum* has been edited and translated by Jonathan and Louise Riley-Smith in *The Crusades: Idea and Reality* (London: Edward Arnold, 1981).

13. In the late eleventh century Anastasius the Librarian translated the Byzantine Theophanes' account of Islam into Latin, which was used by scholars. See Kedar, *Crusade and Mission*, 33–34, 86–87, 89.

14. Daniel, *Islam and the West*, 24; Kedar, *Crusade and Mission*, 87.

15. See Daniel, *Islam and the West*, 22–23; Tolan, *Petrus Alfonsi*, 3–11, 27–33.

16. Jacopo da Voragine, "The Life of St. Pelagius, Pope," in Jacopo da Voragine, *The Golden Legend: Readings on the Saints*, tr. William Granger Ryan (Princeton, N.J.: Princeton University Press, 1993), 2:370–73. See also Daniel, *Islam and the West*, 22–23; Tolan, *Petrus Alfonsi*, 109–10.

17. In bk. 1, chap. 2, he admits the difficulty in refuting the sacrilegious remarks of individual men that "are not so well known to us." See Saint Thomas Aquinas, *Summa contra Gentiles*, bk. 1, ed. and tr. Anton C. Pegis (Notre Dame, Ind.: University of Notre Dame Press, 1975), 62.

18. Aquinas, *Summa*, 73 (bk. 1, chap. 6).

19. Still, Aquinas supported holy war against Muslims when they were judged to be impeding the progress of the faith by means of blasphemy, evil suasions, or outright persecution. Blasphemy, Kedar points out, could be given a dangerously broad definition; see his *Crusade and Mission*, 183–84.

20. See Aquinas, *Summa*, 62 (bk. 1, chap. 2) and 74 (bk. 1, chap. 6).

21. McGinn, *Visions of the End*, 70–73; see also Emmerson, *Antichrist in the Middle Ages*, 48.

22. See David Burr, "Antichrist and Islam in Medieval Franciscan Exegesis," in *Medieval Christian Perceptions of Islam*, ed. Tolan, 147.

23. On Joachim, see Emmerson, *Antichrist in the Middle Ages*, 61, 67; Kedar, *Crusade and Mission*, 112–16. See also Reeves, *Influence of Prophecy*, passim.

24. Villani inserted a rather lengthy discussion on the rise of Islam into his chronicle on the history of Florence, including it among chapters dealing with "other perverse and barbarous people who invaded Italy," such as the Goths and Lombards; see Villani, *Nuova Cronica*, 1:120. I would like to thank Rala Djiakite for her suggestions on Villani.

25. Ibid., 114–15.

26. "e per iscusarsi della sua disordinata vita d'avolterio, si fece una legge seguendo la giudaica del vecchio Testamento, che qual femmina fosse trovata in avolterio fosse morta, salvo che collui, però ch'avea per comandamento da l'angiolo Gabriello ch'usasse le maritate per potere generare profeti" (ibid., 115).

27. See Setton, *Papacy and the Levant*. The foregoing discussion draws on Setton as well as Black, *Benedetto Accolti*; Stinger, *Renaissance in Rome*; Housley, *Later Crusades*; Schwoebel, *Shadow of the Crescent*.

28. Every pope from Nicholas V (1447–53) to Leo X (1513–21) proclaimed crusade, with the exception of Pius III (1503), who reigned only one month before his death; see Smith, "Pope Pius II's Use," 408. See also Riley-Smith, *Crusades*, 238–43, on the crusading activities of popes into the sixteenth century. One notable exception cited by Riley-Smith (*Crusades*, 243) was Paul IV (1555–59), who spent his time battling Protestant heretics rather than the Turkish Infidel.

29. Zoe, the daughter of the former Greek despot, Thomas, had been living in Rome as a ward of the papacy and as a practicing Roman Catholic. Despite Sixtus's generosity to Zoe and his hopes that her marriage to Ivan would pave the way for both Church union and a joint crusade, Zoe immediately took up Orthodoxy once again, helping to make Russia the "third Rome." See Setton, *Papacy and Levant*, 2:314–21.

30. Halil Inalcik believes that Innocent's pact with Bayezid II to keep Djem Sultan (the rival to the Ottoman throne) in Rome prevented him from pursuing crusade; see Inalcik, "A Case Study in Renaissance Diplomacy: The Agreement between Innocent VIII and Bayezid II Regarding Djem Sultan," in Inalcik, *The Middle East and the Balkans under the Ottoman Empire* (Bloomington: Indiana University Turkish Studies, 1993), 342–68. Another view is that Innocent planned on using Djem as a pawn or a potential ally, and that the failure of the crusade may have more to do with the death of King Matthias, who was crucial to the plan.

31. Stinger, *Renaissance in Rome*, 108–13.

32. In this they were using a term that had been popular since the Middle Ages to express, among other things, a concept akin to Europe. See Jordan, " 'Europe' in the Middle Ages," 75.

33. Capistrano preached in the Holy Roman Empire, Transylvania, and Hungary and was present at the battle of Belgrade in 1456; see Schwoebel, *Shadow of the Crescent*, 41–43.

34. On Florence's experience, see Black, *Benedetto Accolti*, 247.

35. Schwoebel, *Shadow of the Crescent*, 39.

36. Roberto Caracciolo, *Specchio della Fede* (Venice: c. 1495), fol. 8v; Schwoebel, *Shadow of the Crescent*, 41.

37. "Cardinal Bessarion's instructions to his crusade preachers," in *Documents on the Later Crusades*, ed. Housley, 148.

38. Ibid., 148–49.

39. John W. O'Malley, *Praise and Blame in Renaissance Rome: Rhetoric, Doctrine, and Reform in the Sacred Orators of the Papal Court, c. 1450–1521* (Durham, N.C.: Duke University Press, 1979), 190. The Franciscan friar Roberto Caracciolo roused audiences with graphic images of the final judgment, hellfire, and torture; he even compared these sufferings to the fall of Constantinople, suggesting that conquest by the Turks would produce suffering comparable to the pains of hell. See Schwoebel, *Shadow of the Crescent*, 39–40.

40. Diane Owen Hughes, "Distinguishing Signs: Ear-rings, Jews and Franciscan Rhetoric in the Italian Renaissance City," *Past and Present* 112 (August 1986): 3–59.

41. Ibid., 15–16.

42. Ibid., 19, 29–37.

43. See Attilio Milano, *Storia degli ebrei in Italia* (Turin: Giulio Einaudi Editore, 1963), Chapter 4, esp. 161–66.

44. Black, *Benedetto Accolti*, 247; see also Gordon Griffiths, "Leonardo Bruni and the 1431 Florentine Complaint against Indulgence Hawkers: A Case Study in Anticlericalism," in *Anticlericalism in Late Medieval and Early Modern Europe*, ed. Peter Dykema and Heiko Oberman (Leiden: E. J. Brill, 1993), 133–43.

45. Schwoebel, *Shadow of the Crescent*, 40.

46. Poggio Bracciolini, *The Facetiae of Poggio and Other Medieval Story-tellers*, ed. and tr. Edward Storer (London: George Routledge and Sons Ltd., n.d.), 59–60.

47. Vespasiano, *Vite*, ed. Greco, 2:198–99.

48. Ottavia Niccoli, *Prophecy and People in Renaissance Italy*, tr. Lydia G. Cochrane (Princeton, N.J.: Princeton University Press, 1990), 104.

49. Cusanus, of course, would later become a supporter of papal primacy, as would another ardent conciliarist, Aeneas Silvius Piccolomini.

50. See Thomas M. Izbicki, "The Possibility of a Dialogue with Islam in the Fifteenth Century," and James E. Biechler, "A New Face toward Islam: Nicholas of Cusa and John of Segovia," both in *Nicholas of Cusa in Search of God and Wisdom*, ed. Gerald Christianson and Thomas M. Izbicki (Leiden: E. J. Brill, 1991), 175–83; 185–202, respectively. See also Southern, *Western Views of Islam*, 86–94.

51. Several essays in Rabil *Renaissance Humanism*, underscore the ambiguity of Cusanus's status. John F. D'Amico calls Cusanus "perhaps the most famous of early northern European humanist theologians"; see D'Amico, "Humanism and Prereformation Theology," in *Renaissance Humanism*, ed. Rabil, 3:368. Maristella Lorch refers to Cusanus as a "fellow humanist and friend of Valla"; see Lorch, "Lorenzo Valla," in *Renaissance Humanism*, ed. Rabil, 1:335. Noel Brann notes that Cusanus "is not generally listed in the textbooks as a humanist" but argues that he "displayed many of the features . . . identified with the humanist personality," such as his love of antiquity; see Brann, "Humanism in Germany," in *Renais-*

sance Humanism, ed. Rabil, 2:143. John of Segovia has not, to my knowledge, been classified as a humanist.

52. Schwoebel, *Shadow of the Crescent*, 223; Southern, *Western Views of Islam*, 89.

53. Gary Remer, *Humanism and the Rhetoric of Toleration* (University Park: Pennsylvania State University Press, 1996), 4–7.

54. James E. Biechler, "Christian Humanism Confronts Islam: The Sifting of the Qur'an with Nicholas of Cusa," *Journal of Ecumenical Studies* 13 (1978): 4.

55. See Kristeller, "Humanism and Moral Philosophy," in *Renaissance Humanism*, ed. Rabil, 3:304; Geanakoplos, "Italian Humanism and the Byzantine Émigré Scholars," in *Renaissance Humanism*, ed. Rabil, 1:360, 339; John Monfasani, "Nicholas of Cusa, the Byzantines, and the Greek Language;" in *Nicholaus Cusanus zwischen Deutschland und Italien*, ed. Martin Thurner (Berlin: Akademie Verlag, 2002), 215–52.

56. Southern, *Western Views*, 89, 93.

57. Ibid., 88.

58. Biechler, "New Face," 192–93. Selections of a letter from Segovia to Cusanus outlining some of his views on converting the Turks have recently been translated by Housley; see Housley, *Documents on the Later Crusades*, 144–47.

59. Southern, *Western Views*, 86.

60. Ibid., 91–92; Biechler, "New Face," 189–90.

61. This point of view was shared by Nicholas of Cusa; see Biechler, "New Face," 193, 200.

62. Biechler points to the stark contrast between the two men and their contemporaries as an illustration of the uniqueness of their "positive and irenic approaches"; see ibid., 200. See also Schwoebel, *Shadow of the Crescent*, 223–25.

63. While John of Segovia sought support for his *contraferentia* by writing letters to Aeneas Silvius Piccolomini, Jean Germain (bishop of Châlon), and Nicholas, only Cusanus seems to have responded supportively. See Southern, *Western Views*, 94–103.

64. Schwoebel, *Shadow of the Crescent*, 41, 223; O'Malley, *Praise and Blame*, 233–34.

65. Biechler, "New Face," 191–96.

66. Nicholas Cusanus, *Nicholas of Cusa's De pace fidei and Cribratio Alkorani: Translation and Analysis*, ed. and tr. Jasper Hopkins (Minneapolis: A. J. Banning Press, 1990), 35. Cf. Biechler, "New Face," 196–97. Izbicki points out that this means one *religio* with a diversity of rites but not a proliferation of sects; see Izbicki, "Possibility of a Dialogue," 178.

67. Southern, *Western Views*, 92.

68. Nicholas Cusanus, *Unity and Reform*, ed. John Patrick Dolan (Notre Dame: University of Notre Dame Press, 1962), 188.

69. "Facile etiam Arabes et omnes sapientes ex his intelligent: trinitatem negare esse negare divinam foecunditatem et virtutem creativam, ac quam admissio trinitatis est negare deorum pluralitatem et consocialitatem facit enim ipsa foecunditas quae est trinitas . . . multo melius Arabes capere poterunt veritatem hoc modo: quam modo quo ipsi loquuntur deum habere essentiam et animam addunt

quam deum habere verbum et spiritum" (Nicholas Cusanus, *Opera* 1514; rcpr., Frankfurt/Main: Minerva, 1962), 117v; English tr. in Cusanus, *Unity and Reform,* ed. and trans. Dolan, 210.

70. Biechler, "New Face," 198; Southern, *Western Views,* 94.

71. Biechler, "Christian Humanism," 11. Cusanus's harsher attitude may have arisen partly from the mounting anti-Turkish sentiment in Europe and partly from his decision to dedicate the work to Pius II for the pope's edification in confronting Islam.

72. Cusanus, *Nicholas of Cusa's De pace fidei and Cribratio,* ed. and tr. Hopkins, 19, 96, 158, 147, 154. On Cusa's medieval sources, see Biechler, "Christian Humanism," 10.

73. Biechler, "Christian Humanism," 10.

74. Ibid., 7.

75. Cusanus, *Nicholas of Cusa's De pace fidei and Cribratio,* ed. and tr. Hopkins, 145.

76. Ibid., 132.

77. For a fuller discussion of *De Pace Fidei* and *Cribratio Alkorani,* see Biechler's "Christian Humanism." See also Jasper Hopkins, "The Role of Pia Interpretatio in Nicholas of Cusa's Hermeneutical Approach to the Koran," in *Concordia Discors: studi su Niccolò Cusano e l'umanesimo Europeo offerti a Giovanni Santinello,* ed. Gregorio Piaia (Padua: Editrice Antenore, 1993), 251–73.

78. Humanist attitudes toward Arabic language and learning will be discussed later in this chapter.

79. Cusanus spent some time in Constantinople during the Council of Basel, and Segovia had engaged Spanish Muslims in religious dialogue. See Biechler, "Christian Humanism," 4–5.

80. Southern calls Pius's letter an "effective reply to [Segovia's] ideas"; see Southern, *Western Views,* 99. If so, it was a very late reply. See also Babinger, *Mehmed the Conqueror,* 199.

81. I have addressed this question at greater length in "Pius II's Letter to Mehmed II."

82. The first phrase comes from Pius's pamphlet on the fall of Constantinople, *De captione urbis Constantinopolitane;* see R. J. Mitchell, *The Laurels and the Tiara: Pope Pius II 1458–64* (London: Harvill Press, 1962), 124. The last two phrases are from Pius's letter to Leonardo Benvoglienti (25 September 1453) in Pertusi, *Caduta di Costantinopoli,* 2:62, 64.

83. Hankins, "Renaissance Crusaders," 128–30; Franz Babinger, "Pio II e l'Oriente maomettano," in *Enea Silvio Piccolomini Papa Pio II,* ed. Domenico Maffei (Siena: Varese, 1968), 6; Mitchell, *Laurels and the Tiara,* 153–54; Setton, *Papacy and the Levant,* 2:233; Franco Gaeta, "Sulla 'Lettera a Maometto' di Pio II," *Bulletino dell'Istituto storico italiano per il medioevo e archivio muratoriano* 77 (1965): 132; Paolo Brezzi, "La lettera di Pio II a Maometto II," in *Pio II e la cultura,* ed. Tarugi, 263–72. See also Margolin, "Place et fonction," in *Pio II e la cultura,* ed. Tarugi, 261.

84. Mitchell, *Laurels and the Tiara,* 172–73.

85. Southern, *Western Views,* 102.

86. Piccolomini, *Epistola ad Mahomatem*, ed. and tr. Baca, English tr., 11; Latin, 115.

87. "Non enim te odio persequimur, neque tuo insidiamur capiti, quamvis nostrae religionis hostis existas et armis Christianam urgeas plebem. Operibus tuis, non tibi sumus infensi" (ibid., English tr., 11; Latin, 115).

88. Ibid., bk. 5.

89. "quem Mahumetea lex, in qua natus es, et virum sanctum et prophetam magnum et virginis filium et miraculis clarum dicit" (ibid., English tr., 11; Latin, 115).

90. Pius may have read and used Nicholas of Cusa's *Cribratio Alkorani* to obtain a better understanding of Islam; see Mitchell, *Laurels and the Tiara*, 171. But, as will shortly be discussed, he drew more directly on other, more hostile, sources.

91. "Tu creatura Dei es et ovis eius, sed errabunda, extra caulas in alienis pascuis, procul ab ovili dominico . . . compatimur tibi et tuorum subditorum infelicitatem deploramus, qui tecum pereunt. Nec te credimus libenter errare, cuius naturam bonam esse confidimus. Ignorantia veri te retinet" (Piccolomini, *Epistola ad Mahomatem*, ed. and tr. Baca, English tr., 38; Latin, 144).

92. Ibid., 25.

93. Black has recently demonstrated that several thinkers including Dante, Petrarch, Guicciardini, and (indirectly) even Aeneas criticized Constantine for single-handedly making the Church political and wealthy; see Black, "Donation of Constantine." But Aeneas's views on the whole seem more positive. In his dialogue Pius depicts Constantine expressing his willingness to return to earth to convene the Christians for a meeting on dealing with the Turks. See Aeneas Silvius Piccolomini, *Aeneae Silvii Piccolomini Senensis qui postea fuit Pius II Pont: Max opera inedita*, ed. Joseph Cugnoni (Rome: Reale Accademia dei Lincei, 1883), 252–54. Hankins cites a passage from this work in "Renaissance Crusaders," 133–34. Incidentally, another humanist, Nicola Loschi, used this model for his *Constantinus Supplex*, which he dedicated to Pius; see Pertusi, *Testi inediti*.

94. Piccolomini, *Epistola ad Mahomatem*, ed. and tr. Baca, Latin, 131; English tr., 26. Augustine voiced a similar opinion of Constantine in *City of God*, bk. 5:25.

95. "Tua origo, sicut accepimus, Scythica est. Inter Scythas multos fuisse viros in armis claros memoriae traditur, qui vectigalem Asiam pluribus saeculis tenuerunt et Aegyptios ultra paludes eiecerunt. Non sunt comparandi aut Aegyptii aut Arabes Scythico generi; non est forti et ignavo aequa societas. Mirandum est tantum potuisse suis fascinationibus Arabes, ut audaces et praestantes Scythas in suam societatem adduxerint" (Piccolomini, *Epistola ad Mahomatem*, ed. and tr. Baca, Latin, 180; English tr., 74).

96. Herodotus, *Histories*, 84–85. Praising the Scythians required the use of a classical source other than Aethicus, Pius's preferred "ancient" source; Pius's use of Aethicus is discussed in Chapter 2 above.

97. "virtus virtuti placet"; "inter aequales consorti[um]" (Piccolomini, *Epistola ad Mahomatem*, ed. and tr. Baca, Latin, 180; English tr., 74).

98. Pius's condescension is apparent, for example, in bk. 5 when he tells Mehmed that if he listens to his advice he is wise. See ibid., 35, 141.

99. "Tua lex in altera vita flumina lactis et mellis et vini promittit, et cibaria delicata et uxores multas et concubinas et virginum coitus et angelorum in turpibus obsequiis ministeria, et quicquid caro deposcit. Bovis haec paradisus et asini potius quam hominis est!" (ibid., Latin, 61, English tr. 167).

100. Ibid., 88, 194.

101. "innumerabiles sunt eius ineptiae et aniles fabulae et pueriles nugae" (ibid., Latin, 91, English tr., 199).

102. Gaeta, "Sulla Lettera a Maometto," 177.

103. Biechler, "Christian Humanism," 14; idem, "New Face," 200, 202. See also Daniel, *Islam and the West*, 307.

104. Gaeta, "Sulla Lettera a Maometto," 163. Although he believes that Segovia's letter may have been somewhat influential, Biechler concurs with Gaeta that Torquemada was Pius's strongest influence; see Biechler, "New Face," 190, 202.

105. Monfasani, *George of Trebizond*, 140–41. George made repeated efforts to gain Pius's ear regarding his apocalyptic visions and the central role that Mehmed's potential conversion might play. George's knowledge of the Greek East and the Ottoman Empire alone should have made him an invaluable tool to Pius had he been serious about trying to reach Mehmed.

106. "Parva res omnium qui hodie vivunt maximum et potentissimum et clarissimum te reddere potest. Quaeris quae sit? Non est inventu difficilis, neque procul quaerenda, ubique gentium reperitur: id est aquae pauxillum, quo baptizeris et ad Christianorum sacra te conferas et credas Evangelio" (Piccolomini, *Epistola ad Mahomatem*, ed. and tr. Baca, Latin, 17–18, English tr., 122).

107. See respectively Babinger, "Pio II," 4; and Gaeta, "Sulla Lettera a Maometto," 190, 193–94.

108. Answering the challenge that his crusade would give too much power to the Venetians, Pius replied: "Would you rather obey Venice or the Turks? No Christian who deserves the name would prefer the rule of the Turks under which the sacraments of the Church must finally be doomed and the gate to the other life be closed to those who desert the Gospel." See Piccolomini, *Commentaries*, tr. Gragg, 5:814–15.

109. We might compare the tone of Pius's baptism remark to that of Louis XI of France, who told a Milanese ambassador in 1466—years before Pius's letter was printed and widely disseminated—"If the Turk were to pour a spoonful of water over his head, professing, 'I am a Christian,' he [Louis] would help him and go to his aid against the Venetians" (*Et s'el Turcho volesse tore un cuchiaro di aqua sopra la testa, dicendo, "io sono Chrystiano," dice lo adiutaria et si voria adiutarlo contra Venetiani*) (Vincent Ilardi, ed., *Dispatches with Related Documents of Milanese Ambassadors in France*, tr. Frank J. Fata [Dekalb: Northern Illinois University Press, 1981], 3:284–85).

110. The letter was printed around 1470, several years after Pius's death. See Babinger, "Pio II," 10. See also Mitchell, *Laurels and the Tiara*, 155. On Pius's silence regarding the letter in other writings, see Franco Gaeta, "Alcune osservazi

oni sulla prima redazione della lettera a Maometto," in *Enea Silvio Piccolomini Papa Pio II*, ed. Domenico Maffei (Siena: Varese, 1968), 178.

111. Gaeta, "Sulla Lettera a Maometto," 127, 192.

112. Piccolomini, *Commentaries*, tr. Gragg, 4:517.

113. Pius may have intended to leak the letter to Emperor Frederick III; see Hankins, "Renaissance Crusaders," 130 n. 57.

114. See my article "Pius II's Letter to Mehmed II."

115. See Chapter 3 for biographical information on George and a discussion of his procrusade works.

116. For further details, see Monfasani, *George of Trebizond*, 132, 189–94.

117. See for example bk. 2, chap. 1 of *On the Eternal Glory of the Autocrat*, ed. and tr. Monfasani, in George of Trebizond, *Collectanea Trapezuntiana*, ed. Monfasani, 493. George later recanted statements praising Mehmed in letters he had written to him; see Monfasani, *George of Trebizond*, 193.

118. Monfasani cites Mercati and Zoras in *George of Trebizond*, 132.

119. Ibid., 135.

120. Ibid., 134–35; see also Chapter 2 above for a discussion of George's oration to Nicholas V (1452).

121. Monfasani, *George of Trebizond*, 131–36.

122. George of Trebizond *Collectanea Trapezuntiana*, ed. Monfasani, 493.

123. See Monfasani, *George of Trebizond*, 133–35.

124. Ibid., 133.

125. See Pertusi's partial translation into Italian and notes in *Caduta de Costantinopoli*, 2:73, 437–38, n. 3; Monfasani, *George of Trebizond*, 131. This concept of a universal faith is also stated in *On the Eternal Glory of the Autocrat* (see note 117 above).

126. An example of George's continuing orthodoxy after 1453 can be seen in his martyrology (1468) of the Blessed Andrea of Chios, reportedly executed by the Turks in 1465 at Constantinople. See *Patrologia Graeca*, 161:883–90.

127. See Exhortations to King Alfonso of Aragon and Emperor Frederick III, in George of Trebizond, *Collectanea Trapezuntiana*, ed. Monfasani, 422–33; see especially 423.

128. It is ironic that Nicholas of Cusa was an enthusiast of Plato and the Neoplatonists and yet both he and George were ardent supporters of conversion of the Turks.

129. Monfasani, *George of Trebizond*, 158–59.

130. George of Trebizond, *Collectanea Trapezuntiana*, ed. Monfasani, 495.

131. Ibid., 495.

132. This appears to be a reference to Gen. 16:10.

133. George of Trebizond, *Collectanea Trapezuntiana*, ed. Monfasani, 565.

134. Ibid., 566–67.

135. O'Malley, *Praise and Blame*, 190–91; see also 195–96, 199, 204.

136. Reeves, *Influence of Prophecy*, 429–30.

137. See Roberto Rusconi, "Gerusalemme nella predicazione popolare quattrocentesca tra millennio, ricordo di viaggio e luogo sacro," in *Toscana e Terransanta nel medioevo*, ed. Franco Cardini (Florence: Alinea Editrice, 1982), 285–98.

138. Among his prophecies of tribulation leading up to the French invasion of 1494, the fiery Dominican preacher often featured the Turk as the Antichrist or the Great Beast of the Apocalypse. After Charles VIII spared the city, Savonarola's prophecies took on a much brighter aspect; tribulation changed to *renovatio*. Florence would be the "new Jerusalem," God's chosen city. Through God's agency it would lead all of Italy in spiritual reform, and its empire and wealth would grow. Moreover, Savonarola claimed that this reform would spread as far as the territory of the Turks, who would be brought to the light of Christ. See Weinstein, *Savonarola and Florence*, 90, 94, 136–46.

139. Niccoli, *Prophecy and People*, passim. Prophecies also acted as heavenly "proof" of God's displeasure over political and social ills such as corruption in the secular and ecclesiastical hierarchy, a decline in civic virtue, or inaction before the Turkish advance; see 190.

140. See Marcel Bataillon, "Mythe et connaissance de la Turquie in Occident au milieu de XVI sièclè," in *Venezia e l'Oriente fra tardo medioevo e rinascimento*, ed. Agostino Pertusi (Florence: G. C. Sansoni, 1966), 453.

141. Heath, *Crusading Commonplaces*, 45.

142. In fact, the apocalyptic genre reached its peak in the late fifteenth and early sixteenth centuries, due in no small part to the intense anxiety provoked by this event. See O'Malley, *Praise and Blame*, 184.

143. See Setton, *Papacy and the Levant*, 2: chap. 11; Imber, *Ottoman Empire*, 247–49.

144. Several eyewitness reports on the siege of Rhodes were printed within months after the victory. Guillaume Caoursin's account was the most widely read; it was printed ten times in four languages. Also popular were the accounts of Giacomo de Curti and Mary Dupuis. See Schwoebel, *Shadow of the Crescent*, 122–31.

145. This was not the first time Turkish forces attacked Italy; Turkish raiders had been pillaging north of Venice in Istria and Friuli (1476–78) during the Venetian war. It was said that the Venetians could see the distant fires from the campanile in Saint Mark's Square. These occurrences, however, were not regarded with nearly as much alarm as that which Otranto would inspire.

146. The Turks did not quickly expand on this conquest, nor could they with their current forces; Gedik Ahmed traveled back to Albania to prepare additional attacks in the following year. See Imber, *Ottoman Empire*, 249–52; Schwoebel, *Shadow of the Crescent*, 131–33; Housley, *Later Crusades*, 111.

147. Babinger, *Mehmed the Conqueror*, 391.

148. See Setton, *Papacy and the Levant*, 2:373–74; Schwoebel, *Shadow of the Crescent*, 132, 144 n. 70; Babinger, *Mehmed the Conqueror*, 391.

149. Tateo, "L'ideologia umanistica," 173–74. See also Tateo's introduction to *Gli umanisti e la guerra otrantina*, ed. L. Gualdo Rosa, 7–8. Donato Moro has shown how one diary used to make the case for canonization in the eighteenth century was a later forgery: "Fonti Salentine sugli avvenimenti Otrantini del 1480/81," in *Otranto 1480*, ed. Fonseca, 2:11–41.

150. See Ilarione, "Copia Idruntine expugnatis" (1480), in *Gli umanisti e la guerra Otrantina*, ed. L. Gualdo Rosa et al., 32–34; Giovanni Albino Lucano, "De

bello Hydruntino" (1481), in ibid., 58; "Relazione d'Acello" (c. 1480), ed. Donato Moro, in Moro, "Fonti Salentine," in *Otranto 1480*, ed. Fonseca, 2:154. A sermon of Roberto Caracciolo printed several years later tells a similar tale; see his *Specchio della Fede* (1495), fol. viii, verso.

151. The dispatches of the Ferrarese ambassador to Naples, Niccolò Sadoleto, and Florentine ambassadorial relations do not mention martyrs. See C. Foucard, ed., "Dispacci degli oratori Estensi," *Archivio storico per le province napoletane* 6 (1881): 88–89; Tateo, "L'ideologia umanistica," 175; ASF, *Missive, Prima Cancelleria* 48, fol. 123r ff.; *Missive* 49, fol. 78v ff. On the Turkish historian Ibn Kemal see Aldo Galotta, "I Turchi e la Terra d'Otranto (1480–81)," in *Otranto 1480*, ed. Fonseca, 2:182, 187.

152. On the enslavement of Otrantines, see Charles Verlinden, "La presence turque à Otrante (1480–1481) et l'esclavage," in *Otranto 1480*, ed. Fonseca, 1:149. Donato Moro has posited that the legend of the eight hundred martyrs grew little by little among the inhabitants after they returned to Otranto in 1481, perhaps as a coping mechanism. The tale of eight hundred martyrs, for all its pathos, was more life affirming and positive than were stories of helpless enslavement and execution. See Moro, "Fonti Salentine," in *Otranto 1480*, ed. Fonseca, 2:7.

153. Many vernacular laments on the fall of Otranto were sold and sung in city squares; see Niccoli, *Prophecy and People*, 16.

154. Venice's excuse for neutrality was understandable; it had fought the Turks for over fifteen years unaided by any Italian power, and now that it was at peace with the Ottomans it was reluctant to violate the treaty. See Babinger, *Mehmed the Conqueror*, 393–94. Venice also bore a grudge against Ferrante for his anti-Venetian policies; see Vincent Ilardi, "Quattrocento Politics in the Treccani *Storia di Milano*," in Vincent Ilardi, *Studies in Italian Renaissance Diplomatic History* (London: Variorum Reprints, 1986), VIII:181.

155. Machiavelli and diarist Lucca Landucci wrote that Florentines rejoiced because the attack on Neapolitan soil meant a cessation of their hostilities against Siena and Florence; see Niccolò Machiavelli, *Florentine Histories*, tr. Laura F. Banfield and Harvey C. Mansfield Jr. (Princeton, N.J.: Princeton University Press, 1988), 342; Schwoebel, *Shadow of the Crescent*, 144 n. 66; Luca Landucci, *A Florentine Diary*, tr. Alice de Rosen Jervis (London: J. M. Dent & Sons, Ltd., 1927), 33. Landucci also noted the celebrations and bonfires that took place in Florence when the city was recovered a year later. The official Florentine response to the capture of Otranto demonstrated support for both Sixtus and Ferrante in their plans to expel the Turks from Italy but supported some negotiations as well. See Lorenzo de' Medici, *Lettere*, vol. 5, ed. Michael Mallett (Florence: Giunti-Barbera, 1989); Machiavelli, *Florentine Histories* (bk. 8, chaps. 21–22); ASF, *Missive* 48, fol. 123r ff.; *Missive* 49, fol. 78v ff.

156. Angelo Poliziano, "dum enim hi barbari Italiae oras obtinuerint, semper mihi crux illa funebris proferri videbitur" (Letter to Piero de Medici, in Angelo Poliziano, *Prose volgari inedite e poesie latine e greche edite*, ed. Isidoro del Lungo [Florence: G. Barbera Editore, 1867], 37). The letter was written in the summer of 1481 as it mentions Mehmed II's death (3 May 1481) but not the defeat of the Turks (10 September 1481). Cf. Garin, *Portraits from the Quattrocento*, 163. Mar-

silio Ficino's letter to King Matthias of Hungary, written in response to Otranto, is discussed in Chapter 2.

157. See Margaret King, "Book-Lined Cells: Women and Humanism in the Early Italian Renaissance," in *Renaissance Humanism*, ed. Rabil, 1:435–40; see also King, *Women of the Renaissance* (Chicago: University of Chicago Press, 1991).

158. Laura Cereta, *The Collected Letters of a Renaissance Feminist*, ed. and tr. Diana Robin (Chicago: University of Chicago Press, 1997), 139–40.

159. On the rhetoric of sermons, see James J. Murphy, *Rhetoric in the Middle Ages: A History of Rhetorical Theory from Saint Augustine to the Renaissance* (Berkeley: University of California Press, 1974), 269–355.

160. See Myron P. Gilmore's introduction to Vespasiano's *Renaissance Princes*, xii.

161. Gilmore suggests that Vespasiano's education was rather modest; see ibid., xi–xii. His compositions were in Tuscan, and when writing letters to high-ranking individuals he required the assistance of humanists such as Acciaiuoli. Margery Ganz takes a closer look at Vespasiano's circle and intellectual interests in "A Florentine Friendship: Donato Acciaiuoli and Vespasiano da Bisticci," *Renaissance Quarterly* 43 (1990): 372–82.

162. Edited by Ludovico Frati in *Vite di uomini illustri del secolo XV scritte da Vespasiano da Bisticci* (Bologna: Romagnoli-Dall'Acqua, 1893), 3:306–25.

163. "Chi darà al capo mio acqua, ed a' mia occhi una fontana di lagrime, acciò ch'io pianga il dì e la notte le fedite del mio popolo" (ibid., 306). This is derived from Jer. 9:1: "And I will weep day and night for the slain of the daughter of my people."

164. "[si può . . .] piagnere [*sic*] e dolersi della cecità, non solo della nostra città che è accecata, indurata e ostinata ne' peccati; ma volesse Iddio ch'ella fusse sola; ma tutta Italia è in questa ostinazione e maladizione. Perchè vedendosi venire addosso tanto fragello, quanto è questo del Turco, che non sia ignuno che si muovi, accecati e ottenebrati et ostinati nel peccato: e vedendo il principio di tanta rovina, della quale non è persona che si muovi, nè che la stimi, nè che creda che fossi toccare a lui" (ibid., 306–7).

165. "Leggete tutta la Santa Scrittura e vedrete che l'onnipotente Iddio sempre ha presi questi modi alle sua punizioni; sempre ha castigati i sua nimici coi sua inimici medesimi" (ibid., 307).

166. Harry M. Orlinsky, *Ancient Israel*, 2d ed. (Ithaca, N.Y.: Cornell University Press, 1960), 97–98.

167. "I profeti sono i sanctissimi predicatori che sono venuti ad annunciare e predicare in Italia l'avvenimento del Turco, la emendazione de' peccati, mostrando la cagione perchè Iddio permetteva che venisse il Turco, e mai sono suti creduti, e ognuno se n'ha fatto beffe, e mai hanno voluto mutare la loro perversa vita, nè i loro perversi costumi." See Vespasiano, *Lamento*, 319.

168. Aulo Greco makes a strong argument that Fra Roberto Caracciolo was a direct influence on Vespasiano. See Greco, "Lamento d'Italia per la presa d'Otranto di Vespasiano da Bisticci," 2:347–51. Similarities between Caracciolo's sermons and Vespasiano's *Lamento* include the loss of Christian cities and lands as a sign of God's anger and a divine call for repentance.

169. See Murphy, *Rhetoric in the Middle Ages*, 273.

170. In a 1461–62 oration Venetian ambassador and humanist Bernardo Giustiniani repeatedly used the image of the Turks as a "fierce and huge beast" to be hunted and destroyed by the king of France. See Labalme, *Bernardo Giustiniani*, 166–67; for another example of Giustiniani's comparison of the Turks to beasts, see his oration to Sixtus IV in the wake of Negroponte (ibid., 198). Marsilio Ficino's letters to Sixtus IV also seem to allude to apocalyptic beasts. See Tateo, "L'ideologica umanistica," 160. Erasmus, as the Epilogue will discuss, was also an advocate of Christian repentance over holy war.

171. Daniel, *Islam and the West*.

172. See Chapter 1.

173. "Quid deo odibilius quam effundere sanguinem innocentium, quam fidelium non solum corpora sed animas perditum ire in Sathane sacrificium detestandum" (Bracciolini, *Lettere*, ed. Harth, 3:67).

174. Benedetto Accolti, Oration delivered at the Congress of Mantua (1459). See Black, *Benedetto Accolti*, 263.

175. Hankins, "Renaissance Crusaders," 169; Hainsworth, *Idea of Epic*, 58–59.

176. Norman Daniel names a few thinkers who employed this notion, including Riccoldo da Montecroce, San Pedro Pascual, and Peter of Toledo; See Daniel, *Islam and West*, 104, 116, 210.

177. Until recently the *Carmen* was only available in manuscript form; according to Hankins, six copies exist, denoting some broad interest in the work. I cite here Hankins's edition and my own transcription of Biblioteca Riccardiana, Florence, Riccardiano 660, fols. 63r–68v.

178. Vespasiano, *Vite*, 1:299–300.

179. F. Flamini, "Leonardo di Piero Dati, poeta latino del secolo XV," *Giornale storico della letteratura italiana* 16 (1890): 58–61.

180. On the date of the work, see Hankins, "Renaissance Crusaders," 169.

181. Literally, Satan "opens the door of the underworld and exits in the company of the agitated Furies" (*horrida Ditis / Porta patet, Sathan Furiis agitantibus exit*); see Hankins, "Renaissance Crusaders," 169; Ricc. 660, 63r.

182. "Aspicit inmitem Mahomet: nuda ille cruentus / Constantinopoli victor veniebat ab urbe" (ibid.).

183. "Hic, ait ille, meus quem tota mente poposci / Hic est ille comes scelerum cui lurida mundi / Sceptra dabo et poterit nihil exitiale videri" (ibid.).

184. Hankins, "Renaissance Crusaders," 170–71; Ricc. 660, 63v-64r; cf. Flamini, "Leonardo di Piero Dati," 66.

185. See Claudian, "In Rufinum," in *Claudian*, ed. and tr. Maurice Platnauer (London: William Heinemann, 1922), 1:28–38. Thanks to Danuta Shanzer for this reference.

186. "Dixit, et horrendum visu mox tempora circum / Illius apponit centum dyadema cerastis / Consertum ac dextre, cui Cerberus ore trifauci / Eminet horrificus, sceptrum implacabile donat / Scrutatusque oculum candenti tetra Megere / Addicit leve digito, et super alligat ensem / In femur, ensem atris immersum Acherontis in undis; / Hinc os allibat patulamque insibilat aurem" (Hankins, "Renaissance Crusaders," 171; Ricc. 660, 64r).

187. Hankins, "Renaissance Crusaders," 170; Ricc. 660, 63v.

188. "Nosti pontificem quo non prestantior alter, / Qui culmen virtutis habet: pater optimus idem / Repperit ecclesiam quassam penitusque ruentem, / Obsessam et vitiis et avaris mille tyrannis" (Hankins, "Renaissance Crusaders," 174; Ricc. 660, 66v).

189. "sublata schismatis umbra / Romanam sponsam ritu stabiliuit honesto. / Ingrati populi sese discordibus armis / Vndique discerpunt ac preda et sanguine fedant" (Hankins, "Renaissance Crusades," 174; Ricc. 660, 67r).

190. "Hi sunt Christicolae, hi sunt quos ipse redemi?" (Hankins, "Renaissance Crusaders," 174; Ricc. 660, 67v).

191. Hankins, "Renaissance Crusaders," 175–76; Ricc. 660, 67v–68v.

192. Petrarch: Latin, *Vita solitaria*, 242; English tr., *Life of Solitude*, 247.

193. More precisely, he is referring here to Muhammad as "the founder of a wicked superstition" (*nefande superstitionis artifex*) (ibid., 244 and 248 respectively).

194. See Sheehan, *Savagism and Civility*; Dower, *War without Mercy*.

195. ASF, *Missive, Prima Cancelleria* 21, fol. 139r; English tr. in Emmert, *Serbian Golgotha*, 47.

196. Black, *Benedetto Accolti*, 299, 301; William of Tyre, *History of Deeds Done*, 1:61; Marin Sanuto, *Liber secretorum fidelium crucis super Terrae Sanctae* (1611; repr., Toronto: University of Toronto Press, 1972), 124–25.

197. "arabe quodam, Maumetto nomine, qui, humili et sordido loco natus, . . . ausus est prophetam se dicere a deo missum qui leges perennes, novissima sacra mortalibus traderet. Nec acre ingenium illi defuit nec peritia sacrarum rerum quam ex iudeis christianisque hauserat. Et quamvis esset perditis moribus, tamen flagitia quadam arte occultabat . . . addens quoque prodigiorum comenta, ludibrium oculis atque auribus, quo magis cresceret hominum fides et suis gestis legibusque maior inesset auctoritas" (Latin and English tr. Black, *Benedetto Accolti*, 264–65; Accolti, *De bello a christianis*, 532).

198. Daniel, *Islam and the West*, 88–91.

199. "At Mahumetis legem quae signa, quae miracula probant? . . . Non habet igitur tua lex testimonium . . ." (Piccolomini, *Epistola ad Mahomatem*, ed. Baca, English tr., 90; Latin, 196–97).

200. Daniel, *Islam and the West*, 105.

201. Piccolomini, *Epistola ad Mahomatem*, 47.

202. Accolti, *De bello a christianis*, 532; Sanuto describes Sergius as a Nestorian monk, 124.

203. Aquinas, *Summa contra Gentiles*, 73 (bk. 1, chap. 6).

204. "Hoc ergo unum Mahumetis inventum fuit, ut legem propagaret suam: ea praecipiens quae grata essent auditoribus et maxime plebibus, quae iumentis similes existunt. Nec fefellit eum opinio in hac parte: placuit nova lex et brevi tempore ita coaluit, ut in multis populis gentibus ac linguis reciperetur, cuius fundamenta in voluptate iacta fuerunt" (Piccolomini, *Epistola ad Mahomatem*, ed. Baca, English tr., 75–76; Latin, 181–82).

205. "Neque ignarus populos magis ad vitia quam ad virtutem pronos esse, . . . eas instituit leges que parum graves videri possent nec fere iuberent quicquam

quod explende libidini adversum esset. Sic enim credidit fore ut multi, christiane severitatis pertesi, posthabita illa, suam sectam sequerentur" (Latin and English tr., Black, *Benedetto Accolti,* 265; Accolti, *De bello a christianis,* 532.

206. Daniel, *Islam and the West,* 147–48.

207. See Piccolomini, *Epistola ad Mahomatem,* 20, 84, 87.

208. Pius evoked Constantine's conversion in the same letter as an example of divine favor resulting in military victories and acquisition of power; see ibid., 26.

209. "Quodsi alia non essent adversus tuam legem indicia, hoc unum sufficere potuit, quia prohibuit eius lator in disputationem veniret" (ibid., Latin, 194; English, 88).

210. Daniel, *Islam and the West,* 146–50. If anything, Daniel argues, governments opposed interfaith disputation because of the potential civil unrest it might produce; scholars disdained dispute out of contempt for Christianity, not for fear of its rational superiority.

211. Sanuto, for example, provides much of the polemic Accolti used on Muhammad and Islamic culture, but Accolti's emphasis on the degradation of learning is new.

212. "Inque hac nova vivendi norma, cum virtuti aut doctrine nullus honos, nullum penitus premium esset, nam vanitati religionis nil erat infestius quam virtus cognitioque bonarum artium, ad luxum homines desidiamque conversi, studium quodque libero dignum abiecerunt, . . . mente capti enervatique animis, vitam ac mores mutarunt suos et, quasi mersi profundis in tenebris, post longa tempora, nec se attollere nec lucem aspicere potuerunt" (Latin and English tr., Black, *Benedetto Accolti,* 265; Accolti, *De bello a christianis,* 533.

213. "Magna olim et florida in Alexandria philosophorum schola fuit. . . . At, postquam lex Mahumatea cursum habuit, paucissimi nominantur, qui, naturae arcana perscrutati, excellentes evaserint: quia non praestat parvulis sapientiam tuus propheta aut tua lex, cuius fundamentum voluptas est et tutela gladius" (Piccolomini, *Epistola ad Mahomatem,* ed. Baca, Latin, 199; English tr., 91).

214. Piccolomini, *Opera quae extant omnia,* 385–86.

215. Piccolomini: "aniles fabulae," *Epistola ad Mahomatem,* 199; Accolti: "anilis superstitio," in Black, *Benedetto Accolti,* 266; Accolti, *De bello a christianis,* 536.

216. "Inter nos vero liberalium artium studia admodum florent. Legitur publice philosophia, auditur in scholis theologia, nullum doctrinae genus praemittitur. . . ." (Piccolomini, *Epistola ad Mahomatem,* ed. Baca, Latin, 199; English tr., 91).

217. See Epilogue for further discussion on how humanist views carried over into modern thought.

218. "tui isti Arabes arceantur, atque exulent, odi genus universum . . . quales medici tu scis. quales autem poetae scio ego, nihil blandius, nihil mollius, nihil enervatius, nihil denique turpius . . . et quid multa, vix mihi persuadebitur ab Arabia posse aliquid boni esse" (Petrarch, *Opera,* 2:1009; English tr., *Letters of Old Age,* 2:472).

219. According to C. H. L. Bodenham, Petrarch appears to be basing this judgment on a Latin translation of Averroes's commentary on Aristotle's *Poetics*

and even duplicating some of the wording, such as *turpis*. See Bodenham, "Petrarch and the Poetry of the Arabs," *Romanische Forschungen* 94, no. 2/3 (1982): 167–78. See also Charles Burnett, "Petrarch and Averroes: An Episode in the History of Poetics," in *The Medieval Mind: Hispanic Studies in Honour of Alan Deyermond*, ed. Ian MacPherson and Ralph Penny (Rochester, N.Y.: Tamesis Press, 1997), 49–56.

220. Francesco Gabrieli, "Petrarca e gli Arabi," *Al-Andalus* 42 (1977): 241–48. Another classical reference in the letter is his invocation of Cicero, who contended that the Romans surpassed the Greeks in talent and style. Building on this, Petrarch sarcastically exclaims, "it can be said with much greater confidence in comparison with other peoples, that is, except those measly Arabs as you would have it." (". . . multo fidentius in comparationem omnium aliarum gentium dici potest Arabiculis, ut vos velle videmini, duntaxat exceptis . . .") (Petrarch, *Opera*, 2: 1010; English tr., *Letters of Old Age*, 2:472–73).

221. See Petrarch's "On his own ignorance," in *The Renaissance Philosophy of Man*, ed. Cassirer et al., 47–133.

222. Despite his criticisms of Islam, Accolti praised Avicenna and Averroes and acknowledged their contributions to scholasticism in his *Dialogus*; see Black, *Benedetto Accolti*, 327. Scholars of Greek literature and philosophy, such as Ermolao Barbaro, opposed scholasticism most likely because they found earlier Greek models to be the purest sources of Aristotelian philosophy. See Geanakoplos, "Italian Humanism," 1:363–64. Moreover, the division between scholasticism and rhetoric was not so firm in the minds of some quattrocento humanists. Kristeller has shown that humanism and scholasticism coexisted and developed alongside one another in Renaissance Italy, see his *Renaissance Thought: The Classic, Scholastic and Humanist Strains* chap. 5. Arthur Field too discusses the close associations in Florence between scholastic theologians and humanists, as well as the use some humanists, for example, Ficino, made of scholastic methods. He points out, however, that these humanists were aware of the tension between scholasticism and their own rhetorical style; see Field, *Origins of the Platonic Academy*, chap. 6.

223. Marsilio Ficino, *Three Books on Life*, ed. and tr. Carol V. Kaske and John R. Clark (Binghamton, N.Y.: Medieval and Renaissance Texts and Studies, 1989), 123, 223. I would like to thank Professor Kaske for her help with this question.

224. Cassirer et al., *Renaissance Philosophy of Man*, 223, 243, 248.

225. Kristeller, *Renaissance Thought and Its Sources*, 205–6.

226. On Ficino's Qur'an and Pico's use of it, see Chaim Wirszubski, *Pico della Mirandola's Encounter with Jewish Mysticism* (Cambridge: Harvard University Press, 1989), 3–4; see also Sebastiano Gentile et al., *Marsilio Ficino e il ritorno di Platone: manoscritti stampe e documenti* (Florence: Casa Editrice Le Lettere, 1984), 787–79; Angelo Michele Piemontese, "Il Corano latino di Ficino e i corani arabi di Pico e Monchates," *Rinascimento*, 2d ser. 36 (1996): 227–73.

227. Cardini, "Crociata mito politico," 208.

228. Kristeller, *Renaissance Thought and Its Sources*, 204. See also Kristeller, "Humanism and Moral Philosophy," in *Renaissance Humanism*, ed. Rabil, 3: 304.

229. Kristeller, *Renaissance Thought and Its Sources*, 204. In his *De christiana religione* (chaps. 36–37) Ficino cites the work of polemicist Riccoldo of Monte-

croce and accuses Muhammad of fabricating Jesus' prophecy of his (Muhammad's) coming; he also invokes the common claim that Islam was spread by violence and concupiscence. See Marsilio Ficino, *Opera Omnia*, 1:74–77.

230. Giuseppe Saitta, *Il pensiero italiano nell'umanesimo e nel rinascimento* (Bologna: Dott. Cesare Zuffi Editore, 1949), 1:522–23.

231. Kristeller, *Renaissance Thought and Its Sources*, 205. For an analysis of Pico's interaction with Jewish scholars and his thoughts on syncretism and Judaism, see David Ruderman, "The Italian Renaissance and Jewish Thought," in *Renaissance Humanism*, ed. Rabil, 1: 382–434. As Ruderman argues, Pico's desire, at its core, was to convert his Jewish friends to Christianity, but he also offered a dialogue with Jews on ways to merge the best aspects of their faith with the best aspects of Christianity.

232. Henri de Lubac, *Pic de la Mirandole* (Paris: Aubier Montaigne, 1974), 287–89.

233. See Chapter 2.

234. Specifically, Aeneas Silvius Piccolomini, Benedetto Accolti, Donato Acciaiuoli, and Ugolino Verino. See Chapter 2.

235. Dannenfeldt, "Renaissance Humanists," 105.

236. Charles Burnett, "The Second Revelation of Arabic Philosophy and Science: 1492–1562," in *Islam and the Italian Renaissance*, ed. Charles Burnett and Anna Contadini (London: Warburg Institute, 1999), 197.

237. See Dannenfeldt, "Renaissance Humanists."

Epilogue

1. For more detailed discussion of Erasmus's views on the Turks and crusade, see Ronald G. Musto, "Just Wars and Evil Empires: Erasmus and the Turks," in *Renaissance Society and Culture*, ed. John Monfasani and Ronald Musto (New York: Italica Press, 1991), 197–216; Norman Housley, "A Necessary Evil? Erasmus, the Crusade, and War against the Turks," in *The Crusades and Their Sources: Essays Presented to Bernard Hamilton*, ed. John France and William G. Zajac (Aldershot: Ashgate Publishing Ltd., 1998), 259–79. For Erasmus on toleration, see Remer, *Humanism and the Rhetoric of Toleration*, 43–101.

2. Musto, "Just Wars," 198–99, 216.

3. Desiderius Erasmus, "Letter to Paul Volz," ed. and tr. John C. Olin, in *Christian Humanism and the Reformation: Selected Writings of Erasmus*, 3d ed. (New York: Fordham University Press, 1987), 109–29.

4. Ibid., 112.

5. "Si ex strepitu nostro plusquam tyrannico perspexerint ambitionem nostram, si ex rapacitate avaritiam, si ex stupris libidinem, si ex oppressionibus seviciam, qua fronte ingeremus illis Christi doctrinam ab hisce rebus longe lateque discrepantem?"; (Desiderius Erasmus, *Opus Epistolarum*, ed. P. S. Allen [London: Oxford University Press, 1913], 3:364; English tr., Olin, *Christian Humanism*, 113).

6. See Chapter 4 above for a discussion of Cereta's letter on the Turkish advance.

7. "Homines sunt et illi, nec ferrum aut adamantem gestant in pectore" (Erasmus, *Opus Epistolarum*, 3:365; English tr., Olin, *Christian Humanism*, 114).

8. For further discussion of sixteenth-century proponents of conversion, both peaceable and forced, see Heath, *Crusading Commonplaces*, 89–99.

9. Desiderius Erasmus, *Consultatio de bello Turcis inferendo* (1643; repr., Athens, 1974).

10. Desiderius Erasmus, *De bello Turcico*, tr. Michael J. Heath, in *The Erasmus Reader*, ed. Erika Rummel (Toronto: University of Toronto Press, 1990), 315, 318–19.

11. Despite his own use of the term "barbarian," he states, "whenever the ignorant mob hear the name 'Turk,' they immediately fly into a rage and clamour for blood, calling them dogs and enemies to the name of Christian"; see Erasmus, *Consultatio*, 33; English tr., *De bello Turcico*, tr. Heath, 317. The Turks, Erasmus continues, cannot be reduced to the level of beasts and idolaters, nor should Christians rail against Turkish cruelty and atrocities when they attack one another just as viciously—as at the recent battle of Asperen; see *De bello Turcico*, tr. Heath, 317–18.

12. See Vitkus, "Early Modern Orientalism," 212–13, 218–19; Schwoebel, *Shadow of the Crescent*, 213.

13. "principe di ingegno mansueto e molto dissimile alla ferocia del padre, e dedito alle lettere e agli studi de' libri sacri della sua religione, aveva per natura l'animo alienissimo dalle armi" (Francesco Guicciardini, *Storia d'Italia*, in *Opere*, ed. Emanuella Lugnani Scarano [Turin: Unione Tipografico-Editrice Torinese, 1981], 2:613; English tr., *The History of Italy*, tr. and ed. Sidney Alexander [1969; repr., Princeton, N.J.: Princeton University Press, 1984], 176).

14. Guicciardini, *History*, 210; *Opere*, 2:863.

15. Guicciardini, *History*, 334; *Opere*, 3:1433–34.

16. "trovato il paese non guardato né sospettando di tale accidente, corsono predando e ardendo insino a Liquenza, e avendo fatto quantità innumerabile di prigioni, quando, ritornandosene, giunsono alla ripa del fiume del Tigliavento, per camminare più espediti, riserbatasi quella parte quale stimorono potere condurre seco, ammazzorono crudelissimamente tutti gli altri" (Guicciardini, *Opere*, 2:474; English tr., *History*, 150–51).

17. Guicciardini, *History*, 298; *Opere*, 3: 1297–98.

18. "in maggiore dispregio della cristiana religione, fece l'entrata sua in quella città il giorno della natività del Figliuolo de Dio . . . fece convertire tutte le chiese di Rodi, dedicate al culto di Cristo, in moschee; che secondo l'uso loro, esterminati tutti i riti de' cristiani." (Guicciardini, *Opere*, 3: 1434; English tr., *History*, 335).

19. Guicciardini, *History*, 335; *Opere*, 3:1434.

20. The plan called for a joint attack on several areas of the Turks' dominions: "Earth and land [being] covered with these preparations, and the empire of the Turks . . . attacked from so many sides, it seemed legitimate to hope, especially with the addition of divine help, that so fearful a war would have a most felicitous conclusion" (Guicciardini, *History*, 301; *Opere*, 3:1301).

21. Machiavelli, *Florentine Histories*, tr. Banfield and Mansfield, 300; Niccolò

Machiavelli, *The Comedies of Machiavelli*, ed. and tr. David Sices and James B. Atkinson (Hanover, N.H.: University Press of New England, 1985), 209.

22. "Questo farebbe più secura e più durabile quella possessione: come ha fatto el Turco, di Grecia: il quale, con tutti gli altri ordini osservati da lui per tenere quello stato, se non vi fussi ito ad abitare, non era possibile che lo tenessi" (Niccolò Machiavelli, *The Prince*, ed. and tr. Mark Musa [New York: St. Martin's Press, 1964], Italian, 12; English tr., 13).

23. See Chapter 2 above for a discussion of this letter.

24. "ma chi nasce in Italia ed in Grecia e non sia diventato o in Italia oltramontano o in Grecia Turco, ha ragione di biasimare i tempi suoi e laudare gli altri; perché in quelli vi sono assai cose che gli fanno maravigliosi, in questi non è cosa alcuna che gli ricomperi da ogni estrema miseria, infamia e vituperio. . . ." (Niccolò Machiavelli, *Discorsi*, ed. Mario Bonfantini [Milan: Riccardo Ricciardi Editore, 1954], in *Opere*, 219; English tr., *The Discourses*, ed. Bernard Crick, tr. Leslie J. Walker, S.J. [London: Penguin Books, 1970], 267).

25. See Cochrane, *Historians and Historiography*, 331–33; T. C. Price Zimmermann, *Paolo Giovio: The Historian and the Crisis of Sixteenth-Century Italy* (Princeton, N.J.: Princeton University Press, 1995), 121–25. Giovio seems especially inclined to use the term "barbarian" when calling for confrontation against the Turks, perhaps indicating his sense of the word as an emotional and persuasive term if not a descriptive one. See ibid., 124, 182.

26. While diplomats may have viewed the Turks more openly and helped to negotiate occasional alliances, we should also note that the Ottomans continued to appear in diplomatic treatises in the sixteenth and seventeenth centuries as the common enemy of Christendom; the underlying sense of "us versus them" did not dissipate even as the political scene opened in other ways. See Hay, *Europe*, 114.

27. On sources such as the *avvisi and relazione* available to historians, see Cochrane, *Historians and Historiography*, 331.

28. As J. R. Hale has commented, the tolerance of thinkers such as Montaigne regarding other cultures should not be taken as representative of later Renaissance attitudes; by 1600 the vast majority of his contemporaries demonstrated a closed, Eurocentric worldview. See Hale, *Civilization of Europe*, 50.

29. Cochrane, *Historians and Historiography*, 336–37. Parts of Aeneas Silvius Piccolomini's works were replicated by the German scholar Johannes Adelphus; see Bernard Gorceix, "Les Turcs dans les lettres Allemandes aux XVI et XVII siècles: Johannes Adelphus et Abraham a Santa Clara," *Revue d'Allemagne* 13, no. 2 (1981): 216–37. Benedetto Accolti's history of the First Crusade was printed and widely read in the sixteenth century; See Cochrane, *Historians and Historiography*, 27.

30. Cochrane, *Historians and Historiography*, 27. Tasso's poem was translated into Italian dialects and sung by members of the peasant and working classes. See Peter Burke, "Learned Culture and Popular Culture in Renaissance Italy," in *The Renaissance in Europe: A Reader*, ed. Keith Whitlock (New Haven, Conn.: Yale University Press, 2000), 75.

31. Heath, *Crusading Commonplaces*, 11, 22, 31–32. Lucinge, like Machiavelli, compared the Turks to the Romans; see ibid., 24. Montaigne argued that the

Turks' scorn of learning made them hardier soldiers; see Chew, *Crescent and the Rose*, 100.

32. Heath, *Crusading Commonplaces*, 31–32, 36. German humanist and reformer Ulrich Von Hutten drew heavily on humanist rhetoric in his exhortation to the princes of Germany to take up war against the barbarous Turks; see Von Hutten, *Opera* (Leipzig: Teubner, 1861), 5:101–34. See also Schwoebel, *Shadow of the Crescent*, 218–19.

33. Heath, *Crusading Commonplaces*, 27–31.

34. See Chew, *Crescent and the Rose*, 117, 134, and passim.

35. See Blanks, "Western Views of Islam," 40; Giambattista Vico, *On Humanistic Education (Six Inaugural Orations, 1699–1707)*, tr. Giorgio A. Pinton and Arthur W. Shippee (Ithaca, N.Y.: Cornell University Press, 1993), 107, 116.

36. Rouillard in particular champions the view that travelers wrote enlightened pieces and helped open the minds of European readers; see his *Turk in French History*.

37. See Housley's useful cautions in *Later Crusades*, 382–83. Schwoebel too provides a more nuanced account of travelers' tales in *Shadow of the Crescent*, chap. 7.

38. Postel was sent by Francis I as part of an embassy to the Ottoman Empire in 1535; he later returned in 1549. His role was scholarly rather than diplomatic, involving the collection of manuscripts and information on the Turks and their religion. Busbecq, an ambassador of the Habsburg emperor Ferdinand, was in Turkey from 1554 to 1562.

39. See Housley, *Later Crusades*, 383; Rouillard, *Turk in French History*, 211, 224; Heath, *Crusading Commonplaces*, 43.

40. Ogier Ghislain de Busbecq, *The Turkish Letters of Ogier Ghiselin de Busbecq*, tr. Edward Seymour Forster (Oxford: Clarendon Press, 1927), xiv. Rouillard stresses the positive aspects of the letters; see his *Turk in French History*, 220–24.

41. Busbecq, *Turkish Letters*, 40.

42. "These tales [of the immortal hero Chederle] are laughable enough, but the following is still more deserving of ridicule: they declare that he was one of the companions and friends of Alexander the Great! The Turks have no idea of chronology and dates, and make a wonderful mixture and confusion of all the epochs of history . . ." Busbecq, *Turkish Letters*, 55.

43. Rouillard, *Turk in French History*, 224, n. 1.

44. First printed in 1567, Nicolas de Nicolay's *Les Navigations, Peregrinations, et Voyages faicts en la Turquie* was translated into English in 1585. See Rouillard, *Turk in French History*, 196, 213.

45. See, for example Nicolay's discussions of Turkish baths and various religious sects in *The Navigations into Turkie* (1585; repr., Amsterdam: Da Capo Press, 1968), 59r, 99r–108v. Also, a strong indication of his reliance on humanist sources may be found in his description of the sack of Constantinople, in which he all but plagiarizes accounts by Pius and others; see ibid., 48v–49r.

46. See J. D. Gurney, "Pietro della Valle and the Limits of Perception," *Bulletin of the School of Oriental and African Studies* 49 (1986): 105.

47. Nicolay, for example, frequently discusses reports of Turkish sexual li-

cense. See Housley, *Later Crusades*, 383. For a fuller discussion of the "lustful and cruel Turk," see Wheatcroft, *Ottomans*.

48. Grafton et al., *New Worlds, Ancient Texts*, 5–6.

49. Anthony Pagden, *Lords of All the World: Ideologies of Empire in Spain, Britain and France c. 1500–1800* (New Haven, Conn.: Yale University Press, 1995), 29–62.

50. Francisco de Vitoria's argument was made in *De indis* (1539). See Anthony Pagden, *The Fall of Natural Man: The American Indian and the Origins of Comparative Ethnology* (Cambridge: Cambridge University Press, 1982), 90. A staunch scholastic, Vitoria nonetheless advocated the study of moral philosophy, which brought him closer to humanist principles; see ibid., 61.

51. Maldonado's address to the arts faculty at the University of Burgos (1545); See Pagden, *Fall of Natural Man*, 92.

52. Pertusi, *Testi inediti*, 76; see Chapter 2 above for more on this letter.

53. Pagden, *Fall of Natural Man*, 109, 114, 116.

54. Greenblatt, *Marvelous Possessions*, 9.

55. Samuel Purchas, *Hakluytus Posthumus or Purchas His Pilgrimes* (Glasgow: James MacLehose and Sons, 1905), 1:486; see also Greenblatt, *Marvelous Possessions*, 9–10.

56. Ficino, *Opera*, 1:722; English tr., *Letters*, 2: 5.

57. See Said, *Orientalism*; idem, *Culture and Imperialism* (New York: Vintage Books, 1993).

58. Greenblatt provides a fascinating discussion of Columbus's actions from an intellectual standpoint; see his *Marvelous Possessions*, 52–85. Columbus, it should be noted, was familiar with Aeneas Silvius Piccolomini's work, probably the *Cosmographia*; see Stefano Pittaluga, "Il 'vocabulario' usato da Cristoforo Colombo," *Columbeis* I (1986): 107–15.

59. See Hay, *Europe*.

60. See Mignolo, "Darker Side of the Renaissance," 808–28.

61. See Lewis, *Muslim Discovery*; Maalouf, *Crusades*, 261–64.

62. Jerry Brotton has argued that lively trade between East and West proves that Renaissance Europeans were far more multicultural. European art and styles were no doubt influenced by the East, but Brotton has not grappled with the vast body of hostile writings produced by humanists beyond dismissing them as mercenary and insincere in nature. See Brotton, *Renaissance Bazaar*.

63. Shelley, for example, chastised the Turks as destroyers of ancient Greek civilization, while praising other Muslim cultures of the East. See Issawi, *Cross-Cultural Encounters*, 47–48.

64. Wheatcroft, *Ottomans*, 233–35.

65. William Ewart Gladstone, *Bulgarian Horrors and the Question of the East* (London: John Murray, 1876), 12–13.

66. See Roy Jenkins, *Gladstone* (London: Macmillan, 1995), chap. 24. The pamphlet, it should be noted, served ancillary political purposes, such as an attack on Disraeli; see Volkan and Itzkowitz, *Turks and Greeks*, 95–96.

67. See, for example, Stephen Kinzer, "First Question for Europe: Is Turkey Really European?," *New York Times*, 9 December 1999, A12.

68. Michael Gunter discusses the many misperceptions of the historical and modern Turks that are still prevalent in American culture; see his "L'image de la Turquie aux États-Unis," in *La Turquie au seuil de l'Europe*, ed. Paul Dumont and François Georgeon (Paris: Editions L'Harmattan, 1991), 257–67.

69. Robert D. Kaplan, *Balkan Ghosts* (New York: St. Martin's Press, 1993), 37–40. On Milosevic's propagandistic treatment of Kosovo, see Volkan and Itzkowitz, *Turks and Greeks*, 43.

70. Aleksa Djilas, "A Nation That Wasn't," in *The Black Book of Bosnia*, ed. Nader Mousavizadeh (New York: New Republic Books, 1996), 21; this article was originally printed in *The New Republic* (21 September 1992).

71. For more on the Balkans from the period of Ottoman rule to the present day, see Robert J. Donia and John V. A. Fine, *Bosnia and Hercegovina*; *The Muslims of Bosnia-Hercegovina*, ed. Mark Pinson (Cambridge: Harvard University Press, 1994); Noel Malcolm, *Bosnia: A Short History* (New York: New York University Press, 1994).

72. Said, *Orientalism*, 52.

73. See Issawi, *Cross-Cultural Encounters*, 148–49; Lewis, *Islam and the West*, 26; Maalouf, *Crusades*, 264–66.

74. Said, *Orientalism*, 287–328; idem, *Covering Islam* (New York: Pantheon Books, 1981).

Bibliography

MANUSCRIPT SOURCES

Archivio di Stato, Florence (ASF)

Legazioni e commissarie. Elezioni ed istruzioni ad oratori 13, 14, and 15.
Missive, Prima Cancelleria 21, 42, 44, 48, and 49.

Biblioteca Laurenziana, Florence

Manetti, Giannozzo. *Oratio ad Calixtum summum pontificem.* San Marco 456,
    fols. 52–59.

Biblioteca Nazionale Centrale, Florence (BNCF)

Acciaiuoli, Donato. (Letters). Magliabecchiano VIII, 1390.
———. *Oratio funebris Joannis Vaivode.* Magliabecchiano IX, 123, fols. 83r–86r.

Biblioteca Riccardiana, Florence

Bessarion, Cardinal (translation of and commentary on Demosthenes). *Olynthiac*
    Orations. Riccardiano 365, fols. 33r ff.
Dati, Leonardo. *Carmen ad Nicolaum Papam V in Thurcum Mahomet.* Riccardi-
    ano 660, fols. 63r–68v. Recently edited by James Hankins in his "Renaissance
    Crusaders"; see below.
Verino, Ugolino. *Carlias.* Riccardiano 838. Recently edited by Niklaus Thurn; see
    below.

Biblioteca Apostolica Vaticana, Rome

Birago, Lampugnino. *Strategicon adversus turcos.* Vaticana, Lat. 3423.
Filelfo, Giovanni Mario. *In turcos adhortatio ad Christianos principes.* Urb. Lat.
    353.
Tignosi, Niccolo. *Expugnatio Constantinopolitana.* Urb. Lat. 923.

PUBLISHED SOURCES

Primary Sources

Acciaiuoli, Donato. *La Vita Caroli di Donato Acciaiuoli.* Edited by Daniela Gatti. Bologna: Pàtron Editore, 1981.

Accolti, Benedetto. *De bello a christianis contra barbaros.* In *Recueil des historiens des croisades.* Vol. 5, pt. 2. Paris: Imprimerie Nationale, 1895.

Aethicus. *Die Kosmographie des Aethicus.* Edited by Otto Prinz. Munich: Monumenta Germaniae Historica, 1993.

Alighieri, Dante. *The Divine Comedy.* 3 vols. Edited and translated by Charles S. Singleton. Princeton, N.J.: Princeton University Press, 1970–75.

Ammianus Marcellinus. *The Histories.* 3 vols. Edited and translated by John Rolfe. Cambridge: Harvard University Press, 1963.

Aquinas, Saint Thomas. *Summa contra Gentiles.* Edited and translated by Anton C. Pegis. Notre Dame, Ind.: University of Notre Dame Press, 1975.

Aristotle. *The Politics.* Edited and translated by Ernest Barker. London: Oxford University Press, 1970.

Augustine of Hippo. *City of God.* Translated by George E. McCracken. Cambridge: Harvard University Press, 1957.

———. *Confessions.* Edited and translated by Henry Chadwick. Oxford: Oxford University Press, 1991.

Balbo, Michael Ben Shabbetai Cohen. "A Hebrew Lament from Venetian Crete on the Fall of Constantinople." Translated by Avi Sharon. *Dialogos: Hellenic Studies Review* 6 (1999): 43–46.

Bernard of Clairvaux. *The Letters of Bernard of Clairvaux.* Translated by Bruno Scott James. London: Burns Oates, 1953.

Bessarion, Cardinal. *Epistolae et orationes.* Paris: Guillaume Fichet. 1471.

———. *Oratio Dogmatica.* In *Patrilogia Graeca*, vol. 161, 543–614. 1866.

———. *Orationes contra Turcas.* Edited by J. P. Migne. In *Patrologia Graeca*, vol. 161, 642–76. 1866.

Biondo, Flavio. *Opera Historica.* Basel, 1531.

———. *Scritti inediti e rari di Biondo Flavio.* Edited by Bartolomeo Nogara. In *Studi e testi*, vol. 48. Rome: Tipografia Poliglotta Vaticana, 1927.

Boccaccio, Giovanni. *Il Decameron.* 2 vols. Edited by Charles Singleton. Bari: Giuseppe Laterza e Figli, 1955.

Bracciolini, Poggio. *The Facetiae of Poggio and Other Medieval Story-tellers.* Edited and translated by Edward Storer. London: George Routledge and Sons Ltd., n.d.

———. *Lettere.* 3 vols. Edited by Helene Harth. Florence: Leo S. Olschki Editore, 1984.

———. *Opera Omnia.* 4 vols. 1538. Reprint, Turin: Bottega d'Erasmo, 1963–69.

———. "Oratio in funere reverendissimi Cardinalis D. Iuliani de Caesarinis Romani." In *Spicilegium Romanum*, vol. 10. Edited by Angelo Mai. Rome: Typis Collegii Urbani, 1844.

Bruni, Leonardo. "Dialogues to Pier Paolo Vergerio"; "Life of Petrarch." In *The*

Three Crowns of Florence: Humanist Assessments of Dante, Petrarch, and Boccaccio. Edited and translated by David Thompson and Alan F. Nagel. New York: Harper and Row, 1972.

———. *History of the Florentine People.* Edited and translated by James Hankins. Cambridge, Mass.: I Tatti Renaissance Library, 2001.

———. *The Humanism of Leonardo Bruni: Selected Texts.* Edited and translated by Gordon Griffiths et al. Binghamton, N.Y.: Medieval and Renaissance Texts and Studies, 1987.

———. *Leonardo Bruni Arretini Epistolarum Libri VIII.* Edited by Lorenzo Mehus. Florence, 1741.

Busbecq, Ogier Ghislain de. *The Turkish Letters of Ogier Ghiselin de Busbecq.* Translated by Edward Seymour Forster. Oxford: Clarendon Press, 1927.

Caracciolo, Roberto. *Specchio della Fede.* Venice, c. 1495.

Cassirer, Ernst, Paul Oskar Kristeller, and John Herman Randall Jr., eds. *The Renaissance Philosophy of Man.* Chicago: University of Chicago Press, 1971.

Catherine of Siena. *The Letters of Catherine of Siena.* Translated by Suzanne Noffke, O.P. Binghamton, N.Y.: Medieval and Renaissance Texts and Studies, 1988.

Cereta, Laura. *The Collected Letters of a Renaissance Feminist.* Edited and translated by Diana Robin. Chicago: University of Chicago Press, 1997.

Christine de Pizan. *Oeuvres Poétiques.* Vol. 2. Edited by Maurice Roy. Paris: Libraire de Firmin Didot et Companie, 1891.

Cicero. *Cicero in Twenty-eight Volumes.* Edited and translated by C. Macdonald. Cambridge: Harvard University Press, 1976.

———. *The Speeches.* Edited and translated by N. H. Watts. Cambridge: Harvard University Press, 1958.

———. *The Speeches.* Edited by H. Grose Hodge. Cambridge: Harvard University Press, 1959.

Ciriaco of Ancona. *Cyriacus of Ancona's Journeys in the Propontis and the Northern Aegean 1444–1445.* Edited by Edward J. Bodnar, S.J., and Charles Mitchell. Philadelphia: American Philosophical Society, 1976.

Claudian (works). Vol. 1. Edited and translated by Maurice Platnauer. London: William Heinemann, 1922.

Cusanus, Nicholas. *De pace fidei.* In Nicholas Cusanus, *Unity and Reform.* Edited and translated by John Patrick Dolan. Notre Dame, Ind.: University of Notre Dame Press, 1962.

———. *Nicholas of Cusa's De pace fidei and Cribratio Alkorani: Translation and Analysis.* Edited and translated by Jasper Hopkins. Minneapolis: A. J. Banning Press, 1990.

———. *Opera.* 1514. Reprint, Frankfurt/Main: Minerva, 1962.

Dati, Leonardo. *Carmen ad Nicolaum Papam V in Thurcum Mahomet.* Edited by James Hankins. In "Renaissance Crusaders: Humanist Crusade Literature in the Age of Mehmed II." *Dumbarton Oaks Papers* 49 (1995).

Dei, Benedetto. *La Cronica dall'anno 1400 all'anno 1500.* Edited by Roberto Barducci. Florence: Francesco Papafava Editore, 1984.

Demosthenes. *Orations.* Translated by J. H. Vince. New York: G. P. Putnam, 1930.

Doukas. *Decline and Fall of Byzantium to the Ottoman Turks*. Edited and translated by Harry J. Magoulias. Detroit: Wayne State University Press, 1975.

Erasmus, Desiderius. *Consultatio de bello Turcis inferendo*. 1643. Reprint, Athens, 1974.

———. *De bello Turcico*. Translated by Michael J. Heath. In *The Erasmus Reader*. Edited by Erika Rummel. Toronto: University of Toronto Press, 1990.

———. "Letter to Anthony Bergen." Edited and translated by Peter Mayer. In *The Pacifist Conscience*. New York: Holt, Rinehart and Winston, 1966.

———. "Letter to Paul Volz." Edited and translated by John C. Olin. In *Christian Humanism and the Reformation: Selected Writings of Erasmus*. 3d edition. New York: Fordham University Press, 1987.

———. *Opus Epistolarum*. 10 vols. Edited by P. S. Allen. London: Oxford University Press, 1906–58.

Euripides. *Bakkhai*. Translated by Robert Bagg. Amherst: University of Massachusetts Press, 1978.

Ficino, Marsilio. *The Letters of Marsilio Ficino*. 6 vols. London: Shepheard-Walwyn, 1978.

———. *Opera Omnia*. 2 vols. 1576. Reprint, Turin: Bottega d'Erasmo, 1962.

———. *Three Books on Life*. Edited and translated by Carol V. Kaske and John R. Clark. Binghamton, N.Y.: Medieval and Renaissance Texts and Studies, 1989.

Filelfo, Francesco. *Cent-dix lettres grecques de François Filelfe*. Edited by Émile Legrand. Paris: Ernest Leroux Editeur, 1892.

———. *Orationes cum quibusdam aliis eiusdem operibus*. Basel, 1498.

Filelfo, Giovanni Mario. *Amyris*. Edited by Aldo Manetti. Bologna: Pàtron Editore, 1978.

Foucard, C., ed. "Dispacci degli oratori Estensi." *Archivio storico per le province napoletane* 6 (1881).

Gabrieli, Francesco, ed. and tr. *Arab Historians of the Crusades*. Translated from the Italian by E. J. Costello. Berkeley: University of California Press, 1969.

Geanakoplos, Deno John, ed. *Byzantium: Church, Society, and Civilization Seen through Contemporary Eyes*. Chicago: University of Chicago Press, 1984.

George of Trebizond. *Collectanea Trapezuntiana: Texts, Documents, and Bibliographies of George of Trebizond*. Edited by John Monfasani. Binghamton, N.Y.: Medieval and Renaissance Texts and Studies, 1984.

———. *Martyrium beatissimi Andreae de Chio*. In *Patrologia Graeca*, vol. 161, 883–90. Edited by J. P. Migne, 1866.

Gladstone, William Ewart. *Bulgarian Horrors and the Question of the East*. London: John Murray, 1876.

Gualdo Rosa, Lucia, Isabella Nuovo, and Domenico Defilippis, eds. *Gli umanisti e la guerra otrantina*. Bari: Dedalo, 1982.

Guicciardini, Francesco. *The History of Italy*. Translated and edited by Sidney Alexander. 1969. Reprint, Princeton, N.J.: Princeton University Press, 1984.

———. *Storia d'Italia*. In *Opere*. 3 vols. Edited by Emanuella Lugnani Scarano. Turin: Unione Tipografico-Editrice, 1981.

Habig, Marion A., ed. *St. Francis of Assisi: Writings and Early Biographies*. Chicago: Franciscan Herald Press, 1972.

Herodotus. *The Histories*. Translated by Aubrey de Sélincourt and edited by A. R. Burn. London: Penguin Books, 1972.

Housley, Norman, ed. and tr. *Documents on the Later Crusades 1274–1580*. New York: St. Martin's Press, 1996.

Ilardi, Vincent, ed. *Dispatches with Related Documents of Milanese Ambassadors in France*. 3 vols. Translated by Frank J. Fata. Dekalb: Northern Illinois University Press, 1981.

Infessura, Stefano. *Diario della città di Roma*. Edited by Oreste Tommasini. Rome: Forzani E. C. Tipografi del Senato, 1890.

Jerome, Saint. *Selected Letters*. Edited and translated by F. A. Wright. London: William Heinemann, 1933.

Jones, J. R. Melville, tr. and ed. *The Siege of Constantinople 1453: Seven Contemporary Accounts*. Amsterdam: Adolf M. Hakkert, 1972.

The Journey of Charlemagne. Edited by Jean-Louis G. Picherit. Birmingham: Summa Publications. 1984.

Kritoboulos. *The History of Mehmed the Conqueror*. Edited and translated by Charles T. Riggs. Princeton, N.J.: Princeton University Press, 1954.

Landucci, Luca. *A Florentine Diary*. Translated by Alice de Rosen Jervis. London: J. M. Dent and Sons, Ltd., 1927.

Leonard of Chios. *Historia Constantinopolitanae urbis a Mahumete II captae*. Edited by J. P. Migne. In *Patrologia Graeca*, vol. 159, 923–41. 1866.

The Little Flowers. In *St. Francis of Assisi: Writings and Early Biographies*. Edited by Marion A. Habig. Chicago: Franciscan Herald Press, 1972.

Machiavelli, Niccolò. *The Comedies of Machiavelli*. Edited and translated by David Sices and James B. Atkinson. Hanover, N.H.: University Press of New England, 1985.

———. *The Discourses*. Edited by Bernard Crick and translated by Leslie J. Walker, S.J. London: Penguin Books, 1970.

———. *Florentine Histories*. Translated by Laura F. Banfield and Harvey C. Mansfield Jr. Princeton, N.J.: Princeton University Press, 1988.

———. *Letters of Machiavelli*. Edited and translated by Allan Gilbert. Chicago: University of Chicago Press, 1961.

———. *Opere*. Edited by Mario Bonfantini. Milan: Riccardo Ricciardi Editore, 1954.

———. *The Prince*. Edited and translated by Mark Musa. New York: St. Martin's Press, 1964.

Marullus, Michael Tarcaniota. *Carmina*. Edited by Alessandro Perosa. Turici: Societas Thesauri Mundi, 1951.

Medici, Lorenzo de'. *Lettere*. Vols. 5 (1480–81) and 6 (1481–82). Edited by Michael Mallett. Florence: Giunti-Barbera, 1989.

Müller, Giuseppe, ed. *Documenti sulle relazioni delle città toscane coll'Oriente cristiano e coi Turchi*. 1879. Reprint, Rome: Società Multigrafica Editrice, 1966.

Nicolay, Nicolas de. *The Navigations into Turkie*. 1585. Reprint, Amsterdam: Da Capo Press, 1968.

Parenti, Marco. *Lettere*. Edited by Maria Marrese. Florence: Leo S. Olschki Editore, 1996.

Pertusi, Agostino, ed. *La caduta di Costantinopoli*. 2 vols. Milan: Arnoldo Mondadori Editore, 1976.

———. *Testi inediti e poco noti sulla caduta di Costantinopoli*. Bologna: Pàtron Editore, 1983.

Peter the Venerable. *Liber contra sectam Saracenorum*. Edited by J. P. Migne. In *Patrologia Latina*, vol. 189, 659–716. 1890.

Peters, Edward. ed. *Christian Society and the Crusades 1198–1229: Sources in Translation*. Philadelphia: University of Pennsylvania Press, 1971.

———. *The First Crusade: The Chronicle of Fulcher of Chartres and Other Source Materials*. 2nd edition. Philadelphia: University of Pennsylvania Press, 1998.

Petrarch, Francesco. *Canzoniere or Rerum vulgarium fragmenta*. Edited and translated by Mark Musa. Bloomington: University of Indiana Press, 1996.

———. *De vita solitaria*. Edited and translated into Italian by Marco Noce. Milan: Arnoldo Mondadori Editore, 1992.

———. *Le Familiari*. Edited by Vittorio Rossi. Florence: G. C. Sansoni Editore, 1933–42.

———. *Itinerario in Terra Santa*. Edited and translated into Italian by Francesco Lo Monaco. Bergamo: Pierluigi Lubrina Editore, 1990.

———. *Letters of Old Age: Rerum senilium libri I–XVIII*. 2 vols. Translated by Aldo S. Bernardo, Saul Levin, and Reta A. Bernardo. Baltimore: Johns Hopkins University Press, 1992.

———. *Letters on Familiar Matters: Rerum familiarum libri*. 3 vols. Translated by Aldo S. Bernardo. Baltimore: Johns Hopkins University Press, 1975–82.

———. *The Life of Solitude*. Edited and translated by Jacob Zeitlin. Urbana: University of Illinois Press, 1924.

———. "On his own ignorance and that of many others." Translated by Hans Nachod. In *The Renaissance Philosophy of Man*. Edited by Ernst Cassirer et al. Chicago: University of Chicago Press, 1971.

———. *Opera Omnia*. 3 vols. 1554. Reprint, Ridgewood, N.J.: Gregg Press, 1965.

———. *Petrarch's Guide to the Holy Land: Itinerary to the Sepulcher of Our Lord Jesus Christ*. Edited and translated by Theodore J. Cachey Jr. Notre Dame, Ind.: University of Notre Dame Press, 2002.

———. *Petrarch's Lyric Poems*. Edited and translated by Robert M. Durling. Cambridge: Harvard University Press, 1976.

Piccolomini, Aeneas Silvius (Pope Pius II). *Aeneae Silvii Piccolomini Senensis qui postea fuit Pius II Pont. Max. opera inedita*. Edited by Joseph Cugnoni. Rome: Reale Accademia dei Lincei, 1883.

———. *Der Briefwechsel des Eneas Silvius Piccolomini*. Edited by Rudolf Wolkan. In *Fontes rerum austriacarum*. Bd. 68. Vienna: Alfred Holder, 1918.

———. *Commentaries of Pius II*. 5 vols. Translated by Florence Alden Gragg and edited by Leona C. Gabel. Northampton, Mass.: Smith College, 1951.

———. *De captione urbis Constantinopolitanae Tractaculus*. Rome: Johannes Gensberg, c. 1474.

———. *Epistola ad Mahomatem II (Epistle to Mohammed II)*. Edited and translated by Albert R. Baca. New York: Peter Lang, 1990.

———. *I Commentarii*. Edited by Luigi Totaro. Milan: Adelphi Edizioni, 1984.

———. *Memoirs of a Renaissance Pope: The Commentaries of Pius II.* Translated by Florence A. Gragg and edited by Leona C. Gabel. New York: Capricorn Books, 1959.

———. *Opera quae extant omnia.* Frankfurt: Minerva, 1967.

Poliziano, Angelo. *Prose volgari inedite e poesie latine e greche edite.* Edited by Isidoro del Lungo. Florence: G. Barbera Editore, 1867.

Polo, Marco. *The Travels.* Edited and translated by Ronald Latham. London: Penguin Books, 1958.

The Portable Renaissance Reader. Edited by James Bruce Ross and Mary M. McLaughlin. New York: Penguin Books, 1953.

Purchas, Samuel. *Hakluytus Posthumus or Purchas His Pilgrimes.* 20 vols. Glasgow: James MacLehose and Sons, 1905.

The Renaissance in Europe: An Anthology. Edited by Peter Elmer, Nick Webb, and Roberta Wood. New Haven, Conn.: Yale University Press, 2000.

Ross, Janet, ed. and tr. *The Lives of the Early Medici as Told in Their Correspondence.* London: Chatto and Windus, 1910.

Salutati, Coluccio. *Epistolario di Coluccio Salutati.* 3 vols. Edited by Francesco Novati. Rome: Forzani E. C. Tipografi del Senato, 1896.

Sanuto, Marin. *Liber secretorum fidelium crucis super Terrae Sanctae.* 1611. Reprint, Toronto: University of Toronto Press, 1972.

The Song of Roland. Translated by Glyn Burgess. London: Penguin Books, 1990.

Spandounes, Theodore. *On the Origin of the Ottoman Emperors.* Edited and translated by Donald M. Nicol. Cambridge: Cambridge University Press, 1997.

Tacitus. *The Complete Works of Tacitus.* Edited by Moses Hadas. New York: The Modern Library, 1942.

A Thirteenth Century Life of Charlemagne. Edited and translated by Robert Levine. New York: Garland Publishing, 1991.

The Three Crowns of Florence: Humanist Assessments of Dante, Petrarch, and Boccaccio. Edited and translated by David Thompson and Alan F. Nagel. New York: Harper and Row, 1972.

Tignosi, Niccolò. *Expugnatio Constantinopolitana.* Edited by Mario Sensi. In "Niccolò Tignosi da Foligno opera e il pensiero." *Annali della facoltà di lettere e filosofia della Università degli Studi di Perugia* 9 (1971–72).

Tursun Beg. *History of Mehmed the Conqueror.* Edited by Halil Inalcik. Minneapolis: Bibliotheca Islamica, 1978.

Two Lives of Charlemagne. Edited and translated by Lewis Thorpe. Middlesex: Penguin Books, 1969.

Usamah Ibn Muquidh. *Memoirs.* In *Arab Historians of the Crusades.* Edited and translated by Francesco Gabrieli. Translated from Italian by E. J. Costello. Berkeley: University of California Press, 1969.

Vergerio, Pier Paolo. *Epistolario.* Edited by Leonardo Smith. Rome: Tipografia del Senato, 1934.

Verino, Ugolino. *Carlias.* Edited by Niklaus Thurn. Munich: Wilhelm Fink Verlag, 1995.

———. *De illustratione urbis florentiae: Libri tres.* Florence, 1636.

———. *Panegyricon ad Ferdinandum regem et Isabellam reginam hispaniarum de saracenae baetidos gloriosa expugnatione.* Edited by Joseph Fogel and Ladislaus Juhasz. Leipzig: Teubner, 1933.

Vespasiano da Bisticci. *Lamento d'Italia per la presa d'Otranto.* Edited by Ludovico Frati. In *Vite di uomini illustri del secolo XV*, vol. 3, 306–25. Bologna: Romagnoli-Dall'Acqua, 1893.

———. *Renaissance Princes, Popes and Prelates.* Edited by Myron Gilmore and translated by William George and Emily Waters. New York: Harper and Row, 1963.

———. *Le Vite.* 2 vols. Edited by Aulo Greco. Florence: Istituto Nazionale di Studi sul Rinascimento, 1970.

Vico, Giambattista. *On Humanistic Education (Six Inaugural Orations, 1699–1707).* Translated by Giorgio A. Pinton and Arthur W. Shippee. Ithaca, N.Y.: Cornell University Press, 1993.

Villani, Giovanni. *Nuova Cronica.* 3 vols. Edited by Giuseppe Porta. Parma: Fondazione Pietro Bembo, 1990.

da Voragine, Jacopo. *The Golden Legend: Readings on the Saints.* 2 vols. Translated by William Granger Ryan. Princeton, N.J.: Princeton University Press, 1993.

William of Tyre, *A History of Deeds Done beyond the Sea.* Translated and edited by Emily Atwater Babcock and A. C. Krey. New York: Columbia University Press, 1943.

Secondary Sources

Abulafia, David. *Frederick II: A Medieval Emperor.* Oxford: Oxford University Press, 1992.

Ahmad, Aijaz. "Orientalism and After: Ambivalence and Metropolitan Location in the Work of Edward Said." In *In Theory: Classes, Nations, Literatures.* Edited by Aijaz Ahmad. London: Verso, 1992.

Akbari, Suzanne Conklin. "From Due East to True North: Orientalism and Orientation." In *The Postcolonial Middle Ages.* Edited by Jeffrey Jerome Cohen. New York: St. Martin's Press, 2000.

Allaire, Gloria. *Andrea Barberino and the Language of Chivalry.* Gainesville: University Press of Florida, 1997.

———. "Portrayal of Muslims in Andrea da Barberino's *Guerrino il Meschino.*" In *Medieval Christian Perceptions of Islam.* Edited by John V. Tolan. New York: Garland Publishing, 1996.

Ashtor, Eliyahu. *Levant Trade in the Later Middle Ages.* Princeton, N.J.: Princeton University Press, 1983.

Babinger, Franz. "Lorenzo de' Medici e la corte ottomana." *Archivio storico italiano* 121 (1963): 305–61.

———. "Maometto II, il Conquistore, e l'Italia." *Rivista storica italiana* 63 (1951): 469–505.

———. *Mehmed the Conqueror and His Time.* Translated by Ralph Manheim. 1953. Rev. ed., Princeton, N.J.: Princeton University Press, 1978.

————. "Pio II e l'Oriente maomettano." In *Enea Silvio Piccolomini Papa Pio II.* Edited by Domenico Maffei. Siena: Varese, 1968.

Balsdon, J. V. P. D. *Romans and Aliens.* London: Duckworth and Co., 1979.

Barker, John W. *Manuel II Palaeologus (1391–1425): A Study in Late Byzantine Statesmanship.* New Brunswick, N.J.: Rutgers University Press, 1969.

Baron, Hans. *The Crisis of the Early Italian Renaissance.* 1955. Rev. ed., Princeton, N.J.: Princeton University Press, 1966.

————. *From Petrarch to Leonardo Bruni.* Chicago: University of Chicago Press, 1968.

Bartlett, Robert. *The Making of Europe: Conquest, Colonization and Cultural Change 950–1350.* Princeton, N.J.: Princeton University Press, 1993.

Bataillon, Marcel. "Mythe et connaissance de la Turquie in Occident au milieu de XVI siècle." In *Venezia e l'Oriente fra tardo medioevo e rinascimento.* Edited by Agostino Pertusi. Florence: G. C. Sansoni, 1966.

Beck, Hans-Georg, Manoussos Manoussacas, and Agostino Pertusi, eds. *Venezia centro di mediazione tra oriente e occidente (secoli XV–XVI) aspetti e problemi.* 2 vols. Florence: Leo S. Olschki Editore, 1977.

Bentley, Jerry H. *Old World Encounters.* New York: Oxford University Press, 1993.

Beye, Charles Rowan. *Ancient Greek Literature and Society.* 2d edition. Ithaca, N.Y.: Cornell University Press, 1987.

Bezzola, Reto R. "L'Oriente nel poema cavalleresco del primo Rinascimento." In *Venezia e l'Oriente fra tardro medioevo e rinascimento.* Edited by Agostino Pertusi. Venice: G. C. Sansoni, 1966.

Bhabha, Homi. *The Location of Culture.* London: Routledge, 1994.

Bianca, Concetta. *Da Bisanzio a Roma: Studi sul Cardinale Bessarione.* Rome: Roma nel Rinascimento, 1999.

Biechler, James E. "Christian Humanism Confronts Islam: The Sifting of the Qur'an with Nicholas of Cusa." *Journal of Ecumenical Studies* 13 (1978): 1–14.

————. "A New Face toward Islam: Nicholas of Cusa and John of Segovia." In *Nicholas of Cusa in Search of God and Wisdom.* Edited by Gerald Christianson and Thomas M. Izbicki. Leiden: E. J. Brill, 1991.

Billanovich, Giuseppe. *Petrarca Letterato.* Rome: Edizioni di Storia e Letteratura, 1947.

Bisaha, Nancy. "The Early Ottoman Empire." In *Trade, Travel, and Exploration in the Middle Ages: An Encyclopedia.* Edited by John Block Friedman and Kristen Mossler Figg. New York: Garland Press, 2000.

————. "New Barbarian or Worthy Adversary? Humanist Constructs of the Ottoman Turks in Fifteenth-Century Italy." In *Western Views of Islam in Medieval and Early Modern Europe: Perception of Other.* Edited by David Blanks and Michael Frassetto. New York: St. Martin's Press, 1999.

————. "Petrarch's Vision of the Muslim and Byzantine East." *Speculum* 76, no. 2 (April 2001): 284–314.

————. "Pius II's Letter to Sultan Mehmed II: A Reexamination." *Crusades* 1 (2002).

Bitterly, Urs. *Cultures in Conflict: Encounters between European and Non-*

European Cultures, 1492–1800. Translated by Ritchie Robertson. Stanford, Calif.: Stanford University Press, 1989.

Black, Robert. *Benedetto Accolti and the Florentine Renaissance*. Cambridge: Cambridge University Press, 1985.

———. "The Donation of Constantine: A New Source for the Concept of the Renaissance?" In *Language and Images of Renaissance Italy*. Edited by Alison Brown. Oxford: Clarendon Press, 1995.

———. "Italian Renaissance Education: Changing Perspectives and Continuing Controversies." *Journal of the History of Ideas* 52, no. 2 (1991): 315–34.

———. "La storia della prima crociata di Benedetto Accolti e la diplomazia fiorentina rispetto all'Oriente." *Archivio storico italiano* 131 (1973): 3–25.

Blanks, David. "Western Views of Islam in the Premodern Period: A Brief History of Past Approaches." In *Western Views of Islam in Medieval and Early Modern Europe: Perception of Other*. Edited by Michael Frassetto and David Blanks. New York: St. Martin's Press, 1999.

Blanks, David, and Michael Frassetto, eds. *Western Views of Islam in Medieval and Early Modern Europe: Perception of Other*. New York: St. Martin's Press, 1999.

Boas, George. *Essays on Primitivism and Related Ideas in the Middle Ages*. Baltimore: Johns Hopkins University Press, 1948.

Boas, George, and Arthur Lovejoy. *Primitivism and Related Ideas in Antiquity*. Baltimore: Johns Hopkins University Press, 1935.

Bodenham, C. H. L. "Petrarch and the Poetry of the Arabs." *Romanische Forschungen* 94, no. 2/3 (1982): 167–78.

Bodnar, Edward W., S.J. *Cyriacus of Ancona and Athens*. Brussels: Latomus, 1960.

Borst, Arno. *Medieval Worlds: Barbarians, Heretics, and Artists in the Middle Ages*. Chicago: University of Chicago Press, 1992.

Boyle, Marjorie O'Rourke. *Petrarch's Genius*. Berkeley: University of California Press, 1991.

Branca, Daniela Delcorno. *Il romanzo cavalleresco medievale*. Florence: G. C. Sansoni, 1974.

Brotton, Jerry. *The Renaissance Bazaar*. Oxford: Oxford University Press, 2002.

Brown, Alison. *Bartolomeo Scala 1430–1497, Chancellor of Florence*. Princeton, N.J.: Princeton University Press, 1979.

———, ed. *Language and Images of Renaissance Italy*. Oxford: Clarendon Press, 1995.

Brown, L. Carl, ed. *Imperial Legacy: The Ottoman Imprint on the Balkans and the Middle East*. New York: Columbia University Press, 1996.

Brown, Peter. *The World of Late Antiquity*. London: W. W. Norton and Co., 1971.

Bull, Marcus. *Knightly Piety and the Lay Response to the First Crusade*. Oxford: Clarendon Press, 1993.

Burckhardt, Jacob. *The Civilization of the Renaissance in Italy*. Translated by S. G. C. Middlemore. New York: Modern Library, 1954.

Burke, Peter. *The European Renaissance: Centres and Peripheries*. Oxford: Blackwell Publishers, 1998.

———. "Learned Culture and Popular Culture in Renaissance Italy." In *The Re-*

naissance in Europe: A Reader. Edited by Keith Whitlock. New Haven, Conn.: Yale University Press, 2000.

Burnett, Charles. "Petrarch and Averroes: An Episode in the History of Poetics." In *The Medieval Mind: Hispanic Studies in Honour of Alan Deyermond*. Edited by Ian MacPherson and Ralph Penny, 49–56. Rochester, N.Y.: Tamesis Press, 1997.

———. "The Second Revelation of Arabic Philosophy and Science: 1492–1562." In *Islam and the Italian Renaissance*. Edited by Charles Burnett and Anna Contadini. London: Warburg Institute, 1999.

Burr, David, "Antichrist and Islam in Medieval Franciscan Exegesis." In *Medieval Christian Perceptions of Islam: A Book of Essays*. Edited by John V. Tolan. New York: Garland Publishing, 1996.

Cameron, Alan. *Claudian: Poetry and Propaganda at the Court of Honorius*. Oxford: Clarendon Press, 1970.

Cammelli, Giuseppe. *I dotti bizantini e le origini dell'umanesimo*. 3 vols. Florence: Valecchi Editore, 1941.

Campbell, Mary. *The Witness and the Other World*. Ithaca, N.Y.: Cornell University Press, 1988.

Cardini, Franco. "La crociata mito politico." *Il pensiero politico* 8, no. 1 (1975): 3–32.

———. *Europa e Islam: storia di un malinteso*. Rome: Laterza, 1999.

———. *Studi sulla storia e sull'idea di crociata*. Rome: Jouvence, 1993.

———. *Toscana e terrasanta nel medioevo*. Florence: Alinea, 1982.

Cartledge, Paul. *The Greeks: A Portrait of Self and Others*. Oxford: Oxford University Press, 1993.

Catologus Translationum et commentariorum: Medieval and Renaissance Latin Translations and Commentaries. Edited by F. E. Cranz and P. O. Kristeller. Washington, D.C.: Catholic University of America Press, 1986.

Chew, Samuel. *The Crescent and the Rose: Islam and England during the Renaissance*. 1937. Reprint, New York: Octagon Books, 1965.

Christianson, Gerald, and Thomas M. Izbicki, eds. *Nicholas of Cusa in Search of God and Wisdom*. Leiden: E. J. Brill, 1991.

Ciarambino, Gerardo C. A. *Carlomagno, Gano e Orlando in alcuni romanzi italiani del XIV e XV secolo*. Pisa: Giardini Editori e Stampatori, 1976.

Clough, Cecil H. "The Cult of Antiquity: Letters and Letter Collections." In *Cultural Aspects of the Italian Renaissance: Essays in Honor of Paul Oskar Kristeller*. Edited by Cecil H. Clough, 33–67. Manchester: Manchester University Press, 1976.

Cochrane, Eric. *Historians and Historiography in the Italian Renaissance*. Chicago: University of Chicago Press, 1980.

Cohen, Beth, ed.. *Not the Classical Ideal: Athens and the Construction of the Other in Greek Art*. Leiden: Brill, 2003.

Cohen, Jeffrey Jerome, ed. *The Postcolonial Middle Ages*. New York: St. Martin's Press, 2000.

Coles, Paul. *The Ottoman Impact on Europe*. London: Harcourt, Brace, and World, 1968.

Colin, Jean. *Cyriaque d'Ancône: le voyageur, le marchand, l'humaniste.* Paris: Maloine Éditeur , 1981.

Collins, Roger. *Early Medieval Europe 300–1000.* New York: St. Martin's Press, 1991.

Constable, Giles, and James Kritzeck, eds. *Petrus Venerabilis 1156–1956.* Rome: Herder, 1956.

Cosenza, Mario. *Biographical and Bibliographical Dictionary of the Italian Humanists and of the World of Classical Scholarship in Italy 1300–1800.* 6 vols. Boston: G. K. Hall, 1962–67.

Coulet, Jules. *Etudes sur l'ancien poème français du voyage de Charlemagne in Orient.* Montpellier: Coulet et Fils Editeurs, 1907.

Cranz, F. E. *Nicholas of Cusa and the Renaissance.* Edited by Thomas Izbicki and Gerald Christianson. Aldershot: Ashgate, 2000.

Cruz, Jo Ann Hoeppner Moran. "Popular Attitudes towards Islam in Medieval Europe." In *Western Views of Islam in Medieval and Early Modern Europe: Perception of Other.* Edited by David Blanks and Michael Frassetto. New York: St. Martin's Press, 1999.

Curtius, Ernst. *European Literature and the Latin Middle Ages.* Translated by Willard R. Trask. 1953. Reprint, with afterword by Peter Godman, Princeton, N.J.: Princeton University Press, 1990.

D'Amico, John F. "Humanism and Prereformation Theology." In *Renaissance Humanism,* vol. 3. Edited by Albert Rabil Jr. Philadelphia: University of Pennsylvania Press, 1988.

———. "Humanism in Rome." In *Renaissance Humanism,* vol. 1. Edited by Albert Rabil Jr. Philadelphia: University of Pennsylvania Press, 1988.

Daniel, Norman. "Crusade Propaganda." In *A History of the Crusades.* General editor, Kenneth M. Setton. Vol. 6, edited by Harry W. Hazard and Norman P. Zacour. Madison: University of Wisconsin Press, 1989.

———. *Heroes and Saracens: An Interpretation of the Chansons de Geste.* Edinburgh: Edinburgh University Press, 1984.

———. *Islam and the West: The Making of an Image.* 1960. Rev. ed., Oxford: Oneworld Publications, 1993.

Dannenfeldt, Karl H. "The Renaissance Humanists and the Knowledge of Arabic." *Studies in the Renaissance* 2 (1955): 96–117.

Davies, Jonathan. *Florence and Its University during the Early Renaissance.* Leiden: Brill, 1998.

Davies, M. C. "Poggio Bracciolini as Rhetorician and Historian: Unpublished Pieces." *Rinascimento* 2d ser., 22 (1982).

Dizionario biografico degli Italiani. Rome: Istituto della Enciclopedia Italiana, 1997.

Donia, Robert J., and John V. A. Fine. *Bosnia and Hercegovina: A Tradition Betrayed.* New York: Columbia University Press, 1994.

Dower, John W. *War without Mercy: Race and Power in the Pacific War.* New York: Pantheon Books, 1986.

Dursteler, Eric. "Identity and Coexistence in the Eastern Mediterranean, ca. 1600." *New Perspectives on Turkey* 18 (spring 1998): 113–30.

Ellis, J. R., and R. D. Milns. *The Spectre of Philip: Demosthenes' First Philippic, Olynthiacs and Speech on the Peace.* Sydney: Sydney University Press, 1970.

Emmerson, Richard. *Antichrist in the Middle Ages.* Seattle: University of Washington Press, 1981.

Emmert, Thomas A. *Serbian Golgotha: Kosovo, 1389.* New York: East European Monographs, 1990.

Englebert, Omer. *St. Francis of Assisi: A Biography.* Translated by Eve Marie Cooper. Ann Arbor, Mich.: Servant Books, 1965.

Favre, Guillaume. "Vie de Jean-Marius Philelfe." In *Mélanges d'histoire littéraire*, vol. 1. Geneva, 1856.

Ferguson, Wallace K. *The Renaissance.* New York: Holt, Rinehart and Winston, Inc., 1940.

Field, Arthur. *The Origins of the Platonic Academy of Florence.* Princeton, N.J.: Princeton University Press, 1988.

Findlen, Paula. "Possessing the Past: The Material World of the Italian Renaissance." *American Historical Review* 103, no. 1 (February 1998): 84–114.

Fine, John V. A., *The Late Medieval Balkans.* Ann Arbor: University of Michigan Press, 1987.

Flamini, F. "Leonardo di Piero Dati, poeta latino del secolo XV." *Giornale storico della letteratura italiana* 16 (1890): 1–107.

Fleet, Kate. "Italian Perceptions of the Turks in the Fourteenth and Fifteenth Centuries." *Journal of Mediterranean Studies* 5, no. 2 (1995): 159–72.

Fletcher, Richard. *Moorish Spain.* Berkeley: University of California Press, 1992.

———. *The Quest for El Cid.* New York: Knopf, 1990.

Fonseca, Cosimo Damiano, ed. *Otranto 1480: Atti del convegno internazionale di studio promosso in occasione del V centenario della caduta di Otranto ad opera dei Turchi.* 2 vols. Lecce: Galatina Congedo Editore, 1986.

Francesco Filelfo nel quinto centenario della morte: Atti del XVII convegno di studi maceratesi. Padua: Editrice Antenore, 1986.

Frank, Tenney. "Race Mixture in the Roman Empire." In *The Fall of Rome.* Edited by Mortimer Chambers. New York: Holt, Rinehart and Winston, 1963.

Frassetto, Michael. "The Image of the Saracen as Heretic in the Sermons of Adhemar of Chabannes." In *Western Views of Islam in Medieval and Early Modern Europe: Perception of Other.* Edited by David Blanks and Michael Frassetto. New York: St. Martin's Press, 1999.

Fubini, Riccardo. "The Italian League and the Policy of the Balance of Power at the Accession of Lorenzo de' Medici." *Journal of Modern History* 67 supplement (December 1995): S166–99.

Gabrieli, Francesco. "Petrarca e gli Arabi." *Al-Andalus* 42 (1977): 241–48.

Gaeta, Franco. "Alcune osservazioni sulla prima redazione della 'lettera a Maometto'." In *Enea Silvio Piccolomini Papa Pio II.* Edited by Domenico Maffei. Siena: Varese, 1968.

———. "Sulla 'Lettera a Maometto' di Pio II." *Bulletino dell'Istituto storico italiano per il medioevo e archivio muratoriano* 77 (1965).

Galotta, Aldo. "I Turchi e la Terra d'Otranto (1480–81)." In *Otranto 1480: Atti del convegno internazionale di studio promosso in occasione del V centenario della caduta di Otranto ad opera dei Turchi*, vol. 2. Edited by Cosimo Damiano Fonseca. Lecce: Galatina Congedo Editore, 1986.

Ganz, Margery. "A Florentine Friendship: Donato Acciaiuoli and Vespasiano da Bisticci." *Renaissance Quarterly* 43 (1990): 372–82.

———. "The Humanist as Citizen: Donato di Neri Acciaiuoli, 1428–1473." Ph.D. thesis, Syracuse University, 1979.

Garfagnini, Gian Carlo, ed. *Lorenzo Magnifico e il suo mondo*. Florence: Leo S. Olschki Editore, 1994.

Garin, Eugenio. *Italian Humanism: Philosophy and Civic Life in the Renaissance*. Translated by Peter Munz. New York: Harper and Row, 1965.

———. *Portraits from the Quattrocento*. Translated by Victor A. and Elizabeth Velen. New York: Harper and Row, 1972.

Geanakoplos, Deno John. *Constantinople and the West*. Madison: University of Wisconsin Press, 1989.

———. *Greek Scholars in Venice: Studies in the Dissemination of Greek Learning from Byzantium to Western Europe*. Cambridge: Harvard University Press, 1962.

———. *Interaction of the "Sibling" Byzantine and Western Cultures in the Middle Ages and Italian Renaissance*. New Haven, Conn.: Yale University Press, 1976.

———. "Italian Humanism and the Byzantine Émigré Scholars." In *Renaissance Humanism: Foundations, Forms, and Legacy*, vol. 1. Edited by Albert Rabil, Jr. Philadelphia: University of Pennsylvania Press, 1988.

Gentile, Sebastiano. "Lorenzo e Giano Lascaris: Il fondo greco della biblioteca medicea privata." In *Lorenzo il Magnifico e il suo mondo*. Edited by Gian Carlo Garfagnini. Florence: Leo S. Olschki Editore, 1994.

Gill, Joseph, S.J. *The Council of Florence*. Cambridge: Cambridge University Press, 1959.

Gilmore, Myron P. *The World of Humanism: 1453–1517*. New York: Harper Torchbooks, 1952.

Ginzburg, Carlo. *The Enigma of Piero della Francesca*. Translated by Martin Ryle and Kate Soper. London: Verso, 1985.

Goffart, Walter. *Barbarians and Romans* A.D. 418–584: The Techniques of Accommodation. Princeton, N.J.: Princeton University Press, 1980.

Gorceix, Bernard. "Les Turcs dans les lettres Allemandes aux XVI et XVII siècles: Johannes Adelphus et Abraham a Santa Clara." *Revue d'Allemagne* 13, no. 2 (1981): 216–37.

Gordan, Phyllis Walter Goodhart. *Two Renaissance Book Hunters: The Letters of Poggius Bracciolini to Nicolaus de Niccolis*. New York: Columbia University Press, 1974.

Gouwens, Kenneth. "Perceiving the Past: Renaissance Humanism after the 'Cognitive Turn.'" *American Historical Review* 103, no. 1 (1998): 55–82.

Grafton, Anthony. *Commerce with the Classics: Ancient Books and Renaissance Readers*. Ann Arbor: University of Michigan Press, 1997.

———. *Defenders of the Text: The Traditions of Scholarship in the Age of Science 1450–1800*. Cambridge: Harvard University Press, 1991.

Grafton, Anthony, and Lisa Jardine. *From Humanism to the Humanities: Education and the Liberal Arts in Fifteenth- and Sixteenth-Century Europe.* Cambridge: Harvard University Press, 1986.

Grafton, Anthony, April Shelford, and Nancy Siraisi. *New Worlds, Ancient Texts: The Power of Tradition and the Shock of Discovery.* Cambridge, Mass.: Belknap Press, 1992.

Gray, Hanna H. "Renaissance Humanism: The Pursuit of Eloquence." In *Renaissance Essays from the Journal of the History of Ideas.* Edited by Paul Oskar Kristeller and Philip P. Wiener. New York: Harper and Row, 1968. Originally published in *Journal of the History of Ideas* 24 (1963).

Greco, Aulo. "Il Lamento d'Italia per la presa d'Otranto di Vespasiano da Bisticci." In *Otranto 1480: Atti del convegno internazionale di studio promosso in occasione del V centenario della caduta di Otranto ad opera dei Turchi,* vol. 2. Edited by Cosimo Damiano Fonseca. Galatina: Congedo Editore, 1986.

Greenblatt, Stephen. *Marvelous Possessions: The Wonder of the New World.* Chicago: University of Chicago Press, 1991.

Grendler, Paul F. *Schooling in Renaissance Italy.* Baltimore: Johns Hopkins University Press, 1989.

Griffiths, Gordon. "Leonardo Bruni and the 1431 Florentine Complaint against Indulgence Hawkers: A Case Study in Anticlericalism." In *Anticlericalism in Late Medieval and Early Modern Europe.* Edited by Peter Dykema and Heiko Oberman, 133–43. Leiden: E. J. Brill, 1993.

Griffiths, Gordon, James Hankins and David Thompson, eds. *The Humanism of Leonardo Bruni: Selected Texts.* Binghamton, N.Y.: Medieval and Renaissance Texts and Studies, 1987.

Gruen, Erich S. *Culture and National Identity in Imperial Rome.* Ithaca, N.Y.: Cornell University Press, 1992.

Gunter, Michael. "L'image de la Turquie aux États-Unis." In *La Turquie au seuil de l'Europe.* Edited by Paul Dumont and François Georgeon. Paris: Editions L'Harmattan, 1991.

Gurney, J. D. "Pietro della Valle and the Limits of Perception." *Bulletin of the School of Oriental and African Studies* 49 (1986).

Haarmann, Ulrich W. "Ideology and History, Identity and Alterity: The Arab Image of the Turk from the 'Abbasids to Modern Egypt." *International Journal of Middle East Studies* 20 (1988): 175–96.

Haines, Keith. "Attitudes and Impediments to Pacifism in Medieval Europe." *Journal of Medieval History* 7 (1981): 369–88.

Hainsworth, J. B. *The Idea of Epic.* Berkeley: University of California Press, 1991.

Hale, J. R. *The Civilization of Europe in the Renaissance.* New York: Atheneum, 1994.

Halecki, Oscar. *From Florence to Brest (1439–1596).* Rome: Sacrum Poloniae Millenium, 1958.

Hall, Edith. *Inventing the Barbarian.* Oxford: Clarendon Press, 1989.

Hamilton, Bernard. *The Leper King and His Heirs: Baldwin IV and the Crusader Kingdom of Jerusalem.* Cambridge: Cambridge University Press, 2000.

Hankins, James. "Chrysoloras and the Greek Studies of Leonardo Bruni." In *Ma-*

nuele Crisolora e il ritorno del greco in occidente. Edited by Riccardo Maisano and Antonio Rollo. Naples: Istituto Universitario Orientale, 2002.

———. *Plato in the Italian Renaissance.* 2 vols. Leiden: E. J. Brill, 1990.

———. "Renaissance Crusaders: Humanist Crusade Literature in the Age of Mehmed II." *Dumbarton Oaks Papers* 49 (1995): 111–207.

Hanson, Victor Davis. *The Western Way of War.* New York: Alfred A. Knopf, 1989.

Hartog, François. *The Mirror of Herodotus.* Translated by Janet Lloyd. Berkeley: University of California Press, 1988.

Hay, Denys. *Europe: The Emergence of an Idea.* Edinburgh: Edinburgh University Press, 1957.

———. "Flavio Biondo and the Middle Ages." *Proceedings of the British Academy* 45 (1959): 97–125.

———. "Italy and Barbarian Europe." In *Italian Renaissance Studies: A Tribute to the Late Cecilia M. Ady.* Edited by E. F. Jacob. London: Faber and Faber, 1960.

Heath, Michael J. *Crusading Commonplaces: La Noue, Lucinge and Rhetoric against the Turks.* Geneva: Librairie Droz, 1986.

———. "Renaissance Scholars and the Origins of the Turks." *Bibliothèque d'humanisme et renaissance* 41 (1979): 453–71.

Held, Joseph. *Hunyadi: Legend and Reality.* Boulder: East European Monographs, 1985.

Hillenbrand, Carole. *The Crusades: Islamic Perspectives.* New York: Routledge, 2000.

Holmes, George. *The Florentine Enlightenment 1400–1450.* 1969. Rev. ed., Oxford: Clarendon Press, 1992.

Holt, P. M. *The Age of the Crusades from the Eleventh Century to 1517.* New York: Longman, 1986.

Housley, Norman. *The Later Crusades, 1274–1580: From Lyons to Alcazar.* Oxford: Oxford University Press, 1992.

———. "A Necessary Evil? Erasmus, the Crusade, and War against the Turks." In *The Crusades and Their Sources: Essays Presented to Bernard Hamilton.* Edited by John France and William G. Zajac, 259–79. Aldershot: Ashgate Publishing Ltd., 1998.

Hughes, Diane Owen. "Distinguishing Signs: Ear-rings, Jews and Franciscan Rhetoric in the Italian Renaissance City." *Past and Present* 112 (August 1986): 3–59.

Huntington, Samuel. *The Clash of Civilizations and the Remaking of World Order.* New York: Touchstone Books, 1998.

Ilardi, Vincent. *Studies in Italian Renaissance Diplomatic History.* London: Variorum Reprints, 1986.

Imber, Colin. *The Ottoman Empire 1300–1481.* Istanbul: Isis Press, 1990.

Inalcik, Halil. *The Middle East and the Balkans under the Ottoman Empire.* Bloomington: Indiana University Turkish Studies, 1993.

———. *The Ottoman Empire.* Translated by Norman Itzkowitz and Colin Imber. London: Weidenfeld and Nicolson, 1973.

Issawi, Charles. *Cross-Cultural Encounters and Conflicts.* Oxford: Oxford University Press, 1998.

Itzkowitz, Norman. *The Ottoman Empire and Islamic Tradition.* Chicago: University of Chicago Press, 1972.

Izbicki, Thomas M. "The Possibility of a Dialogue with Islam in the Fifteenth Century." In *Nicholas of Cusa in Search of God and Wisdom.* Edited by Gerald Christianson and Thomas M. Izbicki. Leiden: E. J. Brill, 1991.

Jardine, Lisa. *Worldly Goods: A New History of the Renaissance.* New York: W. W. Norton, 1996.

Jardine, Lisa, and Jerry Brotton. *Global Interests: Renaissance Art between East and West.* Ithaca, N.Y.: Cornell University Press, 2000.

Jirousek, Charlotte. "More than Oriental Splendor: European and Ottoman Headgear; 1380–1580." *Dress* 22 (1995): 22–33.

Jones, W. R. "The Image of the Barbarian in Medieval Europe." *Comparative Studies in Society and History* 13 (1971): 376–407.

Jordan, William C. "'Europe' in the Middle Ages." In *The Idea of Europe from Antiquity to the European Union.* Edited by Anthony Pagden. Cambridge: Cambridge University Press, 2002.

Kafadar, Cemal. *Between Two Worlds: The Construction of the Ottoman State.* Berkeley: University of California Press, 1995.

Kaplan, Robert D. *Balkan Ghosts.* New York: St. Martin's Press, 1993.

Kedar, Benjamin Z. *Crusade and Mission: European Approaches toward the Muslims.* Princeton, N.J.: Princeton University Press, 1984.

Kedar, Benjamin Z., Jonathan Riley-Smith, and Rudolf Hiestand, eds. *Montjoie: Studies in Crusade History in Honour of Hans Eberhard Mayer.* Aldershot: Variorum, 1997.

Kelsay, John, and James Turner Johnson, eds. *Just War and Jihad.* New York: Greenwood Press, 1991.

Kennedy, George A. *Classical Rhetoric and its Christian and Secular Tradition from Ancient to Modern Times.* 2d edition. Chapel Hill: University of North Carolina Press, 1999.

King, Margaret L. "Book-Lined Cells: Women and Humanism in the Early Italian Renaissance." In *Renaissance Humanism: Foundations, Forms and Legacy.* Vol. 1. Edited by Albert Rabil Jr. Philadelphia: University of Pennsylvania Press, 1988.

———. *Venetian Humanism in an Age of Patrician Dominance.* Princeton, N.J.: Princeton University Press, 1986.

Knös, Börge. *Un ambassadeur de l'hellenisme, Janus Lascaris et la tradition greco-byzantine dans l'humanisme français.* Uppsala: Almquist & Wiksells Boktryckeri AB, 1945.

Krautter, Konrad, Agostino Pertusi, et al., eds. *Lauro Quirini umanista.* Florence: Leo S. Olschki Editore, 1977.

Kretzmann, Norman, et al., eds. *The Cambridge History of Later Medieval Philosophy.* Cambridge: Cambridge University Press, 1982.

Kristeller, Paul Oskar. "Humanism and Moral Philosophy." In *Renaissance Hu-*

manism: Foundations, Forms and Legacy, vol. 1. Edited by Albert Rabil Jr. Philadelphia: University of Pennsylvania Press, 1988.

———. *Renaissance Thought: The Classic, Scholastic and Humanist Strains*. 1955. Reprint, New York: Harper and Row, 1961.

———. *Renaissance Thought and Its Sources*. Edited by Michael Mooney. New York: Columbia University Press, 1979.

Kritzeck, James. *Peter the Venerable and Islam*. Princeton, N.J.: Princeton University Press, 1964.

Kuhrt, Amelie, and Susan Sherwin-White, eds. *Hellenism in the East*. Berkeley: University of California Press, 1987.

Labalme, Patricia. *Bernardo Giustiniani: A Venetian of the Quattrocento*. Rome: Edizioni di Storia e Letteratura, 1969.

Labowsky, Lotte. "Il Cardinale Bessarione e gli inizi della Biblioteca Marciana." In *Venezia e l'Oriente fra tardo medioevo e rinascimento*, edited by Agostino Pertusi. Venice: Sansoni, 1966.

Ladner, Gerhart B. "On Roman Attitudes toward Barbarians in Late Antiquity." *Viator* 7 (1976): 1–26.

Laiou, Angeliki, and Henry Maguire, eds. *Byzantium a World Civilization*, Washington, D.C.: Dumbarton Oaks, 1992.

Laiou-Thomadakis, Angeliki E., ed. *Charanis Studies: Essays in Honor of Peter Charanis*. New Brunswick, N.J.: Rutgers University Press, 1980.

Lane, Frederic C. *Venice a Maritime Republic*. Baltimore: Johns Hopkins University Press, 1973.

Langmuir, Gavin. *Toward a Definition of Antisemitism*. Los Angeles: Center for Medieval and Renaissance Studies, 1990.

Lazzari, Alfonso. *Ugolino e Michele Verino: studi biografici e critici*. Turin: Libreria Carlo Clausen, 1897.

Legrand, Emile. *Bibliographie Hellenique*. 4 vols. Paris: Ernest Leroux Editeur, 1885–1906.

Lewis, Bernard. *The Arabs in History*. New York: Harper and Row, 1966.

———. *Islam and the West*. Oxford: Oxford University Press, 1993.

———. *Istanbul and the Civilization of the Ottoman Empire*. Norman: University of Oklahoma Press, 1963.

———. *The Muslim Discovery of Europe*. New York: W. W. Norton and Co., 1982.

Lines, David. *Aristotle's Ethics in the Italian Renaissance (ca. 1300–1650)*. Leiden: E. J. Brill, 2002.

Lock, Peter. *The Franks in the Aegean 1204–1500*. London: Longman, 1995.

Luiso, Francesco Paolo. *Studi sull'epistolario di Leonardo Bruni*. Edited by Lucia Gualdo Rosa. Rome: Istituto Storico Italiano per il Medioevo, 1980.

Maalouf, Amin. *The Crusades through Arab Eyes*. Translated by Jon Rothschild. New York: Schocken Books, 1985.

Maisano, Riccardo, and Antonio Rollo, eds. *Manuele Crisolora e il ritorno del greco in occidente*. Naples: Istituto Universitario Orientale, 2002.

Malcolm, Noel. *Bosnia: A Short History*. New York: New York University Press, 1994.

Mallett, Michael E. *Florentine Galleys in the Fifteenth Century*. Oxford: Clarendon Press, 1967.

Martin, Ronald. *Tacitus*. London: Batsford Academic and Educational Ltd., 1981.

Martines, Lauro. *Power and Imagination: City-States in Renaissance Italy*. 1979. Reprint, Baltimore: Johns Hopkins University Press, 1988.

———. "The Renaissance and the Birth of Consumer Society." *Renaissance Quarterly* 51, no. 1 (1998): 193–97.

———. *The Social World of Florentine Humanists 1390–1460*. Princeton, N.J.: Princeton University Press, 1963.

———. *Strong Words: Writing and Social Strain in the Italian Renaissance*. Baltimore: Johns Hopkins University Press, 2001.

Matar, Nabil. *Turks, Moors, and Englishmen in the Age of Discovery*. New York: Columbia University Press, 1999.

Mattingly, Garrett. *Renaissance Diplomacy*. 1955. Reprint, New York: Dover Publications, 1988.

Mayer, Hans Eberhard. *The Crusades*. Translated by John Gillingham. 1972. Reprint, Oxford: Oxford University Press, 1989.

Mazzotta, Giuseppe. *The Worlds of Petrarch*. Durham, N.C.: Duke University Press, 1993.

McCarthy, Justin. *The Ottoman Turks: An Introductory History to 1923*. London: Longman, 1997.

McGinn, Bernard. *Visions of the End: Apocalyptic Traditions of the Middle Ages*. New York: Columbia University Press, 1979.

McKee, Sally. *Uncommon Dominion: Venetian Crete and the Myth of Ethnic Purity*. Philadelphia: University of Pennsylvania Press, 2000.

McManamon, John M., S.J., *Funeral Oratory and the Cultural Ideals of Italian Humanism*. Chapel Hill: University of North Carolina Press, 1989.

Menage, V. L. "Devshirme." In *Encyclopedia of Islam*, vol. 2, 210–13. London: E. J. Brill, 1965.

———. "Some Notes on the Devshirme." *Bulletin of the School of Oriental and African Studies* 29 (1966): 64–78.

Meserve, Margaret. "Medieval Sources for Renaissance Theories on the Origins of the Ottoman Turks." In *Europa und die Türken in der Renaissance*. Edited by Bodo Guthmüller and Wilhelm Kühlmann. Tübingen: Max Niemeyer Verlag, 2000.

Michel, Francisque. *Charlemagne: An Anglo-Norman Poem of the Twelfth Century*. London: William Pickering, 1836.

Mignolo, Walter D. "The Darker Side of the Renaissance: Colonization and the Discontinuity of the Classical Tradition." *Renaissance Quarterly* 45, no. 4 (1992): 808–28.

———. *The Darker Side of the Renaissance: Literacy, Territoriality, and Colonization*. Ann Arbor: University of Michigan Press, 1994.

Milano, Attilio. *Storia degli ebrei in Italia*. Turin: Giulio Einaudi Editore, 1963.

Mitchell, R. J. *The Laurels and the Tiara: Pope Pius II 1458–64*. London: Harvill Press, 1962.

Mitter, Partha. "Can We Ever Understand Alien Cultures? Some Epistemological

Concerns Relating to the Perception and Understanding of the Other." *Comparative Criticism* 9 (1987): 9–13.

Mohler, Ludwig. *Kardinal Bessarion als Theologe, Humanist, und Staatsmann.* 3 vols. 1923. Reprint, Aalen: Scientia Verlag, 1967.

Momigliano, Arnaldo. *Alien Wisdom: The Limits of Hellenization.* Cambridge: Cambridge University Press, 1975.

———. *Studies in Historiography.* London: Weidenfeld and Nicolson, 1966.

Mommsen, Theodor E. "Petrarch's Conception of the 'Dark Ages.'" *Speculum* 17 (1942): 226–42.

Monfasani, John. "The Averroism of John Argyropoulos and His *Quaestio utrum intellectus humanus sit perpetuus.*" *I Tatti Studies* 5 (1993): 157–208.

———. *Byzantine Scholars in Renaissance Italy: Cardinal Bessarion and Other Emigres.* Aldershot: Variorum, 1995.

———. *George of Trebizond: A Biography and a Study of His Rhetoric and Logic.* Leiden: E. J. Brill, 1976.

———. "Greek Renaissance Migrations." *Italian History and Culture* 8 (2002): 1–14.

———. "Nicholas of Cusa, the Byzantines, and the Greek Language." In *Nicholaus Cusanus zwischen Deutschland und Italien.* Edited by Martin Thurner, 215–52. Berlin: Akademie Verlag, 2002.

Monfrin, J. "La figure de Charlemagne dans l'historiographie du xve siècle." *Annuaire du bulletin* de la Société de l'Histoire de France (1964–65): 67–78.

Moore, R. I. *The Formation of a Persecuting Society.* Cambridge, Mass.: Blackwell, 1987.

Moro Donato. "Fonti Salentine sugli avvenimenti Otrantini del 1480/81." In *Otranto 1480: atti del convegno internazionale di studio promosso in occasione del V centenario della caduta di Otranto ad opera dei Turchi,* vol. 2. Edited by Cosimo Damiano Fonseca. Lecce: Galatina Congedo Editore, 1986.

Moulakis, Athanasios. "Bruni's Constitution of Florence." *Rinascimento,* 2d ser., 26 (1986).

Mousavizadeh, Nader, ed. *The Black Book of Bosnia.* New York: New Republic Books, 1996.

Munro, Dana C. "The Western Attitude toward Islam during the Period of the Crusades." *Speculum* 6 (1931): 329–43.

Murphy, James J. *Rhetoric in the Middle Ages: A History of Rhetorical Theory from Saint Augustine to the Renaissance.* Berkeley: University of California Press, 1974.

Musto, Ronald G. "Just Wars and Evil Empires: Erasmus and the Turks." In *Renaissance Society and Culture.* Edited by John Monfasani and Ronald Musto. New York: Italica Press, 1991.

Najemy, John M. *Between Friends: Discourses of Power and Desire in the Machiavelli-Vettori Letters of 1513–1515.* Princeton, N.J.: Princeton University Press, 1993.

———. "Dante and Florence." In *The Cambridge Companion to Dante.* Edited by Rachel Jacoff. Cambridge: Cambridge University Press, 1993.

Niccoli, Ottavia. *Prophecy and People in Renaissance Italy*. Translated by Lydia G. Cochrane. Princeton, N.J.: Princeton University Press, 1990.

Nicol, Donald. *The Last Centuries of Byzantium 1261–1453*. Cambridge: Cambridge University Press, 1993.

Nirenberg, David. *Communities of Violence: Persecution of Minorities in the Middle Ages*. Princeton, N.J.: Princeton University Press, 1996.

Norwich, John Julius. *A History of Venice*. New York: Vintage Books, 1989.

Ober, Josiah, and Barry Strauss. "Drama, Political Rhetoric, and the Discourse of Athenian Democracy." In *Nothing to Do with Dionysos?: Athenian Drama in Its Social Context*. Edited by John J. Winkler and Froma Zeitlin. Princeton, N.J.: Princeton University Press, 1989.

O'Malley, John W. *Praise and Blame in Renaissance Rome: Rhetoric, Doctrine, and Reform in the Sacred Orators of the Papal Court, c. 1450–1521*. Durham, N.C.: Duke University Press, 1979.

Orlinsky, Harry M. *Ancient Israel*. 2d. edition. Ithaca, N.Y.: Cornell University Press, 1960.

Orvieto, Paolo. "Un esperto orientalista del '400: Benedetto Dei." *Rinascimento*, 2d ser., 9 (1969): 205–75.

Pagden, Anthony. *The Fall of Natural Man: The American Indian and the Origins of Comparative Ethnology*. Cambridge: Cambridge University Press, 1982.

———. *Lords of All the World: Ideologies of Empire in Spain, Britain and France c. 1500–1800*. New Haven, Conn.: Yale University Press, 1995.

———, ed. *The Idea of Europe from Antiquity to the European Union*. Cambridge: Cambridge University Press, 2002.

Pastor, Ludwig. *History of the Popes*. 40 vols. London: Kegan Paul, Trench, Trubner, and Co., 1899.

Patrides, C. A. " 'The Bloody and Cruell Turke': The Background of a Renaissance Commonplace." *Studies in the Renaissance* 10 (1963): 126–35.

Pertusi, Agostino. "I primi studi in occidente sull'origine e la potenza dei Turchi." *Studi veneziani* 12 (1970): 465–552.

———. "Le Notizie sulla organizzazione amministrativa e militare dei Turchi nello 'Strategicon' Adversum Turcos' di Lampo Birago (c. 1453–55)." In *Studi sul medioevo cristiano: offerti a Raffaello Morghen*, vol. 2. Rome: Istituto Storico Italiano, 1974.

———, ed. *Venezia e l'Oriente fra tardo medioevo e rinascimento*. Florence: G. C. Sansoni, 1966.

Philippides, Marios. "The Fall of Constantinople 1453: Bishop Leonardo Giustiniani and His Italian Followers." *Viator* 29 (1998): 189–225.

———. "Urban's Bombard(s), Gunpowder, and the Siege of Constantinople (1453)." *Byzantine Studies*, n.s., 4 (1999): 1–67.

Piaia, Gregorio, ed. *Concordia Discors: studi su Niccolò Cusano e l'umanesimo Europeo offerti a Giovanni Santinello*. Padua: Editrice Antenore, 1993.

Piemontese, Angelo Michele. "Il Corano latino di Ficino e i corani arabi di Pico e Monchates." *Rinascimento*, 2d ser., 36 (1996): 227–73.

Pinson, Mark, ed. *The Muslims of Bosnia-Hercegovina*. Cambridge: Cambridge University Press, 1994.

Pittaluga, Stefano. "Il 'vocabulario' usato da Cristoforo Colombo." *Columbeis* 1 (1986): 107–15.

Piur, Paul. *Petrarcas 'Buch ohne Namen' und die päpstliche Kurie, ein Beitrag zur Geistesgeschichte der Frührenaissance.* Halle: M. Niemeyer, 1925.

Porter, Roy, ed. *The Renaissance in National Context.* Cambridge: Cambridge University Press, 1992.

Prawer, Joshua. *The World of the Crusaders.* New York: Quadrangle Books, 1973.

Quillen, Carol Everhardt. *Rereading the Renaissance: Petrarch, Augustine, and the Language of Humanism.* Ann Arbor: University of Michigan Press, 1998.

Rabil, Albert Jr., ed. *Renaissance Humanism: Foundations, Forms, and Legacy.* 3 vols. Philadelphia: University of Pennsylvania Press, 1988.

Raby, Julian. "Cyriacus of Ancona and the Ottoman Sultan Mehmed II." *Journal of the Warburg and Courtauld Institutes* 43 (1980): 242–46.

———. "East and West in Mehmed the Conqueror's Library." *Bulletin du bibliophile* (1987): 299–321.

Rees, Valery. "Hungary's Philosopher King: Matthias Corvinus 1458–90." *History Today* 44, no. 4 (March 1994): 18–24.

Remer, Gary. *Humanism and the Rhetoric of Toleration.* University Park: Pennsylvania State University Press, 1996.

Reeves, Marjorie. *The Influence of Prophecy in the Later Middle Ages.* Oxford: Clarendon Press, 1969.

Reynolds, L. D., ed. *Texts and Transmission: A Survey of the Latin Classics.* Oxford: Clarendon Press, 1983.

Richards, Jeffrey. *Sex, Dissidence, and Damnation: Minority Groups in the Middle Ages.* London: Routledge, 1991.

Riley-Smith, Jonathan. *The Crusades: A Short History.* New Haven, Conn.: Yale University Press, 1987.

Riley-Smith, Jonathan, and Louise Riley-Smith, eds. *The Crusades: Idea and Reality.* London: Edward Arnold, 1981.

———, ed. *Oxford Illustrated History of the Crusades.* Oxford: Oxford University Press, 1995.

———. *The First Crusade and the Idea of Crusading.* Philadelphia: University of Pennsylvania Press, 1986.

Robin, Diana. *Filelfo in Milan.* Princeton, N.J.: Princeton University Press, 1991.

Robinson, James Harvey. *Petrarch the First Modern Man of Letters.* New York: Haskell House Publishers Ltd., 1970.

Rodinson, Maxime. *Europe and the Mystique of Islam.* Translated by Roger Veinus. Seattle: University of Washington Press, 1987.

Roscoe, William. *The Life and Pontificate of Leo X.* 2 vols. 1805–6. Rev. ed. by Thomas Roscoe, London: Henry G. Bohn, 1846.

Rouillard, Clarence Dana. *The Turk in French History, Thought, and Literature.* Paris: Boivin et Companie Editeurs, 1941.

Ruderman, David. "The Italian Renaissance and Jewish Thought." In *Renaissance Humanism: Foundations, Forms and Legacy*, vol. 1. Edited by Albert Rabil Jr. Philadelphia: University of Pennsylvania Press, 1988.

Runciman, Sir Steven. "Charlemagne and Palestine." *English Historical Review* 50 (1935): 606–19.

———. *The Eastern Schism.* Oxford: Clarendon Press, 1955.

———. *The Fall of Constantinople 1453.* Cambridge: Cambridge University Press, 1965.

———. *History of the Crusades.* Volumes 1–3. Cambridge: Cambridge University Press, 1951–54.

———. *The Last Byzantine Renaissance.* Cambridge: Cambridge University Press, 1970.

Rusconi, Roberto. "Gerusalemme nella predicazione popolare quattrocentesca tra millennio, ricordo di viaggio e luogo sacro." In *Toscana e Terransanta nel medioevo.* Edited by Franco Cardini. Florence: Alinea Editrice, 1982.

Sabbadini, Remigio. *Le scoperte dei codici latini e greci ne' secoli XIV e XV.* 2 vols. Florence: G. C. Sansoni Editore, 1967.

Said, Edward W. *Covering Islam.* New York: Pantheon Books, 1981.

———. *Culture and Imperialism.* New York: Vintage Books, 1993.

———. "East Isn't East: The Impending End of the Age of Orientalism." *Times Literary Supplement* (3 February 1995).

———. *Orientalism.* New York: Vintage Books, 1978.

Saitta, Giuseppe. *Il pensiero italiano nell'umanesimo e nel rinascimento.* Vol. 1. Bologna: Dott. Cesare Zuffi Editore, 1949.

Samarrai, Alauddin. "Arabs and Latins in the Middle Ages: Enemies, Partners, and Scholars." In *Western Views of Islam in Medieval and Early Modern Europe: Perception of Other.* Edited by David Blanks and Michael Frassetto. New York: St. Martin's Press, 1999.

Schevill, Ferdinand. *A History of the Balkans.* 1933. Reprint, New York: Dorset Press, 1991.

Schiffman, Zachary. *Humanism and the Renaissance.* Boston: Houghton Mifflin, 2002.

Schildgen, Brenda Deen. "Dante and the Crusades." *Dante Studies* 116 (1998): 95–125.

Schmügge, Ludwig. *Die Kreuzzüge aus der Sicht humanistischer Geschichtsschreiber.* Basel: Verlag Helbing & Lichtenhahn, 1987.

Schwoebel, Robert. "Coexistence, Conversion, and the Crusade against the Turks." *Studies in the Renaissance* 12 (1965): 164–87.

———. *The Shadow of the Crescent: The Renaissance Image of the Turk (1453–1517).* New York: St. Martin's Press, 1967.

Seigel, Jerrold. *Rhetoric and Philosophy in Renaissance Humanism.* Princeton, N.J.: Princeton University Press, 1968.

Sensi, Mario. "Niccolò Tignosi da Foligno, l'opera e il pensiero." *Annali della facoltà di lettere e filosofia della Università degli Studi di Perugia* 9 (1971–72): 361–495.

Settis, Salvatore, ed. *I Greci: storia, cultura, arte, società.* 4 vols. Turin: Giulio Einaudi Editore, 2001.

Setton, Kenneth. "The Byzantine Background to the Italian Renaissance." *Proceedings of the American Philosophical Society* 100 (1956): 1–76.

————. *The Papacy and the Levant (1204–1571)*. 4 vols. Philadelphia: American Philosophical Society, 1978.

————, ed. *A History of the Crusades*. 6 vols. Madison: University of Wisconsin Press, 1989.

Seymour, M. C. *Sir John Mandeville*. Aldershot: Variorum, 1993.

Seznec, Jean. *The Survival of the Pagan Gods*. Translated by Barbara F. Sessions. New York: Harper and Row, 1953.

Shahid, Irfan. "Byzantium and the Islamic World." In *Byzantium a World Civilization*. Edited by Angeliki Laiou and Henry Maguire, 49–60. Washington, D.C.: Dumbarton Oaks, 1992.

Shaw, Brent D. " 'Eaters of Flesh, Drinkers of Milk': The Ancient Mediterranean Ideology of the Pastoral Nomad." *Ancient Society* 13/14 (1982–83): 5–31.

Sheehan, Bernard. *Savagism and Civility: Indians and Englishmen in Colonial Virginia*. Cambridge: Cambridge University Press, 1980.

Sherwin-White, A. N. *Racial Prejudice in Imperial Rome*. Cambridge: Cambridge University Press, 1967.

Siberry, Elizabeth. *Criticism of Crusading 1095–1274*. Oxford: Clarendon Press, 1985.

Simon, Eckehard. *The Türkenkalender (1454) Attributed to Gutenberg and the Strasbourg Lunation Tracts*. Cambridge, Mass.: The Medieval Academy of America, 1988.

Sivan, Emmanuel. "Edward Said and His Arab Reviewers." *Jerusalem Quarterly* 35 (spring 1985): 11–23.

Smith, Leslie F. "Pope Pius II's Use of Turkish Atrocities." *Southwestern Social Science Quarterly* 46 (1966): 408–15.

Southern, R. W. "Dante and Islam." In *Relations between East and West in the Middle Ages*. Edited by Derek Baker. Edinburgh: Edinburgh University Press, 1973.

————. *Western Views of Islam in the Middle Ages*. Cambridge: Harvard University Press, 1962.

Spencer, Terence. "Turks and Trojans in the Renaissance." *Modern Language Review* 47 (1952): 330–33.

Spiridonakis, Basile G. *Grecs, Occidentaux et Turcs de 1054 à 1453: Quatre siècles d'histoire de relations internationales*. Thessaloniki: Institute for Balkan Studies, 1990.

Starr, Chester G. *A History of the Ancient World*. 3d edition. New York: Oxford University Press, 1983.

Stinger, Charles L. *The Renaissance in Rome*. Bloomington: Indiana University Press, 1985.

Tarugi, Luisa Rotondi Secchi, ed. *Pio II e la cultura del suo tempo*. Milan: Guerini e Associati, 1991.

Tateo, Francesco. "Gli stereotipi letterari." In *Europa e Mediterraneo tra medioevo e prima età moderna l'osservatorio italiano*. Edited by Sergio Gensini. Commune San Miniato: Pacini Editore, 1992.

————. "L'ideologia umanistica e il simbolo 'immane' di Otranto." In *Otranto 1480: atti del convegno internazionale di studio promosso in occasione del V centenario della caduta di Otranto ad opera dei Turchi*, vol. 1. Edited by Cosimo Damiano Fonseca. Lecce: Galatina Congedo Editore, 1986.

Throop, Palmer A. *Criticism of Crusade*. Amsterdam: N. V. Swets and Zeitlinger, 1940.

Tolan, John V. "Muslims as Pagan Idolaters in Chronicles of the First Crusade." In *Western Views of Islam in Medieval and Early Modern Europe: Perception of Other*. Edited by David Blanks and Michael Frassetto. New York: St. Martin's Press, 1999.

———. *Petrus Alfonsi and His Medieval Readers*. Gainesville: University Press of Florida, 1993.

———, ed. *Medieval Christian Perceptions of Islam*. New York: Garland Press, 1996.

Trade, Travel, and Exploration in the Middle Ages: An Encyclopedia. Edited by John Block Friedman and Kristen Mossler Figg. New York: Garland Press, 2000.

Trinkaus, Charles. *In Our Image and Likeness: Humanity and Divinity in Italian Humanist Thought*. 2 vols. London: Constable, 1970.

Turner, Hilary. "The Expanding Horizons of Cristoforo Buondelmonti." *History Today* 40 (October 1990): 40–45.

Tyerman, Christopher. *The Invention of the Crusades*. Toronto: University of Toronto Press, 1998.

———. "Philip VI and the Recovery of the Holy Land." *English Historical Review* 100 (1985): 25–52.

Ullman, Berthold L. *The Humanism of Coluccio Salutati*. Padua: Editrice Antenore, 1963.

Ugurgieri della Berardenga, Curzio. *Gli Acciaioli di Firenze nella luce del loro tempo (1160–1834)*. 2 vols. Florence: Leo S. Olschki Editore, 1962.

Vacalopoulos, Apostolos. "The Flight of the Inhabitants of Greece to the Aegean Islands, Crete, and Mane during the Turkish Invasions (Fourteenth and Fifteenth Centuries)." In *Charanis Studies: Essays in Honor of Peter Charanis*. Edited by Angeliki E. Laiou-Thomadakis. New Brunswick, N.J.: Rutgers University Press, 1980.

Valensi, Lucette. *The Birth of the Despot: Venice and the Sublime Porte*. Translated by Arthur Denner. Ithaca, N.Y.: Cornell University Press, 1993.

Vast, Henri, ed. *Le Cardinal Bessarion*. Paris: Librairie Hachette et Companie, 1878.

Vaughn, Dorothy. *Europe and the Turk: A Pattern of Alliances 1350–1700*. Liverpool: University Press, 1954.

Verdon, Timothy, and John Henderson, eds. *Christianity and the Renaissance: Image and Religious Imagination in the Quattrocento*. Syracuse, N.Y.: Syracuse University Press, 1990.

Verlinden, Charles. "La presence turque à Otrante (1480–1481) et l'esclavage." In *Otranto 1480: atti del convegno internazionale di studio promosso in occasione del V centenario della caduta di Otranto ad opera dei Turchi*, vol. 1. Edited by Cosimo Damiano Fonseca. Lecce: Galatina Congedo Editore, 1986.

Viti, Paolo. *Leonardo Bruni e Firenze: studi sulle lettere pubbliche e private*. Rome: Bulzoni Editore, 1992.

Vitkus, Daniel. "Early Modern Orientalism: Representations of Islam in Sixteenth- and Seventeenth-Century Europe." In *Western Views of Islam in Medieval and Early Modern Europe: Perception of Other*. Edited by David Blanks and Michael Frassetto. New York: St. Martin's Press, 1999.

Volkan, Vamik D., and Norman Itzkowitz. *Turks and Greeks: Neighbors in Conflict*. Huntingdon: Eothen Press, 1994.

Vryonis, Speros, Jr. "Byzantium and Islam, Seven–Seventeenth Century." In *Byzantium: Its Internal History and Relations with the Muslim World: Collected Studies*. London: Variorum Reprints, 1971.

Wallbank, F. W. *The Hellenistic World*. Cambridge: Harvard University Press, 1981.

Walser, Ernst. *Poggius Florentinus Leben und Werke*. Berlin: B. G. Teubner, 1914.

Watt, W. Montgomery. *The Influence of Islam on Medieval Europe*. Edinburgh: Edinburgh University Press, 1972.

Weinstein, Donald. *Savonarola and Florence*. Princeton, N.J.: Princeton University Press, 1970.

Weiss, Roberto. "Ciriaco d'Ancona in Oriente." In *Venezia e l'Oriente fra tardo medioevo e rinascimento*. Edited by Agostino Pertusi. Venice: Sansoni, 1966.

———. *Medieval and Humanist Greek: Collected Essays by Roberto Weiss*. Padua: Antenore, 1977.

———. *The Renaissance Discovery of Classical Antiquity*. 1969. Reprint, Oxford: Basil Blackwell, 1988.

Wheatcroft, Andrew. *The Ottomans*. London: Viking Press, 1993.

Wilkins, E. H. *The Life of Petrarch*. Chicago: University of Chicago Press, 1961.

———. *Studies in the Life and Works of Petrarch*. Cambridge, Mass.: Medieval Academy of America, 1955.

Wilson, N. G. *From Byzantium to Italy: Greek Studies in the Italian Renaissance*. Baltimore: Johns Hopkins University Press, 1992.

Wirszubski, Chaim. *Pico della Mirandola's Encounter with Jewish Mysticism*. Cambridge: Harvard University Press, 1989.

Witt, Ronald. *Hercules at the Crossroads: The Life, Works and Thought of Coluccio Salutati*. Durham, N.C.: Duke University Press, 1983.

———. "The Humanist Movement." In *The Handbook of European History 1400–1600*, vol. 2. Edited by Thomas A. Brady Jr., Heiko Oberman, and James D. Tracy. Grand Rapids, Mich.: William B. Eerdmans Publishing Co., 1995.

———. *'In the Footsteps of the Ancients': The Origins of Humanism from Lovato to Bruni*. Leiden: Brill, 2000.

Wittek, Paul. "An Eloquent Conquest." In *The Fall of Constantinople*. London: School of Oriental and African Studies, 1955.

Wittschier, Heinz Willi. *Giannozzo Manetti: Das Corpus der Orationes*. Graz: Bohlau Verlag, 1968.

Woodhouse, C. M. *George Gemistos Plethon: The Last of the Hellenes*. Oxford: Clarendon Press, 1986.

Ye'or, Bat. *The Decline of Eastern Christianity under Islam: From Jihad to Dhim-*

mitude Seventh–Twentieth Century. Translated by Miriam Kochan and David Littman. Cranbury, N.J.: Associated University Presses, 1996.

Zachariadou, Elizabeth A. *Trade and Crusade: Venetian Crete and the Emirates of Menteshe and Aydin (1300–1415).* Venice: Istituto Ellenico di Studi Bizantini e Postbizantini, 1983.

Zimmermann, T. C. Price. *Paolo Giovio: The Historian and the Crisis of Sixteenth-Century Italy.* Princeton, N.J.: Princeton University Press, 1995.

Index

Acknowledgments

OVER THE YEARS, many people have contributed to the creation and development of this book, from its beginnings at Cornell University to its final completion at Vassar College. I hope they will recognize the unique and positive imprints they have left on the work; I can certainly no longer imagine what this study would look like without all their advice and support. Any defects that remain are, of course, my own.

First and foremost, I wish to thank John M. Najemy at Cornell, who helped me to develop an interesting idea into a deeply engaging project with nuances and depths that I would not have discovered without his discerning eye and incisive questions. I could not have asked for a more supportive or inspiring mentor and colleague. I want to thank Barry Strauss, James John, and Leslie Peirce, also at Cornell, for their guidance at various stages. A special thanks goes to Danuta Shanzer, who helped with Latin translations and various other suggestions. To all my friends from Cornell, particularly Vicki Szabo and Amy Phelan, many thanks for their continuing collegiality and companionship.

My colleagues and friends at Vassar provided crucial support and advice in developing this study into a more coherent and polished work. James H. Merrell of the history department carefully read and commented on earlier drafts of this book, offering wisdom and valued criticism along with encouragement and humor. Also in the history department, Mita Choudhury, Rebecca Edwards, Anthony Wohl, and Robert Brigham sustained me with their collegiality, suggestions, and friendship at many critical moments. My distinguished predecessor, Benjamin Kohl, and senior colleague David Schalk also generously shared insights and words of encouragement along the way. In the medieval and Renaissance studies program, Karen Robertson has given me numerous forums to share my work with colleagues; I am grateful for her positive attitude toward the project as it unfolded and to all the members of the medieval/Renaissance circle who provided much-needed feedback on portions of my work. Thanks also go to Rachel Friedman, Roberta Antognini, Susan Kassouf, John

Ahern, and Eugenio Giusti for their help on various questions. Also at Vassar, I wish to thank my energetic and intellectually curious students for their questions and ideas, which helped me to reexamine and reposition my arguments on this topic. They are a constant source of inspiration.

Beyond Cornell and Vassar, it is my great pleasure to thank members of the larger scholarly community who helped in the research and writing of this book. Robert Black, whose book on Benedetto Accolti sparked my interest in this topic, was a generous and encouraging correspondent on questions and drafts at various stages in my research. Arthur Field provided cheerful insights into navigating the archives and libraries during my first research trip to Florence, as well as numerous bibliographical suggestions. I also want to thank Carol Helstosky, Myra Best, and countless other friends from Florence for their companionship and academic camaraderie during my year there.

James Hankins, Marios Philippides, John Monfasani, John Van A. Fine, and David Marsh read drafts of the entire book and shared their expertise with me on numerous issues from references to interpretive or factual problems. I am tremendously grateful for their comments and supportive words. Thanks also to Norman Housley, who read portions of this work and was a helpful correspondent on numerous questions along the way. Margaret Meserve and Benjamin Kedar also deserve thanks for their enthusiasm and suggestions. Finally, Alison Brown, Steven Reinert, and John Lenaghan helped with some important sources and translations.

Countless librarians and staff members have helped me find and access materials indispensable to this book. In the United States, warm thanks and praise to the staff of Olin Library at Cornell University, Alexander Library at Rutgers University, Thompson Library at Vassar College, the Firestone Library at Princeton University, the Beinecke and Sterling Libraries at Yale University, the New York Public Library, and the Houghton Library at Harvard University. A special thanks to members of the interlibrary-loan department at Vassar, whose patience and resourcefulness were inexhaustible. In Italy, I wish to thank the staff of the following institutions: in Florence, the Archivio di Stato, Biblioteca Nazionale Centrale, Biblioteca Riccardiana, Biblioteca Medicea Laurenziana, and the Villa i Tatti; in Rome, the Biblioteca Apostolica Vaticana; and in Venice, the Biblioteca Nazionale Marciana. Trips abroad were generously funded by the Mommsen Traveling Fellowship, courtesy of the Cornell history department, and by a faculty research stipend from Vassar College. Additional support was provided by the Mellon Fellowship from the Cornell history department.

Many thanks go to all those at the University of Pennsylvania Press who helped develop and produce this book, especially Humanities Editor Jerome Singerman, Acquisitions Assistant Theodore Mann, and Associate Managing Editor Erica Ginsburg. Their cheerful support of this project, their professionalism, and their help with numerous questions along the way are much appreciated.

Finally, to my family—Mom, Sue, Joe, Sarah, Joan, and Jerry—who encouraged and sustained me countless times along the journey from graduate school to the rigors of the job market to manuscript preparation and completion: I cannot thank them enough. Specifically, I want to thank my husband, David B. Bieler, who had very little to do with the conception and completion of this book in an academic sense but everything to do with making it possible in other ways. For his emotional support and reassuring belief in me, not to mention limitless patience and humor during the many years that we shared our lives with this project, I do not exaggerate when I say I could not have done this without him. Last but not least, to my daughter, Jocelyn Heloise, whose birth made the final stages of this book a bit more challenging, my thanks for also making it a time of infinite joy.

ably more complex, in that it addressed secular and cultural issues, marking a watershed between the medieval and modern. Taking a close look at a number of texts, Bisaha expands current notions of Renaissance humanism and of the history of cross-cultural perceptions. Engaging both traditional methods of intellectual history and more recent methods of cross-cultural studies, she demonstrates that modern attitudes of Western societies toward other cultures emerged not during the later period of expansion and domination but rather as a defensive intellectual reaction to a sophisticated and threatening power to the east.

Nancy Bisaha teaches history at Vassar College.